Programming the
Internet with Java

Programming the Internet with Java

Darrel Ince & Adam Freeman

The Open University

ADDISON-WESLEY

Harlow, England • Reading, Massachusetts
Menlo Park, California • New York • Don Mills, Ontario
Amsterdam • Bonn • Sydney • Singapore • Tokyo • Madrid
San Juan • Milan • Mexico City • Seoul • Taipei

© Addison Wesley Longman 1997

Addison Wesley Longman Limited
Edinburgh Gate
Harlow
Essex CM20 2JE
England

and Associated Companies throughout the World.

Published in the United States of America by Addison Wesley Longman Inc., New York.

Cover designed by odB Design & Communication, Reading, UK
Typesetting and line illustrations by the author

Printed and bound in The United Stated of America.
First printed 1997
ISBN 0–201–17549–5

British Library Cataloguing-in-Publication Data

A catalogue record for this book is available from the British Library

Library of Congress Cataloging-in-Publication Data is available

Preface

This book is intended for students studying a course on Java within a University or College. Typically such a course would form a second or third year module in a computing, computer science, electronics or telecommunications degree. In the book we take you from the fundamentals of Java to the point where you will be able to develop some very sophisticated software indeed, for example multi-threaded, client–server software and threaded applets.

The book is split up into a number of sections based on chapters. The first three chapters form an introduction to Java and the concept of object-oriented programming. If your background is that of procedural programming in languages such as C or Pascal, then it is worth your while reading these chapters carefully. However, if you have encountered object-oriented languages before then you can either miss out this part of the book or skim read it.

Chapters 4 to 10 teach the elements of Java. It will provide you with enough skills to develop the most complex Java code. The remainder of the book mainly covers the application of Java to applets (programs which can be embedded in Web documents) and Java applications. An appendix containing a description of the Java Development Kit concludes the book.

There are a number of elements in this book which you may not have found in any other that you have read. First, in order to make the book suitable for self-study we have written a number of exercises and self-assessment questions (SAQs). The former involve quite a bit of thought and are substantial pieces of work normally involving the development of code. The latter are short questions which test that you have understood the concepts we have just written about. These SAQs are either short, sharp questions which require a written answer, or require you to write some short section of code. The book is supported by a Web site; its URL is http://www.awl-he.com/computing/titles/0-201-17549-5.html.

At this site you will find:

- Web links to other sites which have interesting information about Java.

- A stop press informing you of any typos.

- Further teaching text which will describe new features of Java which will emerge from the 1.1 version of the JDK. This is currently in a beta form and we have incorporated some material from this beta into this book.

However, we intend including extra material in the Web site over the next six months which reflects the changes, particularly those connected with the new event model.

- Applets which check out your understanding of each chapter. These applets are a sort of dynamic multi-choice examination which will provide you with evidence that you are progressing through the book and understanding the main concepts.

- The exercises we mentioned above. These will range from easy exercises which ask you to complete the code of a single method, through medium difficulty ones which ask you to develop a small applet, to difficult exercises which give you a specification of an application and ask you to carry out the programming. *We want to stress, however, that you do not need to have Web access to read this book.* Regard the site as an extra.

If you want to be notified whenever there is an important addition to the Web site such as extra exercises or further teaching material on the JDK 1.1 please email Darrel Ince (`D.C.Ince@open.ac.uk`).

We have also included a number of boxes which describe Internet concepts. Normally the boxes will precede some code or an exercise or SAQ which requires knowledge of the concept.

We would like to thank a number of people associated with the book. First, Sally Mortimore, commissioning editor at Addison-Wesley who supported us during the writing; second, our editor Annette Abel who carried out a superb job in converting our words to readable text and who calmly coped with the changes forced on us during production by the release of the Java 1.1 beta.

Darrel Ince
Adam Freeman

Contents

Publisher's Acknowledgements and Trademark Notice
The publishers are grateful to the following for permission to reproduce the material
listed below.

For extracts from Java documentation on pages 204–5 and 211–13, and for permission
to use screen images featuring the Appletviewer, our thanks to Sun Microsystems, Inc.

Java, HotJava, and Solaris are trademarks of Sun Microsystems, Inc.

Thanks to Netscape Communications Corporation for permission to show on page 10 a
fragment of HTML viewed through the browser Netscape Navigator. Netscape
Communications Corporation has not authorized, sponsored, or endorsed, or approved
this publication and is not responsible for its content.

Netscape, Netscape Navigator and the Netscape Communications Corporate Logos, are
trademarks and trade names of Netscape Communications Corporation.

Ingres is a trademark of Ingres Corporation

Microsoft Access, Internet Explorer, MS-DOS, SQL Server, Windows 3.11 and
Windows 95 are trademarks of Microsoft Corporation.

Macintosh is a trademark of Apple Computer, Inc.

Oracle is a trademark of Oracle Corporation

CHAPTER ONE

Java and the Internet

AIMS

- To outline a brief history of the Java project.
- To describe the main principles underlying the Java programming language.
- To briefly outline the history of Java and Java-compatible browsers.

1.1 Introduction

The past four years have seen a phenomenal rise in interest in the collection of computers known as the **Internet**.

Tens of millions of users regularly access this network to carry out operations such as browsing through electronic newspapers, downloading bibliographies, participating in news groups and emailing friends and colleagues. The number of applications that are hosted within the Internet has also grown; however, there are major problems in developing such applications:

- The first problem is security. There are still many problems concerned with ensuring that unauthorized access is prevented. This is becoming one of the major drag factors why commercial applications - particularly those involving the direct transfer of funds across communication lines - have been relatively slow in developing as compared with academic applications.

- The lack of a specific programming language for Internet applications. Currently applications are written in a wide variety of languages including C, Pascal and Tcl/Tk which have to access fairly low-level facilities such as protocol handlers.

- It is very difficult to build interaction into an Internet application. Most of the applications that have been developed tend to give the impression of being interactive. However, what they usually involve is just the user moving through a series of text and visual images following pointers to other sections of text and visual images. Often the most one gets with the vast majority of Internet applications is some small amount of interactivity, for example an application asking the user for an identity and a password and checking what has been typed against some stored data which describes the user.

- The majority of interactive applications are non-portable: they tend to be firmly anchored within one computer architecture and operating system by virtue of the fact, for example, that they tend to use the run-time facilities provided by one specific operating system.

The Internet

The Internet is a collection of computer networks spread around the world. The key fact about the Internet is that the computers are connected together using standard communication protocols which allow the sharing of information worldwide. There are a number of aspects to the Internet:

- It is a medium for sending electronic messages. One of the most popular applications of the Internet is electronic mail whereby people separated by continents send each other messages which are delivered in no more than a few hours.

- It is a medium for sending large quantities of data using file transfer software.

- It supports the World Wide Web. The Web consists of a number of computers known as **Web sites** which contain documents that are linked to other documents. Typical documents held in the World Wide Web are research reports, advertising material, educational courses and software libraries. Later in this chapter we shall look at the Web in a little more detail.

1.2 The Java programming language

1.2.1 The language

The Java programming language originated at Sun Microsystems. It was developed initially as a programming language for consumer-electronics products; however, its later versions address the problems that have been outlined in the previous section. The developers of the language had a number of design goals:

- *The language should be familiar.* It should have no strange syntax and, as much as possible, it should look like an existing language. However, this principle was not taken to the point where problems with other languages would be carried through to Java. The control structures and data types in Java look like some of those provided in the C programming language, while those facilities which make it object-oriented resemble those in the programming language C++. The developers of the Java language felt that on both commercial and technical grounds Java would have the greatest success if the learning curve was not too steep. Its similarity to the C family of programming languages means that a wide variety of users are able to program in it: ranging from professionals at the cutting edge of Internet technology to the home computer user. However, it is worth pointing out here that Java is not compatible with C or C++: a Java program when processed by a C or C++ compiler will not compile and will generate error messages.

- *The language should be object-oriented.* A programming language is object-oriented if it offers facilities to define and manipulate objects: self-contained entities which have a state and to which messages can be sent. At this stage of the book do not worry too much about the meaning of the term *object-oriented*. In Chapter 2 we provide a tutorial on the concept and, in Chapter 3, we show in detail how object-orientation is provided within the Java programming language.

An object-oriented programming language has two major advantages. First, by adhering to a small set of programming principles it is possible to write systems which are relatively easy to modify. This is massively important in today's world. Customer requirements for systems can change quite quickly, even during the development of an application; for example, a company that contracts for a financial reporting system might be affected by changes in tax laws which require major changes to the system. All the surveys that have been carried out on the amount of resource expended on software development have come up with figures which suggest that companies who have a significant software development capability spend somewhere between 60 and 80% of their development resources in changing existing software – the changes being due to a variety of factors ranging from errors to changes in requirements, with the latter predominating.

As you will see in this book Java, being an object-oriented language, provides facilities whereby systems developed using the Java technology are relatively easy to modify as compared to systems which have been developed using other languages.

The other feature of an object-oriented programming language is that it allows a high degree of reuse; in such a language programmers can develop objects which represent HCI (human–computer interface) items such as buttons, menus and scroll bars and application items such as accounts, invoices and air traffic radars which can be reused time and time again with little extra effort. One of the features of the Java system is a large library which can be used to instantiate objects that can be used for Internet applications.

- *The language should be robust.* One of the problems with some of the more popular programming languages is the fact that it is quite easy to produce applications that collapse. Sometimes this collapse manifests itself immediately; however, it can also occur outside the application because, for example, the application has corrupted some memory which is not used by another application until a few days later. Probably the most notorious programming language guilty of having features which lead to non-robust performance is C. One example of a facility within C which can give rise to problems is the pointer type. Pointers enable variables to contain the address of a location. Such addresses can be manipulated as if they are arithmetic entities: they can be added to, subtracted from, multiplied and even divided. Once a programming error has been committed with a pointer a number of events could happen depending on the nature of the error. Some common events include memory being unusable and memory becoming corrupt, leading to a crash of the application or even the host operating system. One of the design aims of the developers of Java has been to eliminate features of programming languages such as C which lead to such problems. For example, there is no notion of a pointer in Java.

- *The language should have a high performance.* One of the features of the Java programming language is that of **threads**. These are multiple concurrent executions of code which provide a high-level implementation of concurrent processing. This allows a Java program to switch between each of its threads when the processing in one thread reaches a point where it cannot progress. This leads to a highly efficient utilization of processor cycles and a fast response time.

- *The language should be portable.* A major aim of the designers of Java was that a program developed in Java for, say, a Sun workstation running the Solaris operating system should be capable of being ported across to a PC running another operating system, for example Windows NT or Windows 95. This is one of the main achievements of the Java development team. The authors have ported some very large applications written in Java from one computer to another dissimilar computer with no changes made at all.

- *The language should be as simple as possible.* Many languages – Ada is probably the best example – have become overburdened with features. This has a number of effects: first, such languages are often expensive to compile and their run-time support is so large that even a small program occupies a large amount of memory; second, the learning curve for such languages is long and hard; and third, compiling programs in such languages can take quite a long time. The designers of Java have tried to keep the base facilities of the language to a minimum and have provided many extras within a number of libraries.

1.2.2 A simple Java program

In order to give you a flavour of what Java looks like we have reproduced a simple Java program below. You will find this program in Chapter 12 which describes how you develop applets: programs which can be embedded in Web pages.

```java
import java.awt.Graphics;

public class HelloWorld extends java.applet.Applet {
  public void init() {
    resize(100,100);
  }

  public void paint(Graphics g) {
    g.drawString("Hello World!",5,20);
  }
}
```

The first line informs the Java system that the graphics library associated with the system is to be used. The next line introduces a class. A **class** is an object-oriented concept which will be described in Chapters 2 and 3. For the time being just assume that a class implements a series of chunks of code each of which implements some function. The class in the example is known as `HelloWorld`. The keyword `extends` is part of the object-oriented baggage connected with Java. This concept will be discussed at length in Chapter 5; for the time being assume that `extends` implements a facility whereby program code identified by `java.applet.Applet` is made available to the code within `HelloWorld`. `java.applet.Applet` is another example of a class which contains chunks of code useful for developing applets.

The two chunks of code within the class `HelloWorld` are `init` and `paint`. The header line that describes `init` states that it can be used by any other code in the system (`public`) and the code does not return any value (`void`), it just carries out some processing. `init` is called initially when a Java-compatible browser loads the applet. The processing that it carries out is to call a chunk of code called `resize` which forms part of `java.applet.Applet`; all this code does is to increase the amount of space that the applet page occupies to 100 × 100 pixels. The second chunk of code, `paint`, writes the string `"Hello World!"` at the coordinates 5, 20 on the browser page space; this chunk of code is invoked when the applet is first asked to display itself.

Do not be too worried about whether you fully understand the code presented above. You will find that a lot will become clearer during the reading of the first five chapters of this book. If you want further information about writing and running Java programs this can be found in Appendix A.

1.3 The system

1.3.1 How the Java compiler works

It is worth describing the implementation of the Java language in a little more detail. Figure 1.1 shows the implementation of a conventional programming language.The programmer develops a program expressed in what is known as **source code**. This is translated by a **compiler** to the base language of the computer known as **object code**. This object code is then executed and the program carries out its function. The rules governing the way code is written are very strict and if an error has been made the compiler will not carry out the translation but issue a number of error messages which tell the programmer what has gone wrong. This, then, is the conventional way of implementing a programming language. Unfortunately it suffers from one problem: the implementation is specific to just one computer – the object code that has been generated can only be executed by a computer that recognizes it.

In order to produce a portable implementation the developers of Java adopted the strategy shown in Figure 1.2. The compiler in this case does not translate the source code to the object code of the computer but translates it into what is known as a **byte code**. This is a language which is capable of being executed by any computer. However, before it can be executed a program to do this, known as an **interpreter**, has to be constructed. Normally the effort to do this is quite small. If you wish to transfer a Java system to a computer for which it is not implemented two steps are needed. First, move the Java compiler to the new computer.

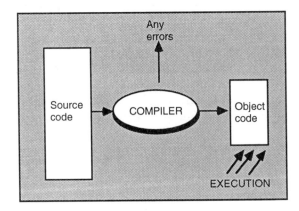

Figure 1.1 A conventional compiler.

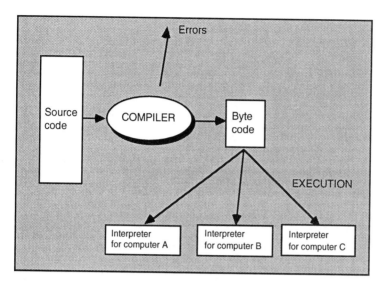

Figure 1.2 The implementation of the Java compiler.

This is usually very easy – normally a matter of days – since the compiler is written in a standard subset of a programming language; next the developer has to write a new interpreter which takes the byte code generated by the Java compiler and executes it. This is a longer process but not too long – usually a few months. After the interpreter has been developed the Java system is ready to be used.

The Java code distribution currently includes the following important components:

- *The Java interpreter.* This is the language processor which has been ported to a number of systems. It works by reading and executing Java byte code.

- *The Java compiler.* This is the language processor which translates Java code to byte code. Normally it is used for the development of high-performance code.

- *The Java disassembler.* This displays files created using the Java compiler.

- *The document generator.* This processes files which contain Java code and displays useful bureaucratic information such as descriptions of what the Java code produced by a programmer is meant to do.

- *The profiling tool.* This produces a listing of where the execution of Java code has occurred.

- *The applet viewer.* This is a utility which enables the developer to examine the output from a Java program.

- *The Java debugger.* This is a hybrid debugger which debugs interpreted code.

1.3.2 The current state of the system

The Java system has been implemented for Sun workstations, PCs running Windows 95 and Macintoshes running the System 7 operating system. There are a number of teams currently developing implementations for other operating systems and hardware; for example, there is a team at IBM currently developing an implementation for Windows 3.11. In December 1996 Sun announced a further upgrade of the JDK to version 1.1.

1.4 The evolution of browsers

Almost certainly the main area of the Internet which has expanded well beyond the wildest hopes of its inventors has been the World Wide Web. The Web was the brainchild of Tim Berners-Lee, a researcher at the European Laboratory for Particle Physics in Geneva (CERN), who proposed a system of interlocking documents within CERN, where references or links to other documents could be embedded in another document with the facility for a user of the CERN system to navigate via these links. Web documents are written in a primitive language known as HTML (Hyper Text Markup Language). The statements in HTML determine how a document will look when it is viewed. An example of a simple HTML document is shown below.

```
<HTML><HEAD><TITLE>Development processes</TITLE></HEAD>
<BODY>
<H1>Aims</H1> After reading this document you will
<UL>
<LI>Have an appreciation of how software development in
the real world is carried out.</LI>
<LI>Have an appreciation of how a software project
consists of interlinked technical processes.</LI>
<LI>Have an appreciation that many factors influence the
software development process, not only technical
ones.</LI></UL>

<H1>Objectives</H1>After studying this part of the course
you will be able to:<UL>

<LI>Identify    the   main    software    development
processes.</LI>
```

```
<LI> Detail the defining characteristics of the technical
and validation processes that are used in software
development.</LI>
<LI>Give reasons why a particular form of software
development has been
adopted.</LI>
</UL><H1>Introduction</H1><P>
Up to this point in the course you will have concerned
yourself with programming and other technical activities
such as sending email. This chunk represents the first
glimpse you will have of the real world of software
development. It describes the various tasks that make up
a software project and how they are put together within a
project. We will be looking at how software is developed
by examining the history of a company's involvement with
information technology from its initial stages, when it
decides to become involved with a computer system, up to
the point where the system is installed and undergoes
change to take account of business conditions.</P>
</BODY>
</HTML>
```

The way that users of the World Wide Web would see this document is shown as Figure 1.3.

There are a number of points to be made about HTML code. First, the elements of the document are introduced by the use of the characters < and > enclosing some keywords. The meaning of the various keywords shown in the fragment above is:

<HTML></HTML> delineates the document and states that the document will be expressed in the HTML language.

<TITLE></TITLE> encloses the title of the document.

<BODY></BODY> encloses the main body of the document.

<UL></UL> introduces a collection of bullet pointed paragraphs.

<LI></LI> encloses a bullet pointed paragraph.

<H1> </H1> encloses a heading which is expressed in bold characters.

<P></P> encloses a new paragraph of text.

It is worth stressing that the example we have given is only a very simple one: HTML is a moderately rich language which provides facilities for incorporating graphics, tables and images.

It also enables links to be embedded in an HTML document which, when clicked by a user, take that user to another Web site. This enables authors of Web documents to reference other documents and provides the characteristics which have led to it being called a web.

Originally Berners-Lee's system was meant only to be a relatively local system for CERN and its early development took place on CERN local area networks and central computers.

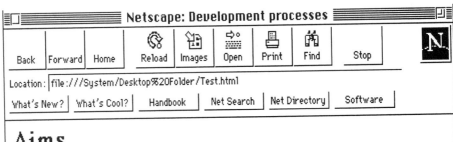

Figure 1.3 The fragment of HTML viewed by Netscape.

Initially the growth of the Web was quite small. However, in 1993 an application was developed which transformed it. This was *Mosaic*, developed by an undergraduate named Marc Andreessen who was then at the University of Illinois at Urbana-Champaign. *Mosaic* was the first usable graphical interface to the Web: it allowed users to navigate through the links in the Web with relative ease. The development of *Mosaic* provided a huge impetus and other tools were developed of which *Netscape* is probably the most used and well known.

Browsers and the World Wide Web

The state of the World Wide Web at the beginning of 1995 was that it was immensely popular, with the main medium used to develop Web pages being the language HTML. The browsers which enabled users to traverse links within documents in the Web implemented in HTML were moderately sophisticated. However, such browsers did not really support very much interaction. Certainly the users of such browsers were able, with little effort, to traverse links which spanned continents but, apart from simple functions such as checking a user's password, the browsers extant at the beginning of 1995 implemented little more than the traversal of links.

This changed in mid-1995 with the release of a browser known as *HotJava* which was the first to provide interactive access to Web documents. The history of Java and HotJava started around 1991 and was preceded by the development of a programming language known as *Oak* at Sun Microsystems. The driving principle behind *Oak* was the development of consumer-electronics products that would be simple and bug free. The direct parent of *Oak* was the programming language known as C++. However, the process of refining *Oak* to the point that it became Java involved the simplification and deletion of some of the facilities within C++.

Java programmers can produce two types of software, **applets** and **applications**. The latter are standalone applications which can run independently. The former are programs which can be included in Web documents. The inclusion of Java code in such documents marks a transition point in the development of the World Wide Web. From being a passive repository of data it became a store of interactive applications – albeit applications embedded in the linking technology. Users of browsers which recognize Java code are now able to execute programs which have the functionality of programs written in any other programming language.

Two specific types of programs that can be written in Java are **protocol handlers** and **content handlers**. The former are programs that can be loaded into a browser and interpret an Internet protocol such as HTTP. The latter are again programs which can be loaded into a Java-compatible browser and interpret differing file formats.

1.5 Running Java applications and Java applets

So far we have discussed general issues with regard to Java. Before looking at the language in a little more detail it is worth describing how to execute Java programs. The details of compiling and running a Java program will differ from implementation to implementation, for example the programs developed in this book were implemented using the Macintosh System 7 version of the Java Development Kit. For this implementation compilation and execution was achieved via a process of dragging and dropping files on top of the compiler and a program known as Java Runner which carried out the execution. In this section we shall assume the base PC implementation.

1.5.1 Compiling and running applications

The process of compiling and running an application is simple:

- Use your favourite editor to create a Java program. The file that contains the program must have the extension .java.

- Compile the program using the Java compiler javac. If you are not using a Java development environment then you will need to use an MS-DOS prompt. So, if you have called your application file MyFile.java, all you need do is to type:

```
javac MyFile.java
```

The program will compile and if you have made some syntax errors the compiler will notify you of their nature. Any errors will need to be corrected.

- Execute the program using the java interpreter java. The file produced by the compilation above will be called MyFile.class, but all you need do is to specify the name in front of the full stop. So, to execute the program held in MyFile.class, all you need type is:

```
java MyFile
```

This, then, is the process of compiling and executing a Java application. The process for producing an applet is a little different.

1.5.2 Compiling and running an applet

Applets are snippets of Java code which can be incorporated into HTML documents. The process of running an applet is described below; the first two steps are identical to those detailed in the previous sub-section.

- Use your favourite editor to create a Java program. The file that contains the program must have the extension `.java`.

- Compile the program using the Java compiler `javac`. If you are not using a Java development environment then you will need to use an MS-DOS prompt. So, if you have called your application file `MyFile.java` all you need do is to type:

```
javac MyFile.java
```

The program will compile and if you have made some syntax errors the compiler will notify you of their nature.

- Prepare an HTML file which embeds the code, using your editor. Normally this file is used for testing the applet and has a minimal form. The code for an HTML file for testing the applet contained in `MyFile.java` is shown below:

```
<HTML>
<HEAD>
<TITLE>MyFile Applet</title>
</HEAD>
<BODY>
<HR>
<APPLET CODE=MyFile.class WIDTH=400 HEIGHT=300>
</APPLET>
<HR>
</BODY>
</HTML>
```

All it contains is a title, instructions to generate two horizontal rules and a section which details where the code which is to be executed can be found and the size of the applet window (400 by 300 pixels). The name of the file should be the same as that adopted for the source code, but should have an extension `html`.

- Use the Java appletviewer to check out that the program works. This program, which is supplied as part of the Java Development Kit, will display your working applet on the computer screen. The command line for this is:

```
appletviewer MyFile.html
```

- When you are happy with the functioning of the applet, embed it in the HTML document that you intend placing it in and check it out with your favourite browser.

Appendix A contains further information about running applications and applets.

1.6 What you will learn from this book

We have set ourselves a number of overall aims:

- To teach you the elements of the Java programming language. In an introductory book such as this we have not set out to teach 100% of the language. We estimate that we will have taught you 90% of the language; however, we would claim that in doing this we will have taught you *all* of the important parts of the language.

- To teach you how to develop both standalone applications and browser-compatible applications known as applets.

- To teach you how you can write Java programs which can interface seamlessly with entities that can be found on the Internet, for example World Wide Web pages.

- To teach you what an object-oriented approach to software development is and how you can use the object-oriented paradigm to develop Internet programs.

- To teach you how to access the extensive library of software that comes bundled with the Java system.

1.7 A note on exercises and SAQs

In the remaining chapters of the book we have included a number of exercises and self–assessment questions (SAQs). The former are mainly programming exercises and involve a substantial commitment of time. The latter are short, snappy questions which enable you to gain confidence that you have grasped the main points of a section of teaching. You will either love or hate SAQs; if you hate them just ignore them. We would, however, advise you to make an attempt at all the exercises.

1.8 SUMMARY

This chapter has described the Web technology that gave rise to Java. We have also shown you how Java can be used to develop both applications (standalone programs) and applets (code which can be included in a Web page). This chapter has also taught enough of the HTML markup language for you to be able to write Web pages that contain Java code.

CHAPTER TWO

Objects

AIMS

- To show how computing applications can be regarded as consisting of objects.
- To introduce the vocabulary terms: *object, message* and *state*.
- To describe how communication occurs in an object-oriented application via messages.
- To show some very simple examples of Java code.
- To show that objects can also, in turn, consist of objects.

2.1 Introduction

The past five years have seen a huge increase in the use of object-oriented technology. Programming languages such as C++ and Objective C are now becoming relatively commonplace, object-oriented databases are starting to become efficient enough to use on commercial projects and every degree course in computing contains at least one course that focuses on object technology. Unfortunately most of the teaching literature on object-orientation tends to be quite difficult to access; since Java is an object-oriented programming language we have decided not to dive straight into a full description of the language, but briefly introduce you to some of the main concepts of object-orientation.

In order to do this a number of examples of computer-based systems will be described and an object view taken of their architecture. In describing these systems we will introduce some very small fragments of Java code.

2.2 Some examples of object-based systems

This section will describe a number of computer applications and show how each can be regarded as consisting of a collection of objects and an outside world where the system executes via the process of message passing.

2.2.1 A simple air traffic control system

The first example that we shall describe is a simple system for keeping track of the planes in the air space surrounding an airport. The system is simple as we do not intend that any detail should come between you and the teaching of object concepts that will be carried out in this section. An example of such a system is shown in Figure 2.1.

This is a very simple view of an air traffic control system. Figure 2.1 is just a snapshot taken at a particular time during its execution and shows that five planes are currently under the control of the human air traffic controllers who supervise the traffic to and from the airport. Each plane is an example of an **object**: some entity which is represented in the store of the computer on which the application runs.

Each object will consist of a unique **identifier** and some stored data which is associated with it; the unique identifiers in this case are the flight numbers attached to each plane in Figure 2.1. The stored data is often referred to as the **state** of an object.

The stored data will be necessary for the functioning of the system in which the objects are embedded. In the example of the air traffic control system there is potentially a large amount of data that can be associated with a flight. Since we are only considering a very simple system we shall assume that only four items of data are associated with each object: the plane's x coordinate position, y coordinate position, z coordinate position and the type of plane.

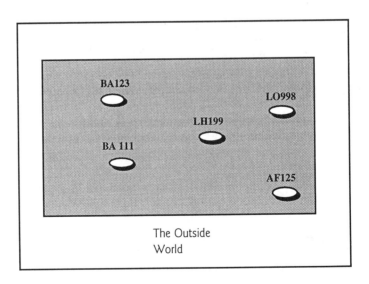

Figure 2.1 A very simple air traffic control system.

These four items of data are important for the functioning of an air traffic control system; indeed the first three items are mandatory as it would be impossible to do very much in such a system without knowing where the planes are. The final piece of data is required in order to assign a runway on which the plane is to land as the airport may have a number of runways suited to different types of plane.

Figure 2.1 is split into two parts. The shaded part represents the air traffic control system, while the unshaded part represents the outside world: the world of real aircraft, human controllers and concrete airports. Events occur in this outside world which affect the object world. A typical event might be a radar informing the system that a particular plane has moved its position or a particular plane has disappeared because it has removed itself from the area of the skies administered by the air traffic control system. These events will access or affect the object world within the computer – normally this is manifested in the destruction of existing objects, the construction of a new object, the updating of an object's state or the retrieval of data from the object world. Let us look at some of these events and how they affect the simple air traffic control system:

- A plane appears in the air space controlled by the system. This results in a new plane object being created and given values for its state.

- A plane disappears from the air space. This can occur for a number of reasons: the plane may have left the air space during its onward journey, it could have landed or, very rarely, it could have crashed. This results in the disappearance of the plane object.

- The plane moves its position in the sky. This is normally monitored by radar equipment and it results in the x, y and z coordinates of the plane being updated.

- Data about a plane's position is sent to a controller on the ground. The object world remains the same; the only thing that happens is that the x, y and z coordinates of a plane are sent to the outside world.

The way in which the object world within the shaded area is altered and accessed is achieved via a mechanism known as a **message**. An example best explains what a message looks like. The line below shows a Java message being set to the aeroplane AF565; the effect of the message is to update the position of the plane to which the message is sent. At this stage don't worry about how such messages are programmed in Java; the important thing you should be concentrating on at this stage in the book is the format of messages:

```
AF565.newPos(12,444,22);
```

The line consists of two components. The first component is an object known as the **receiver object**. In the line above, this is the plane identified by AF565. The second component is the message. The message above consists of four components. The first component is known as the **selector**, which identifies the message that is to be sent. The remaining three components are known as the **arguments** of the message. Thus, in the example above, the receiver object AF565 receives a message identified by the selector newPos and arguments 12, 444, 22 which are associated with the *x* position, *y* position and *z* position of the plane. Do not worry about the semicolon at the end of each statement. In Chapter 4 in which we outline some Java programming constructs we describe the use of semicolons.

As we have implied above, messages are generated by events which occur in the outside world. The message example above might correspond to the event of a plane moving and its new position being detected by a radar. Messages either update objects, update objects and return with some value, or just return with some value without updating any objects.

SAQ

In the Java code shown below write down the receiver object, the selector and the arguments; do not worry about the meaning of each statement.

(i)   newRadar.update()

(ii)   oldRadar.writeDown(12,newPos)

(iii)   planeLH.land(runway12)

Solution

The three answers are:

(i)   The receiver object is newRadar, the selector is update and there are no arguments.

(ii)   The receiver object is oldRadar, the selector is writeDown and the arguments are 12 and newPos.

(iii)   The receiver object is planeLH, the selector is land and the argument is runway12.

Another example of a message associated with the air traffic control system is:

LH123.getxPos();

This message is sent to the receiver object LH123 and returns with the *x* position of the plane. Here the selector is not associated with any parameters so the brackets following it are empty.

This message is differentiated from the previous one that we examined in one way: it does not have any arguments. A message in Java can consist of an arbitrary number of arguments ranging from zero up to some arbitrary number imposed by the Java interpreter you use.

Another example of a message being sent is:

```
AF555.getyPos();
```

This sends the message `getyPos` to the receiver object `AF555` and returns with the *y* position of the plane. Another example of a message associated with the simple air traffic control system is:

```
BA126.removePlane();
```

This removes a plane from the air space. This message would normally be sent when a plane flies outside the air space covered by the system. A final example of a message is:

```
BA133.landPlane();
```

This would result in the receiver object (`BA133`) landing and disappearing from the world of plane objects.

Exercise

A system has been built which monitors the movement of staff within a building. Each member of staff wears a badge which emits a signal that is picked up by sensors situated in the rooms of the building. Can you write some typical *receiver object.messages* that will occur in this application?

Solution

Two examples are shown below.

```
thomas.enterBuilding()
```

The code for this will be executed when the member of staff `thomas` enters the building.

```
roberts.moveFromTo(room12,entrance)
```

The code for this will be executed when the member of staff `roberts` moves from room 12 of the building to the entrance foyer of the building.

It is worth pointing out that the messages which we have discussed are all associated with some Java programming code which carries out the processing associated with the message. However, at this point you should not worry too much about how this code is defined. You will find full details in Chapter 5. An important point to reiterate about messages is that when something happens in an application, messages will be sent to and from the objects which make up the application.

2.2.2 A more complicated air traffic control system

The previous example was used to describe some of the core concepts of object-oriented technology. This example provides some reinforcement of these concepts and also introduces some new properties of messages.

The example involves an air traffic control system in which the planes are held in a number of queues. Each queue will have a collection of planes awaiting landing. Normally a plane lands by being transferred from the front of one queue to the end of another queue below it. The system also keeps track of the planes that have landed. A snapshot of the system is shown in Figure 2.2.

This shows that the air space has been divided into three queues with the topmost queue containing planes which have the longest time to wait before landing. The instance also shows a collection of planes which have landed. The important point to make about this application is that not only does it contain simple objects such as planes, but it also contains objects which themselves contain objects. For example, the collection of landed planes is a set of plane objects and the queues of planes awaiting landing are also objects which, in turn, contain other objects (planes).

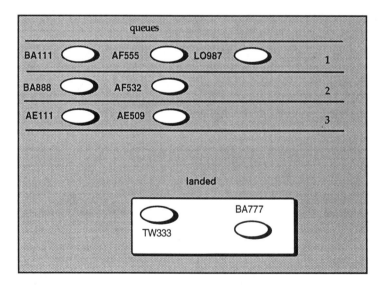

Figure 2.2 An instance of the air traffic control system.

Since this is a more complicated system than that described in the previous subsection it will have more messages associated with it. An example of a message is shown below:

```
queues.moveDown(1);
```

This takes the first plane in queue 1 and places it at the end of the queue below it (queue 2). The receiver object in this case is queues. This illustrates another important point about objects. The receiver object for this message is not a simple object such as a plane but a collection of objects.

Some more examples of typical messages are shown below:

```
queues.moveUp(2);
queues.land();
queues.movePlane(AF555,2,3);
queues.emergencyLand(BA7630);
```

The first message consists of a selector and one argument. Its function is to take the first plane in the second queue and place it at the end of the queue above it; this message might be generated when an air traffic controller is attempting to find some space in a queue – perhaps for a plane that wants to land in a hurry.

The second message lands the plane which is nearest the ground. This message is a frequent one since it corresponds to the normal operation of the air traffic control system and might be generated when a controller lands a plane normally. The third message, which consists of a selector and three arguments, moves a plane from its current position to a new position within a queue. The example shown above moves the plane AF555 to the third position in queue 2.

The final message, which just consists of a selector and a single argument, lands a plane in an emergency: no matter where the plane is in the queues, it joins the planes which have already landed on the ground. Clearly this corresponds to a major incident at the airport. Some further examples of messages are shown below:

```
queues.moveUp(3);
queues.movePlane(TU878,1,3);
queues.adjustPlane(TU878,3,1);
queues.land();
```

With the first message the plane at the head of queue 3 is moved up so that it is at the end of queue 2. Next, the plane TU878 is sent to the third position in queue 1. Then, the same plane is sent to the first position in queue 3. The next line of code results in the plane at the head of the lowermost queue (queue 3) being landed. This is plane TU878.

Again it is important to point out that each of the messages shown above is associated with program code which is executed when the message is sent to the receiver object.

SAQ

Write down the sequence of *receiver object.messages* which are executed when the first three planes in the bottommost queue land and the plane AF555 moves from its current position to the third position in queue 3.

Solution

The solution is:

```
queues.land(); queues.land();
queues.land(); queues.movePlane(AF555,3,3);
```

2.2.3 A print spooler

The next example is a print spooler. This is a piece of system software that forms part of a multi-user operating system. During the operation of such an operating system computer users will ask for files to be printed.

The computer normally has limited printing resources, and so the print requests are queued up for each printer in the system, with the print spooler controlling the addition of print requests to the queues and the selection of those print requests that are to be satisfied. A snapshot of a print spooler is shown in Figure 2.3.

This shows a number of objects. It contains a table which lists all the printers in the system together with their upper and lower print limits. For example, one entry in the table states that printer TH44 will only be available to print files between 5000 and 10 000 lines of text; obviously the technology used in this printer is best for large print runs. Each item in the table is itself an object, so in Figure 2.3 the printer table currently holds six objects which describe the printing limits of individual printers. One thing which is worth noticing in Figure 2.3 is that we give objects names which start with lower case letters.

The other objects shown in this figure are the print requests (the shadowed boxes) which are identified by an initial letter *p*, and a collection which contains the names of the available printers together with a pointer to their queues of print requests – some of which could be empty. Each item in the collection is itself an object, the queues are objects and the print requests in the queues are objects. So it is quite a rich model.

A whole variety of messages might be generated during the execution of such a print spooler. For example:

```
printQueues.addRequest(LA245,p107);
```

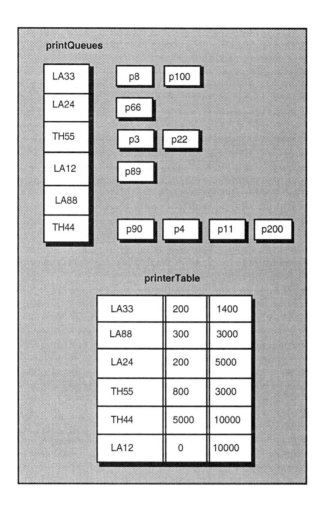

Figure 2.3 An instance of a print spooler.

would add a print request identified as p107 to the end of the queue for the printer LA245. The message addRequest(LA245,p107) would be sent to the object printQueues containing the queue information for the spooler.

Another example of Java code containing a message for the spooler would be:

```
printQueues.removeRequest(LA88);
```

This shows the receiver object printQueues being sent the message removeRequest() which results in the first item in the queue associated with printer LA88 being removed from the queue. As well as the queues being associated with messages, the table holding print details would also be associated with messages. For example, the Java code:

```
printTable.adjustPrinterLimits(LA24,100,3000);
```

contains a message sent to the receiver object `printTable` which adjusts the lower and upper limits of print requests that the printer `LA24` can handle, with the lower limit being 100 lines and the upper limit being 3000 lines. The code:

```
printTable.newPrinter(LA777,100,7000);
```

would add a new printer to the table with a lower print limit of 100 lines and an upper limit of 7000 lines. This message would also give rise to a new message:

```
printQueues.setNewPrinter(LA777);
```

generated by the code associated with the `newPrinter` message which would establish a new object corresponding to LA777 within the print request queues. This message would be generated by the print table object rather than emanating from outside the system. This is an important point: up till now we have described the fact that messages are generated from the outside world by events that happen in that world. While this is true of many messages you will also find, throughout this book, that messages can be generated by objects and sent to other objects. A line of code which contains a receiver object and a message will be referred to in the remainder of this book as a **Java expression**.

SAQ

Write down the Java expressions which are executed when the following occur:

- A new printer `cLaser` is added to the system. It has a lower limit of 1500 lines of print and an upper limit of 8000.

- Two items are removed from the queue associated with printer LA33.

Solution

These are shown below:

```
printTable.newPrinter(cLaser,1500,8000);
printQueues.removeRequest(LA33);
printQueues.removeRequest(LA33);
```

2.2.4 A security monitor

The next example is a security monitor. This is a program which is used to determine whether there have been any unusual accesses to a computer system or network which indicate an intruder has been at work.

Computer systems now contain very valuable materials such as copyrights, trade secrets, personnel details, bank accounts and defence secrets. Large amounts of money can be made by accessing this material; for example, an intruder who gains access to the accounts held on a bank's computer might be able to create a new account, add a large amount of money to that account and then withdraw the money at a bank branch.

There are a large number of ways that a computer system can be illegally accessed. One of the most popular is to masquerade as a genuine user. When a genuine user accesses a computer system the first thing that the system will ask for is his or her password. This is a combination of letters and digits which, theoretically, only the user knows and which is assigned to the user when he or she first registers with the computer system. A popular way of illegally accessing a system is to find out the password of an existing user. There are a number of ways that this can be done: by monitoring the traffic between the user's computer and the network; by searching the user's room – often users will keep a written version of their password in a drawer, wallet or handbag; or by knowing something about the user – often users will employ their wife's, husband's or dog's name as a password. Once the password has been discovered an illegal user can create havoc.

The Security Monitor

One way to detect whether an intruder has gained access to a system is to keep details of the usage of a computer by legal users and to alert the manager of the computer if a user is exhibiting unusual behaviour such as using the computer late at night. Most of us are people of habit: we tend to use a computer between certain times and make a fixed number of accesses. For example, a programmer who works for an industrial company might normally start using a computer at 9.00 o'clock, take a short break from 1.00 to 1.30 and start using the computer again until 5.00 o'clock. A student studying programming might use the computer during the times of the day allocated to the programming class and also early in the evening.

A program which keeps details of the usage of a computer and which checks whether any unusual use is being made is known as a **security monitor**. A security monitor periodically examines the usage data generated by users accessing a computer and looks for any unusual accesses such as a worker accessing the computer past midnight. At its heart is a collection of data which describes the use made of a computer system by its users.

Williams	22
Tompkinson	334
Roberts	4
Ince	77
Freeman	34
Jewson	331
Maltravers	3
Coleman	44
MacDonald	509
MacDougall	28

Figure 2.4 Part of a security monitor.

For this example we shall concentrate on one small part of this data: that concerned with tracking the number of times a user has accessed a computer. The data for this is shown in Figure 2.4.

This data represents a table in which each entry contains the name of a user and the number of times that he or she has accessed the computer since some date in the past. For example, Figure 2.4 shows that user Jewson has accessed the table 331 times.

Exercise

Can you think of messages with which this table would be associated? Don't write them down as Java expressions, but just write them using English.

Solution

The three we would choose would be:

- A message which added a new legal user to the table. This user would be initialized to have zero accesses.
- A message which increased the number of accesses of a legal user by one.
- A message which removed a legal user from the table, for example when that user left employment.

Some examples of *receiver object.message* expressions corresponding to the bullet point answers to the previous exercise are shown below. The first:

```
securityTable.addUser(thomas);
```

adds the user thomas to the table. The expression:

```
securityTable.increaseAccess(roberts);
```

increases the number of times the user roberts has accessed the system by one (we have assumed that roberts is in the table). The expression:

```
securityTable.deleteUser(thomas);
```

removes the user thomas from the table.

Yellow Pages and Network Information Services

Yellow Pages is a service which enables the users of a large number of computers not to worry about the potentially large number of passwords that they would need to keep track of – one per computer. Using Yellow Pages a single file is used to associate one user with a single password that can be used on every computer to which he or she is allowed access. This file is stored on a central computer called the *master* or *ypmaster*. On large networks, and also to serve as a backup, other machines designated as *slaves* or *ypslaves* will maintain this information as well. Because of copyright problems you will now find Yellow Pages called Network Information Services in more up-to-date technical documentation books.

Exercise

List some of the messages you would expect to be sent to the table which stores the user names and passwords in a Yellow Pages file. Write down no more than three.

Solution

Some of them are shown below. No doubt you will have used other names for the selectors and destination objects.

```
passTable.newUser(userJones, "jjhjll");
passTable.deleteUser(userWilliams);
passtable.changePassword(userRoberts, "887&&%%rfop");
```

The first line adds a new user with a password to the table. The next line removes an existing user. The final line changes the password of an existing user.

SAQ ▌

Which of the following statements are true and which are false? if you think that a statement is false explain why.

(i)   A Java expression consists of an object, a selector and one or more arguments enclosed in brackets.

(ii)   A system can be regarded as a collection of objects to which messages can be sent.

(iii) Objects can themselves consist of objects.

(iv)   The state of an object is the size of the object expressed in bytes.

(v)   A message can be used to change the state of an object.

Solution ▌

(i) Almost true: a Java expression can have no arguments as well as one or more arguments (ii) True. (iii) True. (iv) False, the state is the data associated with an object. (v) True.

2.3 SUMMARY

A number of points have emerged from this chapter:

- Collections of objects carry out the functions of the system by sending messages to each other.

- The objects in a system can be simple or can be collections of other objects.

- During execution of a system messages are sent to objects. The object to which a message is sent is known as a receiver object.

- A message can be sent to a receiver object from the outside world or can be sent from another object.

- Messages are normally associated, directly or indirectly, with an event that occurs in the outside world.

- A message consists of a selector and a number of arguments – anything from zero up to a predefined limit.

CHAPTER THREE

Classes and Objects

AIMS

- To show how objects can be described by classes.
- To introduce the vocabulary terms: *instance method, class method, instance variable, class variable* and *inheritance*.
- To describe how the mechanisms of inheritance can be used to develop reusable software.
- To describe how the state of an object can be changed.

3.1 Introduction

The previous chapter described the fact that computing systems can be viewed as consisting of objects which cooperate with each other in order to carry out a task by means of the mechanism of message sending. Events in the outside world such as a user requesting some information from an applet or application will give rise to a series of messages exchanged between objects within that applet or application until one or more objects send some data to the outside world. Often these messages will result in the state of an object being changed. The first part of this chapter examines *some* of the mechanisms whereby a state changes. This material is needed to understand the rest of the book so we would advise you to read it slowly and surely, attempting all the exercises and SAQs.

3.2 State changes

In the previous chapter we told you that objects had a state. The state of an object represents the data that is contained in that object. For example, a system which administered the employees of a company would have employee objects each of which had a state consisting of data which represented the employee's name, his or her address, salary and tax code. The question that we want to address in this section is: how can we modify this data, for example in changing an employee's salary? The aim of this section is to show this with respect to what are known as scalars. These are simple data values such as integers.

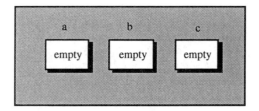

Figure 3.1 The effect of the declaration.

Java has facilities for a number of **scalar values**. These are values which are simple, for example integers, characters and floating point numbers. It is worth pointing out here that the term is used in a slightly different way in other programming languages; whenever we use it in this book it refers to a simple piece of data and not an object. In this section we are going to concentrate on integers; Chapter 4 will examine the other **scalars** that are available in Java. Integers are designated by the keyword int in Java. Since integers will occupy space somewhere in the memory of the computer and will need to be identified Java provides a declaration facility. An example of this is shown below:

```
int a, b, c;
```

What this statement does is to notify the Java system that we will be using three variables a, b and c. Each of these variables represents a location into which an integer can be placed. All that has happened after this statement has been executed is that three locations have been allocated which are big enough for integer values and each of these locations is uniquely identified by a label. This is shown in Figure 3.1. The three scalar variables a, b and c will usually need to be given values. This is achieved in Java by means of a statement known as an **assignment statement**:

```
variable = expression;
```

where expression delivers some value which can be stored in the variable. For the time being we shall assume that expression delivers an integer result. An example of three assignment statements in action is shown below:

```
a = 23;
b = 333;
c = 99;
```

This results in the values being deposited in the area of computer memory identified by a, b and c as shown in Figure 3.2.

Assignments can be combined with declarations. For example, the code:

```
int newVal = 99, oldVal = 33, increment = 1;
```

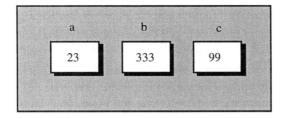

Figure 3.2 Assignment in action.

is equivalent to the code :

```
int newVal, oldVal, increment;
newVal = 99;
oldVal = 33;
increment = 1;
```

So far you have seen some simple assignments in that single values were given to variables. All programming languages – and Java is no exception – allow more complicated assignments which allow for larger expressions to be assigned. Chapter 4 will describe these more complex expressions in more detail. However, it is worth giving you a flavour at this stage in the book. Some examples of more complicated expressions are shown below; + stands for addition, * for multiplication and – for subtraction in Java:

```
newVal = 12 + oldVal;
oldVal = 2*increment + 12;
oldVal = (a+b)*(c+d)
```

What is the meaning of each these statements? The first statement places in the location labelled by newVal the result of adding 12 to the location labelled by oldVal. So, if oldVal contained 33 the result of this operation would be to place 45 into the location labelled by newVal.

The result of the second statement is to multiply the contents of increment by 2, add to the result the integer 12 and then place the result into the location labelled by oldVal. The result of the third statement is to add together the integers in the locations a and b and then multiply this result by the sum of the integers in c and d.

It is worth making an important point about the names you use for variables in Java. As you will see later you should not use variable names with an upper case first letter. The convention that we have adopted in the book is to have a lower case first letter for the first word within the variable name with the second and subsequent words having upper case letters.

Often we will need to be able to use the contents of a variable in modifying that variable; for example, in the security monitor example we needed to increase the number of accesses made by a user by one.

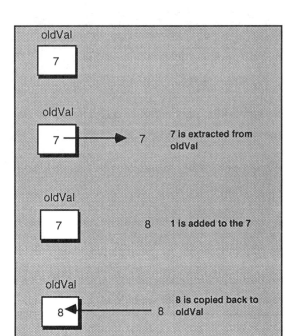

Figure 3.3 The effect of the statement `oldVal = oldVal + 1`.

In order to explain how this is programmed let us examine a single Java assignment statement:

```
oldVal = oldVal + 1;
```

If you have a mathematical background then this statement will mystify you as it seems to state an impossible condition: that `oldVal` is one more than itself. However, if we take the meaning of the = symbol as 'place in the variable on my left hand side the value on the right hand side' then a clear meaning emerges. In order to explain this meaning let us assume that the variable `oldVal` contains the value 7.

Then when this statement is executed the action that is carried out is to extract out the current value of the variable, add one to it and then place this new value into the variable. This is shown in Figure 3.3.

Some further examples of this style of assignment statement are shown below:

```
x = x + 12;
oldVal = oldVal*2;
newVal = newVal*3 + 1;
increment = increment*12 - 33;
holder = holder + (99*old)
```

The first statement adds 12 to the value of the variable x; the second doubles the value of the variable oldVal; the third trebles the value of newVal, adds one to it and places the result back in newVal; the fourth multiplies increment by 12, subtracts 33 from it and places the result back in increment; and the fifth statement multiplies the contents of the variable old by 99, adds the result of this to holder and then places the result back in holder.

SAQ

If the contents of the three variables ia, ib and ic are 12, 33 and 10, what is the result of the following assignment statements?

```
ia = ia + 5;
ib = (ia + ib)*ic;
ia = ia*2 - 3;
ic = ic - 2;
```

Solution

The first statement places the value 17 into ia; the second statement places the value 450 in the variable ib; the third statement places the value 21 into the variable ia; and the final statement places the value 8 into ic.

This concludes the section on state changes. Before leaving it is worth stating that the section has been very limited in concept. All that we have tried to do is to show how scalar variables can be changed and, in particular, we have concentrated on integer variables. As you will see in Chapter 4 there are a number of other types of scalars that Java contains and in Chapter 5 you will see that there is much more to the notion of state change than has been presented here. However, what we have presented is not incorrect: it is just that we do not want to overwhelm you with too much detail at this stage of the book, our aim being to give you enough notions to access the remainder of this chapter and Chapter 4.

3.3 Classes

The previous chapter's description of objects was, of necessity, brief and introductory. The aim of this section is to look at objects in more detail and, in particular, show how they are implemented in the Java programming language. In order to understand this it is worth examining what happens when a message is sent to an object. For example, let us assume that an object obj has been sent a message mess:

```
obj.mess(arguments);
```

What happens is that the object receives the message and decodes it. The decoding consists of looking at a list of all the messages that it can receive and then executing the code corresponding to the message mess. The question that this poses is how does the object access this information? The answer is that objects in Java are defined by means of a mechanism known as a **class**. A class is very much like a template which defines the stored data associated with an object and the program code which is executed when particular messages are received.

The outline architecture of a class is as shown below:

```
class Name {
State
   Method1
   Method2
   Method3
   . . .
   Methodn
}
```

The first line contains the Java language statements which define the name of the class. The state contains declaration statements which define the individual data items that make up an object and the lines labelled method1, method2 and so on contain the code corresponding to each particular message that is sent. We use the term **method** to describe the chunk of code that is executed when a message is sent. For example, if an object can receive a message x then there will normally be code identified by x within the class definition; this code is executed when the message is received by the object.

The state part of a class will contain data items which are important to the object defined by that class. As an example of what might be contained in a typical class used in an Internet application, consider a class which describes the commands found in Telnet.

Telnet _____

The Telnet (Telecommunications Network) program is intended to provide remote login facilities across a network. It enables a user of one computer to log in to another computer which may even be on another continent. Telnet contains a number of commands and options which are used by each computer at the end of a Telnet session. These commands will not be noticed by the user but will form part of the internal processes of the software running the Telnet application. A typical Telnet command is AYT (Are You There) which queries the remote computer to see whether it is functioning. Each Telnet command is associated with options such as an option which outputs a carriage return.

The state would contain data which represented valid Telnet commands stored in a table together with a list of valid command options. Typical methods within such a class would be a method to check that a command is valid, a method to check that a particular option is valid and that a particular option could be used by a certain command. There would also be methods to execute each command.

Web Servers

A Web server is a computer which acts as an interface to a whole series of HTML documents. Such servers form the backbone of the World Wide Web. Users who interact with a Web server use browsers such as Netscape and Internet Explorer. These browsers issue instructions to the Web servers to navigate through the documents that are held at the location. We say that the browsers act as **clients** to the Web server. This an example of what is known as **client–server technology**.

The state which describes a Web server would contain a wide variety of instance variables. Typically this would include the name of the server, variables which describe the structure of the file system used to store the HTML documents lodged on the Web server and also internal data structures used to hold access requests issued by browsers.

As another example, assume that we have written a program which allows password access to some stored data. In such a system there will be an object defined by a class User. In order for users to be processed correctly by this applet there will need to be some means whereby such users can be identified and their passwords stored. The state for each user is hence defined by two items of data: a password and some unique identification such as that given to users when they are registered at their home computer.

In this example where there are two items of data associated with each object, such items will be held in variables known as **instance variables**. These are a realization of what in previous chapters we have called state. Each user object within the program will contain these two items of data.

It is worth lingering a little longer with this example. In the program, user objects will be sent messages such as:

```
user1.getPassword();
daveUser.newPassword("klxxx");
daveUser.newId("Dave33");
rolandUser.changeId("Roland66");
rolandUser.changePassword("zlxxghj");
robUser.checkPassword("xxkoil99");
```

The first expression involves the object identified by user1 being sent the message getPassword(). The result of this communication is that the password for the user is returned and could then be used within the applet. The second expression involves the object identified by daveUser being sent the message newPassword("klxxx"). This communication involves the instance variable corresponding to the password being given a value ("klxxx"). The third expression involves the object identified by daveUser being sent the message newId("Dave33"). This results in the instance variable corresponding to the identity of the user being updated to the string value "Dave33". The fourth expression involves the sending of the message changeId("Roland66") to rolandUser. This would result in the instance variable which holds the user's identity being changed. Similarly the fifth expression would involve the instance variable representing the password of the user rolandUser being changed to a new value ("zlxxghj"). The final Java expression involves the message checkPassword("xxkoil99") being sent to the user identified by robUser. This results in a check being made that robUser has the password value "xxkoil99" in the instance variable which holds the current password of the user.

An important point to make about the messages above is that two pairs of messages look very similar; for example, newPassword and changePassword seem to do the same things. What we have assumed here is that they correspond to slightly different processing. For example, the message corresponding to newPassword might access another instance variable which contains data that describes the date on which the user was first allowed access. This instance variable would not be accessed by changePassword. If the processing required by these two methods and the methods changeId and newId were the same, then they could, of course, be replaced by just one message.

A class template for users that also have associated with them the date of last access would look something like this:

```
class User{
// Declarations of variables for the password of a user,
// the identity and the date of first access
// Code defining the method getPassword
// Code defining the method newPassword
// Code defining the method newId
// Code defining the method changeId
// Code defining the method changePassword
// Code defining the method checkPassword
...

// Code for other methods
...
}
```

Notice that we have started the class name with a capital letter. The symbols // introduce a comment on a single line; these introduce a section of text that documents part of the code. Once you have defined such a class within a Java applet or application new users can be defined and space allocated for them. The code:

```
User rolandUser, daveUser, janeUser;
```

defines three user variables which will identify User objects. Each of these users will eventually contain values in the instance variables which hold their password, their user identity and the date they first accessed the applet.

The statement above just informs the Java system that the variables rolandUser, daveUser and janeUser will be User variables. To allocate space requires a facility known as the new facility. For example, to allocate memory space for the object identified by rolandUser you will need to write:

```
rolandUser = new User();
```

In order to reinforce the ideas just presented let us take another example from a Java application. Let us assume that we have written an applet which allows users to interrogate the prices of shares on a stock exchange. We shall assume that the user of such an application carries out functions such as finding the current price of a share and also examining the price of the shares as far back in the past as 365 days. This means that we will need an object which we shall call ShareHistory. This contains the last 365 days of prices for each share, taken at the end of the dealing day.

The template for this object will look like:

```
class ShareHistory {

// Instance variable holding the last 365 prices for
// each of the shares listed on the stock exchange

// Method code for findCurrentPrice

// Method code for findAnyPrice

// Method code for updatePrice
}
```

The first method, findCurrentPrice, will find the last price posted for a particular share – normally the price for the previous day's close of business. The second method, findAnyPrice, given a day within 365 days of the current day, will deliver the price of a particular share on that day. The third method will update the price of a share at the end of a day's trading.

This can deal with a number of stock exchanges and can be declared as:

```
ShareHistory tokyo, london, newYork;
```

with typical Java expressions being:

```
tokyo.findCurrentPrice("Daiwa");
london.findCurrentPrice("UNISYS");
newYork.findAnyPrice("IBM", "22/09/95");
newYork.updatePrice("General Motors", 333);
```

Notice that even though we refer to cities we still start an identifier with a lower case letter. The first message to the receiver object tokyo results in the current stock price of the Daiwa company being returned, the second message sent to the object london results in the current price of the computer company UNISYS being returned, the third message sent to the New York exchange results in the price of the stock for IBM on 22 September being returned. Finally, the fourth line updates the price of General Motors on the New York stock exchange.

The two examples above are structurally similar. As you proceed through the book you will find that all classes will follow this pattern of class definition, definition of variables and definition of methods.

What are the reasons for defining data in such a way? Later in this chapter you will see how some of the more advanced facilities related to objects lead to a high degree of reuse. Apart from reuse there is also the advantage of maintainability.

Software systems are subject to major changes in their lifetime. Recent surveys have suggested that as much as 80% of the development effort expended by a software company is devoted to modifying existing systems. When you define objects using classes one of the things that you can do is to ensure that no user can use the instance variables of an object: that all access to the information stored in an object is via methods. This principle is known as **information hiding**: the user of an object does not happen to know the details of how that object is implemented. This means that when a developer wants to change an implementation of an object, for example to speed up access to it, then the instance variables and program code of all the methods change but the interface to the object – the method names and arguments themselves – does not change.

For example, after using the stock exchange system detailed above for a number of months the developer may discover that there is a particular pattern of access to objects; he or she may discover that most of the access is to recent data, and that a new way of storing the stock prices which takes advantage of this access leads to an enhanced run-time performance. This new way of storing the price data would inevitably lead to large changes in the code of the methods that the stock exchange object recognized. However, it would not lead to any changes in the format of the messages. For example, users could still send messages such as:

```
tokyo.findCurrentPrice("Daiwa");
london.findCurrentPrice("UNISYS");
newYork.findAnyPrice("IBM", "22/09/95");
newYork.updatePrice("General Motors", 333);
```

as before, without any changes being made to the applet. This means that any applet or Java application which uses the stock exchange class does not need to be changed.

Web Server Performance and Web Pingers _____

One of the most important tasks carried out by a Web administrator is tuning the computer system which acts as a Web server. A tool which is often used when optimizing server performance is known as a **Web pinger.** What the tool does is to issue a series of requests to a destination Web document, carry out some request such as transferring text and then measure the time such requests took. Web pingers can send almost any sequence of requests, known as **workloads**. It is the response of the system to such workloads which determines what strategies the Web administrator will use to optimize the server performance. For example, he or she may discover that increasing the area of memory available to hold data may greatly decrease the response time of the server.

_____

A Web pinger written in Java would contain a number of objects and messages which help carry out its functions. For example, a history object might contain the details of all the requests sent to a particular Web server and the times that these requests took. Typical methods might include those to calculate average response time, total time and the number of requests sent.

3.4 Some concepts

Almost certainly the next question that you are asking yourself is: what is the detailed syntax of a class in Java? This question will be answered fully in Chapter 5. Nevertheless, at this stage in the book we would like to give you an idea of how you write such classes. An example of a simple Java class is shown below. It is simple, and hence unrealistic; however, we have included it for teaching reasons: we do not want to get the detail of classes in the way of understanding what, for many, is regarded as a difficult concept.

3.4.1 A robot

The class below is taken from a screen robot applet. Here the user can direct a robot to move on a two-dimensional board, where the coordinates of the board are expressed as x and y coordinates. When the robot is moved the screen updates itself by showing the next position. The lowest x and y positions are 1 and the highest x and y positions are 8. An example of this board and the current position of a robot is shown in Figure 3.4.

Let us assume that we need to send the robot a number of messages which can send the robot vertically upwards (to the north), vertically downwards (to the south), horizontally leftwards (to the west) and horizontally rightwards (to the east).

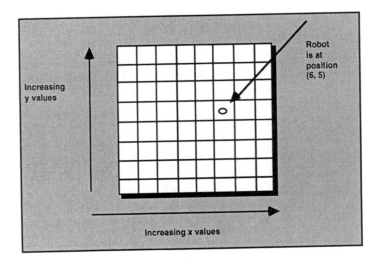

Figure 3.4 A robot board.

We also want to be able to send messages to the robot to send it upwards and to the right, upwards and to the left, downwards and to the left and downwards and to the right.

Exercise

What variables would you use for the state of a Robot object?

Solution

We would use two: the x position of the robot and the y position.

Examples of these messages are shown below:

```
newRobot.up(); oldRobot.down();
newRobot.left(); oldRobot.right();
oddRobot.leftUp(); oddRobot.rightUp();
smallRobot.leftDown(); smallRobot.rightDown();
```

All these messages affect the state of a robot object. For example, the message right() which sends a robot one position right would incremement the value of the x position by one.

The first part of the Java class definition for a robot is shown below:

```
Class Robot {
int x, y;
```

This states that the class is known as Robot and that there will be two instance variables x and y which define where the robot is on the grid; these variables will hold integer values.

This allows us to declare robots as in:

```
Robot newRobot, oldRobot, oddRobot, smallRobot;
```

which declares that four robots named newRobot, oldRobot, oddRobot and smallRobot are to be Robot objects.

In the discussion that follows we shall assume that there is no possibility that the robot will travel beyond the confines of the square grid. This would normally be ensured by means of messages sent to a robot to check that it was not on the edge of the grid. These will not be defined here.

The definition of the up and down messages is shown below:

```
public void up() {
   y = y + 1;
}

public void down() {
   y = y - 1;
}
```

All of the method definitions above start with the keyword public. This specifies that they can be used by other objects and by code written outside the class. The keyword void states that no value is to be returned by the method; this keyword is followed by the name of the method and a list of its arguments; in the case of the four methods above there are no arguments. The first method up moves the robot one grid upwards and the code following the first curly bracket does this. The code for the down message is similar except that it decrements the instance variable y by one, hence moving the robot downwards.

Exercise

Write down code for the messages right and left. Each of these messages takes no arguments. The method right moves a robot one square to the right and left moves a robot one square to the left. Again assume that the movement does not take the robot out of the board.

Solution

The code is shown below:

```
public void right() {
   x = x + 1;
}
```

```
public void left() {
   x = x - 1;
}
```

Exercise

Write down code for the messages upLeft and downLeft. The former moves a robot diagonally upwards to the left and the latter moves a robot diagonally downwards to the left.

Solution

The code is shown below:

```
public void upLeft() {
   y = y + 1;    x = x - 1;
}
```

```
public void downLeft() {
   x = x - 1;    y = y - 1;
}
```

The code for the methods upRight and downRight is shown below; remember that the former moves a robot one square diagonally upwards to the right while the latter moves a robot one square diagonally downwards to the right.

```
public void upRight() {
   y = y + 1;
   x = x + 1;
}
```

```
public void downRight() {
   y = y - 1;
   x = x + 1;
}
```

Let us assume that as well as methods which move the robot we require methods which find out the position of the robot, for example to discover whether the robot is in a position where it is possible to move. Assume that the two methods we need will be called findxPos and findyPos. When a message corresponding to findxPos is sent to a receiver object what is returned is the x position of the object and when a `findyPos` message is sent to a receiver object what is returned is the y position of the object. The code for these two methods is shown below:

```
public int findXPos() {
   return x;
}

public int findYPos() {
   return y;
}
```

There are a number of things to notice about this code. First, the two methods are declared as public; this means that they can be accessed by other methods and by code outside the class which defines robots. The second thing to notice is that the keyword `int` is used instead of the previously used `void`. This means that the method will return with an integer value. The final thing to notice about the code is that in the body of the method, between the curly brackets, the keyword `return` is used. This means that the value specified by `return` is the one that is returned by the method. In the case of the `findXPos` method this is the value of the x instance variable.

Since these methods return integers they can be used in other Java statements that expect integer values. For example, the statement:

```
currXPosition = robotCharlie.findXPos();
```

places in the variable `currXPosition` the current x position of the robot identified by the name `robotCharlie`.

Before looking at other robot methods it will be instructive to look at what happens when you use some of these methods within a Java program. The code below shows some fragments of Java code within a single Java program.

```
...
Robot arthurRobot, joeRobot;
int newXPos, oldXPos;
...
arthurRobot.downRight();
joeRobot.upLeft();
...
oldXPos = joeRobot.findXPos();
joeRobot.left();
newXPos = joeRobot.findXPos();
...
```

The first line of code declares the variables `arthurRobot` and `joeRobot` to be Robots. The next line declares `newXPos` and `oldXPos` to be integers. The third line moves `arthurRobot` down and to the right. When the Java system finds such an expression it discovers that the receiver object is a robot; it then looks in the class for a method that corresponds to the selector used in the message; and when that selector is found the code defined in the class for the method is executed. Thus, for the third line the Java system would look for the method downRight, find its description and then execute the code which increments the *x* position and decrements the *y* position of arthurRobot. This not the full story, as you will see in Chapter 5. However, it suffices for this chapter.

SAQ

Explain what happens when the fourth line in the fragment above is executed.

Solution

The fourth line moves joeRobot up and to the left. When the Java system finds such an expression it discovers that the receiver object is a robot; it then looks in the class for a method that corresponds to the selector used in the message; and when that selector is found the code defined in the class for the method is executed. Thus, for the fourth line the Java system would look for the method upLeft, find its description and then execute the code which increments the *x* position and the *y* position of joeRobot.

When the fifth line is executed the Java system will examine joeRobot, find out from its declaration that it is a robot and then look up the name of its selector (findXPos) within the class definition of Robot; it will then execute the code corresponding to the method findXPos. This code will return the value of the *x* position of the robot joeRobot which will then be assigned to the variable oldXPos.

When the fifth line is executed the Java system will determine that joeRobot is a robot and then execute the code corresponding to the left selector. This will result in the *x* position of that robot being decremented by one. Finally the seventh line will place the new *x* position of joeRobot into the variable newXPos.

So far we have described methods without arguments. The next collection of methods show how arguments can be used. The first method checkAtPoint checks whether a robot is at a specific point on the grid. The second method moveToPoint moves a robot from its current point to a new point specified by two arguments. The code for these two methods is shown below:

```
public boolean checkAtPoint(int xPos, int yPos) {
    return (x==xPos && y==yPos);
}

public void moveToPoint(int xPos, int yPos) {
```

```
    x = xPos;
    y = yPos;
}
```

The first method is headed with the `boolean` keyword. This means that it will return a value which is either true or false. The two arguments to the method are `xPos` and `yPos` which represent a possible position of the robot. The body of the method returns true if the `x` instance variable contains the same integer as the `xPos` argument and the `y` instance variable contains the same value as the `yPos` argument. The `==` symbol stands for arithmetic equality while the operator `&&` stands for Boolean *and*.

Thus, when the Java interpreter executes the code shown below:

```
strangeRobot.checkAtPoint(3,4);
```

it checks whether the receiver object `strangeRobot` is at the point (3, 4).

What happens is that the interpreter first recognizes `strangeRobot` as of class `Robot`, because it will have been defined previously in the Java program which uses the code as, say:

```
Robot strangeRobot;
```

The interpreter will look for a method corresponding to the selector `checkAtPoint`. It will find the method and execute the code. However, before executing the code it will copy the values 3 and 4 to the arguments `xPos` and `yPos`. It will thus evaluate the expression:

```
x==3 && y==4
```

and will return either true or false depending on whether the receiver object is at the point (3,4); the robot's position is defined by the contents of its instance variables.

SAQ

Look at the definition of the method shown below.

```
public void addCoordinates(int incX, incY) {
    xPos = xPos + incX;
    yPos = yPos + incY;
}
```

Explain what happens when the code below is executed.

```
oldRobot.addCoordinates(2,8)
```

Assume that the instance variables `xPos` and `yPos` of the object `oldRobot` have the values 7 and 8 respectively.

Solution

First the Java system determines what class oldRobot is derived from. It discovers that it is defined by the Robot class. It then looks for the method addCoordinates. It finds the definition and copies the values in the messsage to the arguments incX and incY. This code results in the values 2 and 8 being added to the values of the instance variables xPos and yPos. The current values of these variables are 7 and 8 so they become 9 and 16. Since the method is preceded by the keyword void no value is returned.

SAQ

Look at the definition of the method shown below.

```
public boolean checkDiagonal(int diagVal) {
   return xPos==diagvVal && yPos==diagVal;
}
```

Explain what happens when the code below is executed.

```
oldRobot.checkDiagonal(3)
```

Assume that the instance variables xPos and yPos of the object oldRobot have the values 2 and 9 respectively.

Solution

First the Java system determines what class oldRobot is derived from. It discovers that it is contained in the Robot class. It then looks for the method checkDiagonal. It finds the definition and copies the value in the message to the argument diagVal. The code of the method is then executed and 3 is compared with the xPos and yPos instance variables of the Robot object oldRobot. The comparison will return false since the method is preceded by the boolean keyword.

So far in this section we have described methods which access the state (instance variables) of an object and which update those variables. There is, however, one class of method which we have omitted: methods which create an object. We have said very little about how objects are created apart from the fact that the new facility is used; for example, the declaration:

```
Robot fredRobot = new Robot();
```

declares a variable fredRobot, allocates space for a Robot object and identifies this space as fredRobot.

The one problem with this form of declaration and allocation of space is that the instance variables of the objects declared in such a way are uninitialized. Java contains a facility whereby an object can be given a value when it is declared as above. In order to do this all that is required is to declare a new method within the class template which has the same name as the class. So, for example, in our Robot class we would need to define Robot as:

```
Robot() {
   x = 1;
   y = 1;
}
```

The effect of this is that whenever you declare a Robot object, for example in:

```
Robot slowRobot = new Robot();
```

the Java interpreter will first examine the methods defined in Robot looking for a method which has the same name as the class name. If it does not find such a method, then it will just create an object which has uninitialized instance variables. However, if it discovers a method with the same name, then the code for the method is executed. In the case of the code shown above this will create a robot which is initially positioned on the bottom left square of the grid. The method, known as Robot, is called a **constructor**. Constructors can have specified defaults such as Robot shown above where the default is that a newly created Robot object is placed on the square (1,1). However, constructors can also be associated with arguments which represent a user's specified initial value. An example of a Robot constructor which sets the *x* position and *y* position of a robot taken from values supplied by the programmer is shown below:

```
Robot(int xPos, int yPos) {
   x = xPos;
   y = yPos;
}
```

An example of its use with the new facility is shown below:

```
Robot denseRobot = new Robot(6,5);
```

This line of code declares an object denseRobot which is created by applying new to the Robot method. This method requires two arguments (in the example above these are 6 and 5) which are used to update the x and y instance variables within denseRobot.

It is worth reproducing the whole code for the Robot class. This is shown below.

```
class Robot {
int x, y;
```

```
Robot () {
   x = 1; y = 1;
}

Robot (int xPos, int yPos) {
   x = xPos; y = yPos;}

public void up() {
   y = y + 1;}

public void down() {
   y = y - 1;}

public void right() {
    x = x + 1;}

public void left() {
   x = x - 1;}

public void upRight() {
   y = y + 1; x = x + 1;}

public void downRight() {
   y = y - 1; x = x + 1;}

public int findXPos() {
    return x;}

public int findYPos() {
    return y;}

}
```

It follows the general structure described earlier in this chapter: the keyword class followed by the class name and the instance variables and methods enclosed within curly brackets, with some of the methods being constructors.

3.4.2 A two-person race

This subsection describes the definition of an object known as a twoPersonRace. It will have two instance variables which represent two riders in a cycle race. Each instance variable will be an integer which represents the number of yards that the rider has achieved in the race. The class heading will be:

```
class twoPersonRace{
int riderAYards, riderBYards;
```

The constructor for this method is shown below. The method will initialize the number of yards achieved by each rider to zero.

```
class twoPersonRace{
riderAYards = 0;
riderBYards = 0;
}
```

The code for a method which increases the number of yards achieved by the first rider is shown below:

```
public void increaseYardA(int increment){
   riderAYards = riderAYards + increment;
}
```

The code for the dual of this method which increases the yards achieved by the second rider is very similar. It is shown below:

```
public void increaseYardB(int increment){
   riderBYards = riderBYards + increment;
}
```

Exercise

Write down a method isAAhead which returns a Boolean value. This value will be true if the first rider is ahead of the second rider. Use the operator > in your return statement.

Solution

```
public boolean isAAhead(){
   return riderAYards > riderBYards;
}
```

The whole code for the class is shown below:

```
class twoPersonRace{
int riderAYards, riderBYards;

public void increaseYardA(int increment){
   riderAYards = riderAYards + increment;
}
```

```
public void increaseYardB(int increment){
   riderBYards = riderBYards + increment;
}

public boolean isAAhead(){
   return riderAYards > riderBYards;
}

}
```

Again notice the terminating curly bracket which marks the end of the class.

3.4.3 Messages and classes

Before leaving this section and looking at the key idea of object-oriented programming it is worth recapping, yet again, the mechanisms used within Java for sending messages and what happens to these messages. When the Java interpreter encounters an expression such as:

```
receiverObject.message(arguments);
```

it will first determine which class the destination object is defined by. To do this it will scan all the declarations within the code of the applet or Java application. If it finds the name of the object within a declaration then it recovers the name of the class which describes it. It will then scan the code of the methods associated with this class.

Firewalls

A **firewall** is a collection of hardware and software technology which is used to protect a computer or network of computers against data coming from untrusted sources. For example, a firewall for a network used within a defence environment will almost invariably restrict non-defence computers from sending data into the network. There are a number of firewall configurations that can be used in computer networks. Some of them have become so common that they have gained their own names, such as dual homed gateway, screened host and screened subnet. Probably the simplest type of firewall protection is that provided by **packet filtering routers**. These are often implemented as hardware but sometimes as software. What they do is to look at some of the bureaucratic information in the data that is coming in to a computer: the source network, the destination network and the port of the source and destination addresses would be typical items that it would examine. A system administrator would set up a filtering rule base which determined which sets of data would be allowed through the firewall based on decisions, for example, about which networks to exclude.

If it finds a method with the same name as the message name then the code is executed; if not an error is flagged. If the message is associated with any arguments these are copied through as the arguments of the method and the code associated with the method is executed. This is a slight simplification as you will see in the next section. However, in essence, it represents the action of the processing cycle that occurs.

You have seen some examples of classes which represent robots and cycle races. Needless to say, classes can be used to represent Internet entities. Two short examples of this follow. First, a class can be used to implement packet filtering routers. The general structure of such a class would be:

```
class PackFilter{
// Instance variables holding filter information such
// as names of networks to exclude, computers
// to exclude etc.

// Method to add untrusted networks

// Method to remove untrusted networks

// Method to remove untrusted ports

// Method to add untrusted ports

// Method to add trusted ports

// etc

}
```

Mail Filers

One of the most popular uses of the Internet is email. A huge amount of traffic is transferred over the Net by users; this traffic consists of letters sent by mailing programs and handled by mail protocols in both receiving and sending computers. This mail may be personal or may be part of a UseGroup. These are groups of users who have some interest and who form news groups. There are thousands of these groups in existence ranging from groups dedicated to cookery and humour to the more technical groups such as those which are interested in the UNIX operating system.

One of the problems faced by users of email is connected with the large amount of mail that can be generated. It can be something of a nightmare storing this mail and remembering exactly what you have received. Consequently a number of applications known as mail filers have been constructed. At their most primitive level they contain facilities for storing mail in folders, sub folders and sub-sub folders. At their most sophisticated they contain further facilities for retrieving mail which enable the user to carry out requests such as: find all the mail sent to me by Davis before 11 July which refers to the UNIX operating system.

Mail filers can be designed as classes. A typical template for a class which could be used for a mail filer is shown below:

```
class MailFiler
// Instance variables containing folders,
// sub, folders etc.

// Instance variables containing indexes
// used to retrieve emails

// Instance variables referencing the various
// files in which the emails are stored

// Methods for retrieval of emails using
// some search criteria

// Methods for storing new emails

}
```

3.5 Inheritance

So far we have outlined a number of powerful facilities contained in the Java programming language which are used to construct objects and define the methods which correspond to the messages that Java objects receive. This section introduces what is certainly the most powerful facility within Java: that of **inheritance**. In order to introduce the idea we will first describe three increasingly complex examples of where inheritance is useful. The first example will introduce the idea of inheritance in an abstract way. Later chapters of the book show how inheritance is used within more realistic applets and applications.

3.5.1 The augmented set

The first example concerns a collection of unique objects known as a set. We shall assume that we need methods which find out the number of items in the set and add integers to the set, together with an operation which finds the sum of the elements in the set. One very efficient way of implementing such a set in such a way that summation is not too inefficient an operation is to have a class which has two instance variables: one which will hold the collection of integers and an integer sum which contains the current sum of the integers. This is an efficient implementation because any method which needs to find the sum only needs to look it up in the variable sum rather than summing all the values in the set.

An example of an object described by this class is shown in Figure 3.5. Here the instance variable sum contains the current sum of the integers in the instance variable intSet (at this stage in the book do not worry about how the set is defined).

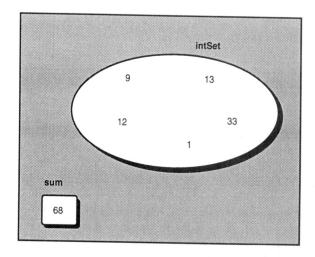

Figure 3.5 An implementation of a set of integers.

Let us assume that we have already implemented a set of integers described by the class intSet shown below, where the code for each of the classes is not shown and where we have not listed the instance variables. The class does not require a summation method and hence does not require an instance variable to contain a sum. However, it does contain an instance variable intSetVar which will hold the collection of integers. For the time being do not worry about how collections are defined in Java or any of the mechanisms used to access collections. These will be discussed in the next chapter.

```
class IntSet {
//   Definition of the instance variables holding the
//   collection of integers. The name of the instance
//   variable is intSetVar

    public boolean includes(int no) {
    . . .
    }

    public int size(int no) {
    . . .
    }

    public void add (int no) {
    . . .
    }
```

```
public void remove(int no) {
  ...
}
}
```

Let us assume that this set has been implemented for another project and is associated with the four methods shown above which check that a particular number is in the set, find the size of the set, add an element to the set and remove an element from the set.

Now let us assume that we need a set to which we wish to send messages that calculate its sum. We are faced with one choice immediately: we can program a new class from scratch. However, another choice is to use a facility known as inheritance which takes advantage of the set class we have just written. Before seeing it in action it is worth providing some definitions.

Inheritance is a relationship between two classes: if a class A inherits from a class B, then class A, as well as being able to use all of its own instance variables and methods, can use all the methods that B can use and can also use any instance variables that B can use.

As an example of this consider the two classes X and Y below without the code for their methods.

```
class X {
// Declarations for instance variables u, v and w

  // Code for method A

  // Code for method B

  // Code for method C

}


class Y {
// Declarations for instance variables l and m

  // Code for method R

  // Code for method S

  // Code for method T
}
```

If class Y inherits from class X, then, firstly, all the methods in class Y can refer to not only the instance variables in class Y but also the instance variables in class X; and secondly an object described by class Y can have messages corresponding not only to the methods R, S and T but also the methods A, B and C.

Classes can inherit from classes which inherit from other classes. As an example consider the three classes shown below:

```
class X {
// Declarations for instance variables u, v and w

  // Code for method A

  // Code for method B

  // Code for method C
}

class Y {
// Declarations for instance variables l and m

  // Code for method R

  // Code for method S

  // Code for method T
}

class Z {
// Declarations for instance variables n and o

  // Code for method G

  // Code for method H

  // Code for method I
}
```

Here, if class Z inherits from class Y which, in turn, inherits from class X, then objects described by class Z can be sent messages which correspond to the methods which class Y can use; these not only include the methods R, S and T but also the methods inherited from class X, namely methods A, B and C. This means that objects described by class Z can be sent messages corresponding to the methods G, H, I, R, S, T, A, B and C.

The same holds for the instance variables: methods in class Z can refer to not only the instance variables n and o defined in Z, but also the instance variables l and m which it inherits from Y and also the instance variables u, v and w which Y inherits. We can represent this relationship graphically as shown in Figure 3.6.

This diagram, which shows that class Z inherits from class Y which, in turn, inherits from class X, is known as a **class hierarchy diagram**. Class hierarchies are a very powerful way of describing the relationship between classes. This relationship lies at the heart of the use of an object-oriented programming language as a medium for software reuse.

Consider the classes described below where B inherits from A:

```
class A {
// Declarations of the instance variables a, b and c
```

```
// Code for method J

// Code for method K

// Code for method L

}
class B {
// Declarations of the instance variables e, f, g and h

// Code for method X

// Code for method Y

// Code for method Z
}
```

Also consider the statements:

- An object of class B can be sent a message associated with method K.
- An object of class A can be sent a message associated with method B.
- Method Z in class B can refer to the instance variable a.

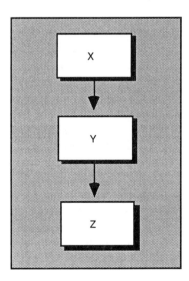

Figure 3.6 A diagrammatic representation of hierarchy.

- Method Y in class B can refer to the instance variable e.
- Method K in class A can refer to the instance variable g.

Which of these statements are true?

The first is true since A contains a method K which B inherits. The second is false since there is no method called B, only a class called B. The third is true since there is an instance variable a in A which is inherited by B. The fourth is true since the instance variable e is defined in the class B. The final statement is false.

SAQ

Consider the code skeleton shown below for the two classes V and W, where W inherits from V.

```
class V {
// Declarations of the instance variables l, m and n
  // Code for method A
  // Code for method B
  // Code for method C
}

class W {
// Declarations of the instance variables r, s, t and u
  // Code for method G
  // Code for method H
  // Code for method I
}
```

Which of the following statements are true?

(i)   An object of class V can be sent a message associated with method B.

(ii)   An object of class W can be sent a message associated with method G.

(iii) An object of class V can be sent a message associated with method H.

(iv)   Method B in class V can refer to the instance variable r.

(v)   Method H in class W can refer to the instance variable l.

Solution

(i) True. (ii) True. (iii) False, class V does not inherit from class W – the reverse is actually true. (iv) False, again V does not inherit from W. (v) True.

There is only one further rule that needs to be explained about inheritance before we return to the example that started this section. This concerns classes which contain methods that have the same name as methods in the class which they inherit. Consider the classes shown below, where class B inherits from class A.

```
class A {
// Declarations a, b and c

   // Code for method J

   // Code for method K

   // Code for method L
}
```

```
class B {
// Declarations e, f, g and h

   // Code for method X

   // Code for method K

   // Code for method Z
}
```

If a message with the name K was sent to an object of class B which method would be executed?

The answer is that it would be the method in class B. The general rule is that whenever a class inherits from another class and there is duplication of method names between the class and the one it inherits from, then the method from the class that inherits is the one invoked.

Consider the classes shown below:

```
class D {
// Declarations of a, b, and c

   // Code for method J

   // Code for method K

   // Code for method L
}
```

```
class E {
// Declarations of e, f, g, h, i and j

   // Code for method J

   // Code for method K

   // Code for method Z
}
```

The following statements are true:

- When a message is sent to an object described by class E and the message uses the selector J, then the method J defined in E is invoked.

- When a message is sent to an object described by class E and the message uses the selector Z, then the method Z defined in E is invoked.

- When a message is sent to an object defined by class E and the message uses the selector L, then the method L defined in class D is invoked.

However, the following statement is not true:

- When a message is sent to an object defined by class D and the message uses the selector K, then the method K defined in E is invoked.

Because D does not inherit from E, the method corresponding to K defined in D is invoked. This rule about similar names for methods holds whatever the level of the inheritance hierarchy. For example, consider the three classes shown below:

```
class A {
// Declaration of r and s

   // Code for method J

   // Code for method K

   // Code for method L
}


class B {
// Declarations of e, f and g

   // Code for method J

   // Code for method U

   // Code for method V
}

class C {
// Declarations of l, m, n and o

   // Code for method U

   // Code for method R

   // Code for method S
}
```

If class C inherits from class B which, in turn, inherits from class A, then when a message involving the selector U is sent to an object defined by C, the method U defined in C is invoked; when a message using the selector J is sent to the same type of object, the method J defined in class B is invoked.

SAQ

Consider three classes X, Y and Z. Class X has three methods a, b and c; class Y has two methods b and d; and class Z has four methods a, c, e and f. Z inherits from Y which, in turn, inherits from X. Which of the following are true?

(i)   When a message with selector c is sent to an object defined by Z the method c defined in Z is executed.

(ii)   When a message with selector a is sent to an object defined by Y then the method a defined in Z is executed.

(iii) When a message with selector f is sent to an object defined by Y then the method f defined in Z is executed.

(iv)   When a message with selector a is sent to an object defined by Y then the method a defined in Z is executed.

(v)   When a message with selector a is sent to an object defined by Z then the method f defined in Y is executed.

(vi)   When a message with selector b is sent to an object defined by Y then the method b defined in Y is executed.

(vii) When a message with selector c is sent to an object defined by Z then the method c defined in X is executed.

Solution

The solutions are:

(i)   True, the Java system need look no further.

(ii)   False, the Java system does not find a within Y and then looks in the class above it in the inheritance hierarchy, namely class X. The method a within X is thus executed.

(iii) False, there is no f within Y or the next class above it (X) and so an error will occur.

(iv)   False, the Java system will not find a within Y and so will look in the class above it, namely X. It finds a method a within X and executes it.

(v)   False, the method a defined within Z is executed.

(vi)   True, there is a method b defined within Y.

(vii) False, there is a method c within Z and this is the method which is executed.

Before returning to the summable set example it is worth defining a concept that you will meet a number of times later in the book. The **protocol** of a class is the list of messages that can be sent to an object defined by that class. The protocol will contain those method names defined within the class, together with the methods from those classes it inherits from. For example, the protocol of the class C defined above contains the messages corresponding to the methods U, R, S, J, V, K, L.

It is now worth continuing with the summable set example. You will remember that we had already defined a set of integers as:

```
class IntSet {
//   Definition of an instance variable holding the
//   collection of integers. The name of the instance
//   variable is intSetVar

    public boolean includes(int no) {
    ...
    }

    public int size(int no) {
    ...
    }

    public void add(int no) {
    ...
    }

    public void remove(int no) {
    ...
    }
}
```

and that we wanted to define a new class which provided all the facilities of IntSet but also provided a method which summed the integers within the set.

You will remember that the way to do this is to somehow define a new class which has an instance variable which holds the current sum of the values and an inherited instance variable which holds the members of the set. We can easily define this new set by writing down its name, specifying the names of the instance variables and then writing code for the five methods. However, inheritance allows us to save some time, since by using inheritance we can reuse some of the elements of IntSet.

We shall assume that the new class which describes summable sets is called SummableSet. The code skeleton describing its structure is shown below:

```
Class SummableSet ...

int sum;
```

```
   public int totalSum() {
   ...
   }
}
```

Here a new method `totalSum` is defined which returns with the sum of the set; also defined is an instance variable `sum` which holds the current sum of the set.

In Java if we wish to specify that a set inherits from another set then we write this using the keyword `extends`. The full definition of `SummableSet` is then:

```
class SummableSet extends IntSet {

int sum;

   public int totalSum() {
   ...
   }
}
```

This states that we have defined a new class called `SummableSet` which inherits the instance variables and the methods from the existing class `IntSet`. If this class inherits from `IntSet`, then an object described by `SummableSet` can be sent messages corresponding to the methods `includes`, `size`, `add` and `remove`. There seems to be no reason why we cannot now write code such as:

```
SummableSet sms;

sms = new SummableSet();
sms.add(23);
```

where the semicolon is used as with most C-like programming languages to terminate individual Java statements.

Unfortunately, there is a problem: the code for the methods `add` and `remove` is incorrect. The code for `add` and `remove` would correctly alter the set of integers by adding and removing items from it; however, they do not affect the current sum. For example, there may be three integers in the summable set which are 45, 3, 10 with the instance variable `sum` holding 58 which is the sum. If `add` is invoked with the argument 20, then 20 would be deposited in the set but the sum would remain at 58. What we need are new versions of `add` and `remove`.

These need to be embedded in the class `SummableSet`, making its code skeleton look like:

```
Class SummableSet extends IntSet {
int sum;

   public int totalSum() {
   ...
   }
```

```
public void add(int no) {
...
}

public void remove (int no) {
...
}
}
```

The code for the method add would add no to the set by sending a message to the instance variable defined in IntSet and also add the value of no to the instance variable sum. The code for the method remove would remove no from the set and subtract its value from the instance variable sum. Perhaps we could then expect the code for add to look something like:

```
public void add(int no) {
intSetVar.add(no);
sum = sum + no;
...
}
```

where the first line introduces the method, the second line uses the method add declared in the class IntSet to carry out the insertion of no into SummableSet and the third line adjusts the instance variable sum so that it is up to date and contains the current sum. We might also expect the code for remove within SummableSet to look like:

```
public void remove(int no) {
intSetVar.remove(no);
sum = sum - no;
...
}
```

There is one problem, however: which version of add does the first extract refer to: the one defined in IntSet or the one defined in SummableSet? Similarly which version of remove does the second extract refer to: the one defined in IntSet or the one defined in SummableSet? Well, the rule that we have given previously states that when a method *M* is invoked associated with a class *C*, then method *M* is searched for in *C*, and if it is there it is invoked; if it isn't there then the search continues in the next class that it inherits from, namely the class in the next level in the inheritance hierarchy. This means that, for example, inside the method add defined in SummableSet there is a call to itself. When this is invoked there would be another call to itself, and so on. This means that the method could be in a continuous loop and never exit. The same would, of course, be true of remove.

The way to get over this is to use a device which slightly overrides the way in which methods are searched for when they are invoked. This involves the use of a dot notation. In order to refer to the method in the class that `SummableSet` inherits we refer to it as `super.add`.

In order to see how this works, examine the code shown below for the correct version of add within `SummableSet`:

```
public void add(int no) {
intSetvar.super.add(no);
sum = sum + no;
. . .
}
```

This instructs the Java interpreter to start its search for a method to execute not within the class which describes the object `SummableSet`, but within the class `IntSet` (the keyword `super` instructs the Java system to look at the class above).

The code for `remove` would be similar:

```
public void remove(int no) {
intSetvar.super.remove(no);
sum = sum - no;
. . .
}
```

It is worth recapping the points that the example and supporting text have illustrated. First, it has shown how inheritance works. Second, it has illustrated reuse to a certain extent: the reuse of `IntSet` was not massive since we had to redefine the methods add and remove within `SummableSet`, but nevertheless some reuse was employed. Finally, the text described the way in which the Java system looked for methods to execute: by traversing the inheritance hierarchy, normally starting with the class that was defined by the object which is being sent a message, but with the use of the dot notation facility overriding this starting point when required.

We have used inheritance in order to extend the functions of an object: objects defined by `IntSet` could be sent a variety of messages which correspond to functions such as adding an integer to a set, but these objects could not be summed. By using inheritance we have, by creating the class `SummableSet`, added functionality to `IntSet`.

3.5.2 Invoices

A common document used by many companies is the invoice. This is used to bill another company or individual for goods or services. A typical invoice is shown in Figure 3.7.

If you look at a number of invoices, you will see many common items of information. These include the items or services that are being invoiced, the address of the company being invoiced and the address of the company doing the invoicing.

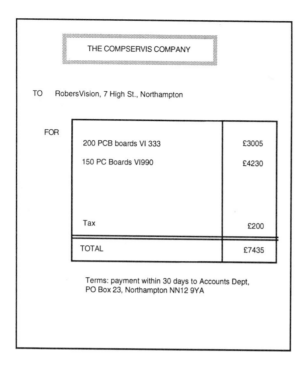

Figure 3.7 A typical invoice.

These are shown in Figure 3.7 and can be found on invoices from a wide variety of sources: electrical companies, catering companies, individual consultants and educational establishments.

A general invoice class is shown below. The keyword string represents a Java data type which contains a collection of characters. For example, `"Darrel Ince"` is an example of a string.

```
class Invoice {
// Definition of instance variables which hold the name
// of the invoiced company and the individual items
   public string invoicedCompanyName( ) {
   . . .
   }

   public void setInvoicedCompanyName(String name) {
   . . .
   }

   public void addItem(String itemName) {
   . . .
   }
```

```
public void addCost(String itemName, int itemCost) {
    ...
}

public void addNumber(String itemName, int no) {
    ...
}

public int calculateTotalCost() {
    ...
}
```

}

A selection of the possible methods is shown. invoicedCompanyName is a method which returns the name of the company that is to be invoiced, setInvoicedCompanyName adds the name of the company to be invoiced to the instance variable invoicedCompany, addItem adds an item which is to be invoiced, addCost sets the cost of an item, addNumber sets the number ordered of an item and, finally, calculateTotalCost calculates the total cost of an invoice. These are just a sample of the methods which might be available for sending messages to invoices.

Sometimes, however, a company might require something which is specific to them or to the type of company they are. For example, many companies often experience trouble getting customers to pay within the time that they allow. In order to provide some incentive they will often quote two prices for an invoice: the normal price and a price which holds if the invoice is paid within a particular period; for example, they might apply a discount if the invoice is paid in 15 days.

Someone who wishes to send invoices which contain discount information would, quite naturally, develop a new class called, say, DiscountedInvoice which inherited the instance variables and methods from Invoice and which added new methods. For example, such a new class might contain a method which calculated the discount for an early payment.

This is just one example of a new invoice class being derived by inheritance from a general invoice class – there are many other examples. For example, a class could be developed for companies which have rules for determining discounts based on a complicated formula which gives discounts for quantities ordered for particular items. If this class does not require any facilities for handling early payment, then it could inherit from the class Invoice direct; however, if it does require these facilities, then it would inherit from the class EarlyPayInvoice which contains these facilities and which was formed by inheritance from the Invoice class. This latter case is shown in Figure 3.8.

In this case inheritance has been used to modify the functions of an object. The top-level class of the inheritance hierarchy contains a method to calculate the cost of the items ordered, but the two levels down from this represent classes where the calculation of the cost is carried out in a different manner.

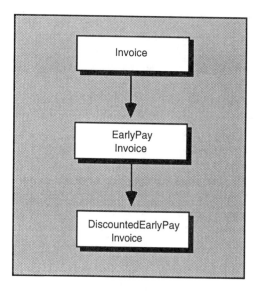

Figure 3.8 A two-level inheritance hierarchy.

This modification of function is in contrast to the previous example where functionality was added.

These are the two main uses of inheritance; and it is these that give object-oriented programming languages their power. What such diagrams represent is a hierarchy showing different levels of generality. As you proceed down the hierarchy the objects defined by the class at a lower level are much more specialized than those that are defined at an upper level; thus Discounted-EarlyPayInvoice is a much more specialized version of an Early-PayInvoice which is a more specialized version of Invoice.

3.5.3 Employee records

One of the most common systems found in commercial companies is a personnel system. Such a system keeps track of the employees in a company: their names, their current salary, where they work, and so on. Such systems are used in a number of ways: normally they are used for providing data which is used in the calculation of the monthly or weekly pay of staff; sometimes they are used to keep track of the training received by staff and sometimes they are used for keeping track of benefits such as a company car.

Such a class would normally have as its instance variables the name of the member of staff, their department, their sex, their annual pay and some indication of a coding which determined how much tax would be deducted from their pay.

In order to see how a hierarchy of employee records might be built up using inheritance we shall first assume that the company that wishes to use this general employee record has two types of employee: weekly paid employees and monthly paid employees. The former are paid on the basis of the number of hours worked: normally a weekly paid employee would work 40 hours per week, but the company we are considering sometimes asks its hourly paid staff to work evenings and pays them at an increased rate. If the company just had this simple division of staff the inheritance hierarchy would look like the hierarchy shown in Figure 3.9.

Now let us assume a further complication: that some monthly staff are allowed to drive company cars. Personnel systems often have information about the car that a current member of staff drives.
This information is used for a wide variety of purposes, from finding out who has misparked the car in the company car park to determining whether a new car is needed for a staff member. We now need a class which will contain instance variables connected with the car an employee runs.

The hierarchy showing this new situation is given in Figure 3.10. The new class will inherit from MonthEmployee since only monthly employees are allowed to drive company cars.

SAQ

Does the inheritance used in CarMonthEmployee represent a modification of the functions of MonthEmployee or an addition of functionality?

Solution

It represents an addition since it will involve adding new instance variables to represent the car and also new methods which access and modify car details.

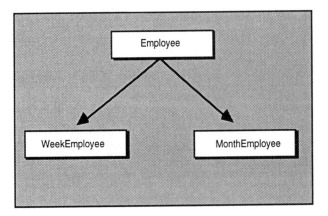

Figure 3.9 The initial hierarchy for the personnel system.

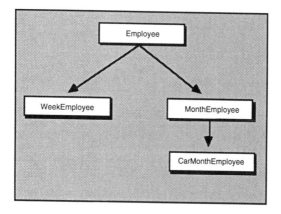

Figure 3.10 The modified hierarchy.

Let us examine a further complication: the company employs sales staff whose job is to sell the items that the company manufactures. These sales staff are monthly employees and need a company car since they travel long distances visiting customers' premises. They differ from other monthly employees in that their pay is made up of two elements: a basic monthly pay and a commission based on the amount of sales they make in their current pay month. The company wishes to keep data on sales in their staff's payment record; typically this data will include the monetary value of the current month's sales and the sales that have been made this year to date. This means that a new class will need to be developed. Figure 3.11 shows one attempt.

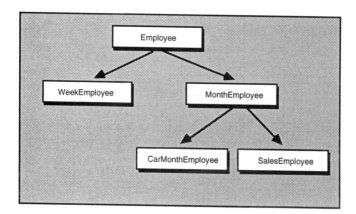

Figure 3.11 A new hierarchy showing sales staff.

Exercise

Is this a correct version of the hierarchy?

Solution

This is not the correct version of the hierarchy since it ignores the fact that a `SalesEmployee` is allowed to drive a car. The position of the `SalesEmployee` class in the hierarchy means that it will not inherit all the facilities available for processing car data that are available in the class `CarMonthEmployee`. The correct version of the hierarchy is shown in Figure 3.12.

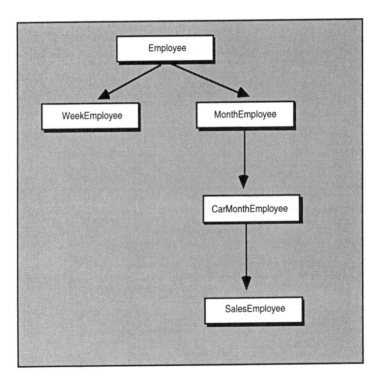

Figure 3.12 The correct version of the inheritance hierarchy showing the correct position of `SalesEmployee`.

Again with this hierarchy you can see that as we proceed downwards the classes become more specific and hence less generally useful: at the top of the hierarchy is a class which contains common information that almost every personnel system could use, at the second level are classes which only companies that employ both weekly and monthly staff could use, at the third level is a class which only companies that provide company cars could use and at the bottom of the hierarchy is a class which only companies that have a sales force could use.

As you proceed down the hierarchy more and more methods and instance variables will be included in classes. For example, the class `CarMonthEmployee` shown in Figure 3.12 would probably contain an instance variable which provides details of the type of car that the member of staff described by this class is currently driving and would also contain an instance variable which details the date on which this employee was given this car so that the company can replace it within a specified time period. This class would also contain methods which access, update and use these instance variables, for example a method `carType` which returns the type of the car that is currently driven by an object described by this class. The class `SalesEmployee`, further down the hierarchy, might contain instance variables which detail the current sales for the month for a sales person and the current sales for the year for the same sales person. There would also be methods associated with these instance variables, for example methods which add a new sale to these variables and which retrieve the values stored in them.

3.6 Class libraries

At this stage in the book it is worth providing some vocabulary. When a class A inherits methods and variables from a class B, then A is known as the **subclass** of B and B is known as the **superclass** of A. Modern object-oriented programming languages such as C++, Smalltalk and, of course, Java provide extensive class libraries which contain a large number of facilities useful to the programmer.

One concept that is useful to know about when using a class library is that of an **abstract class**. Such an abstract class will contain methods known as **abstract methods**. These methods carry out no actions at all but are just place holders which are filled when a subclass is formed by means of inheritance from the abstract class. In order to explain what you might think is a weird idea it is worth looking at an example of an abstract class.

```
class A {
// Instance variables for the class
   // Code for method 1
   // Code for method 2
   // Code for method 3
   abstract AbsMethod { }
```

```
// Code for method n

}
```

Class A is regarded as abstract because one of its methods (AbsMethod) contains no code at all and is headed by the keyword abstract.

You will not be able to use AbsMethod direct; however, you will be able to use AbsMethod in a subclass by employing inheritance. For example, if we want a class B which inherits the methods and variables of A and provides code to implement AbsMethod then we would write:

```
class B extends A {

// Any new instance variables

// Code for method AbsMethod
}
```

Using the rules for inheritance, B would become a class from which objects can be created since the new code for AbsMethod would be used whenever a message involving AbsMethod is sent.

You may think that this is a somewhat strange way to proceed. However, class libraries get much of their power from abstract classes. For example, a class library may contain an abstract class which represents window objects on a screen. It could be that such a class would contain abstract methods which define the way that the border is displayed: that whenever you wish to develop a new screen object which has a different border all you need to do is to extend the abstract window class with a new method which carries out the drawing of the border. We will be describing abstract classes and a number of associated ideas in detail in Chapter 8.

The Java system contains a very large class library in which many of the classes are linked via inheritance. There are five main class libraries:

- *The language foundation classes*. These classes implement low-level data types such as integer and contain the code for the methods which operate on these basic data types.

- *The I/O class library*. This contains classes which provide facilities for low-level input/output, for example for the reading of data from files.

- *Abstract window toolkit class library*. This contains all the classes needed for the interaction between an applet and the user. It contains classes for basic HCI components such as fonts, colours, events, buttons and scroll bars. This library is described in Chapter 11.

- *The utility class library*. This library contains useful facilities such as a data class, tables, vectors and stacks. This library is introduced in Chapter 7.

- *The network interface class library.* This vitally important library contains classes which are used to communicate within a network. They extend the facilities that are available in the I/O class library and provide ways of, for example, connecting to other interfaces such as Web sites.

This has been a very brief introduction to the extensive library of classes that are provided with the Java system.

3.7 SUMMARY

This is probably the key chapter in the book. It describes a deceptively simple idea: that Java contains a mechanism known as inheritance which enables a class to use methods and instance variables from other classes. This is the main mechanism for reuse in an object-oriented programming language like Java. The chapter also describes an importance graphical device known as an inheritance hierarchy, often called a **class hierarchy**. Such a device describes the relationship between classes. It shows how classes are related to each other in terms of the methods and instance variables they inherit from each other. An important point made in this chapter about the inheritance hierarchy is that as you proceed down it, the classes at the bottom become more and more specialized. There is still much more to learn about classes. However, this detail will be presented later in Chapter 5. Before doing this it is necessary to provide a tour of the programming facilities within Java. This is the subject of the next chapter.

CHAPTER FOUR

Java

- To describe the main data types within the Java language.
- To describe the main control structures within the Java language.
- To present some examples of Java code.

4.1 Introduction

There are two aspects to any programming language: there is the variety of different types of data that the language provides and there is the way in which it provides facilities for altering the way it is executed. This chapter will explore both these topics. So far in the book you have seen some very simple sections of code: those mainly associated with the assignment of values to variables. These sections of code were embedded in the methods defined in a class. In this chapter we will look at a wide variety of types of data and also show how Java provides the facilities whereby the execution of a Java program can be controlled. Our discussion is still within the framework that we adopted in the previous chapter: that this code is embedded in methods which access and sometimes modify instance variables.

4.2 Data types

4.2.1 Scalar data types

Java contains all the primitive data types you would expect in a modern programming language. There are four integer numeric data types. These are `byte`, `short`, `int` and `long`. These correspond to stored integers of a maximum length 8 bits, 16 bits, 32 bits and 64 bits respectively. Data type lengths in Java are fixed to ensure portability across implementations of the language.

Variables are given types by writing the name of their type before them, so, for example, the code:

```
int newSocket, oldSocket;
```

declares two variables which will hold 32-bit integers and:

```
long userCodeId, userSwitchId;
```

declares two variables which will hold 64-bit integers. When a variable is declared it can be given a value by means of the = symbol, so, for example:

```
byte lastByte, controlByte = 12;
```

will declare two 8-bit variables `lastByte` and `controlByte` and will assign the value 12 to the second of these, leaving the first variable uninitialized. Integer values can be denoted by writing them as shown above or by writing them in an octal or hexadecimal base. If you wish to specify an integer in octal, the integer needs to be preceded with a zero; if you wish to write an integer in hexadecimal, you precede the integer with a 0 followed by an x. Thus:

```
int    streamId = 017, streamControlId = 0xF,
       switchId = 0xBB;
```

declares three 32-bit integer variables. The first declaration sets `streamId` to be octal 17 (decimal 15), the second declaration sets the 32-bit integer variable `streamControlId` to be hexadecimal F (decimal 15) and the third declaration sets the 32-bit integer variable `switchId` to be hexadecimal BB (decimal 187).

There are two real number types in Java. The first is `float` which represents 32-bit floating point numbers and the second is `double` which represents 64-bit floating point numbers. Thus the statement:

```
float cashValue = 23.8, newCashValue, oldCashValue;
```

declares three variables `cashValue`, `newCashValue` and `oldCashValue` with the first variable being set to 23.8. Floating point numbers are denoted either by writing them as *integerpart.fractionalpart*, or by using scientific notation where the character e or E denotes the fact that the number is to be raised to the power of ten of the integer following the e or E. Thus:

```
float newTotal = 1.56e2, oldTotal = 2.34E4;
```

declares two floating point variables `newTotal` and `oldTotal` with the first variable holding the value 156 and the second variable holding the value 23 400.

There is a char data type called `char` in the Java language. This uses the 16-bit Unicode character set with characters being denoted by the value enclosed within single quotes. Thus:

```
char senseChar, ringChar = 'e';
```

declares two character variables `senseChar` and `ringChar`, with the second of these variables being initialized to contain the character e.

There is a Boolean data type known as `boolean`. Variables of this type can hold either the value `true` or the value `false`. Thus,

```
boolean loopSensor, pollSensor = true;
```

declares the Boolean variables `loopSensor` and `pollSensor` and sets the second of these to the value true.

SAQ

Write down the declaration statements which define two integer variables `oldValue` and `remValue`; three character values `buffA`, `buffB` and `buffC`; and two byte values `controlVal` and `endVal`. The integer variable `oldValue` is to be given the initial value 88 and the character variable `buffC` is to be given the value 'd';

Solution

The code is shown below:

```
int oldValue = 88, remValue;
byte controlVal, endVal;
char buffA, buffC = 'd', buffB;
```

All the scalar data types that are provided in Java are associated with operators which are used to build up expressions. Binary arithmetic operators can be used both with floats and with the various integer types. A list of these is shown in Table 4.1.

The only operator which needs a little explanation is the % operator which is applied to data that is of an integer type. It returns the value which is the remainder when its left operand is divided by its right operand. For example, the value of 34 % 5 is 4 since this is the remainder when 34 is divided by 5. This is similar to modulo arithmetic.

Table 4.1 Arithmetic operators.

Operator	Symbol	Written as	Meaning
Multiplication	*	a * b	*a* times *b*
Division	/	a / b	*a* divided by *b*
Remainder	%	a % b	The remainder of *a* divided by *b*
Addition	+	a + b	*b* added to *a*
Subtraction	−	a − b	*b* subtracted from *a*

SAQ

If the integer variables a, b and c contain the values 11, 55 and 2 respectively what happens when the following three assignment statements are executed?

```
a = a + b - c;
c = c % 3;
c = (a + 22) % 2;
```

Solution

The first statement places the value 64 in the variable a; the second statement places the value 2 in the variable c; and the final statement places the value 1 in the variable c.

There is also a class of operators known as **arithmetic assignment operators**. These mainly carry out some arithmetic operation such as addition and then assign the result to one of the variables used in the expression containing the operator. These are shown in Table 4.2. Each of the operators, apart from = which we have already described in the previous paragraph, corresponds to those in Table 4.1. As an example of the use of these operators consider the section of code shown below:

```
int a = 12, b = 22;
a+=b;
```

This results in the sum of a and b being formed (34) and the result being deposited into a.

Table 4.2 Assignment operators.

Symbol	Operator	Written as	Meaning
=	Assign	a = b	Put the value of b into a
+=	Add and assign	a += b	Put the value of $a+b$ into a
-=	Subtract and assign	a -= b	Put the value of $a-b$ into a
*=	Multiply and assign	a *= b	Put the value of $a*b$ into a
/=	Divide and assign	a /= b	Put the value of a/b into a
%=	Remainder and assign	a %= b	Put the value of $a\%b$ into a

---

| SAQ |

What happens when each of the three Java statements is executed? The variables a, b and c contain 23, 3 and 1 respectively.

```
a+=b;
c*=c;
b%=3
```

| Solution |

The first statement adds b to a and places the result (26) into a. The second statement multiplies c by itself and places the result (9) back into c. The third statement divides b by 3, forms the remainder and places the result (0) back into b.

There are two operators which you will find yourself continually using in Java programs; they are the increment and decrement operators ++ and -- . These exist in two forms: postfix form and prefix form. The ++ operator increments the variable it is associated with by one and the -- operator decrements the value of the variable it is associated with by one. The postfix variant returns the old value of the expression to which it is applied and the prefix form returns the new value. For example, the statement:

```
newInc++;
```

increments the value of the variable `newInc` and places this value back into `newInc`. It then returns the old value of `newInc`. So, for example, if the value of `newInc` was 44 the result of this expression would be to modify the variable `newInc` to contain 45 and then return the value 44. The processing associated with the prefix version of the prefix `++` operator can be shown by looking at the execution of:

```
++newInc;
```

if `newInc` has the current value 79. First 79 is incremented by 1 and this value is placed back in the variable `newInc`. This *new* value is then returned.

Java assignments always deliver a value. So, for example, the assignment:

```
a = 12;
```

would deliver the value 12. This can be used within other parts of a Java program which expect a value. For example, in another assignment statement as in:

```
b = (a = 12);
```

which would set both the int variables a and b to 12.

Since the increment and decrement operators deliver results, they can be used in any context where their value can be used, for example in assignments:

```
int j = 0, k;
k = j++;
```

first increments the variable j by 1 to give it a value of 1 and then sets k to be the value 0 which was the old value of j. The action of the `--` operators is the same, except that subtraction rather than addition occurs. The properties of the `++` and `--` operators are shown in Table 4.3.

Java also contains a number of familiar relational operators which give rise to Boolean values. These operators can be applied to both integer and floating point numbers. They are summarized in Table 4.4. So, for example, if the values of the variables a, b and c were 34, 56 and 3 respectively, then the value of:

```
a+b < c
```

would be false and the value of the expression:

```
a+81 == b*2 + c
```

would be true.

Table 4.3 Increment and decrement operators.

Symbol	Operator	Written as	Meaning
Postfix increment	++	x++	Add 1 to x and return the old value
Prefix increment	++	++x	Add 1 to x and return the new value
Postfix decrement	--	x--	Take 1 from x and return the old value
Prefix decrement	--	--x	Take 1 from x and return the new value

Table 4.4 Relational operators.

Symbol	Operator	Written as	Meaning
==	Equal to	x == y	True if x equals y, otherwise false
>	Greater than	x > y	True if x is greater than y, otherwise false
<	Less than	x < y	True if x is less than y, otherwise false
>=	Greater than or equal to	x >= y	True if x is greater than or equals y, otherwise false
<=	Less than or equal to	x <= y	True if x is less than or equals y, otherwise false
!=	Not equal to	x != y	True if x is not equal to y, otherwise false

It is worth pointing out that the operators deliver Boolean values and hence can be used in assigning values to Boolean variables. For example, the code:

```
int a = 12, b = 23;
boolean checkList, newList;
```

```
checkList = (a < 12);
newList = (b >= 23);
```

first sets checkList to be false since the value of a is 12 and then sets the value of newList to be true since b has the value 23.

Java also provides a number of logical operators which correspond to the natural language words 'and', 'or' and 'not'. The and operator && takes two arguments and returns with a true value if both these arguments are true; the or operator || takes two arguments and returns false if both its arguments are false and true otherwise; and the not operator ! reverses the truth of its single argument: if is true then it becomes false and if it is false it becomes true.

These are similar to logical operators in most other languages. Table 4.5 provides a summary of these operators. Such operators can be used in expressions involving relational operators and variables having numeric types. For example, the code shown below:

```
int a, b, c = 44;
boolean newVal, oldVal;
a = 22;
b = 33;
newVal = (a < 10) && (b == 33);
oldVal = !newVal && !(b<22 && a<23);
```

first assigns values to the integer variables in the Java program. It then assigns Boolean values to the variables newVal and oldVal. The value false is placed in the variable newVal because a is not less than 10 and hence the whole expression to the right of the = operator evaluates to false. The second assignment results in the value true being placed in the Boolean variable oldVal. This is because the expression on the right hand side of the = symbol evaluates to true (the value of the expression is actually true && true).

Table 4.5 Logical operators.

Symbol	Operator	Written as	Meaning
&&	Logical and	a && b	Returns true if both *a* and *b* are true, false otherwise
||	Logical or	a || b	Returns false if both *a* and *b* are false, true otherwise
!	Logical negation	!a	Returns false if *a* is true, returns true if *a* is false

SAQ

What are the values of the following expressions? Assume that the variables a, b and c have the values 44, 10 and 12.

```
a + b
a < b+2
a==12 && b==23
a<55 || b<2
a<55 || b<22
c == b+2 && c == 12
```

Solution

The first expression has the value 54 which is the sum of 44 and 10. The second expression is false since 44 is not less than 12. The third expression has the value false since both the arguments of the and operator are false. The fourth expression is true. The fifth expression is true since both the arguments of the or operator are true. The sixth expression is true.

SAQ

Examine the fragment of Java code below and explain what it does.

```
int newVal, oldVal = 12;
boolean setVal;
oldVal++;
...
newVal = oldVal + 3;
...
setVal = oldVal < newVal;
```

Solution

The first line declares two integer variables and sets one of them (oldVal) to be 12. The next statement declares a Boolean variable setVal. The third statement increments the value in oldVal by one to give 13. The fourth statement adds three to the contents of the variable oldVal placing the result (16) in newVal. Finally the last statement places the Boolean result of 13 < 16 (true) in the variable setVal.

A very important point to make about variables is that if you do not give them a value, then an incorrect result will occur. For example, in the code:

```
int a, b = 12, c;
```

```
c = a + b;
```

an error will occur because there is an attempt to add the values in the variables a and b together without there being a value placed in a.

An important point to make about Java is that you cannot assign values of one type to variables of another type. For example, the code shown below is illegal:

```
int a = 1, b = 12, d = 13;
char c;
c = a + b + d;
```

If you try to execute it the Java system will give you an error since you cannot assign an integer to a character variable.

In Java if you want to do this, you have to use a device known as a **cast**. Casting involves the enclosure of a data type within round brackets. An example of this is shown below:

```
int cVal = (int) realVar;
```

Here the integer variable cVal is given the value of the integer part of the real variable realVar.

SAQ

What is wrong with the following fragment of Java code?

```
int w, x, y, z;
boolean indicator = true
x = 12;
y = 13;
w = z;
z = indicator;
```

Solution

There are two problems. The first occurs in the fifth statement where an attempt is made to update w by copying the contents of z into it. Unfortunately, at this stage in the program z does not have a value contained in it. The second problem is that the int variable z is being assigned a Boolean value.

4.2.2 First class objects

Java treats some data types as objects and hence the message passing mechanism shown in the previous chapter can be used with these data types. The two important examples of data types treated as objects are arrays and strings.

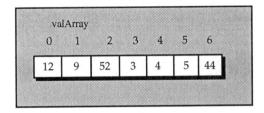

Figure 4.1 An example of an array.

Before looking in more detail at how this works it is necessary to look at the idea of an **array**. Such a data type is a collection of items all of the same type. Each item is indexed by means of integers. Figure 4.1 shows a simple array.

This array contains seven values all of which are integers. The first item in the array is 12, the second is 9 and so on. You can look on an array as a collection of variables: the array `valArray` shown in Figure 4.1 can be regarded as a collection of seven variables. Given this perspective, how can we refer to each item in the array? The answer is that we use an integer called an **index**. In Java the index which identifies the first value in an array is zero and the last is $n-1$, where there are n items in the array. Always remember this as it is a major source of error when writing Java programs. When arrays are declared in Java they start at element zero as shown in Figure 4.1. So if we refer to the third value in `valArray` we write:

```
valArray[2]
```

Indexes allow us to refer to any item in an array. For example, the fragment of code shown below adds the third and fourth items in the array `oldArray` and places the result in the integer variable `result`.

```
i = 2;
result = oldArray[i] + oldArray[i+1];
```

The code shown below multiplies the first three items in the integer array `peopleCount` and places the result in `medFactor`.

```
medFactor =
  peopleCount[0]*peopleCount[1]*peopleCount[2];
```

So far we have only looked at arrays of integers. It will be no surprise to you that Java allows us to build arrays containing virtually any type of data, for example arrays of booleans, bytes and characters.

Another important point to make about arrays is that if an array contains n items and you attempt to access any item further along than the nth item, then an error will occur. For example, if the array `newVals` contained five items and you had the statement:

```
a = newVals[5];
```

in your program then the Java system would report an error. Arrays are a very important facility in a programming language and you will find yourself using them time and time again, so make sure that you are happy with the concept. A correct answer to the following two SAQs is an indication that you have understood the main concepts associated with arrays.

SAQ

Explain what happens when the following section of code is executed. Assume that the variable `select` is an integer array which contains the five values 1, 0, 22, 0 and 15; and that a and b are integers, with a being 99 and b being 10.

```
a = select[2] + select[3] - select[4];
select[0]++; select[2]--;
b = select[0] + select[1];
```

Solution

First a is set to 7 which is the result of adding 22 and 0 together and subtracting 15. Then the contents of the first item in `select` are incremented by one and the contents of the third item in `select` are decremented by one. Finally b is set to 2 which is the sum of 2 and 0.

SAQ

Explain what happens when the following section of code is executed. Assume that the variable `fib` is an integer array which contains four values 12, 3, 5 and 19 and the variable `i` is an integer variable.

```
i = 2; fib[i] = fib[i-1] + fib[i-2];
i++; fib[i] = fib[i-1] + fib[i-2];
```

Solution

The first two statements have the effect of setting the third item of the array equal to the sum of the previous two items. The final two statements have a similar effect: of setting the fourth item in the array to the sum of the previous two items. Thus the array `fib` will contain 12, 3, 15 and 18.

An important question that needs to be answered is: how do we declare arrays in Java? Already we have seen that integers can be declared by means of a statement such as:

```
int oldValue, medianValue;
```

An example of an array declaration is shown below; it differs somewhat from those we have already dealt with.

```
int[] newBuffer = new int[10];
```

This declares the variable `newBuffer` to be an array of integers which will have space for ten integers. This can be read as:

> The variable `newBuffer` is going to be an array of integers and it will contain ten elements.

Other array types can be declared, for example, the declaration:

```
char[] streamChars = new char[20];
```

declares an array called `streamChars` which will contain 20 characters.
An alternative way of declaring arrays is shown below:

```
int tempValues[];
```

which is equivalent to:

```
int[] tempValues;
```

In this book we will normally use the former way.
The elements of an array can also be initialized in a declaration by writing the initial values within curly brackets and preceding the list of initial values by the = operator. For example, the declaration:

```
int[] holder = {0, 0, 0, 0, 0};
```

declares an array with five elements which are integers with the initial value of these elements being zero. Note that there is no need for there to be any indication of how many items there are to be in the array: the Java system will assume that you have written the values of all the items within the curly brackets and take the count of these as the length of the array. The statement:

```
char[] firstLetters = {'a','b','c','d','e','f'};
```

will set up an array `firstLetters` containing six characters, with the initial values of the array being the first lower case letters of the alphabet.
One of the important ideas of this section is that some data types, which in other languages would be treated as scalars, are regarded as objects in Java and hence can be sent messages and are associated with instance variables. For example, arrays are associated with an instance variable `length` which gives the size of the array. Thus, the expression:

```
buffArray.length
```

represents the number of items in the array `buffArray`. The concluding parts of this chapter will look at this idea in more detail; all that you should really know at this stage is that arrays are regarded as objects and, hence, messages can be sent to them.

It is also possible to create two-dimensional arrays in Java. A declaration of the two-dimensional array `meshVals` containing integer values is shown below:

```
int[][] meshVals;
```

The code:

```
meshVals = {{1, 3}, {2, 13},{9, 2},{10, 13}};
```

sets the array to contain two columns and four rows with each row being initialized to the integers written within each innermost curly bracket pair.

Another important type of object is the string: a sequence of characters. Strings can be defined in the same way that primitive data types such as `int` and `char` can be defined. For example, the code:

```
String nodeName, nodeDestination;
```

declares two variables which will contain strings, both of which will be uninitialized.

Strings are denoted by enclosing their characters in double quotation marks. Thus, the statement:

```
String lpLocation, user = "David Jones";
```

declares two string variables: `lpLocation` which will be uninitialized and `user` which will contain the string `"David Jones"`. An important point to make about strings is that they are extensible. For example, a string variable `name` could be declared as:

```
String name = "David";
```

and then later be given a new value in an assignment statement:

```
name = "Roderick";
```

In the same way that arrays are regarded in Java as objects, so are strings. There is, for example, a method associated with strings called `length` which can be used when sending a message to a string in order to ascertain its length. For example, the expression:

```
telnetId.length();
```

delivers the number of characters in the string `telnetId`. It is worth making a point about the `length` method associated with strings compared with the use of `length` in conjunction with arrays.

You will have seen the expression:

```
buffArray.length
```

which gives the number of elements in the array `buffArray` and you might have wondered why it was different to the use of `length` with strings as in:

```
telnetId.length();
```

The answer is that `length` is an instance variable associated with arrays, while `length()` is a method associated with strings. This is a small design fault in the Java language. Another important point concerning arrays and strings is that an array is a fixed length entity: it cannot be extended or even shrunk. It is also important to point out that `length()` will give the number of locations within an array, not the number of initialized values within an array. For example, examine the code shown below which initializes some of the values of the integer array `persLink`:

```
int[] persLink = new int[5];
int noInArray;
persLink[0] = 12;
persLink[1] = 22;
persLink[2] = 33;
noInArray = persLink.length;
```

The final statement will place the value 5 in the variable `noInArray` since the instance variable `length` holds the size of the array – not the number of values which it currently holds.

Ports

A computer connected to the Internet via the Internet protocol TCP/IP has a set of port numbers attached to it that identify the application that is to be run. The port numbers from 0 to 255 are used for frequently used processes and applications. For example, port 21 is used for File Transfer Protocol, the method whereby large files can be transferred from one computer to another, port 110 is used for email services and port 37 provides the time of day. Port numbers above 255 are used for private applications.

As you will see later in the book, arrays are capable of holding anything from scalars to complicated objects. For example, you can have an array of strings. The code below declares an array containing services which are attached to some of the ports of a computer which is connected to the Internet. Notice that the first element of the array is empty since ports are numbered from 1.

```
String[] ports = {"",
        "TCPMUX",
        "RJE",
        "ECHO",
...
}
```

Caching

Web documents have varying degrees of popularity. Some are accessed very frequently by a large number of users, while others may only be accessed a few times in a year by a small number of users. Many Web documents can be found on computers which may be situated very remotely on other networks well away from a Web server. When a request to process such a document comes into a Web server, it has to retrieve the document from the remote site. If the document is very popular, then the amount of resources and bandwidth which are consumed can be huge, with a considerable degradation of performance. In order to get over the resource problems Web servers cache frequently used remote documents. The term **cache** refers to the process of storing these documents at the Web server's site so that few overheads are expended when the documents are accessed.

Another example of the use of strings and arrays is connected with Web server caches. The statement below declares two arrays cachedDocs and nonCachedDocs. These contain strings which represent the addresses of documents which are cached and not cached by a Web server.

```
String[] cachedDocs, nonCachedDocs;
```

As you have previously seen, the scalar data types within Java can be given values by means of assignment statements. For example, the code shown below:

```
int a, b, c;
a = 10;
b = 23;
c = 45;
```

declares three variables a, b and c and then uses assignment statements to give them the values 10, 23 and 45. The code:

```
char newStopChar;
float total;
```

```
int buffSize = 23, newTelLocation;
newStopChar = 'u';
newTelLocation = 017;
total = 1.2e2;
```

declares a character variable, a floating point variable and two integer variables. The third declaration sets the variable buffSize to 23 with the remaining assignment statements setting newStopChar to the character u, the variable newTelLocation to octal 17 and the floating point variable total to 120.

Normally in Java if you wish to give an object a value you will need to send a message to it. However, an exception is made for strings and arrays. If you wish to give a string object a value then an assignment can be made just as with primitive data types. So, for example, the code shown below:

```
String userId;
userId = "Thom Gunn";
```

would initialize the value of userId to the string "Thom Gunn". As you have seen before, arrays can be initialized in the same way. For example, the code shown below:

```
int commsSteps[] = new int[5];
commsSteps = {1, 3, 5, 6, 9};
```

initializes the integer array commsSteps declared in the first line to contain the five integers 1, 3, 5, 6 and 9, starting with 1 in the first (0) position of the array.

4.3 Control structures

As befits a modern programming language Java contains the main programming constructs usually found in other languages such as C and Pascal. These **control structures** determine the way in which a Java program is executed. The aim of this section is to describe the main control structures in Java through their use in small code fragments and in methods.

The first facility to describe is the way in which statements in the Java programming language are terminated. As you will have seen by now this is achieved by means of a semicolon written after a statement. A sequence of statements in Java should be written as:

```
statement1;
statement2;
statement3;
```

Groups of statements in Java can be treated as a compound statement by enclosing them in curly brackets. For example, the statement:

```
{int i, j = 24;
String newName = "Ince", oldString;
```

```
i = j++;
oldString = newString;}
```

is an example of a **compound statement** consisting of four statements, two of which declare variables. As you will see later this enables a whole series of statements to be treated in the same way.

4.3.1 Conditional processing

In any programming language there is a need to carry out some processing if a certain condition holds; for example:

- If a member of staff is a manager his or her salary will be calculated using a productivity bonus.

- If the signal that has just been received is from an insecure computer, then the message that accompanies it is not allowed into the main computer network.

- If the stock of a particular product in a warehouse is empty, then inform the sales clerk that the order cannot be met.

- If the satellite has not emitted a signal for over 30 minutes, inform the main controller of this fact.

Java contains **conditional processing** facilities which allow whole sections of code to be executed if a certain condition is true or if that condition is false.

The first form of this conditional processing is shown below:

```
if (condition)
    true statements;
```

Here, the condition within the round brackets evaluates to a Boolean value. If that value is true, then the statements following are executed. If the value is false, then they are not executed. Three examples of this simple conditional facility are shown below:

```
if (a == 12)
    b = 23;

if (c==12 && d==23)
    signal = true;

if (a<=203 || b==22)
    newValue = "settings";
```

The first statement sets the integer variable b to 23 if the current value of the integer variable a is 12; the second statement sets the Boolean variable signal to be true if the value of the integer variable c is 23 and the value of the integer variable d is 23; and, finally, the third statement sets the string variable newValue to be the string value "settings" if the integer variable a is less than or equal to 203 or the integer variable b is equal to 22. This facility is known as an **if statement**.

Before looking at more complicated examples of the if statement it is worth pointing out that we will be adopting a style of writing Java programs which includes indentation to indicate the structure of a program. For example, in the if statements above we have indented the statement within the if condition to show that it is the one that is to be executed if the if condition is true.

The actions that are executed when a true condition is encountered can be written as a compound statement. For example:

```
if (a == i){
    h = 12;
    b = 23;
    c = "new Employee";
}
```

Here, the three variables a, b and c are given values if the integer variable a has the same value as the integer variable i.

There is a slightly more complicated form of the if statement which caters for the fact that if a Boolean expression is true some processing is carried out and if the value is false some other processing is carried out. For example:

> If the user has indicated that he or she is a novice then set the interface to its verbose mode, else set it to normal mode.

This has the form:

```
if (condition)
    true statements;
else
    false statements;
```

where true statements are executed if the condition is true and false statements are executed if the condition is false. The statements that are executed can be a single statement or a compound statement which is enclosed in curly brackets. For example, the code:

```
if (a == 204)
    found = true;
else
    i++;
```

has two single statements. The first found = true is executed if the contents of the variable a are equal to 204, the second i++ is executed if this condition does not hold. Another example is shown below. The code:

```
if (userCount > 1) {
   userCount++;
   nextId = "first";
}
else{
   sourceSwing++;
   networkSwitchId++;
}
```

consists of two compound statements. The first:

```
{
   userCount++;
   nextId = "first";
}
```

is executed if the variable `userCount` is greater than 1, while the second is executed if the variable is less than or equal to 1.

If statements can be nested within each other. An example of this is shown below:

```
if(a == 34){
   s = 23;
   i++;
   if (i < 23){
      b++;
      c++;
   }
}
```

Here you can see the value of using an indentation style: the structure of the two `if` statements is displayed and it becomes clear which statements are going to be executed when each of the two conditions is true.

If statements tend to be used very frequently in any program, irrespective of what programming language is being used. However, sometimes there are occasions when the use of an `if` statement can be somewhat clumsy and verbose. The main occasion is where a number of outcomes are required to occur based on the value of a variable or an expression. For example, assume that we have a variable `ipBreak` which is going to have values ranging from 1 to 5, and that, at a particular point in the code, some statements need to be executed if the value of this variable is 1, some other statements need to be executed if the value of the variable is 2, and so on.

This can be implemented using `if` statements but the result is usually quite verbose and rather unreadable. Java contains a switch facility which enables this form of multiconditional processing to take place. The general format of the switch facility is:

```
switch (argument){
   case firstcase   : statements;
   case secondcase  : statements;
   case thirdcase   : statements;
   case fourthcase  : statements;
   case fifthcase   : statements;
...
   case nthcase     : statements;
}
```

Each of the cases firstcase, secondcase, thirdcase and so on can be integers or characters. The statements that are associated with each case can be a single statement or a series of statements. Each set of statements is executed when the case corresponding to the set of statements is delivered by the argument following the switch keyword.

Once a statement, or set of statements, associated with a case keyword is executed, transfer of control is made to the set of statements associated with the next case unless a statement known as a break statement is encountered. If such a statement is encountered, then control passes to the end of the switch statement. As an example of this consider the switch statements shown below:

```
switch (bufferId) {
   case 1: statements1;
   case 2: statements2;
   case 3: statements3;
   case 4: statements4;
}
```

where bufferId is an integer variable. If bufferId has a value 1, then the statements labelled statements1 are executed, if the variable has a value 2 then the statements labelled statements2 are executed, and so on. If the value of bufferId is 1 and statements1 does not contain a break statement, then execution carries on with the statements in statements2; if these statements still do not contain a break statement, then execution proceeds to those statements labelled statements3, and so on. It is normally quite unusual for this form of processing to occur where a set of statements associated with a case keyword drops though to the next set of statements. Normally the break statement is used to take the processing to the end of the switch statement. An example of this is shown below:

```
switch (telControlChar) {

   case 'a':     videoId = 3;
                 break;

   case 'b':     videoId = 19;
                 soundId = 12;
```

```
                break;
  case 'c':     videoId = 11;
                link++;
                break;
}
```

Here the character variable `telControlChar` determines which chunk of code is to be executed. If the value of this variable is the character `'a'` then the integer variable `videoId` is set to 3 and the `break` statement transfers control to the end of the `switch` statement, effectively transferring control to the statement following. If the value of the `telControlChar` variable is the character `'b'`, control is then passed to the three statements:

```
videoId = 19;
soundId = 12;
break;
```

After the first two statements have been executed the `break` statement is invoked and, again, control is passed to the statement following the `switch` statement. The final part of the `switch` statement:

```
videoId = 11;
link++;
break;
```

is executed when the variable `telControlChar` contains the value `'c'`. The final statement is the `break` statement; this again transfers control to the end of the `switch` statement. This statement is strictly not necessary since, if it was omitted, the processing would pass to the end of the `switch` statement anyway. However, we regard it as good programming practice: you will often find that you will need to modify a program after it has been tested, and one common set of modifications involves adding new cases to a `switch` statement. If you needed to make a change to the code above which required a new case following the last case, and had not inserted a final break, then you would need to remember to add this break to the case corresponding to character `'c'`; often you will forget and this would mean that your code would look like:

```
switch (telControlChar) {
  case 'a':     videoId = 3;
                break;
  case 'b':     videoId = 19;
                soundId = 12;
                break;
  case 'c':     videoId = 11;
                link++;
```

```
newcase:        code for new case
}
```

When the processing for the case corresponding to the character 'c' has completed, the processing will fall through to the new case that you have added, which is not what you intended. This sort of error is really difficult to detect. Thus, even though the final break is vestigial, it is good practice to include it: it may waste a small amount of memory, but you could find yourself being saved a very large amount of development time.

It is worth pointing out that in the examples above when a series of statements are to be executed in a switch statement there is no need to enclose them within curly brackets.

Another important facility associated with switch statements needs to be mentioned. This is a facility which enables you to specify what processing is required when none of the conditions you expected occurs. One of the disadvantages of the code that you have seen above is that the variable telControlChar could take on other values, apart from those specified following the case keyword; for example, the variable could have a value 'z'. What happens here is that none of the statements in the switch statement are executed. This may not be the processing that we require; for example, if the variable telControlChar contained another character rather than 'a', 'b' or 'c', then this might be a serious error; we might want to pick it up and carry out some processing for it.

The switch statement contains a facility which enables this type of processing to occur: this uses the keyword default to indicate a section of code that is to be executed when none of the other cases in a switch statement conforms to the value of the variable in the switch part of the statement. So, if in the example above, we wish some error processing to take place, then all that we need to do is to label a set of statements which carry out the error processing with the word default. This is shown below:

```
switch (telControlChar){
  case 'a': videoId = 3;
            break;

  case 'b': videoId = 19;
            soundId = 12;
            break;

  case 'c': videoId = 11;
            link++; break;

  default:
            // Code for carrying out some error
            // processing
            break;
}
```

An integer variable i can hold values from 1 to 10. If the value is 1 then an integer variable tOld is incremented by one, if the value is 2 then an integer variable uTerm is decremented by one and an integer variable h is decremented by one; if the value is 3 then a string variable nameId is set to "TelNet". If the variable has none of these values, then a variable linkLose is incremented by four. Write down the code which achieves this.

Solution

The code is shown below. It uses a switch statement:

```
switch (i){
   case 1:     tOld++;
               break;

   case 2:     uTerm--;
               h--;
               break;

   case 3:     nameId = "TelNet";
               break;

   default:
               linkLose+=4
               break;
}
```

Notice the use of the break keyword in the last section of the switch statement.

4.3.2 Repetitive processing

All programming languages contain facilities which enable sections of code to be executed repeatedly, either while, or until, some condition is satisfied or for a fixed number of times. It is these facilities that give a programming language its power. It enables similar sections of code to be repeatedly executed. For example, the facilities described in this section would enable the contents of an array to be summed without writing a long summation involving every element of the array.

The first repetitive facility that we will introduce is the while statement. This has the form:

```
while(Boolean expression)
   statements;
```

where `statements` can be either a single statement or a compound statement. The semantics of the `while` statement is:

> While the Boolean expression is true the statements are executed.

A very simple example of the use of the `while` statement is shown below:

```
int i = 0, sum = 0;
while (i < 5) {
    sum+=vals[i];
    i++;
}
```

This simple piece of code first carries out an initialization and then repeatedly adds the `i`th element of the array `vals` into the variable `sum`; after this it increments the variable `i` which is used to index the array by one. The effect of the code is to find the sum of the first five elements of the array `vals`.

SAQ

Write down the Java code which examines the array `usersFreq` which contains integers and places in the variable `countVals` the number of integers that it contains which lie between 7 and 15 inclusively.

Solution

The code is shown below:

```
int i = 0, countVals = 0;
while (i < usersFreq.length){
    if (usersFreq[i]>=7 && usersFreq[i]<=15)
        countVals++;
    i++;
}
```

SAQ

Write down Java code which examines the array `expData` which contains integers and finds the sum of those values in it which are larger than 70, placing it in `sum`.

Solution

The code is shown below:

```
int i = 0, sum = 0;
while (i < expData.length){
    if (expData[i] > 70) sum+=expData[i];
```

```
    i++;
}
```

Hop Routing

In a computer network the transmission software is faced with the problem of there being a number of paths from one computer to another computer to which it is to send data. One popular way of determining a route is based on hops. A **hop** is the distance between two computers across a communication link. When a computer uses hop routing it finds the route from one computer to another, often via a number of intermediate computers, by choosing the shortest set of hops. This is a simple algorithm to implement since all it requires is a table of distances from one computer to the other computers to which it wishes to send a message.

SAQ

The array `hopDistances` contains the hop distances from a sending computer to another computer. Write down code which finds the minimum distance and places the value in the variable `minHop`. Use a `while` statement and assume that there are `noOfDistances` values in the array.

Solution

```
int minHop = hopDistances[0], i = 1;
while(i < noOfDistances){
  if (hopDistances [i] < minHop)
    minHop = hopDistances[i];
  i++;}
```

The only point worth remaking about the code we have shown is that whenever you write nested control statements, always carry out some indenting of the code in order to increase readability and make sure that all the opening curly brackets are associated with a closing curly bracket.

It is worth showing at this point how a disciplined form of unconditional transfer of control can be used within Java. In the text which described the `switch` statement we described the use of the `break` statement. The effect of this statement, within the context of the `switch` statement, was to transfer control to the end of the statement, that is, to the statement which followed the `switch` statement. This use of the `break` statement can be generalized to any statement which implements repetitive processing. If you write `break` within a repetitive statement, then when the Java interpreter encounters this statement it will transfer control to the statement following the repetitive statement in which it is embedded. For example, the code fragment below shows a code skeleton in which a break statement is embedded:

```
statement;
while(expression) {
    statement1;
    statement2;
    statement3;
    statement4;
    if (some expression)
       break;
    statement5;
    ...
    statementn;
}
nextstatement;
```

When the loop starting at statement is executed and some expression is true, the Java interpreter will transfer control to the statement following the loop. This is statement nextstatement.

A more concrete example of this in action is shown below. It is a fragment of code which looks for a user "Jones" within an array of strings identified by userTable. The code assumes that the array contains totUsers strings and will return with the Boolean variable in set to be true if the name is found and false otherwise. If the name is found, then the integer variable index is set to contain the position of the name within userTable. Again it is worth pointing out that the code uses the method equals to check for equality of strings.

```
boolean in = false;
String nameToBeSearchedFor = "Jones";
int counter = 0, index;
while(counter < totUsers ) {
    if (userTable[counter].equals(nameToBeSearchedFor)) {
       in = true;
       index = counter;
       break;
    }
    counter++;
}
```

The break statement here transfers control to the statement following the while statement.

Java contains a second repetitive statement which is similar to the `while` statement described above. This is the `do-while` statement. It is similar to the `while` statement in that it implements repetitive processing *while* a certain condition is true. However, the test as to whether a loop needs to be terminated occurs at the end of the statement as compared with the `while` statement where the test is made at the beginning. The general form is:

```
do
   statements;
while (expression);
```

The semantics of this statement is: execute the statements identified by `statements` while the expression on the third line is true. However, the check whether it is true or false occurs *after* `statements` is executed. This means that `statements` will be executed at least once; this is in contrast to the `while` statement where it is possible for the statements within the loop to be just skipped over, for example where the `while` statement is processing an array and there are no elements currently stored in the array.

An example of some code involving the `do-while` statement is shown below:

```
int i = -1;
do
   i++;
while (!names[i].equals(lastNodeName));
```

This code searches for the string contained in the string variable `lastNodeName` in the string array `names`. It repeatedly increments the integer variable `i` until the name is found. It is important to point out that this code assumes that the name is contained in the array; if it wasn't, the loop would eventually index over the bounds of the array and the Java interpreter would flag a run-time error. Another example of the use of the `do-while` statement is shown below:

```
int firstIndex, lastIndex, i;
String[] nameArray = new String [100];
...
i = firstIndex - 1;
do{
   i++;
   nameArray[i] = "";
}
while (i != lastindex);
```

This sets a section of the string array identified by `nameArray` to contain null or empty strings. The section is identified by `firstIndex` and `lastIndex` which delimit the first item in the array and the last item respectively.

These are statements which carry out repetitive processing *while* some condition is true. We find that we use the `while` statement much more than the `do-while` statement, as the latter involves carrying out some subtraction on a variable before the loop is entered, and while subtraction is not too inefficient an operation in Java it is easy to forget it and cause a programming error which is quite difficult to spot.

The final repetitive statement which implements repetitive processing in Java is the `for` statement. The general form of this statement is:

```
for (expression1; expression2; expression3)
    statements;
```

The semantics of the `for` statement is as follows:

> The statements are executed continually with a variable, which we shall call a **control variable**, being given a value in `expression1`; each time the statement(s) are executed `expression3` defines the new value of the variable as it progresses through each iteration of the statements; the loop terminates when the condition expressed in `expression2` becomes false.

An example of the use of the `for` statement is shown below:

```
for(int i = 0; i < 10; i++)
    a[i] = 0;
```

Here the statement `a[i] = 0;` is continually executed. On the first pass through the statements the value of i is zero (i = 0 corresponds to `expression1`). The next time that the statement `a[i] = 0` is executed i will be incremented by 1 (i++ corresponds to `expression3`). When the statements are finally executed i will be equal to 10.

This was a very simple example of a loop which started at 0, was incremented by 1 and stopped after a single integer value was encountered. For statements can be more complex. For example:

```
for(int i = start + newList; i <= followBitSum; i+=2)
    statements;
```

executes `statements` repeatedly, starting with the control variable having the value `start + newList`, with it being incremented by two each time that it traverses the statements, finishing when i is greater than the contents of the integer variable `followBitSum`.

The `for` statement:

```
for (expression1; expression2; expression3)
    statements;
```

is equivalent to the code:

```
expression1;
while(expression2){
    statements;
```

```
    expression3;
}
```

The `for` statement exists in a number of forms, each of which represents the original form specified above, but with one or two of the expressions missing; usually these are either `expression1` or `expression3` but not both. If `expression1` is missing the control variable will have been assigned a value in a section of code which has been executed previous to the execution of the `for` statement. If `expression3` is omitted then, within the `statements` of the `for` statement, there is some updating of the control variable. Thus all the following are equivalent:

```
for(int i = 0; i < 10; i++)
    a[i] = 0;
```

and

```
int i = 0;
...
for(; i < 10; i++)
    a[i] = 0;
```

and

```
for(int i = 0; i < 10;) {
    a[i] = 0;
    i++;
};
```

The main thing to notice is that whenever an expression is omitted between the round brackets of the `for` statement the semicolon associated with it is not omitted. It is also worth saying that very rarely do you find Java code with both `expression1` and `expression3` omitted since writing a `for` statement in this way is equivalent to a `while` statement; also it is very rare to find `expression2` missing since there is almost always a need to have a terminating condition for the loop and it would be unwieldy to write the terminating condition within the loop using an `if` statement and a `break` statement.

SAQ

Write down the code which adds up the first ten elements of the integer array `arrCont` and places the result in the integer variable `sumUp`.

Solution

The code is shown below:

```
int sumUp = 0;
```

```
for(int i = 0; i < 10; i++)
  sumUp+=arrCont[i];
```

Write down code which forms the sum of every fifth element of the integer array arrCont and places it into the integer variable sum5Up. This array contains exactly 50 elements.

The code is shown below:

```
int sum5Up = 0;
for(int i = 0; i < 50; i+=5)
  sum5Up+=arrCont[i];
```

Write down code which examines the arrays left and right and places in the Boolean variable compare the value true if the former array contains more zeros than the latter array. The array left contains 100 integers, while right contains 150 integers. Write down two fragments of code: the first declares all the variables including the arrays, the second carries out the processing.

The first fragment is:

```
int rightSum = 0, leftSum = 0;
boolean compare;
int[] left = new int[100]; int[] right = new int[150];
```

The second fragment is:

```
for(int i = 0; i < 100; i++)
  if (left[i] == 0)
    leftSum++;
for(j = 0; j < 150; j++)
  if (right[i] == 0)
    rightSum++;
compare = leftSum > rightSum;
```

Mailing Lists

Mailing lists are collections of users who wish to receive common information. These lists may be internal to a company, for example, they may be the members of a current project, or may range across continents and cover some topic of interest such as Thai cooking, the Fortran programming language or alien life. Lists may be moderated or unmoderated. With the latter any email sent by one of the members of the list is automatically sent to all the other users. When a group is moderated it is first sent to a moderator who will either pass it on to the members of the list, modify it (for example, it may contain inflammatory material) or reject it as it contains some advertising scam.

Organizing mailing lists is a complicated and tedious task when the number of users gets larger and larger: for example, many of the groups devoted to technical computing subjects on the Internet contain tens of thousands of members. Because administering a mailing list is difficult a number of utilities have been developed. The best known of these is Majordomo. This provides facilities such as placing new users on a mailing list, removing users, and determining which users have had emails bounce because their email address does not exist any more.

Before leaving the topic of repetitive processing it is worth mentioning another device similar to break which allows a limited form of flow of control. This is the continue statement. You will remember that the break statement, when executed, results in the current loop that is being executed being exited. The continue statement interrupts the processing in a loop, but in a less drastic manner. When the continue statement is encountered in a loop the Java interpreter will terminate the current execution of the loop and will return the thread of processing to the beginning of the loop. For example, consider the code shown below:

```
for(int i = 1; i < newVal; i++) {
   statement1;
   statement2;
   statement3;
   if (condition)
      continue;
   statement4;
...
   statementn;
}
```

SAQ

Mailing list utilities maintain a list of those users whose emails have bounced. There are a number of reasons for this: the user could have left the institution whose computer he or she is using or there could have been some technical problem with the link between the computer sending the email and the computer receiving it. Assume that two arrays are used to store bounce lists. The first is bounceAddress which stores the addresses that have bounced and noOfBounces which stores the number of times that emails to that address have bounced. Write code that sets the array lotsOfBounces to contain those addresses which have bounced more than 20 times. Assume all the declarations have been made and that there are currently bounceCount entries in the arrays, where bounceCount is an int.

Solution

The code is shown below:

```
int overCount = 0;
for (int i = 0; i < bounceCount; i++){
   if (noOfBounces[i] > 20){
      lotsOfBounces[overCount] = bounceAddress[i];
      overCount++;
   }
}
```

If, during the execution of the set of statements, the condition within the if statement is true, then the execution of the loop will be interrupted and resumed at statement1. This assumes that the condition i < newVal is true; if it wasn't then the loop would terminate.

An example of Java code which shows this facility being used is displayed below.

```
for(int i = 0; i < arrayNumber; i++) {
   if ((signalSensor[i] >= 10) && (signalSensor[i]
      <= 20))
      continue;
   signalSensor[i]++;
   modifyFlag = true;
}
```

Here the loop traverses through the integer array signalSensor. If the value at each element lies outside the limits 10 and 20 inclusively, then it is incremented and a Boolean variable called modifyFlag is set to become true. This is achieved by means of the continue statement within the if statement. Once this is executed it transfers control to the end of the loop, thus missing the final two statements which carry out the processing.

You have now seen a number of examples of break and continue being used. It is worth providing you with a warning about them: the frequent use of these facilities often leads to making your code unreadable. In many cases there is a much better solution to the problems that you intended solving using break and continue. For example, the code above could have eliminated the continue by rewriting the for statement as:

```
for(int i = 0; i < arrayNumber; i++) {
  if ((signalSensor[i] < 10) && (signalSensor[i] > 20)){
    signalSensor[i]++;
    modifyFlag = true;
  }
}
```

4.3.3 Developing some methods

Before leaving this section it is worth providing some more examples of code which involves conditional and repetitive processing in order to provide you with a little more practice. This code will be associated with some methods. We will not show you whole classes being coded – this is left to the next chapter; however, by the time you leave this section you should feel you have some degree of facility with methods and also feel much more confident about repetitive and conditional processing.

The first set of methods which we shall develop are those associated with an object that contains a collection of computer names. These names represent the computers currently connected together in a network. There will be two instance variables associated with this object: computerNames which is an array of strings which represent the names of computers and noOfComputers which is an integer variable that contains the current number of computers connected together in the network. We shall not worry about the declaration of these instance variables now but concentrate on the methods. We shall assume that four methods are required:

- A method which returns with the number of computers in the network;

- A method which adds a computer to the network;

- A method which removes a computer from the network;

- A method which checks whether a particular computer is contained in the network.

In developing the code we shall make the simplifying assumption that no errors will occur, for example we will not be inserting a computer with a name which is equal to a computer already in the network and we shall always have enough room in the instance variable `computerNames` to hold all the computers we want to add to the network.

We require two instance variables: one which contains the number of computers in the network and another which contains the names of the computers. We shall assume that the first instance variable is `noOfComputers` and will be an integer variable and the second instance variable is `computerCollection` which is an array of strings each of which represents a computer name. The first method returns the number of computers:

```
public int noOfComputers(){
   return noOfComputers;
}
```

Remember that the keyword `public` specifies that any other user can use this method and the keyword `int` indicates that an integer value is returned from the method. The method which adds a computer to the collection of computers is shown below:

```
public void addComputer (String addedComputer){
   computerCollection[noOfComputers] = addedComputer;
   noOfComputers++;
}
```

Since the instance variable `noOfComputers` marks the next empty location in the array the code for this method is straightforward.

The method which checks whether a particular computer is contained in the network is shown below. The strategy we shall adopt in programming this method is to place the name of the computer that is to be searched for at the end of the array and then increment a variable `i`, which is initialized to zero until the computer is found. If the computer is found before the one that has been inserted, then it is in the network; if it isn't then it was not in the network.

```
public boolean isInNetwork(String lookedForComputer){
int i = 0;
computerCollection[noOfComputers] = lookedForComputer;
do
   i++;
while(computerCollection[i] != lookedForComputer);
return i < noOfComputers;
}
```

The final method removes a computer from the network. This is achieved by finding the point in the array where the computer is stored and then shifting down each computer that lies after it.

```
public void removeComputer(string removedComputer){
int i = 0;
```

```
do
   i++;
while (computerCollection[i] != removedComputer);
for(int j = i; j < noOfComputers - 1; j++){
   computerCollection[j] = computerCollection[j+1];
}
noOfComputers--;
}
```

The code for these methods can now be used in any program. For example, the fragment of code below adds a computer VAXa to a collection of computers localComputers, then removes the computer Vaxb and finally places in the integer variable collCount the current number of computers in localComputers.

```
localComputers.addComputer("Vaxa");
localComputers.removeComputer("Vaxb");
int collCount = localComputers.noOfComputers();
```

Again notice the format of the expressions which all involve messages being sent to objects and the lack of arguments within the third method which does not require them.

The next example we shall describe is that of a bag. A **bag** is a collection of data which keeps track of the number of times an item is contained in it. In this example we shall develop the code for methods which are associated with a simple bag which just keeps track of the number of times the integers ranging from 0 to 100 are stored in itself. We shall assume that three methods are required:

- A method which adds an integer to a bag;

- A method which removes an integer from a bag;

- A method which returns with the number of occurrences of a particular integer within a bag.

Again we shall assume that there will be no complications with the data: that all the arguments passed to methods will be in the range 0 to 100. We shall, for the time being, ignore the initialization of the bag.

A natural way of storing the items in this bag would be an array which has 101 locations corresponding the 101 possible integers that it could contain. We shall assume that this instance variable will have the name bagVals.

The code for the method addToBag is shown below. It takes one argument which is the integer to be added. This integer will be found within the range 0 to 100.

```
public void addToBag(int toBeAdded){
   bagVals[toBeAdded]+=1; }
```

SAQ

Write down the code for a method removeFromBag which removes an integer from a bag. Assume that the name of the argument to the method is removedFrom.

Solution

The code is shown below:

```
public void removeFromBag(int removedFrom){
    bagVals[removedFrom]-=1;
    }
```

SAQ

Write down the code for a method reset which sets all the elements in the bag to zero.

Solution

The code is shown below:

```
public void reset(){
    for(int i = 0;i < bagVals.length;i++)
      bagVals [i]= 0;
}
```

The code for the method which returns with the number of occurrences of a particular integer within a bag is shown below. It has one argument noToBeLookedFor.

```
public int findNo(int noToBeLookedFor){
return bagVals[noToBeLookedFor];
}
```

The next example we shall deal with is part of a statistical package. At its heart is a collection of integers with a number of methods for their manipulation. We shall assume that the methods which are required are:

- A method which finds the smallest integer in the collection;

- A method which finds the largest integer in the collection;

- A method which finds the number of occurrences of a particular integer in the collection;

- A method which inserts an integer into the collection;

- A method which finds the number of occurrences of integers which lie between two end values;

- A method which returns with the number of integers in the collection.

We shall develop two versions of the collection of methods. The second version will be a more efficient implementation which uses inheritance.

We shall assume that the integers are stored in an integer array `values` and the variable `noInValues` contains the number of integers stored in the array. The code for the method which finds the number of occurrences of a particular integer in the collection is shown below:

```
public int findNo(int no){
int count = 0;
for (int i = 0; i < noInValues; i++)
   if (values[i] == no) count++;
return count;}
```

SAQ

Write down the code for the method which inserts an integer into the collection and which returns with the number of integers in the collection.

Solution

The code for the two methods is shown below:

```
public void insertValue(int toBeInserted){
values[noInValues] = toBeInserted; noInValues++;
}

public int getNumber(){
return noInValues;
}
```

The code for the remaining three methods which find the maximum, find the minimum and find the number of occurrences of integers between two limits is shown below. In the first two methods we have assumed that there will be at least one value contained in the collection.

```
public int findMax(){
int maxSoFar = values[0];
for(int j = 1; j < noInValues; j++)
if (values[j] > maxSoFar)
   maxSoFar = values[j];
return maxSoFar;}
```

```
public int findMin(){
int minSoFar = values[0];
for(int j = 1; j < noInValues; j++)
if (values[j] < minSoFar)
  minSoFar = values[j];
return minSoFar;
}
```

```
public int findBetweenLimits(int upper, lower){
int count = 0;
for(int i = 0; i < noInValues; i++)
if(values[i]>=lower && values[i]<=upper)
  count++;
return count;
}
```

The code for findMax examines each element of the array and compares it with the maximum value that it has found so far; if the element examined is larger than this maximum value then the maximum value becomes the element. The method for findMin is similar.

This method allows us to write sections of code such as:

```
max = experimentalValues.findMax();
min = experimentalValues.findMin();
experimentalValues.insertValue(12);
```

Let us assume that the code above would be encapsulated in a class called DataCollection. The code for this class would look like:

```
class DataCollection{
int noInValues;
int[] values;
```

```
// code which initializes the
// instance variables
```

```
public int findNo(int no){
int count = 0;
for (int i = 0; i < noInValues; i++)
  if (values[i] == no)
    count++;
return count;
}
```

```
public void insertValue(int toBeInserted){
values[noInValues] = toBeInserted;
noInValues++;}
```

```
public int getNumber(){
return noInValues;
}


public int findMax(){
int maxSoFar = values[0];
for(int j = 1; j < noInValues; j++)
if (values[j] > maxSoFar)
   maxSoFar = values[j];
return maxSoFar;
}


public int findMin(){
int minSoFar = values[0];
for(int j = 1; j < noInValues; j++)
if (values[j] < minSoFar)
  minSoFar = values[j];
return minSoFar;
}


public int findBetweenLimits(int upper, lower){
int count = 0;
for(int i = 0; i < noInValues; i++)
if(values[i]>=lower && values[i]<=upper)
   count++;
return count;
}

}
```

We have ignored the methods which are used to construct `DataCollections`. This topic will be dealt with in much more detail in the last part of the next chapter.

Let us now assume that we want to develop a class which is a more efficient version of `DataCollection`. The major inefficiency with this class is that when a maximum or a minimum is found the whole of the array `values` needs to be searched. One way to develop a more efficient version of `DataCollection` is to have two further instance variables `max` and `min`. The former will hold the current maximum value in the collection, while the latter will hold the current minimum value. Each time an integer is inserted into the collection it is compared with `max` and `min` and they are updated depending on whether the integer is greater than `max` or less than `min`. This can be achieved by means of the inheritance mechanism that we discussed in Chapter 3. It would mean developing a new class which inherits its instance variables from `DataCollection` and also inherits some of the methods - but with other methods being overridden.

| SAQ |

Which of the methods within DataCollection would not need to be overridden?

| Solution |

The methods findNo, getNumber and findBetweenLimits would not need to be overridden as they all retrieve values and do not add any integer to the collection.

The code for the new data collection is shown below. We have given it the name EfficientDataCollection.

```
class EfficientDataCollection extends DataCollection{
int max, min;
// methods which initialize max and min

public void insertValue(int toBeInserted){
// code for InsertValue
}

public int findMax(){
// code for findMax
}

public int findMin(){
// code for findMin
}
```

The user of such a class will have the original methods findNo, getNumber and findBetweenLimits available together with the instance variables values and noInValues (inherited from DataCollection) and the new instance variables max and min.

Let us now look at the code for insertValue which overrides the old method insertValue contained in DataCollection:

```
public void insertValue(int toBeInserted){
if (toBeInserted > max) max = toBeInserted;
if (toBeInserted < min) min = toBeInserted;
super.insertValue(toBeInserted);
}
```

The first if statement adjusts max if the value encountered is the largest inserted; the next if statement adjusts min if the value encountered is the smallest inserted; and finally the last line of code carries out this insertion.

The words super.insertValue refer not to the insertValue method within the class EfficientDataClass but to the insertValue method within the superclass (DataCollection). This has the effect of inserting the integer toBeInserted into the array values. Whenever an insertValue message is sent to an object described by the class EfficientDataCollection, it is sent to this method, which in turn uses the insertValue in the superclass.

SAQ

Write down the code for the two remaining methods findMax and FindMin.

Solution

These are very simple: all they do is to return the values held in max and min.

```
public int findMax(){
return max;
}

public int findMin(){
return min;
}
```

Whenever a user sends a findMin or findMax message to an object described by EfficientDataCollection it will be these methods that will be called.

4.3.4 Strings as objects

The previous two sections of this chapter have concentrated on the basic data types and control structures of Java. To conclude the chapter we are returning to strings. There are a number of reasons behind this. First, strings in Java are regarded as objects and we feel that before reading the next chapter it would be useful for you to see more messages being sent to objects and, also, since many of you will be familiar with strings within other programming languages it would be easy for you to understand the main object concepts that you need to program in Java. Second, strings, while being regarded as objects in Java, have some properties of basic data types; these properties have been designed to appeal to C programmers who may have used strings in their programs in a non-object-oriented way. Strings represent something of a halfway house and it is entirely appropriate that we deal with them here, just after discussing scalar data types and before discussing objects.

Before proceeding it is worth reminding you of an item of vocabulary which will be used within this section. A *message* is something that is sent to an object. A message consists of a name and some arguments with the possibility of there being zero arguments. When a message is sent to an object a variety of things could occur: first, the state of the object could be changed; second, the state of the object could be changed and a value returned from the message; third, the state of the object could remain unchanged and a value be returned.

Messages will correspond to the methods associated with the class that describes the receiver object. When a message is sent to a destination object its class is discovered and the code corresponding to the message executed.

In Java there are two types of sequences of characters. These are `String` and `StringBuffer`. Objects described by the former are constants which cannot be changed, while objects described by the latter can be modified. Normally Java code involves strings being converted into StringBuffers, modified and then reconverted into strings.

There are a number of ways of creating Strings and StringBuffers. The first is to declare them using the normal declaration facility that you have seen previously. For example, the declaration:

```
String filename, rootDirectory;
StringBuffer userName;
```

declares two strings called `filename` and `rootDirectory` and a `StringBuffer` called `userName`. These can be initialized by means of an assignment. For example:

```
userName = "James Davis";
```

sets the contents of `userName` to be the string `"James Davis"`. This is very straightforward but hides a subtle point that we made in the first paragraph: in Java strings are regarded as slightly imperfect objects: there are facilities for strings within Java which are not object-oriented, but which have been included to smooth the path of programmers who are used to other languages (most notably C) when they program in Java. If strings were pure objects in Java, then assignments such as the above would be disallowed. The only way to communicate properly with a real object is via a message, so if strings were pure objects the way of setting the value of a string would be to write an expression such as:

```
newUser.setStringValue("James Davis");
```

which sets a string value within the object `newUser`.

There are other examples of this compromise within Java. For example, when you want to join together (concatenate) two strings and set a `StringBuffer` variable equal to the result of this operation, you would use the + operator. For example, the code:

```
String pcFile = userId + "." + extension;
```

concatenates the string in `userId` with the single character string " . " and the string in `extension`. The + operator carries out this concatenation and returns with the string which has been so formed. If strings were pure objects in Java the concatenation process would have to be achieved by sending a series of concatenation messages to `pcFile`.

Note that the + operator will take a wide variety of scalars as an argument and turns them automatically into strings before carrying out a concatenation operation. Thus, there is no need to carry out any conversions to strings before using this operator.

Sockets

All communication by computers in the Internet is carried out by means of sockets. A socket is made up of two entities: a port (defined earlier in the book) and an IP address. The IP address is the address of a computer expressed as four integers separated by full stops. For example,

12.33.4.69

is an IP address.

The combination of socket and address is unique and can hence be used by Internet software to determine the communication circuit along which an application such as email is to run. In this way computers on the Internet can be easily connected together..

For example, to create a socket of a computer from its address and a port number all that would be needed would be the code:

```
String address;
int portNo;
. . .
socket newSock = address + ":" + portNo;
. . .
```

All the conversions to strings would be taken care of by the Java system.

Since strings are objects – albeit slightly impure objects – there are still a large number of messages that can be sent to them. A list of the five most frequently used methods is shown in Table 4.6. These methods give rise to the messages which we shall describe later in this section.

The `length` method is an example of one of those messages that do not affect the receiver object but which return a value. For example, the code below declares two string objects `str1` and `str2` and then sends a `length` message to them. Notice that the `length` method does not require any arguments.

Table 4.6 Some string messages.

Method	Meaning	Returns
length()	Finds the length of a string and returns it.	An integer
charAt(ch)	Finds the character ch at a specified place within a string.	A character
indexOf(str)	Searches for a particular string str within the destination object and returns the position of the string. The search starts at the front of the string.	An integer
lastIndexOf(str)	Searches for a particular string str within the destination object and returns the position of the string. The search starts at the back of the string.	An integer
substring(int1, int2)	Returns with a specified substring of a string which starts at int1 and finishes at int2.	A string

Each of these messages will return a value and the sum of these values is placed in the integer variable sumUp.

```
int sumUp;
String str1, str2;
...
// Code in which the strings are given values
...
sumUp = str1.length() + str2.length();
```

In object terms the receiver objects (str1, str2) have been sent length messages. These messages have no arguments, but result in a value being returned which is the length of the strings in terms of the number of characters found.

The charAt() method has one argument which represents the position within a string of a particular character. When a string object is sent a charAt() message the string is not modified (it wouldn't be a string if it was) but the character at the position given by the argument is returned. So, for example, if the string fileName has the value "dataPlex.txt" then the result of:

```
fileName.charAt(2);
```

would be for the message charAt(2) to be sent to the receiver object fileName with the character in the third position of the file name ('t') being returned.

Since messages such as the one above return values, they can be placed in any part of a Java program which expects the type of data which is to be delivered. For example, the code below finds out how many times the vowels 'a', 'e' or 'i' occur within a string:

```
int count = 0;
String nameOfId;
...
// Code which gives a string value to nameOfId
...
int i = 0;
while (i < nameOfId.length()) {
    char value = nameOfId.charAt(i);
    if (value == 'a' || value == 'e' || value == 'i')
        count++;
    i++;
}
```

This code involves two messages. First, the message length() is sent to the receiver object nameOfId. This results in the value of the length of the string being returned and then compared with i during the execution of the body of the while statement. The second example of a message being sent is within the body of the while statement where the message charAt(i) is sent to the receiver object nameOfId. This results in the character at the ith position in the string being returned.

The method indexOf() searches a string for a substring within the receiver object. When it finds the string it returns with the index within the receiver object of the substring that has been found. The search for the substring starts at the beginning of the receiver object. For example, if the receiver string object receiver that is being searched is "newLinknearNext" and the substring is "ne", then the processing that takes place when:

```
receiver.indexOf("ne");
```

is executed is that the message indexOf("ne") is sent to the receiver object (receiver). The method indexOf associated with the string class is located and the code executed: this results in the search for "ne" from the beginning of the string; this is found at the leftmost part of the string and the result is that the value 0 is returned since it represents the first index within the string object where the "ne" string was found (remember that strings and arrays within Java start at 0). If a different message was sent, for example:

```
receiver.indexOf("near");
```

then the result would be different; the result of the message being sent to `receiver` would be 7 which represents the starting index of the substring `"near"` within the destination object `"newLinknearNext"`.

The method `lastIndexOf()` is similar to `indexOf()` in that it searches for a string within a particular string which is the receiver object. However, it differs in that the search for the substring within the destination object starts at the end of the destination object. For example, the code:

```
receiver.lastIndexOf("ne");
```

would return with 7 which is the first occurrence of the substring `"ne"` when the search starts from the end of the receiver object.

At this stage it is worth reiterating the statement that the programming examples that we are presenting are all well behaved. In the case of the demonstration of `lastIndexOf()` and `indexOf()` above we have assumed that the receiver object contains the substring that is being searched for. Real life is very rarely like that and frequently we will carry out actions where there is scope for some error to occur or some action to fail. Java contains a facility known as the **exception** facility which provides facilities for monitoring such events and carrying out some processing corresponding to them. For the time being we will ignore what might be called this deviant processing and assume a perfect world. However, Chapter 6 will discuss exceptions in more detail.

The final string method that we need to discuss here is `substring()`. What this method does is to extract out the substring of the string which is the destination object. It has two arguments which delimit the substring. For example, assume that the variable name contains the string `"Darrel Ince"`. When:

```
name.substring(2,5);
```

is executed the `substring` message is sent to name. This results in a string being returned which is the substring of the destination object that is indexed by 2 and 5. Therefore the string `"rrel"` is returned. Java contains an extensive set of facilities for handling strings; however, we have found that the five discussed here are the ones that we have most frequently used.

The other type of string object is the `StringBuffer` object. This differs in two ways from String objects in that objects which are StringBuffers can be changed and are treated as pure objects. For example, it is incorrect to write:

```
StringBuffer lanLocation = "Node12";
```

in a similar way to that found when initializing strings. You will need to declare `StringBuffer` identifiers and then use new to create the string. To achieve the effect of the incorrect statement above we would have to write:

```
StringBuffer lanLocation = new StringBuffer("Node12");
```

`StringBuffer` objects also recognize the five methods outlined above. However, since `StringBuffer` objects can be changed they can also respond to methods which alter their state. The three popular methods for changing a string buffer are `append()`, `insert()` and `setCharAt()`.

The `append()` method adds a character to the end of a string buffer. An example of its use is shown below:

```
newName.append('c');
```

This results in the message `append('c')` being sent to the receiver object `newName`. The message adds the character `'c'` to the end of `newName`. If `newName` is empty, then the string so formed would just consist of the single character `'c'`.

The method `insert()` takes two arguments. The first is an index and the second is a string. The result of a message corresponding to this method being sent to a receiver object is that the string which is the second argument is added to the receiver object at the position specified by the index. For example, the code:

```
StringBuffer fileName = new StringBuffer ("DataFilter");
...
fileName.insert(4,"1.txt");
```

results in the message `insert(4,"1.txt")` being sent to the object `fileName`. The result of this message is that the string `"1.txt"` is added to the string stored in `fileName` at the position indexed by the first argument of the message (4). This results in `fileName` being changed to `"Data1.txt Filter"`.

The final method useful for StringBuffers is `setCharAt()`. This has two parameters. The first is a character and the second is the position within a string. When a message involving `setCharAt` is processed by the Java interpreter the receiver object, which is a string, is modified by overwriting the character at the position indicated by the first argument by the character which is the second argument.

For example, the code:

```
StringBuffer ipName = new StringBuffer("NewLog");
...
ipName.setCharAt(4,'h');
```

results in the message `setCharAt(4,'h')` being sent to the receiver object `ipName` with the character at the fourth indexed position (`'o'`) in the object being replaced by the character `'h'`; this ensures that the value of the receiver object is now `"NewLhg"`.

As one example of the use of Strings and StringBuffers, consider an application which processes email addresses.

Email Addresses

Email is one of the most popular applications of the Internet. It allows messages to be sent from one user of the Net to another on another continent in a fraction of the time required for letters. Usually mail is delivered within minutes to recipients who may be continents away from the sender. An email user will have a unique address which is used to direct mail to them. British addresses have the general form:

UserName@Location.Type.UK

where *UserName* is the name of the sender of the email (usually some convenient abbreviation), *Location* is their location – often the name of a company or an educational institution – and *Type* is the type of institution that the sender of the email currently works in, for example ac stands for an academic institution while co stands for a company. UK email addresses are often terminated by the final string "UK".

First let us assume that we have an applet which has managed to store a series of addresses in an array of strings called addressList. The first example of string processing that we will show is the construction of a new array ukAddressList which will contain all the email addresses from the United Kingdom. The code for this is shown below; in the code the identifier maxListSize contains the limit of the number of email addresses that can be found in the lists and the variable noOfAddresses contains the current number of addresses that are found in addressList.

```
. . .
String []   ukAddressList = new String[maxListSize],
            addressList = new String[maxListSize];
int         noOfAddresses, noOfUkAddresses,
            lastDotPosition, ukCount;
. . .

// Code which sets up the list addressList
// ready for processing
. . .

ukCount = 0;
for (int i = 0; i < noOfAddresses; i++) {
  lastDotPosition = addressList[i].lastindexOf(".");
  If (addressList[i].substring(lastDotPosition+1,
    addressList[i].length()-1).equals("uk")) {
      ukAddressList[ukCount] = addressList[i];
      ukCount++;}
}
```

This item of code contains a number of `String` and `StringBuffer` messages. The `for` statement has the effect of moving through the addresses contained in the string array `addressList` examining each item in the array to see whether it represents a United Kingdom address. The first statement in the body of the `for` statement:

```
lastDotPosition = addressList[i].lastindexOf(".");
```

finds the index of the substring consisting of the dot character in the destination object. The destination object is the `ith` item in the array containing email addresses. The message uses the `lastIndex` method since we want to search from the end of the address as the country designator is found at the end. The `if` statement then extracts the substring delineated by the index after the dot and the end of the string and compares it with the string `"uk"` (we have made an artificial assumption that all the email addresses stored in `addressList` have the country in lower case). Once an email address has been found that satisfies this condition, it is written to the array containing United Kingdom email addresses.

Let us now assume that we wish to process the list of email addresses from the United Kingdom in order to discover how many times users who have the address `"open"` are in the array.

The code for this is shown below; we have again made another artificial assumption that user names do not contain a full stop character.

```
int atPosition, dotPosition, openCount = 0;
for(int i = 0; i < ukCount; i++) {
   atPosition = ukAddressList[i].indexOf("@");
   dotPosition = ukAddressList[i].indexOf(".");
   if(ukAddressList[i].substring(atPosition+1,
     dotPosition-1).equals("open"))
       openCount++;
}
```

Three variables are declared: `atPosition` will contain the position of the `@` character within the email string, `dotPosition` will contain the position of the first dot character within the email string (remember that we are assuming that user names do not contain dots) and `openCount` will contain the count of the number of email addresses which have `"open"` as their location.

The `for` statement will iterate over the email addresses within the string array `ukAddressList`. Each element of this array will be a string object and two messages are sent to these objects; the first extracts the position of the `@` character within the email string, the second extracts the position of the first dot character. The search for these characters starts at the leftmost part of the string since the method `indexOf` is used. Once these positions are found a further message:

```
substring(atPosition+1,dotPosition-1)
```

is sent to each email address in the string array ukAddressList. This selects the substring starting after the @ character and before the first . character. This results in the location of the email address being returned; this is then compared with the string "open" and the count openCount is incremented if equality is found.

The URL

This is a string which enables the communication software of a computer to locate a document on the World Wide Web. An example of a URL is shown below:

```
http://www.acme.com/newDir/home.html
```

It has a number of components: *http:* indicates a Web site, *www.acme.com* represents the location of the computer, *newDir* represents a file directory and *home.html* represents the file containing the Web document. URLs have a fixed format: any deviation will mean that any attempt to access the Web document will fail.

SAQ

The string variable holderURL contains a URL. Write down code which sets the Boolean variable isWeb to true if the first four characters are "http" and false otherwise, and then sets the Boolean variable htmlEnd to true if the last substring following a full stop is "html" in lower case and false otherwise.

Solution

```
isWeb = (holderURl.substring(0,3) == "http");
int l = holder.length();
htmlEnd = (holder.substring(l-4,l-1) == "html");
```

4.3.5 Comments

Comments can be written in two ways in Java. For comments written after programming statements the characters // start a comment and the end of the line concludes the comment. For example:

```
newTelId = 0;      // Initialization of TelNet variables
fileType = vaxFile;
interfaceId = "NewSocket";
```

The second type of comment is used where the comment text spans a number of lines or occupies a single line: the characters / * start the comment, while the characters * / conclude the comment. For example:

```
/*
Initialization of the TelNet variables
These are only accessed by the methods which form part of
the classes NewInterface and Telinterface
*/
newTelId = 0;
fileType = vaxFile;
```

4.4 SUMMARY

Much of the material in this chapter will have been familiar to you if you have used a modern programming language; it should certainly be very familiar if you are a C programmer and certainly familiar in concept if you are a programmer in another language. What we have tried to do in this chapter is to introduce you to the main data types and control structures that are used within Java and display some small fragments of code. Towards the end of the chapter we have tried in a very gentle way to orient you towards the major change that will occur in the next chapter. This chapter will describe the key ideas of an object-oriented programming language and their implementation in Java. We have tried to prepare the ground by devoting some time to the string data type in Java. The Java language is a little schizophrenic in its treatment of strings: in some respects it treats them like any other data type in a non-object-oriented programming language, at the same time as providing facilities for sending messages to string objects. It is this latter facet that we have concentrated on. We would hope that by explaining that the main processing mechanism in Java involves messages being sent to receiver objects, and by continually using sentences which usually contain the words message and receiver object, we have prepared you for the conceptual change that will occur in the next chapter.

CHAPTER FIVE

Classes in Java

- To show how Java defines objects using the class facility.
- To describe the concepts of instance variable, static variable, instance method and static method.
- To show how inheritance can be used within Java.
- To briefly introduce the Java class library.

5.1 Introduction

The previous chapter has described the processing facilities and data types that are available within Java. A casual reader who has just read that chapter without reading the rest of the book would be forgiven for assuming that Java was not substantially different from other programming languages; in particular the programming language C. You could say that it had a somewhat strange syntax for calling what looked like subroutines, but apart from that there is little that differentiates Java from other programming languages. The aim of this chapter is to dispel this notion. It is not difficult to write Java programs in a way resembling those of conventional procedural programming languages. However, to derive the most power from Java it is necessary to develop code which is object-oriented. By the end of this chapter you should be able to do this.

5.2 Objects

It is worth carrying out a little revision before looking at how Java implements objects. An object is something which has a state: it is associated with some stored data values. Everything can be regarded as an object. The user of an email system is an object whose state may contain data that describes his or her location and name. A bank account is an object whose state may be the name of the account holder, the current balance, the overdraft limit and a list of recent transactions. A plane in an air traffic control system is an object; its state might consist of data which identifies the plane, its position and its eventual destination. A pull-down menu in the user interface of an applet can be regarded as an object; its state might consist of a list of the commands for the pull-down menu, the type of box that encloses the menu when it is instantiated on a screen and the colour of the pull-down menu. Thus, the first thing that needs saying is that the object paradigm is universal.

Another important point is that objects can receive messages. By now you will have seen plenty of examples of messages in Java and should be totally familiar with the dot notation that is used to indicate that a message is being sent to an object. The expression:

```
obj.mess(arg1, arg2,...,argn);
```

has the interpretation that the message `mess` is sent to the object `obj`. The message consists of *n* arguments which are used when the code corresponding to the message is executed (*n* could be zero).

An applet or application can be regarded as a set or collection of objects which communicate with each other by means of messages in order to achieve some processing demanded by the world outside the applet. For example, assume that we have an application which is a simple word processor and a user wishes to count the number of words in the document. The user will pull down a menu which contains the word count command, instantiate this command and the count will be displayed on the screen. This seemingly simple piece of processing will contain quite a large amount of processing which involves messages being sent to receiver objects. First, the mouse object will send a message to the pull-down menu object; this will result in the display of the pull-down menu, and the mouse will then send a message to the pull-down menu when it has selected the word count command. This will generate a message sent from the pull-down menu to the object which represents the document whose word count is to be found. This document will then send a series of messages to the words in the document with a count being incremented each time a word is found. When this processing has finished a message will be sent to a window asking it to display the word count on the user's computer monitor.

Java contains facilities for defining an object, naming an object and creating an object. Naming an object requires a simple declaration of the form:

```
ObjectType objectname;
```

Here `ObjectType` is the name of an object type and `objectname` is the identifier which is used to refer to the object. Thus, if the user had defined an object `emailUser` the code:

```
emailUser john, jim, angela;
emailUser[] forbiddenUsers;
```

would declare three objects john, jim, angela and an array of user objects identified by forbiddenUsers. It is important to point out that such a declaration does not create the objects, but just informs the Java system that the names will be used to designate the objects.

In order to create an object you will need to use a facility known as new. This creates an object and binds a name to the object. For example, the code:

```
emailUser john = new emailUser();
```

results in an emailUser object being created which is identified by the name john. As you will see later in this chapter there are a number of variants which can be used when constructing new objects. The one above is the simplest: it has no arguments and results in a new object being created with its instance variables uninitialized. The next section of this chapter will describe a number of ways of writing code which creates objects with a wide variety of initial values.

One keyword which you will sometimes encounter in a Java program is null. This represents an empty object. It is similar to zero in arithmetic. An example of the use of null is shown below:

```
User john = null;
```

This creates a User variable named John but does not put any data in it.

5.3 Classes

5.3.1 Defining classes in Java

The class is the key concept in Java. A **class** represents a description of an object. A table containing class details is consulted by the Java interpreter when it is asked to create a new object. A class has two functions. The first is to define the state of an object described by the class, that is, what items of data make up the state and what sort of data they are; for example, whether they are integers, strings or objects defined by other classes. The second function of a class is to define the behaviour of an object, where we use the word *behaviour* to mean the messages that a class can respond to. An example of the initial lines of a class are shown below. We shall use this class as an example in this section of the book:

```
class User {
   String userId, emailAddress;
   int noOfAccesses, dateRegistered;
   . . .
   // Methods
   . . .
}
```

The keyword `class` introduces the name of the class. The declarations following this first line describe the state of an object defined by this class. The class shown above describes the user of an applet. Such a user will have an identity and an email address, both of which are strings. We shall also assume that we are interested in the number of accesses that each user has made to the applet and the date on which they were registered. We shall assume that this date can be represented by an integer which represents some number of days from a base date such as 1 January 1900. This is a little artificial since Java contains a date class in one of its libraries which we could have used here; however, we have not yet taught it so just assume for the time being that an integer value is enough to represent the date on which a user was registered.

These initial lines define the contents of an object. The lines following are used to define the methods, or chunks of code, which correspond to the messages that can be sent to an object. Java distinguishes between two types of methods: accessor methods which access and modify the instance variables and constructor methods which create new instances of an object.

It is worth concentrating on accessor methods first. We shall assume that a number of methods are required: update each of the instance variables (four methods in all, one for each instance variable), read and return the values of the instance variables (another four methods) and a method which indicates that the user has used the applet and updates the instance variable which holds the number of accesses.

The program code for these nine methods is shown below. The first four set the values of the four instance variables while the next four access and return the values:

```
public void setUserId(String usIdVal) {
   userId = usIdVal;
}

public void setEmailAddress(String emailAddressVal) {
   emailAddress = emailAddressVal;
}

public void setNoOfAccesses(String NoOfAccessesVal) {
   noOfAccesses = NoOfAccessesVal;
}

public void setdateRegistered(String dateRegisteredVal){
   dateRegistered = dateRegisteredVal;
}

public String getUserId() {
   return userId;
}

public String getEmailAddress() {
   return emailAddress; }
```

```
public int getNoOfAccesses() {
  return noOfAccesses;
}
public int getDateRegistered() {
  return dateRegistered;
}
public void access() {
  noOfAccesses++;
}
```

The keyword `public` in front of a method indicates that the method can be used outside its class. Because we have not placed this keyword in front of the instance variables, any program that creates objects described by this class, for example:

```
userJohn = new User();
```

is not allowed to access the instance variables directly; for example, you will not be allowed to write statements such as:

```
userJohn.noOfAccesses = 23;
```

Later in this chapter we shall discuss ways in which this rule can be overridden. However, good programming practice dictates that we rarely do this. The reason why classes are written in such a way that the instance variables cannot be accessed directly, but are accessed via methods, is to do with a concept known as **information hiding**.

The core idea behind information hiding is that the programmer who employs a class is not allowed to know anything about the way in which instance variables are stored and the detailed coding within a method. If a user was allowed to access an instance variable directly within his or her programs, then, if the class that implemented the instance variables changed, large amounts of code within the program would need to be changed. Take the `User` class as an example. Let us assume that we implemented the class in the way shown above and that users were allowed to access the instance variables. But now assume that later in the life of the class we decided to replace the two instance variables which hold the user's identity and his or her email address with a single string which merged this information, the decision being made for space efficiency reasons. Every program which referred to these variables would need to be modified. However, if access to these instance variables was just via the methods defined in the class, the only rewriting needed would be to change the declaration of the instance variables and the code which accessed the two string variables whose format would have changed.

The code for the methods in the class is straightforward, the only slightly complicated aspect being the use of the `return` statement. What this does is to return a value when the message corresponding to the method is terminated.

It is worth looking at some more methods. Assume that the application in which the `User` class is embedded requires a method which checks whether a user has made any accesses before: let us call this method `zeroAccesses`; it returns a true value if the user has made no accesses and a false value if he or she has made at least one access.

```
public boolean zeroAccesses() {
   return noOfAccesses == 0;
}
```

Let us also assume that there is a need for a method which returns an integer which holds the number of days since the user accessed the applet. For this the method will need an argument which would be set to the day that the method was invoked. The code for this method, known as `daysFromRegistered`, is shown below:

```
public int daysFromRegistered (int today) {
   return today - dateRegistered;
}
```

All this method does is to subtract `dateRegistered` from the date `today`; it then returns this value for use by the application or applet code.

5.3.2 Access mechanisms

The classes that you have seen in the book have so far all been constructed in such a way that the instance variables *have not* been allowed to be accessed outside their class and the methods *have* been able to be accessed. This corresponds to good programming practice. However, Java does recognize that there are circumstances when other levels of access should be allowed.

Access Control Matrices

In a secure computer network users will usually be given various privileges depending on what types of software they are allowed to use. This information is displayed in an access control matrix which relates users to the software they can use. An example of such a matrix is shown in Figure 5.1. Here a number of programs and files from A to E are specified along with a number of users. R means a file can be read from, W means that a file can be written to and X means that a program can be executed. Thus, the user *Thomas* can execute the programs B and E and can write to the file C. When the operating system encounters user actions such as a file being read it will first check that the action is valid by accessing the matrix.

	A	B	C	D	E
Roberts	R		W		
Thomas		X	W		X
Hall			R		
Davis					X
Dimson		X			
Le Carre	R			R	
Christie	W				

Figure 5.1 Access privileges.

Exercise

What sort of instance variables would you find in a class which described an access control matrix? What methods would you also expect to encounter?

Solution

You would find the table shown in Figure 5.1. You would also find instance variables which held the total of current users and the total of files and executables that are being controlled.

Typical methods would include methods to: add a new user with specified privileges, remove a user, add a file or executable, remove a file or executable and change the privileges of a user with respect to a file or executable.

There are four levels of access known as **public, protected, private** and an access state known as **friendly**. If you precede an instance variable or a method with the keyword public, then any class outside the class in which the declarations occur can access the instance variables and the methods directly. For example, the class skeleton:

```
Class newId {
    public int xCoord, yCoord;

    public int a() {
        ...
    }
```

```
public void b() {
   ...
   }

}
```

defines two instance variables xCoord and yCoord which can be directly referred to in other classes and two methods a and b which again can be referred to in other classes.

By prefacing a method or instance variable with the keyword protected the programmer specifies that the methods and instance variables can only be referred to in any class which inherits from the class in which the protected keyword occurs and in the class itself.

By prefacing a method or instance variable with the keyword private the programmer specifies that the methods and instance variables which are prefaced can only be referenced within the class that they were defined in.

The last access level is *friendly*. This is specified by the programmer not prefacing the instance variables and methods with any of the three keywords described above. Friendly access means that any class which is declared in the same package as the friendly class can access it. A package, as you will see in Chapter 8, is a collection of related classes. The various accesses that have been described here can be mixed throughout a class definition. Most of the Java classes that you will encounter will have most, if not all, of their methods declared as public with their instance variables declared as private. Sometimes some of the methods are declared as private within a class. These methods usually carry out some housekeeping task which is needed by other methods which might be public; usually such methods provide an internal facility which is not needed by the user of the class and, indeed, they often provide internal information which destroys the principle of information hiding. Such methods are often known as **helper methods** or **helpers**.

If you have defined a class in such a way that the instance variables are allowed to be accessed outside the class, then you would use a dot notation to carry out this access. For example, you may have defined a class Point which represents the *x, y* point on a screen. This class might be defined by:

```
class Point {
   public int xCoord, yCoord;
   ...
   methods
   ...
}
```

Then, in order to access the xCoord instance variable of an object identified as edgePoint, all that is required is to write the name of the object followed by a full stop followed by the name of the instance variable as shown below:

```
edgePoint.xCoord;
```

As you will have seen in the previous chapter the dot notation can also be used for referring to methods. For example, if a method m is defined in a class C then that method can be referred to as C.m by other classes, provided, of course, that these classes are allowed to use the method.

5.3.3 Static variables and static methods

So far we have described instance variables and instance methods. The former are variables which hold data associated with each object. For example, if you defined a class as:

```
class newId {
   int a, b, c;

   // Definition of methods
}
```

then, whenever you created a new object described by class newId, and were able to look at the instance so created, you would find three memory locations corresponding to the instance variables a, b and c. There is, however, another type of variable which is known as a **static variable**. This is often referred to as a **class variable**. When you declare a static variable in a class, what you are specifying is that the class itself will be associated with that variable, and that no objects defined by that class will contain data associated with that variable.

Static variables and methods are introduced by means of the keyword static. By prefacing a variable declaration with this keyword you are specifying that the identifiers following are to be variables associated with the class, *not* with each object. There are a limited number of uses of static (or class) variables. Two common ones are to define some constant associated with the class. For example, the Java package associated with mathematical processing implements Pi in this way. The second use of class variables and methods is to implement some data which does not need to be duplicated for every object of that class. One common example of this is to declare a static variable to keep count of the number of objects described by the class that have been created. This class variable might be used when space is limited and the applet or application which uses the class would degrade badly in performance when an upper limit of objects described by the class is reached. Static (or class) methods are specified in the same way: by prefacing the definition of the method with the keyword static.

A static method differs from a normal method in that it is only allowed to access static variables: it is not allowed to read or write to instance variables. A typical use of a static method would occur with the scenario described in the previous paragraph where a static method would increment the class variable which describes the number of objects of the class which have been created.

You will also find class methods in the Java libraries where they carry out general functions not associated with objects. For example, the static method sin within the class `Math` returns the sin of the angle provided to it as a double argument. Thus, the code:

```
double val = Math.sin(angleAz);
```

calculates the sin of the angle `angleAz` and places the result within the double variable `val`.

Another use of class variables would be for identifying the version of a class. Classes undergo many revisions and it is useful to keep track of the current version of the class that is being used within a program. If the programmer uses a major version/minor version numbering scheme, where a major version number represents a big revision to an existing version and a minor version number represents some small tinkering, then this can be represented as two class variables, say `majorVersion` and `minorVersion`, declared in the class. Static methods can then be used to access this information but not change it. An example of this is shown below:

```
class X {
    static int majorVersion, minorVersion;

    // Method to extract the major version number
    // and return it

    // Method to extract the minor version number
    // and return it
}
```

Some examples of static methods and variables will be presented in the remainder of this chapter.

One keyword which you will find yourself using quite a bit is `final`. When you preface a variable name with the keyword `final` this means that the name represents a constant and that nothing in your code can change its value. Thus, the declaration:

```
Static final int MAX_VALUE = 12;
```

declares a constant `MAX_VALUE` which has the value 12. The constant is associated with a class rather than with objects derived from the class. We will adopt the convention that when static constants are declared they are written in upper case letters.

It is now worth looking at two final concepts associated with the notion of a class. The first is that of a **constructor** method. Such a method is used in conjunction with the new facility to create an object. You may have noticed that in describing classes in the previous chapter we only touched on how objects were initialized and only scantly mentioned the mechanisms used to create objects. The time has now come to look at this topic in some detail.

SAQ

Do you think you would ever find yourself writing the two statements below?

```
final int maxValue = 33;
final int constValue;
```

Solution

No, the first associates a constant with every object within the class in which it is defined. This is a waste of memory since the value would not be changed and hence, it would be much more efficient to define the constant once and make it a class variable. You will not find yourself writing the second statement since the constant is not given a value; it would be illegal to write statements such as

```
constValue = 33;
```

later in the code.

In order to write a constructor method all you do is to name the method with the same name as the class within which it is embedded. An example of a constructor method is shown below:

```
Class Coordinate {
   int xPos, yPos, zPos;
   . . .
   public Coordinate(int xVal, int yVal, int zVal) {
   xPos = xVal;
   yPos = yVal;
   zPos = zVal;
   }
   . . .
   // Other methods
   . . .
}
```

Here the constructor has three arguments which represent initial values of the three instance variables. Constructors are used in conjunction with the new facility which creates an object. For example, the code:

```
Coordinate newCoord = new Coordinate(2,2,02);
```

creates a new object described by the class Coordinate and sets its three instance variables to two. Every class has associated with it an implicit constructor which creates an instance of an object described by the class, but which does not initialize any of the instance variables associated with the class. So, for example, even though we have defined a constructor above for the class Coordinate there is still a constructor method available for use which does no initialization, so that we could write code such as:

```
Coordinate newCoord = new Coordinate();
```

Often, when you are writing classes, you will provide a number of constructors which cater for a selection of initialization possibilities. For example, the code for the class `Coordinate` shown below contains three constructors as well as the implicit constructor. These initialize one, two or three instance variables respectively. It is good practice in constructors which only initialize some of the instance variables to set the other variables to some default. In the case of the example below this is 0.

```
Class Coordinate {
  private int xPos, yPos, zPos;
  . . .
  public Coordinate(int xVal, int yVal, int zVal) {
  xPos = xVal;
  yPos = yVal;
  zPos = zVal;
  }
  . . .
  public Coordinate(int xVal) {
  xPos = xVal;
  yPos = 0;
  zPos = 0;
  }
  . . .
  public Coordinate(int xVal, int yVal) {
  xPos = xVal;
  yPos = yVal;
  zPos = 0;
  }

  // Other methods

}
```

The remaining chapters of the book will describe the Java class library and you will find it is the rule rather than the exception for a number of constructors to be provided for classes in the library.

In order to describe some more examples of constructors consider a class which is used to keep track of the names of the users of a computer network and their email addresses. This class makes use of objects defined by the class below:

```
class UserEntries{
private String userName, eMailAddress;
```

```
public UserEntries(String uName, String eAddress){
userName = uName;
eMailAddress = eAddress;
}

public String getEmailAddress(){
return eMailAddress;
}

public String getUserName(){
return userName;
}

}
```

This is an example of a simple class which just consists of two instance variables, a constructor which forms a UserEntries object from two strings and two methods which retrieve the values of the instance variables. We shall use this class in one which contains methods that:

- add a new user and their email address to a set of users and email addresses;

- return with the current number of users who have email addresses;

- return with the email address of a specific user;

- remove the details of a user when he or she no longer uses an email facility.

The code for the header of the class is shown below:

```
class EmailTable{
private int noOfUsers;
UserEntries[] userTable;
```

Let us assume that two constructors are required: one which sets up a table that contains 100 user entries and another which allows the user to set up as many entries as he or she wishes. The code for the two constructors is shown below:

```
public EmailTable(){
userTable = new UserEntries [100];
noOfUsers = 0;
}

public EmailTable(int size){
userTable = new UserEntries[size];
noOfUsers = 0;
}
```

There is some duplication here as the variable noOfUsers is initialized twice: what we really need is some way that the constructor which has no argument can call the other constructor. Later in this chapter we shall show how to do this.

Exercise

Write down the code for all the methods that are required for the EMailTable class.

Solution

These are shown below.

```
public int findNoOfUsers(){
return noOfUsers;
}

public void addUser(UserEntries u){
userTable[noOfUsers] = u;
noOfUsers++;
}

public String findAddress(String userName){
int i = findIndex(userName);
return userTable[i].getEmailAddress();
}


public void deleteUser(String userName){
int i = findIndex(userName);
for(int j = i; j < noOfUsers - 1 ; j++)
   userTable[j] = userTable[j+1];
}

private int findIndex(String userName){
int j = 0;
while (!(userTable[j].getUserName()).equals(userName))
   j++;
return j;
}
```

There is one thing of note in this list of methods. This is the method findIndex which is declared private. This means that it cannot be used outside the class by any other class. This is an example of a helper method which is used by other methods within the class but is unavailable to other classes. The reason why we do not make this method available to other classes is that it betrays a design decision: that the table of users and their email addresses are implemented in some data structure which is indexable. The principle of information hiding which we discussed earlier dictates that we hide such decisions away from the users of the class.

The other important concept associated with classes is the **finalizer**. A finalizer is a method which is executed when an object disappears. Before looking at the way in which this type of method is written it is worth examining the concept of disappearance when applied to an object.

When an object is created, for example by means of the statement:

```
Classname identifier = new Classname();
```

the Java interpreter will create enough space for it to exist; in particular, it will allocate enough memory for its instance variables. When an object is no longer needed the Java interpreter will destroy the object and return the space allocated to the object back to a free reservoir of space used for new objects. For example, within a method a declaration:

```
Classname newObjIdentifier = new Classname();
```

would create space for an object `newObjIdentifier` described by `Classname`; however, when the method completes its processing the space allocated to `newObjIdentifier` will be marked as unused. Periodically the Java interpreter will examine all the unused memory which is not occupied by objects – those that have effectively disappeared - and will return it to the reservoir of free space.

Programmers are allowed to write methods which are invoked when an object disappears within their classes. Such methods are given the name `finalize` and are made protected since they should not be accessed by classes outside the one in which they are declared.

In order to illustrate the use of constructors and finalizers consider the problem that we mentioned earlier: that we are developing a program where space for objects is very limited and, for some objects, we want to establish an upper limit to the number that can be active in a program. In order to do this we need to keep a count of the number of objects created and destroyed. We shall make the assumption in this example that programmers are unable to use the implicit default constructor method to create objects.

Let us assume that the class whose objects we need to monitor is called `IdPool` and that it has two static variables which are both integers. The code for the methods which create and destroy `IdPool` objects is shown below:

```
class IdPool {
  int oldIdPool, newIdPool;
  static int classCount, totIdPoolObjects;
```

```
    public idPool(int firstVal, int secondVal) {
      if (classCount < totIdPoolObjects) {
        oldIdPool = firstVal;
        newIdPool = secondVal;
        classCount++;
      }
      else {
        // Code which handles the problem of too many
        // objects being created
      }

      protected void finalize {
        classCount--;
      }
      ...
      // Other methods
}
```

There are a number of things to notice about this code. First, two static variables are declared; as you will remember these are associated with the class rather than being created every time an object defined by the class is created. The first static variable `classCount` contains the count of the number of `IdPool` objects that have been created and the second static variable `totIdPoolObjects` contains the limit of the number of objects that can be created. Only one constructor method is defined. This takes two integer parameters and initializes the instance variables of an `IdPool` object with the values within the arguments. Before carrying out this initialization the method will check that the upper limit on the number of objects has not been breached. If it hasn't, then the initializations will take place; however, if it has, then some code which will cope with this problem will be executed. We have omitted details of this code which raises what is called an exception, since we have not yet taught exceptions. The finalize method is given the name `finalize` and returns no value. It carries out the simple processing of decrementing the count of objects by one so that when an object disappears the tally of active objects still remains the same. The method is preceded by the keyword `protected`. This means that the method can be used by subclasses of `IdPool` but not any other methods.

An example of a static method which might be used in connection with the class `IdPool` is a method which returns with the current number of `IdPool` objects which have been created. The code for this method is shown below:

```
public static int noOfIdPoolObjects() {
return classCount;
}
```

This method is defined to be public so that other classes can use it and static which tells the Java interpreter that it is a static method and will not be associated with individual objects. When a user of this method wishes to find out how many objects described by `IdPool` are currently active all that would be needed is to send the `noOfIdPoolObjects` message to the class name:

```
IdPool.noOfIdPoolObjects();
```

This expression will then deliver the total. The important point to make is that the message is sent to the class, *not* to an object described by the class. This is one of the most common errors made when programming an object-oriented language and Java is no exception to this.

Passwords

In computer networks passwords are one of the main tools for establishing security. When users are allowed access to a computer they are initially given some default password which they are then allowed to change. Every time that they attempt to use the computer its operating system will ask them for their password. If the password does not match the current one owned by the user then that user will not be able to access the computer. This seems to be a secure way of making sure that intruders do not access a computer system. However, users tend to pick passwords which are easy to guess.

In 1979 two American researchers, Morris and Thompson, studied the passwords from many users over a long period of time. The results from their study give huge cause for concern. They found that 86% of the passwords could be discovered very easily by exhaustively trying sequences of characters. For example, 14% of the sample involved only three-character strings being chosen as a password. One solution to this is that instead of allowing users to choose their own passwords the computer does it for them by means of a password generating program.

As an example of the use of static methods we will use one contained in the Java class library to develop code for a random password generator. This generator will produce eight-character passwords whose characters are chosen randomly from those stored in the array:

```
char[] randomChars = new char [128];
```

The method for doing it is shown below. Do not worry about what sort of class the method is contained in. The method uses the library method `random` contained in the `java.lang.Math` library; it generates a double length number between 0 and 1. In order for it to index the array we will need to multiply it by 127 and cast it to an integer. The code for the method which generates the eight-character string is shown below:

```
StringBuffer pass = "";
for(i=0;i < 8;i++){
   int index = (int)(Math.random()*127);
   pass = pass.append(randomChars[index]);
}
```

The first line creates a string buffer. The loop then randomly generates an integer in the required range. This is used to index the array of characters with the character chosen being appended to the end of the string buffer that we are building up. The method append can be found in the Java string library: it just adds a character to the end of a string buffer.

SAQ

Can you explain why a StringBuffer object was used above rather than a String object?

Solution

The reason is that the object is written to. String objects can be assigned to but never altered.

5.3.4 Inheritance in Java

In Chapter 3 we described the concept of inheritance. In this chapter we will add a little more detail, but first it is useful to summarize what inheritance is all about. First and foremost it is a mechanism for exploiting the reuse of existing classes. When a class W is defined which inherits from another class X, what happens is that all the methods and instance variables of the class can be used by the class W.

To specify that a class inherits from another class you will need to write the keyword extends. An example of its use can be seen below:

```
class PrivilegedUser extends User {
   // Definition of any instance or static variables
   // Definition of any instance or static methods
}
```

Here the class PrivilegedUser is able to access the methods within the class User together with any instance or static variables which are defined.

The only exception to the rule concerning the use of methods and variables from the inherited class is that if we have two classes X and W, W inherits from X and contains methods which have the same name as methods in X, then when you invoke one of these methods from outside W and if the methods are public, it is the methods which are defined in W that are executed. For example, consider the code shown below which represents two classes A and B, where B inherits from A.

```
Class A {
  // Declaration of instance and static variables

  public method s {
    ...
  }

  public method t {
    ...
  }

  public method u {
    ...
  }
}


Class B extends A {
  // Declaration of instance and static variables

  public method q {
    ...
  }

  public method p {
    ...
  }

  public method u {
    ...
  }

}
```

If we encountered the code:

objA.u()...

then, assuming that the object objA was described by class A, the method u embedded within the class definition of A would be executed. If we encountered the code:

objB.u()...

then the method u associated with class B would be invoked. When a class has a method which has the same name as a method in one of its superclasses, this is termed **overloading**.

Inheritance is the key property of the Java programming language. The wise use of inheritance enables the programmer to reuse large chunks of software – not only software that he or she has written, but also software contained within the Java class library. As a simple example of using inheritance for reuse, consider a class which describes the users of an applet. This class would contain instance variables which contain data on each user: their name, their host computer, their email address and access data such as the number of times that they have accessed the applet. The class would also contain methods which access and update these instance variables.

Let us say that we have developed a number of applets using this class, but that we now want to write a new class where we want to differentiate between two types of users: normal users similar to the users of previous applets and privileged users. The former will be allowed to access some of the facilities of the applet; the latter will be able to access all the facilities of the applet but will need to pay for the privilege.

In order to cater for the privileged users we will need to keep track of the amount of use that they are making of the applet and also provide them with a password in order to prevent other users accessing the facilities they are allowed to use.

The important point to make at this juncture is that we can immediately use the class which described users for this applet, and since privileged users will still require the instance variables and methods associated with users we can develop a new class called `PrivilegedUser` which inherits from `User`. This is shown below:

```
Class User {

    // Instance and static variables defining users, for
    // example their email address


    //  Methods for accessing and updating users' instance
    //  variables
}


Class PrivilegedUser extends User {

    // Instance and static variables required in addition
    // to those in User. For example, a string instance
    // variable which contains the current password of a
    // privileged user.

    // Instance and static methods which access the
    // instance variables and static variables for a
    // privileged user. For example, a method which
    // changes a privileged user's password.
}
```

SAQ

In the previous chapter we differentiated between two uses of inheritance: one where the functionality of a class was modified and one in which the functionality of a class was extended. Which of these two is the class `PrivilegedUser` an example of?

Solution

It is an example of extending the functionality as it involves new methods such as the one used to assign passwords.

This reuse through inheritance extends throughout an applet. For example, the Java class library contains facilities for defining windows, menus and buttons which can be used directly and also inherited. For example, you may want to modify a window so that its borders are different or the colour of the window is different.

5.3.5 Some examples of Java classes

The aim of this section is to present some simple examples of classes in order to reinforce some of the ideas that we have described in the chapter. In the following chapters you will discover how to use classes – particularly those associated with the Java class library – but the aim of this chapter is to show you how such classes are developed.

Our first class is comparatively simple. It defines a line in an applet which has a line drawing facility. A line defined by this class has four components: its starting x coordinate, its starting y coordinate, its finishing x coordinate and its finishing y coordinate. This is shown in Figure 5.2.

A number of methods are needed to implement such lines: a constructor method which creates a line given the four coordinate values, methods to access the four coordinate values, methods which alter the coordinate values, a method which returns with the length of a line and a method which checks whether a line is greater than a specified length. The code for this class is shown below:

```java
class Line {
    int startX, startY, finishX, finishY;

    public Line (int startXValue, int startYValue, int
                   finishXValue, int finishYValue) {
    startX = startXValue;
    startY = startYValue;
    finishX = finishXValue;
    finishY = finishYValue;
    }
```

```java
public void changestartXValue(int newStartXValue) {
    startX = newStartXValue;
}

public void changestartYValue(int newStartYValue) {
    startY = newStartYValue;
}

public void changefinishXValue(int newFinishXValue) {
    finishX = newFinishXValue;
}

public void changefinishYValue(int newFinishYValue) {
    finishY = newFinishYValue;
}

public int getStartXValue() {
    return(startX);
}

public int getStartYValue() {
    return(startY);
}

public int getFinishXValue() {
    return(finishX);
}

public int finishYValue() {
    return(finishY);
}

public double lengthLine() {
    return Math.sqrt(Math.pow((double)(finishX
            - startX),2.0)+ Math.pow((double)(finishY
            - startY),2.0));
}

public boolean greaterThan(double lengthGiven) {
    return (this.lengthLine() > lengthGiven);
}
```

}

By now you should be able to understand most of these methods. The only one which might give you some difficulty is the final method greaterThan which returns a Boolean value depending on whether the receiver object is greater in length than the argument of the method and which uses the method lengthLine() defined within the class.

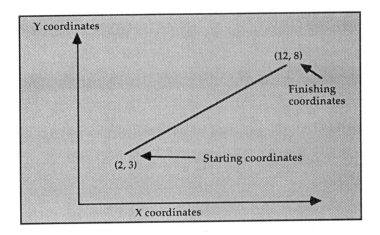

Figure 5.2 A coordinate system.

This method contains the keyword `this`. This is used whenever you want to refer to the destination object within a method. Thus, the semantics of:

```
return(this.lengthLine() > lengthGiven);
```

is that the message `lengthLine()` is first sent to the object which is the destination object of the `greaterThan` method. This results in the length of the receiver object being returned. This is compared with the argument of `greaterThan` and a Boolean true or false returned depending on whether the length was greater or less than or equal to the parameter. The `sqrt` operator in the Math library requires a double length numeric and the cast:

```
(double)(finishY - startY);
```

is needed because the power operator which raises a number to its power requires a double length number.

The next class is one which provides facilities for the processing of queues of users who are waiting to gain access to some of the facilities of a multi-user Java application. The queue will be organized in a first-in-first-out fashion, whereby whoever joins the queue at the earliest point will be the first to be removed from the queue and gain access to the applet. We shall assume that users are defined by the class `User` and that one of the methods within `User`, called `userName`, will retrieve the unique name of the user.

We shall also assume that a number of methods are required: a constructor method which creates an empty queue; a method `addUser` which adds a user to the queue; a method `removeUser` which removes the first user in the queue from the queue; a method `isQueueFull` which checks whether the queue is full; a method `isQueueEmpty` which checks whether the queue is empty; a method `isUserInQueue` which checks whether a user is contained in the queue; and `noOfUsersInQueue` which returns with the number of users currently being stored within the queue.

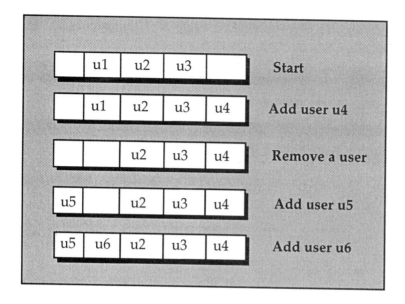

Figure 5.3 A circular queue.

We shall organize the queue as what is known as a *circular list*. This means allocating an array to store the users with the front of the queue being indexed by the variable `frontOfTheQueue` (initially this variable would be set to zero). Users will be stored in the array sequentially, starting from the front of the queue, with a new user being placed in the first location after the last member of the queue. When the last member of the queue is at the final position in the array a new user is placed in the first location in the array. The insertion process is shown in Figure 5.3 for a queue implemented using an array with five locations. Initially the array contains three users (*u1*, *u2* and *u3*) starting with the first user at the second location.

Figure 5.3 shows what happens as a user is added, a user removed and two more users added. When user *u5* is added the queue is wrapped around to the next position in the array that can take an element.

The class for this queue can be described as:

```
Class UserQueue {
  int noOfItemsInQ, frontOfTheQueue, queueCapacity;
  String[] queue;

  public Queue(int capacity) {
  ...
  }
```

```
public void addUser(User name) {
...
}

public User removeUser() {
...
}

public boolean isQueueFull() {
...
}

public boolean isQueueEmpty() {
...
}

public boolean isUserInQueue(User usName) {
...
}

public int noOfUsersInQueue() {
...
}
}
```

The instance variable noOfItemsInQ contains the number of users in the queue, the instance variable frontOfTheQueue contains an integer which points at the first element in the queue and the instance variable queueCapacity contains the capacity of the queue in terms of the maximum number of users that can be stored in the queue. Let us now examine the detailed code for each of these methods. First the constructor:

```
public class UserQueue {
    int noOfItemsInQ, frontOfTheQueue, queueCapacity;
    User[] queue;

    UserQueue(int capacity) {
    queueCapacity = capacity;
    frontOfTheQueue = 0;
    noOfItemsInQ = 0;
    String queue[] = new String[queueCapacity];
    }
```

This just sets the queue to be empty with the first insertion position of a user being the first element of the array (don't forget that Java arrays start at index 0).

The code for the method addUser is shown below:

```
public void addUser(User name) {
  noOfItemsInQ++;
  if (noOfItemsInQ > queueCapacity) {
    // Code to handle the error condition of a user
    // being added to a queue which is full
  }
  else
    addNthUser(noOfItemsInQ, name);
}
```

This code first increments the number of users in the queue by one and then places the user known as name into its position in the queue. This position is calculated by the helper method addNthUser which we shall define later. This adds an item to the queue at its nth position where the argument does not represent the index but the position in the queue. It is very tempting to specify that this position will be one larger than the end of the queue; however, don't forget that the queue may wrap around and start again at the beginning of the array so when we come to write the code we must cater for this wrap-around. We have also omitted the code that would need to be written in order to cater for the error which would happen if someone used addUser to add a user to a queue which was already full. The code for the method isQueueFull is straightforward:

```
public boolean isQueueFull() {
return noOfItemsInQ == queueCapacity;
}
```

It just returns a Boolean value which depends on whether the capacity of the array has been reached. Similarly the code for isQueueEmpty is straightforward:

```
public boolean isQueueEmpty() {
return noOfItemsInQ == 0;
}
```

The code for noOfUsersInQueue is shown below. Again this is straightforward:

```
public int noOfUsersInQueue() {
return noOfItemsInQ;
}
```

SAQ

Write down the code for the method removeUser. Do not worry about writing any code which caters for a user being removed from an empty queue.

Solution

```
public void removeUser() {
  if (noOfItemsInQ > 0) {
    noOfItemsInQ--;
    if(frontOfTheQueue == queueCapacity-1)
      frontOfTheQueue = 0;
    else
      frontOfTheQueue++;
  } else{
      // Code to cater for the error of a user being
      // removed from an empty queue
  }
}
```

The code first checks whether there is a user in the queue to be removed. If the queue is empty, then code which responds to this error is specified; we have omitted it for the time being. The code which is executed if there is at least one user in the queue first decrements the number of users within the receiver object and then increments the pointer which points at the first item in the queue. Again you might have been tempted to increment the value of this instance variable by one. However, don't forget that this pointer may be at the end of the array which represents the queue and it will then need to be reset to 0. Instead of incrementing the pointer by one we have used an if statement to check if the queue needs to wrap around.

The final method that needs to be described is isUserInQueue. This checks whether there is a user in the queue who has a specified name. The code for this method is shown below:

```
public boolean isUserInQueue(User usName) {
  int  count = 0;
  while (count < noOfItemsInQ) {
    count++;
    if (getNthUser(count).equals(usName))
      return true;
  }
  return  false;
}
```

This just loops around each user in the queue, starting at the first user, and returns true when the user has been found. It makes use of the method userName which we have assumed is defined for the class User and which returns the name of the user which is the destination object.

The code for the class now looks like:

```java
public class UserQueue {
  int noOfItemsInQ, frontOfTheQueue, queueCapacity;
  User[] queue;

  UserQueue(int capacity) {
  queueCapacity = capacity;
  frontOfTheQueue = 0;
  noOfItemsInQ = 0;
  String queue[] = new String[queueCapacity];
  }

  public void addUser(User name) {
  noOfItemsInQ++;
  if (noOfItemsInQ > queueCapacity) {
    // Code to handle the error condition of a user
    // being added to a queue which has reached its full
    // capacity;
  }
  else
    addNthUser(noOfItemsInQ, name); }

  public void removeUser() {
  if (noOfItemsInQ > 0) {
    noOfItemsInQ--;
    if(frontOfTheQueue == queueCapacity-1)
      frontOfTheQueue = 0;
    else
      frontOfTheQueue++;
  } else{
    // Code to cater for the error of a user being
    // removed from an empty queue
  }
  }

  public boolean isQueueFull() {
  return noOfItemsInQ == queueCapacity;
  }

  public boolean isQueueEmpty() {
  return noOfItemsInQ == 0;
  }

  public int noOfUsersInQueue() {
  return noOfItemsInQ; }
```

```
public boolean isUserInQueue(User usName) {
int   count = 0;
while (count < noOfItemsInQ) {
   count++;
   if (getNthUser(count).equals(usName))
     return true;
}
return   false;
}
```

}

The only remaining part of the class which is not defined are the methods getNthUser and addNthUser. The former gets the *n*th user in the queue, where by the *n*th user we do not mean the user indexed by *n* in the string array but logically the *n*th user. The latter adds a user into the *n*th position in the queue where again we take the interpretation of *n* in the previous sentence. The first decision that needs to be made about these methods is what access status they should have. Since we have already stated that items are only added to the end of a queue we should not make the method addNthUser generally available, as an outside user of this method could, in theory, use it to write to the middle of the queue. We shall, hence, make this method private. Since there may be some applications which want to examine the *n*th item in a queue it is permissible to make getNthUser a public method.

The code for these methods is shown below:

```
private void addNthUser(int n, User userToBeAdded) {
int index;
index = frontOfTheQueue + n - 1;
if (index >= queueCapacity)
   index = index % queueCapacity;
queue[index] = userToBeAdded;
}

public User getNthUser(int n) {
int index;
index = frontOfTheQueue + n - 1;
if (index >= queueCapacity)
   index = index % queueCapacity;
return queue[index];
}
```

The code uses the remainder operator % to obtain the correct position. The final example forms part of the security system of an applet. One of the major concerns of the developers of software for the Internet is that of preventing illegal access to a system's resources and also identifying illegal access when it happens as quickly as possible. One of the most common ways of illegally accessing a system is via the password of a known user. There are a number of ways in which such passwords can be made available to a potential intruder. One way has been for the intruder to log in under a user's identity and try a number of passwords which the intruder has guessed. This can be a very successful strategy if the intruder knows anything about the personal circumstances of the user, as many employ their spouse's name, their own Christian name, the name of their dog or other related words as their password.

Another way of obtaining a password is via physical theft. Users often keep their passwords in diaries or in drawers in their offices; one of us has even visited a company where some of the employees seemed to keep their passwords on a whiteboard in their office. A third way of appropriating a password is to tap a communication line and read the password letters as they are being typed in. These are just a few of the ways in which valid passwords can be obtained by an intruder. Given that there is a moderate risk that this would happen, how can a system determine that an intrusion has happened?

One way is to take advantage of the fact that the vast majority of users of computer systems are people of habit. For example, one of us tends to use a computer to access programs in the early morning and to log in three or four days a week. A sales clerk for a company may only access a system twice: log on in the morning, stay logged on up until lunchtime, log off and then, after lunchtime, log on again.

In order to determine whether a user is behaving in an unpredictable way, and hence may be being impersonated by an intruder, applications keep details of the accesses made by users. This data would include: the date of last logging on, the number of accesses since the beginning of the month, the average number of accesses per day and so on. A program known as a **security monitor** would scan through this data and display the identity of any users who were behaving in a different way to that in which they have behaved in the past. Normally applications keep large amounts of security data on users and it would be too ambitious to develop a class which stored all this data. For the sake of the aim of this chapter – that of learning about classes in Java – we shall assume that only two items of data are kept: the time of last access to the system and the number of accesses made in the current day.

We shall assume that we require a class known as `SecurityRecord` which holds security data. This class will require access to a class called `User` which will contain the time at which a user last accessed the system and the number of accesses that have occurred within the current day. This `User` class will look like:

```java
class User {
    int lastAccessTime, noOfAccessesToday;
    String userId;

    // Other instance variables such as the email address
    // of the user.

    public int getNoOfAccessesToday() {
```

```
    // Code for getNoOfAccessesToday
    }

    public int getLastAccessTime() {
    // Code for getLastAccessTime
    }
    public void setNoOfAccessesToday(int accesses) {
    // Code for setNoOfAccessesToday
    }
    public void setLastAccessTime(int time) {
    // Code for setLastAccessTime
    }
    public String getUserId() {
    // Code for getuserId
    }

    // Code for other methods which correspond to messages
    // that can be sent to a user.

}
```

The SecurityRecord class will contain an instance variable which is an array of
UserRecords. Let us assume that a number of methods are required: a method
logsOn which has two parameters, namely a userId and a time at which the
user whose identity is userId has logged on; a series of methods which, given a
userId, access the security information associated with that user; constructors
which initialize the array containing the security information; and a method which
adds a new user to the array. The class description of this class will look like:

```
Class SecurityRecord {
    User[] accessTable;
    int noOfUsers;

    public SecurityRecord() {
    // Code for this constructor method which initializes
    // the table. Assumes a default of 100.
    }

    public SecurityRecord(int arraySize) {
    // Code for this constructor method which initializes
    // the table containing security information. Assumes
    // that the default initialization is arraySize
}

    public int getNoAccessesForUser{String userIdentity) {
    // Code for getNoAccesses
    }
```

```
public int getLastAccessforUser(String userIdentity) {
// Code for getLastAccess
}

public void logsOn(userIdentity: String, time: int) {
// Code for logsOn
}

public void addUser(User us) {
// Code for addUser
}
```
}

The main thing to notice about this class is that there are two constructors provided. The first allocates 100 elements to the array which holds user security details, the second allocates a number of elements specified by the user of the class.

SAQ

Write down the code for these two constructors.

Solution

The code is shown below:

```
public SecurityRecord() {
    noOfUsers = 0;
    accessTable = new User[100];
}

public SecurityRecord(int arraySize) {
    noOfUsers = 0;
    accessTable = new User[arraySize];
}
```

SAQ

Write down the code for the method which updates the instance variables when a user logs on. You should use the private method findIndex to determine the position of the user within the security table.

Solution

The code is shown below:

```
public void logsOn(String userIdentity, int time) {
    int index = findIndex(userIdentity);
    accessTable[index].setLastAccessTime(time);
    accessTable[index].
    setNoOfAccessesToday(accessTable[index].
      getNoOfAccessesToday()+1);
}
```

Here, the index of the user is found using findIndex, then the new time of access is set by sending the message setLastAccessTime and the number of accesses incremented by one by sending the message:

```
setNoOfAccessesToday(accessTable[index].
getNoOfAccessesToday()+1)
```

The code for the method which provides the number of accesses that a user has made, given the user's identity, is shown below. It uses a helper method findIndex. This private method finds the position within the array of the specified user and returns with the index of this position. For the time being do not worry about the operation of this method: its code will be shown later. The code is:

```
public int getNoAccessesForUser(String userIdentity) {
    int index = findIndex(userIdentity);
    return accessTable[index].getNofOfAccessesToday();
}
```

The code for the method which provides the time of last access is shown below. It is similar to getNoAccessesForUser.

```
public int getLastAccessforUser(String userIdentity) {
    int index = accessTable.findIndex(userIdentity);
    return accessTable[index].getLastAccessTime();
}
```

The final code, that for addUser, is shown below. All it does is to increment the total number of users and add the new user to the end of the array holding users.

```
public void addUser(User us) {
    noOfUsers++;
    accessTable[noOfUsers] = us;
}
```

The final method is the private method `findIndex` which finds a specified user within the table containing security details. We shall make the rather simplistic assumption that a simple linear search is used. If the array contains a large number of users, then such a search would be inefficient. However, for the time being let us make this simplifying assumption. We shall also make the assumption that the user being searched for is contained in the array.

```
private int findIndex(String usId) {
    int i = 0;
    while (i < noOfUsers) {
      if (accessTable[i].getUserId.equals(usId))
      return i;
      i++;
    }
    return i;
  }
```

Again this is defined as a private method since it has knowledge of how the security information is stored. This gives the full definition of the class as:

```
class SecurityRecord {
  User[] accessTable;
  int noOfUsers;

  public SecurityRecord() {
    noOfUsers = 0;
    accessTable = new User[100];
  }

  public SecurityRecord(int arraySize) {
    noOfUsers = 0;
    accessTable = new User[arraySize];
  }

  public int getNoAccessesForUser(String userIdentity) {
    int index = findIndex(userIdentity);
    return accessTable[index].getNofOfAccessesToday();
  }

  public int getLastAccessforUser(String userIdentity) {
    int index = accessTable.findIndex(userIdentity);
    return accessTable[index].getLastAccessTime();
  }

  public void logsOn(String userIdentity, int time) {
    int index = findIndex(userIdentity);
    accessTable[index].setLastAccessTime(time);
```

```
    accessTable[index].
      setNoOfAccessesToday(accessTable[index].
      getNoOfAccessesToday()+1);
  }

  public void addUser(User us) {
    noOfUsers++;
    accessTable[noOfUsers] = us;
  }

  private int findIndex(String usId) {
    int i = 0;
    while (i < noOfUsers) {
      if (accessTable[i].getUserId.equals(usId))
      return i;
    i++;
  }
  return i;
  }
}
```

5.4 Objects and references

In the previous chapter we described scalar data types and described how scalar data was stored. For example, the declaration:

```
int a = 12, b = 44, c = 4;
```

resulted in the situation shown in Figure 5.4.

Here, three locations are identified by variable names and values written into them. When objects are declared the situation is more complicated. Let us assume that we have declared a class known as Employee which contains three items of data about an employee: a string representing a name, a string representing the country of domicile and an integer representing a monthly salary. These items of data will be held in the instance variables defined by the class.

When we write the code:

```
Employee jonesObject =
  new Employee(1200, "Jones", "France");
Employee robertsObject =
  new Employee(2200, "Roberts", "Germany");
Employee inceObject =
  new Employee(1300, "Ince", "Wales");
```

something rather different happens. Figure 5.5 shows the effect of these three statements.

Three locations are given the name chosen by the programmer. However, the locations are not filled with scalar values but with the address of a set of locations which contain the instance variables for each object. Object variables in Java do not contain values but contain pointers to their collection of instance variables. Thus, `robertsObject` does not contain the values of the three instance variables with which it is associated but a pointer to an area of computer memory where the three variables are stored.

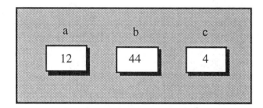

Figure 5.4 The declaration of three scalar variables.

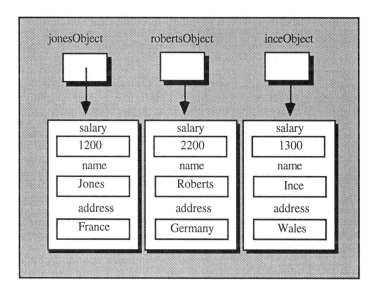

Figure 5.5 The effect of object declarations.

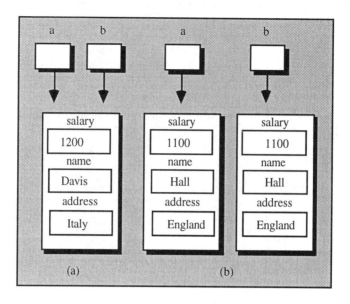

Figure 5.6 Two examples of object equality and inequality.

There are a number of implications of this way of storing data about objects. The first concerns the use of equality operators. When we write code such as:

```
int a, b, c;
...
if (a == b) {
...
}
```

the condition within the if statement compares the values in the variables a and b and executes the true branch of the statement if they are equal to each other.

However, the effect of the code:

```
Employee a, b, c;
...
if (a == b) {
...
}
```

is different. The true branch of the if statement will only be executed if the object variables a and b point at the same object. Figure 5.6(a) shows a situation where this would be true and Figure 5.6(b) shows one where it is false. Figure 5.6(a) represents a value true since the two variables point at the same set of data, while Figure 5.6(b) represents a false value as the variables point at two separate collections of data, even though the values of the instance variables are the same.

This means that, for example, the `if` statement below does not execute the true branch but the false branch.

```
Employee jonesObject =
  new Employee(1200, "Jones", "France");
Employee anotherObject =
  new Employee(2200, "Roberts", "Germany");
...
if (jonesObject == anotherObject){
..
}
else{
...
}
```

You may now be asking: how do we compare objects for equality, where equality means that instance variables are equal? Many of the objects within Java have a method `equals` associated with them which carries out the comparison of contents. Already you have seen `equals` in connection with strings. If you are defining your own objects then you will have to write your own `equals` method for these objects. For reasons which will become clearer later we give the method the name `equals`.

So, for example, if we wanted to test for equality of `Employee` objects the method to do this would be:

```
public boolean equals(Employee e){
return (this.address == e.address
&& this.name == e.name
&& this.salary == e.salary);
}
```

Notice the use of the `this` keyword. Remember that it refers to the object to which the message is being sent. So if the code:

```
oldEmployee.equals(robertsEmployee)
```

was executed then the `this` keyword would refer to `oldEmployee`.

Since object variables will contain pointers to instance variables you will need to be very careful when updating these variables. For example, consider the code:

```
Employee a = new Employee(1300, "Jones", "Wales"), b;
...
...
b = a;
```

This creates a new `Employee` object which is pointed at by a and then arranges for the `Employee` variable b to point at it. If the statement:

```
b.setAddress("Spain");
```

is executed which sets the address instance variable of the object b to become the string "Spain" then the address variable pointed at by a will become "Spain" since a and b both point to the same collection of instance variables.

Exercise

A class UserTable has two instance variables: an integer variable noInTable which contains the number of items in a table and an integer array arrTable which represents the table. Write down a method which checks for the equality of two objects defined by UserTable. Assume that two arrays are equal if they contain the same number of elements in the same order.

Solution

The code is shown below:

```
public boolean equals(UserTable u){
int j = 0, count = 0;
this.arrTable[noInTable] = 1; u.arrTable[noInTable] = 2;
while (this.arrTable[j] == u.arrTable[j])
   j++;
return (this.noInTable == u.noInTable
        && j == u.noInTable);
}
```

The method first places two different values after the last location in the arrays. It then examines each pair of items in the array until it finds two unequal elements. If the two arrays are not equal the place at which it exits will be somewhere before the locations which were filled with non-equal values.

If you want to create a new object which has the same values of instance variables as an existing object then you should normally use the copy method. This method can be applied to all object variables. So, for example, if the object variable a refers to the object with the values 1200, "Jones" and "Denmark" and the code:

```
Employee oldEmployee, currentEmployee;
oldEmployee = new Employee(1200, "Jones", "Denmark");
currentEmployee.copy(oldEmployee);
```

is executed, then what happens is that a new object currentEmployee is created with the same instance variable values that are associated with oldEmployee. It is important to point out that the pointers in oldEmployee and currentEmployee will be different since two separate objects will have been created.

Some of you may have worried about what happens when object variables are reassigned. For example, let us assume that we have objects which describe users in a computer system:

```
Users superUser, jones, williams;
...
// code which gives the three
// variables superUser, jones
// and williams values
...
// code which gives the three variables further values
```

What happens to the collection of instance variables assigned to the three user objects in the first chunk of code? Well, the answer is that they just hang around until the Java system discovers that it needs more space - perhaps because lots of memory space has been used for objects and the system is close to exhaustion. The Java system continually examines all the memory that is allocated to it and identifies any memory that is not pointed at by object variables. This memory is returned to the space available for new objects. When returned it is used again. This process is called **garbage collection** and is the reason why, unless you make massive memory demands, you will never run out of space for objects.

SAQ

Examine the code below and write down the values of the Boolean expressions underneath.

```
Employee a, b, c, d;
a = new Employee (1200, "Jones", "Denmark");
b = new Employee (1300, "Roberts", "Denmark");
c = b; d.copy(b);
```

The expressions are:

    (i)   `a == b`   (ii)   `c == b`
    (iii) `c.salary == b.salary` (iv)   `a.salary == c.salary`
    (v)   `a == d`

Solution

(i) is false since two new objects are created, so a and b will point to different collections of instance variables; (ii) is true since b points at the same object as c; (iii) is true since the two variables point at the same object; (iv) is false since the salary instance variable of a is different to the salary instance variable of c; and (v) is false since a and d refer to different objects.

5.5 The class hierarchy

Before looking at how we can develop more general classes in the next section it is worth describing an important concept which you will need to understand when carrying out serious object-oriented programming. This is the idea of the inheritance hierarchy. It was briefly introduced in Chapter 3.

You will remember that in Chapter 3 we described inheritance and a graphical notation which describes the inheritance hierarchy. An example of this notation is shown in Figure 5.7. This shows the fact that class C and class D inherit from Class B which, in turn, inherits from class A.

All the classes in Java form part of a massive inheritance hierarchy. There will be two types of class in this hierarchy: those that programmers have created and those within the Java class library. Later we will be looking at many of the facilities within this library - all that you need to know at this stage is that it consists of a large number of classes which represent useful objects necessary for Internet programming.

Internet File Security

There is huge potential for crime on the Net. For example, billions of pounds of transactions are sent from banks to other banks every day. If an intruder can capture a transfer funds message being sent from a bank, change the account to his or her account and transfer funds into this account, then this could seriously compromise our banking systems. In order to make this difficult a number of techniques have

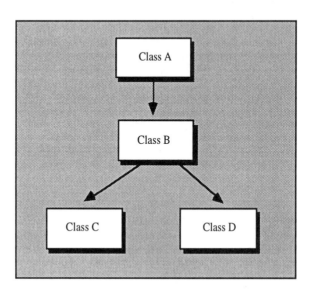

Figure 5.7 An inheritance hierarchy.

been used. The first is to encrypt messages: change the message by transforming the characters in it by applying a coding program which uses a sophisticated algorithm which is secret and cannot be copied. Another technique is to transmit a checksum with any data that is sent. This checksum is formed by another algorithm whose details are secret. A typical checksum algorithm adds the integer values of the bytes transmitted and then applies some secret mathematical function to the bytes. This value, known as a checksum, would be the last item transmitted. When a computer received a file it would then calculate the checksum and if it differed from the one transmitted then someone has altered the message.

Files transferred across the Internet can be of a number of types: encrypted and unencrypted and each of these types could contain a checksum or not contain a checksum.

The classes that programmers develop will either explicitly inherit from the classes within the class library or implicitly inherit. As an example of this consider the declaration:

```
class ClassName{
//instance variables
//methods
. . .
. . .
}
```

even though this class does not include the keyword `extends` which indicates that the class inherits from another class, Java assumes that this class will inherit from a sort of super object known as `Object`. The inheritance hierarchy for the whole Java system is shown in Figure 5.8.

This shows that every object that Java programs create is inherited from `Object`. Is this an academic point? The answer is, of course, no. You will see in the next section that having a sort of superclass `Object` at the top of the class hierarchy enables us to develop very powerful classes.

Exercise

What would the class hierarchy for the secure files described in the inset above look like? What extra functionality would be introduced by lower level classes?

Solution

The class hierarchy would contain seven classes. At the top would be `File`. `EncryptedFile` and `UnEncryptedFile` would inherit from `File`. There would also be the classes `EncryptedFileWithCheckSum` and `UnEncryptedFileWithoutCheckSum`, which would inherit from `EncryptedFile`; finally there would be the two classes `UnEncryptedFileWithCheckSum` and

`EncryptedFileWithoutCheckSum` which would inherit from `UnEncry-ptedFile`. The methods in the lower level classes would be concerned with the extra functionality of calculating checksums, comparing checksums, encrypting and decrypting.

5.6 General classes and constructors

So far the classes that we have described have dealt with specific data types. For example, the queue example that we used earlier processed queues of users of a computer system. If we wish to take the reuse idea of object-oriented technology further, then we really need to be able to develop more general classes. For example, queues are ubiquitous in computing: they are used in operating systems to contain the names of processes which are awaiting execution by a processor; they are also used in operating systems to hold print requests which are to be processed by a printer; in an air traffic control system they are used to hold the identity of planes awaiting landing; and in a computer network they are used to hold packets of messages awaiting processing by the computers in the system. Clearly, for queues there is some leverage in being able to write general-purpose packages which can process a wide variety of data. This holds not only for queues but also for many other classes.

Java contains facilities for developing general-purpose classes. In order to describe them we shall use a simple example of a look-up table which can contain a wide variety of data.

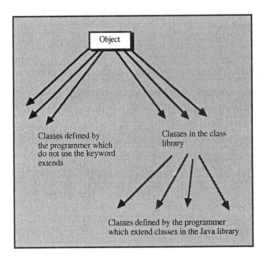

Figure 5.8 The Java class hierarchy.

The function of such a table is to hold items, for example integers or strings, where an important message which can be sent to a look-up table is one which checks that an item is stored in the table. We shall assume that a number of methods are required: two constructor methods which set up look-up tables, one of which has a default value for the maximum number of items in the table with the other setting up a specified number of entries provided by the user of the class. We shall also assume that the class describing such look-up tables requires methods which insert an item in the table, remove an item, check whether the table is full, find the number of items in the table and check whether an item is in the table.

Before looking at the code for such a general class it is worth looking at the way in which we can declare objects and allocate space for them. For example, let us assume that the class describing look-up tables is called `LookUpTable`. We can tell the Java system that certain variables are to hold look-up tables by the declaration:

```
LookUpTable variable-list;
```

So, for example:

```
LookUpTable newTable, oldTable, midTable;
```

tells the Java system that three identifiers are to be used which will be look-up tables. This is just a declaration: *it does not allocate any space*. To allocate space the new facility is required. For example, the statement:

```
LookUpTable symbols = new LookupTable();
```

will allocate the space required for a look-up table `symbols`. If a constructor method corresponding to `LookUpTable()` has been defined, then the amount of space allocated would be found in the code associated with that method.

It is also worth looking at the use of the `this` keyword. When `this` is used within an instance method it refers to the receiver object. When it is used within a constructor method the effect is subtly different. When `this` is encountered it is taken as a reference to the name of the class. So, for example, if the Java interpreter encounters the statement:

```
this(1000, 300);
```

within a constructor method for the class `ClassName` then it will assume that this is a reference to a constructor `ClassName` which has two arguments. It will then look for the constructor and execute the code for it.

The discussion above must have seemed a little abstract so it is worth looking now at an example which illustrates both the use of `this` in constructors and also the use of the `Object` class described in the previous section. Let us first look at the instance variables and the two constructor methods for look-up tables. These are shown below:

```
class LookUpTable {
   int noOfItems, size;
   Object[] holder;

   public LookUpTable(int sizeTable) {
      noOfItems = 0;
      size = sizeTable;
      holder = new Object[sizeTable];
   }

   public LookUpTable() {
      this(100);
   }

   // Code for the remaining methods within LookUpTable.

}
```

There are a number of important points to be made about this code. The first is that one of the instance variables is an array which is to hold objects. Also, remember that `Object` is a built-in type within the Java system and every object type that is declared within a Java program inherits directly or indirectly from `Object`. Using `Object` effectively informs the Java system that we can add items of any type to a look-up table.

The code for the two constructor methods is also of note. The first constructor just sets up a table with the number of elements in the table defined by its argument.

The second constructor method sets up a look-up table which will contain, as a default, 100 objects. The method calls the constructor method defined previously to set up the look-up table with a hundred values. In this code the keyword `this` is used to denote the class `LookUpTable`, so the statement:

```
this(100);
```

is equivalent to:

```
LookUpTable(100);
```

The code for the remaining methods is shown below.

```
public void insertItem(Object item) {
   holder[noOfItems] = item;
   noOfItems++;
}
```

```
public void removeItem(Object item) {
  int i = findIndex(item);
  while (i < noOfItems-1) {
    holder[i] = holder[i+1];
    i++;
  };
  noOfItems--;
}

public boolean fullTable() {
  return noOfItems == size;
}

public int noInTable() {
  return noOfItems;
}

public boolean inTable(Object item) {
  int i = findIndex(item);
  return i == noOfItems;
}
```

The code for these methods is fairly self-explanatory. Two of the methods, inTable and removeItem, require the use of the helper method findIndex. The code for this method is shown below:

```
private int findIndex(Object item) {
int i = 0;
while (i < noOfItems){
  if (holder[i].equals(item))
    return i;
  i++;
  }
return i;
}
```

Again a simple sequential search is employed. The method looks for the object item within the array holder. If it encounters it then it returns with its index. However, if it does not encounter item, it returns with a value one greater than the number of items in holder. The one important thing to notice about this code is that in comparing equality we have not used == since we are comparing values rather than pointers.

We have assumed that in the class that defines the objects that can be inserted there is a method called equals which carries out some equality comparison between two objects. For example, if we were going to insert User objects into the look-up table and the User class defined these objects in terms of instance variables which contained a user's identity, email and so on, then we would need to define a method `equals` within this class which took two users and compared their identities. Only then could we start inserting users into the look-up table as, for example, in:

```
User newUser;
LookUpTable newCreatedUsers;
...
newCreatedUsers.insertItem(newUser);
```

When you encounter an object of type `Object` within a Java program you will often need to identify what type of object it is. The operator `instanceof` does this. Its left hand operand is an object and its right hand operand is the name of a class. It returns true if the object is of the class and false otherwise. For example:

```
stObj instanceOof StringBuffer
```

returns true if the object `stObj` is a `StringBuffer` and false otherwise.

Given this way of developing general classes, how do we recover values from the instance variables that contain objects of type `Object`? For example, is it legal to write:

```
User inceUser = userCollection.getImportantUser();
```

where the method `getImportantUser()` returns an object described by `Object`? The answer is no since the variable on the left hand side of the assignment refers to an object of a different type to that found on the right hand side of the assignment: the left hand side refers to a `User` variable while the right hand side delivers an object described by `Object`. The solution is to use the cast mechanism described in Chapter 3.

```
User inceUser = (User)userCollection.getImportantUser();
```

This converts the object delivered to the required type. Given this cast mechanism you can now see how it is possible to write classes which can contain objects of any type.

The final topic to look at in this section is the use of `super` as a constructor. This keyword is used when a class inherits from another class and wishes to use a constructor in that class. For example, consider the code shown below which contains the skeletal description of a class A which has three instance variables p, q and r.

```
class A{
int p, q, r;

public A(){
this(0, 0, 0);
}
```

```
public A(int a){
this(a, 0, 0);
}

public A(int a, b){
this(a, b, 0);
}

public A(int a, b, c){
p = a; q = b; r = c;
}

//Methods associated with A
}
```

Here the three constructors initialize one, two or all three instance variables. Now let us assume that we want to extend A by adding a further integer instance variable and a few other methods and that we need four constructors similar to those shown above. Some possible code for this is shown below:

```
class B extends A{
int s;

public B(a, b, c, d){
super.p = a; super.q = b; super.r = c; s = d;
}

public B(int a){
this(a, 0, 0, 0);
}

public A(int a, b){
this(a, b, 0, 0);
}

public A(int a, b, c){
this(a, b, c, 0);
}

//Methods associated with B
}
```

There is nothing wrong with this code but B can be written in a more elegant way as:

```
public B(a, b, c, d){
super(a, b, c);
s = d;
}
```

The code super (a,b,c) results in the three-argument constructor of the super class of A being executed. This results in the values of a, b and c being assigned to the instance variables p, q and r associated with this class. After this the instance variable associated with B is then given a value.

5.7 Java programs

So far in the book we have described the elements of Java but have not fully described the structure of a Java program. You may remember from the first chapter that you can construct two types of entities using the Java programming language: applets, which are code fragments which can be embedded in any Java-compatible browser, and applications which are standalone programs. Chapters 12 and 14 describe how to develop each of these types of software in much more detail. However, it is worth describing the program structure of a Java application here for completeness' sake. The code below is that of a very simple Java application which can be executed:

```
public class HelloWorld {
     public static void main (String args[]) {
     System.out.println("Hello World");
     }
}
```

To construct a Java application all you need do is to declare a single class – the one above is called HelloWorld – and then declare a method within it called main which has a single argument that is an array of strings. The method will be static and will not return any values. The string arguments are used to pass data from the world outside to the application, although this is not done in the application above; however, you will always need to declare the arguments as part of the method main. Chapter 14 describes the use of these arguments in much more detail. The only processing that occurs within the main method is for the string "Hello World" to be displayed. This is achieved by means of the message println("Hello World") being sent to the object System.out. The Java system contains an extensive library used for stream-oriented input/output and that the statement:

```
System.out.println ("Hello World")
```

is just an example of its use.

5.8 A running example

Throughout the rest of the book we shall be using a single software example to illustrate the various Java facilities we will be describing. This example will start out as being somewhat simple but will be added to, modified and enhanced as we progress through the book. The example is that of a search engine used to find information in the World Wide Web.

Search Engines

The Internet consists of a massive amount of textual data. Because of its very size it can be immensely difficult to find relevant information on a subject in the Internet. Happily there are specialized computer programs which enable you to specify what information you require and they will then consult a database of sources which they have built up. Three of the most popular programs are *Alta Vista, Lycos* and *Yahoo.* They are collectively known as **search engines**. The user of one of these search engines usually types in a series of terms for which information is required and the search engine will then return with a list of the Web sites which contain data or information relevant to the search criterion that has been communicated. For example, if you wanted information about the composer Elgar and his influence on the composer Finzi you might type in the keywords:

```
Elgar + Finzi
```

The search engine which you employed would then look for all the documents containing both these words. If you wanted anything on either Finzi *or* Elgar you would type in:

```
Elgar || Finzi
```

Search engines usually employ a data structure known as an inverted file to contain the information searched for.

In order to keep track of the occurrences of words in Web documents such a search engine needs to access a data structure which relates a word with the Web documents that contain it. An example of such a data structure is shown in Figure 5.9.

The data structure contains the words which are in the Web documents which are to be searched (since this is a small example only a few are shown). Associated with each word is a fixed length array of locations where the words can be found. For the time being assume that the words are represented by strings, as are the locations. The first class that we present is that for holding the link between a word and the locations. The code for this is shown below:

```
class Links{
private int noOfLocations, maxLocations;
private String word;
private String[] locations;
```

```
public Links(String wordToBeCreated){
this (20, wordToBeCreated);
}

public Links (int  size,  String wordToBeCreated){
noOfLocations = 0;
locations = new String [size];
maxLocations = size;
word = wordToBeCreated;
}

public int getnoOfLocations(){
return noOfLocations;
}

public String getWord(){
return word;
}

public String[] getLocations(){
return locations;
}

public void addLocation(String locationToBeAdded){
if (noOfLocations < maxLocations){
  locations[noOfLocations] = locationToBeAdded;
  noOfLocations++;
  }
else{
  String[] temp = new String [2*maxLocations];
  for (int i = 0;i < maxLocations; i++)
    temp[i] = locations[i];
  maxLocations = 2*maxLocations;
  locations = temp;
  }
}

}
```

The class has four instance variables: noOfLocations contains the number of locations associated with a word, maxLocations contains the maximum number of locations that can currently be associated with a word, word contains the string which is the word which might be searched for, and locations is a string array containing the name of the locations where the word can be found; these can be file names or the address of a Web page.

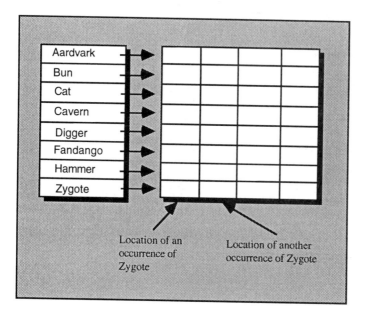

Figure 5.9 A data structure used to hold details for a search engine.

The class has two constructors: one which sets up a string and a default of 20 locations and one which allows the user to set up the number of locations. There are also a number of methods associated with the class:

getnoOfLocations returns with the current number of locations associated with the word.

getLocations returns with the array containing the locations.

addLocation adds another location to the list associated with a word. If the list of locations is full then the size of space is doubled and the location added.

getWord retrieves the word associated with the locations.

It is worth pointing out that the implementation is a little inefficient in terms of space: each word is associated with a fixed size of memory. However, it does have the advantage of being very simple.

Once we have the class for words and their locations the next step is to define a class which holds data on a collection of words and their links. The code for the class is shown below. It is important to point out that there is no error checking contained in the code. For example, if a user inserts a duplicate word then no errors will be signalled. This will be remedied in the next chapter.

```
public class LinksData{
Links [] wordInfo;
```

```
int noOfWords, maxWords;
public LinksData(){
this(100);
}

public LinksData(int size){
maxWords = size;
noOfWords = 0;
wordInfo = new Links[size];
}

public int getNoOfWords(){
return noOfWords;
}

public int getmaxWords(){
return maxWords;
}

public void addWord(String word){
int i = 0;
while(i<noOfWords &&
   (word.compareTo(wordInfo[i].getWord())>0))
   i++;
for(int j = noOfWords; j > i; j--){
   wordInfo[j] = wordInfo[j-1];
}
wordInfo[i] = new Links(20, word);
noOfWords++;
}

public boolean checkWordIn(String word){
int val = findWordIndex(word);
return val != -1;
}

private int findWordIndex(String word){
int first = 0, last = noOfWords - 1, middle = 0;
boolean found = false;
while (!found && (first <= last)){
middle = (first+last) / 2;
if(word.compareTo((wordInfo[middle].getWord())) == 0)
   found = true;
else{
   if (word.compareTo((wordInfo[middle].getWord())) < 0)
```

```
        last = middle - 1;
    else first = middle + 1;
    }
}
if (!found) return -1;
else return middle;
}


public void addLocation(String loc, String word){
int pos = findWordIndex(word);
wordInfo[pos].addLocation(loc);
}


public String[] getLocations(String word){
int pos = findWordIndex(word);
return wordInfo[pos].getLocations();
}

}
```

The class consists of three instance variables: `wordInfo` contains the word and location information, `noOfWords` contains the total number of words stored and `maxWords` sets an upper limit to the number of words stored. The last instance variable is not used in this class yet; however, you will see it used in the next chapter.

There are two constructors. The first sets the number of word-location items given by its argument and the second sets a default of 100 word-location items. There are a number of methods defined:

`getNoOfWords` returns with the number of words stored.

`getMaxWords` returns with the maximum number of words stored.

`addWord` adds a word to the collection of word-locations. It adds the word given by its single argument.

`checkWordIn` checks that a particular word has been stored.

`findWordIndex` is a helper method: it finds the index of a word within the instance variable `wordInfo`. If it finds it then it returns with the position of the word, if it doesn't then it returns with -1. This method uses a binary search mechanism. It employs the built-in method `compareTo` which is associated with strings. This method returns 0 if the argument is the same as the destination object, returns a negative number if the destination object lies alphabetically before the argument and returns a positive number if the argument lies before the destination object.

`addLocation` adds a location to a specific word.

getLocations returns with an array containing the locations associated with a particular word.

5.9 SUMMARY

In terms of Java programming this has been the most important chapter of the book that you have so far read. It has described the facilities in Java for defining classes and also extending classes by means of inheritance. It has also shown how you can use objects defined by classes and the nature of the inheritance hierarchy supported by the Java system. This chapter forms the core of your Java knowledge and the ideas in it will be used time and time again in developing useful programs.

CHAPTER SIX

Exceptions

- To introduce the idea of an exception.
- To show how exceptions are defined in Java.
- To describe the main mechanism whereby exceptions are declared.
- To show how exceptions are used within class definitions.

6.1 Introduction

So far the examples which we have presented have had an air of unreality about them. For example, when we inserted items in a table we assumed that the table had enough room to contain each item, and when we removed an item from a table we assumed that the item was in the table. This is, of course, something of a simplification and it is now necessary to look at some of the techniques that can be used to cater for such error conditions.

The first technique is to use a method to check out a particular error condition before executing code which might encounter that condition. For example, assume that we are writing a method which inserts an item into some data structure such as a table. Before executing this method it would be wise to invoke another method which would check that the table had space for the item to be inserted. If it didn't then the method would not carry out the execution.

The second technique - really a variation on the second method - is to associate with a method some parameter which will indicate whether the error condition was met when performing the code within the method. For example, assume that we have defined a class which implements a queue and we wish to take the first element off the queue. If the queue is empty, an error will occur. Normally the method which takes an element from a queue will have no parameters and just return the element which has been removed. However, in order to cater for this error condition a Boolean parameter would be used. For example, the definition of such a method for a queue of strings might be:

```
public String removeFirst() {
if (noOfItems == 0) {
  empty = true;
  return "";
}
else
{
// Code which is executed when the queue contains at
// least one entry
}
```

If the queue is empty, then a Boolean variable is given the value true and the method returns the empty string.

This is a style of coding that can be adopted for Java. However, there is a more robust facility within Java which is often used to handle error conditions. It is known as the **exception** facility.

An exception is an object which is created when something untoward happens in some Java code. Exceptions can be used by a Java programmer to allow a program to die gracefully or recover from a potentially disastrous occurrence such as an array going out of bounds or a floating point overflow occurring. Within the Java class libraries there are a number of exceptions provided which cover the most important exceptions that can occur within a Java program. Before looking at the exception mechanism in more detail it is worth looking at some of the errors that could occur within a Java program.

- A program accesses an array element whose index is larger than the upper limit of the array.

- A program reads a file of integers into which a string has been inserted.

- An overflow condition occurs when the result of some arithmetic operation exceeds the limit for the scalars involved.

- A program attempts to carry out some disallowed operation on the null value.

- A program reads past the end of a file.

- A program runs out of memory.

- A program tries to connect to a Web site which has a wrong address.

These are all events that can occur which will terminate your program. Before looking at how exceptions can overcome many of the problems associated with such terminations it is worth looking at the exception hierarchy in Java. Figure 6.1 shows the exception classes that are available to the programmer.

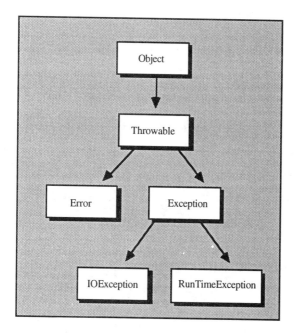

Figure 6.1 The Java exception hierarchy.

The root of the exception inheritance tree is the class `Throwable`. This represents the most general class for describing exceptions. The class `Error` describes exceptions that occur when some internal Java error has happened, for example when it runs out of memory. There is little that a programmer can do about such errors: the Java system monitors them and exits your program with some indication of what has happened being displayed.

It is errors that are described by the class `Exception` that can be monitored and acted on. There are two types of error corresponding to the exception classes `IOException` and `RunTimeException`. The latter corresponds to errors that have been made by a programmer, for example erroneous code giving rise to an illegal array access; while the former is usually out of the control of the programmer, for example an exception being raised when the file being processed does not contain the type of data that it expects.

Java contains facilities for catching the errors that can occur during the running of a program. However, it is worth pointing out that it is only worth catching certain classes of error. For example, there is no point in catching system errors described by the `Error` class: these are almost invariably fatal and the programmer can do nothing about them. It is also not worth catching errors which are described by the class `RunTimeException`. These are programming errors and should be eradicated by proper design, careful coding and exhaustive testing.

SAQ

Which of the following errors should you be able to catch and monitor in a Java program?

- An error that occurs when an empty file is provided where your program assumes that at least one item of data will be contained in the file;

- An array being accessed past the last element;

- The system running out of file space during the process of your program creating a file;

- A hardware error affecting the execution of your program.

Solution

The only error that you should cater for is the first; the second arises from sloppy programming while the last two are irrecoverable system errors.

Errors which are derived from the class `Error` or `RunTimeException` are often referred to as **implicit exceptions**, while errors that arise from the class `IOException` are known as **explicit exceptions**. The general rule that you should adopt when programming exceptions is that you should monitor and catch explicit exceptions. The way this is done is described in the next section of this chapter.

6.2 Defining and throwing exceptions

Whenever one of your methods contains code that discovers that an exception has occurred you have to signal this by naming the exception that has been found after the keyword `throws`. An example of this is shown below:

```
public int valOfId(String userIdentity)
throws IllegalArgumentException{

//code for valOfId
}
```

Here the method `valOfId` processes a string which contains details about a user of a network. Part of that data includes the number of hours of access the user is allowed per week enclosed within dollar characters. If the string between the dollar arguments was not an integer then the code within the method would throw an `IllegalArgumentException` (this is an exception provided by the Java class library; it inherits from `IOException`).

The keyword `throws` advertises to the world that the method is going to throw an exception: that in the code that you write which uses this method some action will need to be taken to cater for this exception.

There are a number of built-in exceptions provided by the Java class library. Some of these are shown below:

- *IllegalArgumentException.* An example of this exception was used above. It is raised when some object or scalar is given a value which is not expected, for example a value outside some range.

- *EOFException.* This is an exception which occurs when a program makes an attempt to read past the end of a file.

- *FileNotFoundException.* This occurs when a program attempts to open an existing file or write to an existing file. If the file cannot be found, then the exception is raised.

- *ArithmeticException.* This occurs when an exceptional arithmetic condition occurs such as a division by zero.

- *IndexOutOfBoundsException.* This occurs when a program accesses an array out of the bounds that have been declared for it.

These are just a selection of the exceptions that are available. As we have stressed before, it is not normal practice to cater for many of these; for example, it is better to program carefully rather than include exception code which checks for an `IndexOutOfBoundException` every time you access an array.

Given that we have described how you communicate to the outside world that an exception occurs the next natural question is: how do we create an exception? The answer is that we use the keyword `throw`. An example of the use of this facility is shown below:

```
public void checkSubString(String s, int low, int up)
throws IllegalArgumentException{
...
if (s.length() > up || low < 0 || low > up)
   throw new IllegalArgumentException();
else
   //code for processing the string s
...
}
```

The method `checkSubString` carries out some processing of the substring of s which is delineated by the arguments `low` and `up`. The former represents the lower, smaller index while the latter represents the upper index. If these indexes are out of the range of the array or the lower index is larger than the upper index then an `IllegalArgumentException` is thrown. Notice that we use the keyword `new`. Since exceptions are objects this has to be used to carry out the process of creating a new exception. Also notice the round brackets; these indicate that we use a no-argument constructor of `IllegalArgumentException`.

The exceptions within the Java class library can be created using a no-argument constructor and a single argument constructor. The single argument constructor is used when a string is to be returned. This string usually indicates what has happened to cause the exception. For example, if we wanted to pass more information back to the code which calls the `checkSubString` method above then we would write the method as:

```
public void checkSubString(String s, int low, int up)
throws illegalArgumentException{
...
if (s.length() > up || low < 0 || low > up)
   throw new IllegalArgumentException
   ("Illegal arguments: low =" + low + "up = " + up);
else
     //code for processing the string s
}
```

This returns with a string consisting of some message and the values of the arguments up and `low`. The use of the + operator in this way is quite common. When it is used with data types which are not strings, then it usually converts them to strings before concatenating them.

SAQ

Write a method which has three arguments. The first two are integer arrays a and b and the third is an integer n. The method copies the first n items from b into array a. In the code you should throw an `IllegalArgumentException` if any of the following conditions occur:

(i) n is zero; (ii) less than n items in a; (iii) less than n items in b.

Solution

```
public void copy(int[] a, int[] b, int n)
throws IllegalArgumentException{

if(n == 0 || a.length < n || b.length < n)
   throw new IllegalArgumentException();
else
   for (int i = 0; i < n; i++)
     a[i] = b[i];}
```

We now know how to indicate that a method throws an exception and how to carry out that throwing. The only part of the story that remains is how to write code that detects that an exception has been thrown.

This is achieved by a further facility of the Java language known as the try–catch block. The general form of a try–catch block is:

```
try{
    code to be checked
}
catch(ExceptiontypeA a){
    handler for ExceptiontypeA}
catch(ExceptiontypeB b){
    handler for ExceptiontypeB}
catch(ExceptiontypeC c){
    handler for ExceptiontypeC}
. . .
```

The code to be checked is executed; if an exception is thrown the code is exited and an exception handler is executed. The code that is executed depends on which exception has been thrown. If the exception was an object described by the class A, then the code immediately following

```
catch(ExceptiontypeA a){
```

is executed, if the exception was described by the class C, then the code immediately following

```
catch(ExceptiontypeC c){
```

is executed. When this code is executed it will find the exception object that has been thrown within the variable specified in the handler. For example, in the handler for ExceptiontypeA the object will be referenced by the variable a. If the code throws an exception which is not catered for in the catch–try block then the program aborts.

We have now discussed how a method advertises the fact that it throws an exception, how to do the throwing and how to write code that executes when a thrown exception has been detected. An important point about exceptions and methods is that if the code within a method throws an exception then you must do one of two things: catch the exception and act upon it using a try–catch block or do nothing but always advertise the fact that an exception is thrown. The Java compiler enforces the rule that if you execute any code which throws an exception then you must either handle it, or advertise the fact that the method has not processed it by using the keyword throws. If the latter is adopted you are assuming that some other method which uses the method that threw the exception will carry out the processing.

You may remember that an exception could be created using a zero-argument or a one-argument constructor; in the latter case the argument will be a string. If the code that caught an exception wants to examine this string a method called getMessage() can be used. What this method does is to take an exception object and return the string. This string is the value associated with the string instance variable associated with each exception class and is normally used to provide some indication of what has happened when the exception has been thrown. Thus the code:

```
try{
  //code which raises an IllegalArgumentException
}
catch (IllegalArgumentException i){
   String errorMessage = i.getMessage();
   //rest of handler code
}
```

contains an assignment to the string errorMessage which is the string associated with the IllegalArgumentException i. Thus, if the code:

```
throw new
IllegalArgumentException("computer name error");
```

occurs during the execution of the code enclosed by the try–catch block, then errorMessage will become equal to the string "computer name error".

6.3 Creating your own exceptions

Even though the Java class library contains a large number of exceptions there will often be times when you want to define your own exceptions which match error conditions that are specific to the application that you are writing. Since exceptions are just objects all you need do is to create a new class which inherits from one of the exception classes that are provided as part of the Java class library. For example, let's say that we are writing a program which examines the state of all the interfaces to a computer network and carries out functions such as sending a packet of data from one computer to another. Assume that we require an exception which indicates that a computer interface can be in one of two error states: *not working*, where a hardware defect has occurred which prevents messages being sent out, and *switched-off* where the interface may be working but has been disconnected from the network for some reason. Let us assume that we require an exception called ComputerInterfaceException which we shall create by inheriting from IllegalArgumentException. This new exception will be associated with a string which indicates the reason for the interface not being able to function and the name of the computer. The code for creating this exception is shown below:

```
class ComputerInterfaceException
```

```
extends IllegalArgumentException{
String computerValue, reasonValue;

public ComputerInterfaceException(
private String errorMessage, computer, reason){
  super(errorMessage);
  computerValue = computer;
  reasonValue = reason;
}


public ComputerInterfaceException(
super(errorMessage);
}

public string computerVal(){
return computerValue;
}


public string reasonVal(){
return reasonValue;
}
```

Two constructors are provided; the first assigns values to the superclass string instance variable and the two instance variables associated with the class; the second constructor just initializes the superclass instance variable.

This exception can then be used within code in the same way that class library exceptions can be used: in try–catch statements and in conjunction with throws and throw as, for example, in the code:

```
try{
  //code to be checked
}
catch (ComputerInterfaceException c){
...
  String comId = c.computerVal();
  String reasonMess = c.reasonVal();
...
}
```

6.4 Exceptions in action — a data structure for a Web crawler

The World Wide Web contains a huge number of documents written in the text processing language HTML. In Chapter 1 you saw an example of this language.

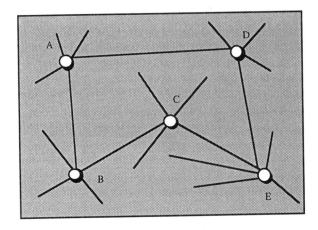

Figure 6.2 A very small fragment of the World Wide Web.

What we did not show you in that fragment was the powerful facility in HTML that allows you to navigate through the World Wide Web.

A fragment of the World Wide Web is shown in Figure 6.2. This shows five HTML documents with links to each other and to other documents which are not shown. These links usually indicate some connection between the Web documents. For example, a document which has been set up by a Java programming interest group might contain links to other groups throughout the world. Within a Web document a reference to another Web document is documented as a Uniform Resource Locator (URL).

Web Crawlers

One of the most useful pieces of software on the Internet is known as a Web crawler. This is a program which wanders around Web sites looking for documents which have certain properties. For example, the user of a Web crawler may ask for all those documents connected to a specific URL which contain the words *Java*, *compiler* and *interpreter*. The Web crawler will start wandering around the Web using the URLs written in each Web document to access another document until the end of the search has occurred. With the large amount of ill-structured information being deposited within the Internet the technology of Web-crawling is set for a major boost in the next decade.

This part of the chapter examines a class which might be used within a Web crawler to describe the connectivity of documents within the World Wide Web. What we effectively want is a class which describes the links between the documents as shown in Figure 6.3.

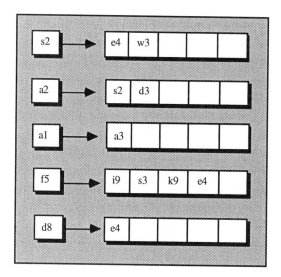

Figure 6.3 Links between World Wide Web documents.

We have referred to the documents by writing an alphabetic character followed by a numeric character. This is to cut down on space in the diagram; normally document URLs would be stored.

In the code that we shall develop towards the end of this section we shall use URLs. In Figure 6.3 we can see that the document *s2* is linked to two other documents and that the document *f5* is linked to four documents.

Our aim is to develop a class which can generate objects such as the one above. In order to do this we will first need to define a class which describes the connectivity of a Web document with other Web documents. This class is shown below. It is worth pointing out that this is not a very efficient solution in terms of memory as many locations will remain empty for each document. Better ways of handling this problem will be described later in the book.

```
class WebConnect{
URL document;
URL[] connectedDocuments;
int noOfConnectedDocs;

public WebConnect(URL base){
this(30, base);
}

public WebConnect(int size, URL base){
connectedDocuments = new URL[size];
noOfConnectedDocs = 0;
```

```
document = base;
}

public void addLink(String toBeAdded)
throws MalformedURLException, AccessException{
if (noOfConnectedDocs != connectedDocuments.length){
  URL i = new URL (toBeAdded);
  connectedDocuments[noOfConnectedDocs] = i;
  noOfConnectedDocs++;
  }
else
  throw new AccessException("locations full");
}

public URL baseDocument(){
return document;}

public int noOfDocuments(){
return noOfConnectedDocs;}

public URL[] linkedDocuments(){
return connectedDocuments;}

}
```

Exercise

Write down the class `AccessException`. Assume that it inherits from an exception known as `IllegalArgumentException`.

Solution

The code is shown below:

```
class AccessException extends IllegalArgumentException{
public AccessException(){}

public AccessException(String mess){
super(mess);}

}
```

There are a number of things to notice about this code. First, there is the use of the class URL. This, not surprisingly, is provided by the Java class library and contains valid URL values. Second, the class throws two exceptions. The first is the user-defined exception `AccessException` which we shall define below. The second exception is `MalformedURLException`. This could be thrown when the assignment statement:

```
URL i = new URL (toBeAdded);
```

is executed. This creates a new URL object which has the URL address given by the string `toBeAdded`. If this address represents a wrongly formed address then the `MalformedURLException` is thrown. This information can be found in the documentation for URLs in the Java class library; later in Chapter 7 we shall describe how to access and use this information.

All that remains is to define a class which contains the connectivity data for a *number* of documents. We shall assume that the class is known as `ConnectTable` and that it contains two constructors. The first will set the number of individual documents that can have entries as 50 and the number of links to each document as 100. The second constructor will have two arguments which set these values to those provided by the user.

```
public class ConnectTable{
WebConnect[] connectionTable;
int maxLinks, maxDocuments, noOfBaseDocuments;

public ConnectTable(){
this (50, 100);
}

public ConnectTable(int noDocs, int noLinks){
noOfBaseDocuments = 0; maxLinks = noLinks;
maxDocuments = noDocs;
}
```

Exercise

Write down the code for the following methods defined in `ConnectTable`:

- A method which returns with the current number of documents.

- A method which returns with the number of links that have been established from all the documents whose information is being stored.

- A method which checks if a particular URL is connected to another URL. This method has two string arguments. If they do not represent URLs then a `MalformedURLException` exception is thrown.

- A method which adds a new document to the connectivity table. If the document already exists then an `AccessException` object will be thrown with a suitable message. This method has a string argument which represents the document. If the string does not represent a valid URL then a `MalformedURLException` exception is thrown. When the document is added 20 locations will be set up for linking information.

Assume the existence of a helper method `findIndex()` within `ConnectTable` which returns an integer that represents the position in the table of the URL of a document that is to have links added. If the URL has not been found then it returns with the value one greater than the number of documents in the table.

Solution

The code is shown below.

```
public int noOfLinkInfo(){
return noOfBaseDocuments;
}

public int totalNoLinks(){
int count = 0;
for(int i = 0; i < noOfBaseDocuments; i++){
   count+=connectionTable[i].noOfDocuments();
}
return count;
}


public boolean findLink(String base,  String link)
throws MalformedURLException, AccessException{

URL ubase = new URL(base), ulink = new URL(link);
boolean found;
int i = findIndex(base);
if (i == maxDocuments+1)
   throw new AccessException("URL not found");
else{
   int j = 0;
   found = false;
   while (!found && j<connectionTable[i].noOfDocuments()){
      found = connectionTable[j].equals (link);
      j++;
   }
}
return found;
}
```

```
public void newDocument(String toBeAdded)
throws MalformedURLException, AccessException{

URL baseURL = new URL(toBeAdded);
int i = findIndex(toBeAdded);
if (i < maxDocuments+1)
   throw new AccessException("URL already in the table");
else{
   connectionTable[noOfBaseDocuments] =
   new WebConnect(20, baseURL);
   noOfBaseDocuments++;
   }
}
}
```

6.5 Extending the running example

In Section 5.8 we described the development of a data structure which related words stored in Web documents to the locations of these words. This enabled retrieval queries to be carried out. Two classes were developed in Section 5.8 to support the data structure. One weakness which we pointed out in that section was the fact that little error processing was attempted. In this section we shall use exceptions to implement this. First let us examine the class which described the link between a word and its locations. The code for this class is shown below:

```
class Links{
private int noOfLocations, maxLocations;
private String word;
private String[] locations;

public Links(String wordToBeCreated){
this (20, wordToBeCreated);
}

public Links (int size, String wordToBeCreated){
noOfLocations = 0;
locations = new String [size];
maxLocations = size;
word = wordToBeCreated;
}

public int getnoOfLocations(){
return noOfLocations;}

public String getWord(){
return word;}
```

```
public String[] getLocations(){
return locations;}

public void addLocation(String locationToBeAdded){
if (noOfLocations < maxLocations){
  locations[noOfLocations] = locationToBeAdded;
  noOfLocations++;}
else
  {
  String[] temp = new String [2*maxLocations];
  for (int i = 0; i < maxLocations; i++)
    temp[i] = locations[i];
  maxLocations = 2*maxLocations;
  locations = temp;
  }}

}
```

SAQ

Which of the methods shown above would benefit from the use of exceptions?

Solution

The method `addLocation` would. The majority of the methods only retrieve data; however, `addLocation` adds a location and there is a danger that a duplicate location might be added.

We thus need to modify this method to ensure that it throws an exception. We shall assume that an `IllegalArgumentException` will be thrown.

Exercise

Write down the code for the version of `addLocation` which throws an `IllegalArgumentException` if a duplicate location is to be added.

Solution

The code is shown below. It uses a sequential search which involves placing the string to be searched one element after the last element in the array `locations` and then checking whether the string to be searched for is this element; if so then there is no duplicate.

The code for the new version of `addLocation` is shown below:

```
public void addLocation(String locationToBeAdded)throws
IllegalArgumentException{
int j = 0;
locations[noOfLocations] = locationToBeAdded;
while(!word.equals (locations[j]))
   j++;
if (j != noOfLocations)
   throw new IllegalArgumentException(
   "Duplicate location " + locationToBeAdded +
   " tried to be added");
else{
   if (noOfLocations < maxLocations){
      locations[noOfLocations] = locationToBeAdded;
      noOfLocations++;
      }
   else{
      String[] temp = new String [2*maxLocations];
      for (int i = 0;i < maxLocations; i++)
      temp[i] = locations[i];
      maxLocations = 2*maxLocations;
      locations = temp;
   }
}
}
```

The class LinksData also needs to be augmented with some form of error
processing. The code for the class is shown below:

```
public class LinksData{

Links [] wordInfo;
int noOfWords, maxWords;

public LinksData(){
this(100);
}

public LinksData(int size){
maxWords = size;
noOfWords = 0;
wordInfo = new Links[size];
}

public int getNoOfWords(){
return noOfWords;
}
```

```
public int getMaxWords(){
return maxWords;
}

public void addWord(String word){
int i = 0;
while(i<noOfWords &&
(word.compareTo(wordInfo[i].getWord())>0))
  i++;
for(int j = noOfWords; j > i; j--){
  wordInfo[j] = wordInfo[j-1];
}
wordInfo[i] = new Links(20, word);
noOfWords++;
}

public boolean checkWordIn(String word){
int val = findWordIndex(word);
return val != -1;
}

private int findWordIndex(String word){
int first = 0, last = noOfWords-1, middle = 0;
boolean found = false;
while (!found && (first <= last)){
middle = (first+last) / 2;
if(word.compareTo((wordInfo[middle].getWord())) == 0)
  found = true;
else{
  if (word.compareTo((wordInfo[middle].getWord())) < 0)
    last = middle - 1;
  else first = middle + 1;
  }
}
if (!found) return -1;
else return middle;
}

public void addLocation(String loc, String word){
int pos = findWordIndex(word);
wordInfo[pos].addLocation(loc);
}

public String[] getLocations(String word){
int pos = findWordIndex(word);
```

```
return wordInfo[pos].getLocations();
  }

  }
```

SAQ

What error handling is needed in the LinksData class?

Solution

The first error processing is that connected with the method addWord. This method will need to throw an exception if a user attempts to add a duplicate word or the addition overflows the capacity of the data structure. The second error processing is that connected with the method addLocation. This uses the method addLocation defined in Links. Previously we added some error processing to this method which resulted in it throwing an Illegal-ArgumentException. The method addLocation in LinksData either needs to handle the exception or pass it on to the method that calls it.

The code which caters for the error processing detailed in the previous SAQ is shown below. The method addWord is augmented by code which uses the method checkWordIn to check for duplication and by code which checks that the table is full. The method addLocation just throws up the exception generated within its code.

```
public void addWord(String word)
throws IllegalArgumentException{
int i = 0;
if (noOfWords == maxWords)
   throw new IllegalArgumentException("Table too full");
int pos = findWordIndex(word);
if (pos == -1)
   throw new IllegalArgumentException("Word already in
table");
while(i < noOfWords &&
   (word.compareTo(wordInfo[i].getWord()) > 0))
   i++;
for(int j = noOfWords; j > i; j--){
   wordInfo[j] = wordInfo[j-1];
}
wordInfo[i] = new Links(20, word);
noOfWords++;}

public void addLocation(String loc, String word)
throws IllegalArgumentException{
```

```
int pos = findWordIndex(word);
wordInfo[pos].addLocation(loc);
}
```

6.6 SUMMARY

Exceptions are a very powerful means of detecting and acting on events which are unexpected. Exceptions are objects; they are thrown using the throw facility and are monitored using `try-catch` blocks. If the code in a method throws an exception then either the exception has to be caught using a `try-catch` block or the header for the method must advertise the fact that the method throws the exception by using the keyword `throws`.

CHAPTER SEVEN

Libraries

- To introduce the idea of the Java class library.
- To introduce the concept of a Java package.
- To describe the main components of the Java library.
- To use the Java util package as an example of a package, concentrating specifically on the Vector and Hashtable classes.
- To describe the concept of collections of general objects.
- To provide you with practice in using the class library.

7.1 Introduction

The Java system contains a number of class libraries which enable the programmer to create a wide variety of objects that implement much of the functionality required for the type of network applications that Java is targeted at. This chapter and Chapters 11 and 13 describe the most important of these libraries and give you plenty of practice in their use. The aim of this chapter is to provide an introduction to the concept of a library.

It is easy to write abstractly about libraries so we have decided to focus our introduction onto one of the more useful and easy-to-understand collections of classes: the Java utility package util and, in particular, two parts of the library, the Vector class and the Hashtable class.

A package is the name given in Java to a collection of classes which have some connection with each other. There are a number of packages which are provided by the Java system. The ones that are dealt with in this book are:

- *The language foundation classes.* These classes implement low-level data types such as integer and contain the code for the methods which operate on these basic data types.

- *The I/O class library.* This contains classes which provide facilities for low-level input/output, for example for the reading of data from files.

- *Another window toolkit class library.* This contains all the classes needed for the interaction between an applet and the user. It contains classes for basic HCI components such as fonts, colours, events, buttons and scroll bars.

- *The utility class library.* This library contains useful facilities such as those for data structuring and contains classes which describe tables, vectors and stacks.

- *The network interface class library.* This vitally important library contains classes which are used to communicate within a network. They extend the facilities that are available in the I/O class library and provide ways of, for example, connecting to other interfaces such as Telnet.

- *The Java database connectivity library.* This contains classes which are used to connect to and process data contained in relational databases. They implement an interface using the query processing language SQL.

These classes are referred to in Java programs as:

```
java.lang
java.io
java.awt
java.util
java.net
java.sql
```

Each package contains a number of classes which the designers of Java knew would be useful in the application areas that Java was intended to address. For example, the java.net package has a class URL which manipulates Uniform Resource Locators, this class being referred to as:

```
java.net.URL
```

If you wish to use one or more classes from one of the above packages then you need to write an import statement as the first statement of the file which contains the classes that you have coded. For example, if you require access to the URL class in the net library, then the first statement should be:

```
import java.net.URL;
```

If you require other classes then separate import statements are needed. For example, if you require the URL class and the Vector class in the util package then you should write

```
import java.net.URL;
import java.util.Vector;
```

What the import statement does is to inform the Java system where to look if it cannot find any class which it does not recognize. If you require a number of classes within the same package then, rather than write a series of import statements, a wild card facility would be used.

Writing an asterisk at the end of a package informs the Java system that all the classes within a specified package are to be searched. Thus,

```
import java.util.*;
```

placed at the beginning of a Java program allows the programmer to use any of the classes contained in the `util` class.

The only exception to this explicit naming is the `lang` package. Since this package contains classes which every Java program will use you do not need to specify it within an import statement – the Java system will automatically search it for the classes that are used within a program.

We hope to do a number of important things within this chapter:

- Introduce you to the way in which Java classes are documented within the class library.

- Provide you with an introduction to the `util` package, This is a package which contains quite a number of useful data structures.

- Describe two very important data structures provided within the `util` package, the classes `Vector` and `Hashtable`. You will find these data structures so useful that you will use them time and time again in your Java programs.

- Provide you with some practice in using the `Object` class. The data structure classes within the `util` library are very general: they can be used to store all sorts of scalars and objects. The mechanism that they use to carry out this important function involves the `Object` class which was described in Chapter 5. We will show you how this class is used. This is a really important topic since the `Object` class is used extensively in constructing general classes.

7.2 The documentation of packages

Part of the Java system contains documentation which describes what each class does. This documentation is written in HTML and, hence, can be examined by a Web browser such as Netscape. An example of this documentation is shown in Figure 7.1.

At this stage do not worry too much about the details of this documentation; just realize that Figure 7.1 is an index which describes the facilities – instance variables, constructors and some of the methods – associated with `Vector`.

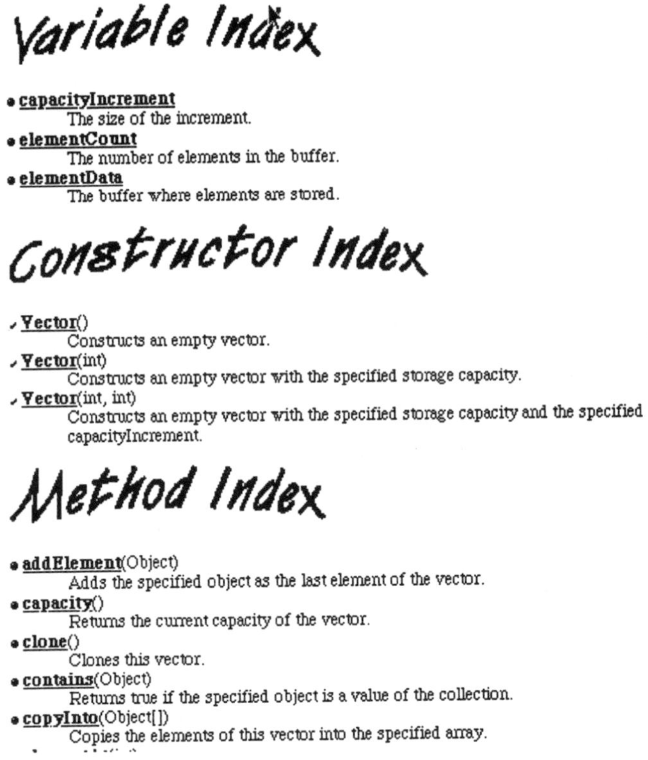

Variable Index

- **capacityIncrement**
  The size of the increment.
- **elementCount**
  The number of elements in the buffer.
- **elementData**
  The buffer where elements are stored.

Constructor Index

- **Vector()**
  Constructs an empty vector.
- **Vector**(int)
  Constructs an empty vector with the specified storage capacity.
- **Vector**(int, int)
  Constructs an empty vector with the specified storage capacity and the specified capacityIncrement.

Method Index

- **addElement**(Object)
  Adds the specified object as the last element of the vector.
- **capacity**()
  Returns the current capacity of the vector.
- **clone**()
  Clones this vector.
- **contains**(Object)
  Returns true if the specified object is a value of the collection.
- **copyInto**(Object[])
  Copies the elements of this vector into the specified array.

Figure 7.1 Part of the documentation of the Vector class.

The parts which are underlined represent links which, if clicked within a browser, will take you to the detailed entry for an instance variable, constructor or method. Figure 7.2 represents a fragment of this detailed information describing some of the methods associated with the Vector class.

Again notice the underlined words. These are again links which, if clicked within the browser, will take you to that part of the documentation describing the word that has been underlined; in the fragment displayed in Figure 7.2 it is the class Object.

An important point that is worth making here is that Java is a rather sparse language in terms of what it can do. Where it gains its huge functionality is from its libraries - not only the libraries that we have described above, but in the large number of special-purpose libraries that commercial developers are currently producing. Because much of the functionality of Java is embedded in these libraries, and because the libraries are too big for one person to remember, you will find yourself continually consulting them: this normally means that you will need to keep your browser open while you are programming in Java, with it pointing at the Java documentation.

● **indexOf**

`public final int indexOf(Object elem)`

Searches for the specified object, starting from the first position and returns an index to it.
Parameters:
elem - the desired element
Returns:
the index of the element, or -1 if it was not found.

● **indexOf**

`public final synchronized int indexOf(Object elem,`
`                                       int index)`

Searches for the specified object, starting at the specified position and returns an index to it.
Parameters:
elem - the desired element
index - the index where to start searching
Returns:
the index of the element, or -1 if it was not found.

● **lastIndexOf**

`public final int lastIndexOf(Object elem)`

Searches backwards for the specified object, starting from the last position and returns an index to it.
Parameters:
elem - the desired element
Returns:
the index of the element, or -1 if it was not found.

Figure 7.2 Part of the documentation of the `Vector` class.

At this very moment as one of us is writing this section (DCI) he has Netscape open on the documentation for the `Vector` class.

The current documentation for the packages provides standard bureaucratic details such as the version number, the date of the version and the developer who was responsible for it. After this comes the important documentation:

- *The constructor index*: a list of the constructors which can be used in Java programs. Most of the classes in the Java library have a number of constructors associated with them. There is usually a constructor which creates an uninitialized object described by the class and a series of constructors which initialize part or the whole of an object described by the class.

- *A list of instance variables*. Some of the classes within the Java library list the instance variables associated with the class. Almost invariably these are private and hence the user of the package is not allowed to access them directly. This is in accordance with the information hiding principle described in Chapter 5.

- *The method index*. This lists the methods which can be used by someone who employs the class within his or her applet or application. The current Java documentation gives the types of the parameters, the name of the method, its access status and a brief description of what it does.

It is important to point out that some of the classes found within the Java library are abstract classes: classes which have place holder methods which do not implement any code (for a fuller explanation of such abstract methods see Chapter 8). A good example of such a method within the `util` package is the class

Dictionary. This class is inherited by the class Hashtable to produce a class which is not abstract.

It is also important to point out that quite a large number of classes store objects which are described by the class Object. This means that they can store a wide variety of objects as we shall describe below.

Another important point to make is that the description of the methods within the Java class library will reference the exceptions which will be raised whenever an error condition occurs such as an attempt to store a value within a data structure when that data structure is full.

7.3 The java.util package

The util package consists of a number of classes which are used to implement useful data structures and facilities. Briefly, the util package consists of:

- Data structure classes: these implement storage structures which programmers tend to use in most applications. These include bitset, hash table, dictionary, stack and vector.

- The Date class: this implements dates in a variety of representations.

- The StringTokenizer class: this class provides the facility whereby a string can be converted into its constituents. For example, the class provides facilities which would convert the string "Hello there I am a Java programmer" to the seven strings "Hello" "there" "I" "am" "a" "Java" "programmer".

- The Properties class implements a file-based data structure which implements system properties.

- The Observer and Observable classes implement objects which can 'watch' the state of other objects. For example, such objects can respond when another object has one of its instance variables changed.

- The Random class implements methods used for the generation of random numbers.

These, then, are the classes which form part of the Java utility package java.util. Each set of related classes is identified by a name which informs the reader that it forms part of the Java library and gives the name of the package and the name of the facility that the classes implement. For example, the BitSet facility within the util package is identified by the name:

```
java.util.BitSet;
```

Remember, if you wish to use the facilities of a particular library you inform the Java system by means of the `import` directive. For example, the statement:

```
import java.util.Hashtable;
```

informs the Java interpreter that the `Hashtable` class within `util` is to be used by the program that follows. If you wish to import all the classes in the `util` library then you can use the `*` character as a wild card. For example:

```
import java.util.*;
```

means import all classes in the package `java.util`.

7.4 Two useful data structures

The aim of this section is to examine two classes which implement some very useful data structures that you will need time and time again. Using the `util` classes alone will considerably shorten the amount of code that you will need to write in a Java applet or application.

7.4.1 The `Vector` class

This is one of the most useful classes in the `util` package; one which we find ourselves using quite a lot within applets or applications. It describes objects which look like arrays in that they are indexable, but they differ from arrays in that they can extend themselves. This means that if a `Vector` object finds itself running out of space it can request more space from the Java run-time system to extend itself. It is important to point out that by describing the `Vector` class we are not elevating it in importance above other classes in the Java libraries – we are just using it as an example.

The `Vector` class is associated with three instance variables. The first is `capacityIncrement` which specifies the increase in storage which will be added to a vector when it runs out of space. If this instance variable is zero then the capacity of a `Vector` object is doubled when it runs out of space. The second is `elementCount` which contains the number of elements in the vector. The third is `elementData` which is an array where the items in the `Vector` object are stored.

There are three constructor methods associated with vectors. `Vector` with two int arguments sets up an empty vector with the first parameter holding the number of items that the vector is assumed to hold and the second parameter specifying the increase in size when the vector becomes full. `Vector` with one argument sets up an empty vector with the sole argument specifying the initial capacity of the vector. This constructor sets the `capacityIncrement` instance variable to zero, ensuring that the capacity of a `Vector` object is doubled whenever it runs out of space. The final constructor is `Vector` without any arguments. The size of the vector is set to a system-defined default with any `Vector` objects instantiated in this way doubling their size when they run out of capacity.

At this point it is worth making an important point about vectors: while they represent an advance over the use of arrays, they still suffer from a memory problem in that there will always be empty locations within a vector: as soon as it becomes full the Java system will allocate more room for it depending on which constructor you used. This means that it is still a slightly profligate solution to the problem of storing variable amounts of data. A much better solution will be described in Chapter 8.

Thus:

```
Vector    smallQ = new Vector(20, 3),
          largeQ = new Vector(),
          medQ = new Vector(1100);
```

declares three `Vector` identifiers. It declares the first vector `smallQ` to initially contain 20 elements with the size of the object being incremented by 3 whenever it runs out of space. It declares the vector `largeQ` to contain the system default of the number of items initially assumed to be held in the vector and assumes the vector's size will be doubled whenever it runs out of space. The final declaration informs the Java system that the vector `medQ` will initially contain 1100 elements and will be doubled in size whenever it runs out of space.

There are a large number of methods associated with `Vector` objects. The aim of this section is not to detail all of them but to briefly describe a small number in order to give you a flavour of the sort of facilities a data structure class will provide within the Java system.

- `public void addElement(Object)` adds the object which is its argument to the end of the vector object to which it sends the message corresponding to this method. Notice that the parameter of the method is `Object`; this means that any objects can be held in a vector.

- `public int capacity()` returns with the capacity of the vector object to which this message is sent. This integer represents the current upper limit of items that can be stored in the object.

- `public int size()` returns with the current number of objects stored in the vector. This is different to the capacity: the latter represents the current maximum number of elements which can be contained in the vector before the vector is increased; the former represents the number of items actually stored.

- `public boolean contains(Object)` returns the Boolean value true if the object which is the argument of the method is currently stored in the vector object which receives the message corresponding to the method.

- `public int lastIndexOf(Object)` searches for the object which is the argument to the method and returns an index to it if it is found; however, if it is not found, then it returns the value -1.

- `public Object firstElement()` returns with the first object in the `Vector` object to which the message corresponding to this method is sent.

- `public void removeElements()` removes all the elements from the object to which the message corresponding to the method is sent. The vector becomes empty.

These, then, are a small selection of methods which are associated with vectors. Before leaving this section it is worth developing some code which involves vectors in order to give you an idea of the power of the class library.

The example that we have chosen is the data structure which contains the details of a computer together with all the computers to which it is connected in a network. The class we developed for this suffered from the problem that we were only able to store a fixed upper limit of computers in the array which contained linked computers. When the method which inserted a computer into this data structure encountered a full array an exception was raised which indicated that the computer could not be inserted. We shall use a `Vector` object to overcome this problem.

The first part of the class which describes the linkage is shown below:

```
class LinkingInfo {
String computer;
Vector linkedComputers;
```

The string `computer` contains the computer which is linked, while the vector `linkedComputers` contains the computers that are linked to `computer`.

We shall assume that a number of methods are required. These are specified below:

`computerName()`. This returns with the name of the computer which is linked.

`noOfLinkedComputers()`. This returns with the number of computers that are linked.

`isLinked(String comp1)`. This returns with a true value if the computer which is the argument is linked to the computer which is the receiver object and a false value otherwise. The argument will or will not be contained in the collection of computers which are linked.

`addComputer(String comp1)`. This adds the computer which is the argument to the method to the list of linked computers. If the computer is already in the list of linked computers, then a `ComputerError-`

Exception exception is raised with the message "Computer already in links".

removeComputer(String comp1). This removes the computer comp1 from the linked computers. If the computer is not in the list of linked computers, then a ComputerErrorException exception is raised with the message "Computer not in links".

For the sake of this exercise assume that the exception ComputerError-Exception has been defined elsewhere. We are going to ask you to carry out the coding of these methods as an exercise and would warn you that you will *not* need to use very many repetitive control structures as, for example, you used in Chapter 4: the Vector class contains methods which carry out functions such as adding items to a Vector and removing items from a Vector, where the detailed programming is hidden from view.

First we need to develop the constructors. We shall assume that there will be two constructors. The first is provided with the name of the computer for which the linking information is to be held and an initial value of the number of locations to hold linked computers. The second is provided with the name of the computer and will default to an initial size of 50 locations. Both constructors will specify that as the vectors become full 10 more locations are added to their end. The code for these two constructors is shown below:

```
LinkingInfo(String computerName, int size){
linkedComputers = new Vector(size, 10);
computer = computerName;
}


LinkingInfo(String computerName){
this(computerName, 50);
}
```

These two constructors set up the vectors using the two-argument Vector constructor described in the Java class documentation as:

⋏ Vector

```
public Vector(int initialCapacity,
              int capacityIncrement)
```

Constructs an empty vector with the specified storage capacity and the specified capacityIncrement.
Parameters:
initialCapacity - the initial storage capacity of the vector
capacityIncrement - how much to increase the element's size by.

We now need to develop the methods. The first one is noOfLinkedComputers(). It returns with the number of linked computers.

```
public int noOfLinkedComputers(){
```

```
return linkedComputers.size();
}
```

This uses the `size` method for vectors defined in the documentation as:

● **size**

```
public final int size()
```

> Returns the number of elements in the vector. Note that this is not the same as the vector's capacity.

This returns with the number of items in a vector. Some of you may have been wondering why we had not stored an instance variable which contained the number of computers that are linked. The reason is that this information is held within the `Vector` instance variable and can be accessed by means of the `size()` method. The code for the method `computerName()` is shown below. It is trivial as it merely returns with the name of the computer.

```
public String computerName(){
return computer;
}
```

Exercise

Write down the code for the methods `isLinked(String comp2)` and `addComputer(String comp1)`. Before doing this it is worth scanning the Vector class documentation. You will find methods in here that will cut down on your programming considerably. If `addComputer` encounters the computer that is to be added within `linkedComputers`, then a `ComputerError-Exception` must be thrown.

Solution

The code is shown below.

```
public boolean isLinked(String comp1){
return linkedComputers.contains(comp1);
}

public void addComputer(String comp1)
throws ComputerErrorException{
if(linkedComputers.contains(comp1))
   throw new ComputerErrorException
   ("Computer already in links");
else
```

```
        linkedComputers.addElement(comp1);
}
```

These two methods use the Vector methods contains and addElement defined in the Java documentation as:

● addElement

```
public final synchronized void addElement(Object obj)
```

> Adds the specified object as the last element of the vector.
> **Parameters:**
> obj – the element to be added

and

● contains

```
public final boolean contains(Object elem)
```

> Returns true if the specified object is a value of the collection.
> **Parameters:**
> elem – the desired element

At this stage in the book do not worry about what the meaning of the term *synchronized* is. It will be described in Chapter 9 which deals with concurrent processing; its meaning does not affect the code that you will see in this chapter.

SAQ

Write down the code for the final method removeComputer(String comp1); again remember that it raises an exception if the computer to be removed is not contained in the object linkedComputers.

Solution

The solution is shown below.

The code for removeComputer is:

```
public void removeComputer(String comp1)
throws ComputerErrorException{
if (!linkedComputers.contains(comp1))
throw new ComputerErrorException
   ("Computer not in links");
else
   linkedComputers.removeElement(comp1);
}
```

This uses the `Vector` method `removeElement` defined as:

● **removeElement**

```
public final synchronized boolean removeElement(Object obj)
```

> Removes the element from the vector. If the object occurs more than once, only the first is removed. If the object is not an element, returns false.
> **Parameters:**
>> obj - the element to be removed
>
> **Returns:**
>> true if the element was actually removed; false otherwise.

We have given you some practice in using the `Vector` class. We have also emphasized the importance of using the Java class documentation. To conclude this chapter we describe another very important Java class, `Hashtable`.

7.4.2 The `Hashtable` class

In many applications we require two types of objects to be associated. Some examples of this are:

- Users of an operating system need to be associated with an email address.

- Users of an operating system may need to be associated with bureaucratic information such as the maximum amount of file space they are allowed to use and their current password.

- Members of staff in a personnel system will need to be associated with bureaucratic details such as their salary, address and tax number.

An abstract view of this association is shown in Figure 7.3 which shows the associations between computer users and their passwords. One set of values in a Hashtable is known as the keys. A **key** is an object or a scalar which is used to look up another object or scalar in a Hashtable. In the example shown in Figure 7.3 the keys are the names of the users. The name is used to retrieve the value of the password.

Ince	A88uiUijUU
Williams	Diana
Robson	llOkJ&&*
Timms	yyhYTRGF44$
Jones	RoverTTHG
Roberts	lki**7YGHFss
Graham	jNBVfG%^$$

Figure 7.3 A logical view of a Hashtable.

The Hashtable data structure allows a programmer to set pairs of objects or scalars and look up a values associated with objects and scalars. There are a wide variety of methods which access data and write data to a Hashtable. You will encounter a number of these in the example which follows. However, it is worth describing some of them here.

The method `size()`, which has no arguments, returns with the number of items in a `Hashtable`, the method `containsKey(Object key)` returns true if an element associated with `key` is contained in a Hashtable, the method `get(Object key)` returns an object of class `Object` associated with `key` and the method `put(Object key, Object value)` places a new entry in a Hashtable corresponding to a key value key and an associated `Object` value.

These, then, are some of the methods associated with the `Hashtable` class. The rest of this section looks at the use of a Hashtable in a simple application.

IP Addresses

In the Internet, computers are identified by means of a unique address. This address is referred as the IP (Internet Protocol) address. This 32-bit address is written as a set of four numbers separated by full stops. For example, 103.12.13.60 is an example of such an address. There are four types of IP addresses: class A through class D. Class A addresses are for networks which have many computers attached to them, class B addresses are for intermediate size networks, class C addresses are for much smaller networks and class D addresses are used in a special way within the Internet when multiple broadcasts of messages are to be sent. The notation used is often referred to as **dotted quad notation** and bears the same relationship to computers in the Internet as memory addresses do in a computer: they uniquely identify a computer. They are allocated by an organization called the Network Information Centre (NIC).

IP addresses are difficult to remember and an organization will name its computers using some easy-to-remember mnemonics. The final part of this section describes the use of a hash table in relating Class A IP addresses to the name of the computer which they represent. The format of class A addresses is shown in Figure 7.4.

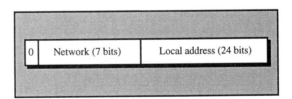

Figure 7.4 A class A IP address.

The first, single-bit field in the address is zero, the second field which is seven bits long represents the network and the final field contains three eight-bit integers which represent the computer address.

The class which we will describe will relate class A IP addresses to a string which is used to name the computer. So, for example, this class might relate the address 10.33.51.12 to the computer identified by the string "BigMacVax".

Before writing down this code we will develop a class which describes class A addresses. The skeleton for the code is:

```
class classAIPAddress{
int networkInt, compAdd1, compAdd2, compAdd3;

classAIPAddress(String fullAddress)
throws InvalidIPAddressException, NumberFormatException{
// Code for constructor
}

public boolean equals (classAIPAddress c){
// Code for equals
}

public int hashCode(classAIPAddress c){
// Code for hashCode
}

}
```

Before looking in detail at the code within the constructors and the methods it is worth describing each of them. There are four instance variables associated with the class, each of them representing the four components of the class A IP address.

There is one constructor: this takes a single string argument which represents a class A IP address. It throws an `InvalidAddressException` exception if this does not represent a valid value. We will assume that we have written a class which describes `InvalidAddressException`. For example, the addresses below do not represent valid class A addresses:

12.3.56

10567.34.12.12

12.56666.1.1

The first has too few fields. The second has too large a value for the network (only eight bits are allowed) and the third has too large a value for the second field. The constructor also throws a `NumberFormatException` if there are non-valid characters within an IP Address, for example as in:

12.3r.45.67

This exception forms part of the Java class library. There are two further methods specified for this class. The first is equals which returns with a Boolean value if two addresses are the same. This method is required by the Hashtable class. Every object that you intend using as a key in a Hashtable requires this method to be defined in its class. A Hashtable object will use this method when carrying out a lot of its processing, for example when it is retrieving a value given a key.

The second method is also required by the Hashtable class. Every object that is to be used as a key in a Hashtable should define this method within the class that describes the object. This method should generate an integer for each value of the key which would have a high chance of being unique: it doesn't *have* to be unique, but for the efficient functioning of the Hashtable class it should have a high probability of uniqueness. The code for both equals and hashCode is shown below:

```
public boolean equals (classAIPAddress c){
return     (networkInt == c.networkInt &&
           compAdd1 == c.compAdd1 &&
           compAdd2 == c.compAdd2 &&
           compAdd3 == c.compAdd3);
}


public int hashCode(classAIPAddress c){
return     (c.networkInt + c.compAdd1
           + c.compAdd2 + c.compAdd3);
}
```

The hashCode method forms the sum of the individual fields of the IP address. It is not a brilliant way of generating a nearly unique value – but it is good enough for our purposes.

The code for the constructor is shown below. It does not attempt to do anything with the exceptions that it generates but propagates them up towards to whatever code uses it. The code first passes over the string argument and extracts out all the full stops within it. If there are three it then checks whether the values of the four fields are correct. If they are then the IP address is formed.

```
classAIPAddress(String fullAddress)
throws InvalidIPAddressException, NumberFormatException{
int[] dots = new int[3]; int dotCount = 0;
for(int i = 0; i < fullAddress.length(); i++)
if (fullAddress.charAt(i) == '.'){
dots[dotCount] = i;
dotCount++;
};
```

```
if (dotCount == 3){
  networkInt = Integer.parseInt
  (fullAddress.substring(0,dots[1]-1));
  compAdd1 = Integer.parseInt
  (fullAddress.substring(dots[1]+1,dots[2]-1));
  compAdd2 = Integer.parseInt
  (fullAddress.substring(dots[2]+1,dots[3]-1));
  compAdd3 = Integer.parseInt
  (fullAddress.substring(dots[2]+1,fullAddress.length()))
  ;};
if (networkInt > 255 || compAdd1 > 511 || compAdd2 > 511 ||
compAdd3 > 511 || dotCount < 3)
  throw new InvalidIPAddressException();
}
```

There are a number of things of note here. First, the static method parseInt, which takes a string and converts it to an integer and throws a Number-FormatException if the string is an invalid integer, for example it contains alphabetic characters. This method can be found in java.lang.Integer.

The method substring has two arguments which delimit a substring of the receiver object. This method can be found in Java.lang.String. The function of the last lines of the method, then, is to extract out the substring representing the four integers and place them within the instance variables. If the values are too large, then an InvalidIPAddressException is thrown.

Given this class we can write a class for associating IP addresses with computer names representing strings.

The skeleton for this class is shown below:

```
class IPRTable{
Hashtable associations;

IPRTable(){
associations = new Hashtable();}

public int noInTable(){
//code for noInTable;
}

public void addToTable(String ipAdd, String name)
throws    InvalidIPAddressException,
          NumberFormatException{

//code for addToTable;
}

public string returnName(String ipAdd)
```

```
throws InvalidIPAddressException, NumberFormatException{

//code for returnName;
}

public boolean isInTable (String ipAdd)
throws InvalidIPAddressException, NumberFormatException{

//code for isInTable;
}

}
```

All of the methods, apart from the constructor and noInTable, will throw the two types of exception that indicate a malformed IP address. This will happen when a classAIPAddress is formed by using its constructor. The method noInTable returns with the number of items in the table; the method addToTable adds an IP address-computer name pair to the table; the method returnName returns with the name of the computer which corresponds to the IP address that is its argument; and isInTable checks whether a particular IP address is contained in the table.

Exercise

Write code for the methods described above. Before doing this consult the Java documentation for the Hashtable class since it will contain many methods which you can use.

Solution

The code is shown below:

The code for the class is:

```
class IPRTable{
Hashtable associations;

IPRTable(){
associations = new Hashtable();
}

public int noInTable(){
return associations.size();
}

public void addToTable(String ipAdd, String name)
throws InvalidIPAddressException, NumberFormatException{
```

```
classAIPAddress ip = new classAIPAddress(ipAdd);
associations.put(ip, name);
}


public String returnName(String ipAdd)
throws InvalidIPAddressException, NumberFormatException{
classAIPAddress ip = new classAIPAddress(ipAdd);
return (String) associations.get(ip);
}


public boolean isInTable (String ipAdd)
throws InvalidIPAddressException, NumberFormatException{
classAIPAddress ip = new classAIPAddress(ipAdd);
return associations.contains(ip);
}
}
```

It calls a number of methods associated with the Hashtable class such as put which places a pair of objects in a Hashtable and contains which returns with a Boolean value if its argument occurs as a key within a Hashtable.

7.5 The Object class and object wrappers

One of the most useful things about data structures such as Vectors and Hashtables is that it is easy to place any objects and scalars into them; indeed it is possible to mix them.

However, we are faced with a problem. For example, let us say that we have declared a class User. We can place an object described by this class into a vector v just by writing the code:

```
v.addElement(u)
```

Getting it out is a little more difficult. The reason for this is that it is stored as an object of class Object in v. Let us say that we use the method lastElement to retrieve the last element in the vector and we write:

```
User lastuser = v.lastElement();
```

What will happen? If you try to execute this statement you will be given a compiler error.

The problem is that lastElement() delivers an Object and the right hand side of the assignment is an object variable which will contain a User. The way to get over this problem is to use the cast facility that was described in Chapter 4 to convert the Object object delivered by lastElement to a User object. This would mean writing:

```
User lastUser = (User) v.lastElement();
```

This seems to solve our problem. Almost, but not quite. Let us assume that we are trying to add `int` values to the vector and we have an `int` variable `i`. We could write:

```
v.addElement(i)
```

Would this work? The answer is no, for a very subtle reason.

Exercise

Can you think why the Java compiler would object to such a statement?

Solution

The reason is that ints are not objects. You may remember that scalar values such as ints are not treated as objects by Java. Any attempt to insert a scalar value into a vector which expects objects to be inserted will result in an error being signalled by the Java compiler.

How does Java get over this problem? It is important that it is solved since it is a fairly common occurrence to want to store scalars. The answer is that many of the scalars within Java are associated with classes which are known as object wrappers. An **object wrapper** for a scalar such as `int` encapsulates `int` values within a class and allows them to be treated as objects. The object wrapper for ints is the class `Integer`. It contains constructors for creating `Integer` objects from ints and also for converting between `Integer` objects, ints and other scalars such as strings. If we want to insert an integer `i` into a vector `v` then the code we would write is:

```
v.addElement(new Integer(i))
```

This first calls the constructor for the class `Integer` which has a single int argument. This forms an `Integer` object which has the value `i`. Since the argument to `addElement` is now an object it can be added to the vector `v`.

How do we retrieve object wrapper values? This is done in the same way as we saw for `User` objects:

```
Integer i = (Integer) v.lastElement()
```

This casts the object to an `Integer` variable. However, what do we do if we want the value to be assigned to an `int`? This would be the normal thing that would happen because Java's facilities for manipulating `Integer` objects are very limited. Happily the `Integer` class contains many conversion methods. One of these, `intValue()`, returns an integer value. Thus if we wished the last element in the vector v to be assigned to the scalar variable `in`, then all that would need to be written would be:

```
int in = ((Integer) v.lastElement()).intValue()
```

7.6 Mixing objects

Before concluding this chapter it is worth saying something about the ability of many of Java's data structures to hold many types of object simultaneously. For example, assume that we have three classes, `Computer`, `User` and `Link`, and three variables, c, u and l, which are defined by these classes respectively; then it is perfectly possible to write code such as:

```
vec1.addElement(c);
vec1.addElement(u);
vec1.addElement(l);
```

where `vec1` is a vector. This would make `vec1` heterogeneous. The only problem that we then face is how to find out what individual objects we have in a vector element when they are retrieved, since we will often have to process each object differently from others. The answer is that we use the operator `instanceof` which we briefly described in Chapter 5. This has two operands: an object and a class. It returns true if the object is defined as a member of the class. Thus it is possible to include code such as:

```
Object o = v.lastElement()
if (o instanceof User){
//code to process User object
...
if (o instanceof Link){
//code to process Link object
...
```

7.7 Further extension of the running example

To conclude the chapter we will carry out some extension of the running example that we have introduced and coded in earlier chapters. The code for this running example – that of the data structure for a Web search engine – is shown below:

```
public class LinksData{
Links [] wordInfo;

int noOfWords, maxWords;
```

```
public LinksData(){
this(100);
}

public LinksData(int size){
maxWords = size;
noOfWords = 0;
wordInfo = new Links[size];
}

public int getNoOfWords(){
return noOfWords;
}

public int getmaxWords(){
return maxWords;
}

public void addWord(String word)
throws IllegalArgumentException{
int i = 0;
if (noOfWords == maxWords)
   throw new IllegalArgumentException("Table too full");
int pos = findWordIndex(word);
if (pos == -1)
   throw new IllegalArgumentException("Word already in
table");
while(i < noOfWords &&
   (word.compareTo(wordInfo[i].getWord()) > 0))
   i++;
for(int j = noOfWords; j > i; j--){
   wordInfo[j] = wordInfo[j-1];
}
wordInfo[i] = new Links(20, word);
noOfWords++;
}

public boolean checkWordIn(String word){
int val = findWordIndex(word);
return val != -1;
}

private int findWordIndex(String word){
int first = 0, last = noOfWords-1, middle=0;
boolean found = false;
```

```
while (!found && (first <= last)){
middle = (first+last) / 2;
if(word.compareTo((wordInfo[middle].getWord())) == 0)
  found = true;
else{
  if (word.compareTo((wordInfo[middle].getWord())) < 0)
    last = middle - 1;
  else first = middle + 1;
  }
}
if (!found) return -1;
else return middle;
}

public void addLocation(String loc, String word)
throws IllegalArgumentException{
int pos = findWordIndex(word);
wordInfo[pos].addLocation(loc);
}

public String[] getLocations(String word){
int pos = findWordIndex(word);
return wordInfo[pos].getLocations();
}

//
//Links class
//

class Links{
private int noOfLocations, maxLocations;
private String word;
private String[] locations;

public Links(String wordToBeCreated){
this (20, wordToBeCreated);
}

public Links (int  size,  String wordToBeCreated){
noOfLocations = 0;
locations = new String [size];
maxLocations = size;
word = wordToBeCreated;
}

public int getnoOfLocations(){
```

```
return noOfLocations;
}

public String getWord(){
return word;
}

public String[] getLocations(){
return locations;
}

public void addLocation(String locationToBeAdded)
throws IllegalArgumentException{
int j = 0;
locations[noOfLocations] = locationToBeAdded;
while(!word.equals (locations[j]))
   j++;
if (j != noOfLocations)
   throw new IllegalArgumentException(
   "Duplicate location " + locationToBeAdded +
   " tried to be added");
else{
   if (noOfLocations < maxLocations){
     locations[noOfLocations] = locationToBeAdded;
     noOfLocations++;
     }
   else{
     String[] temp = new String [2*maxLocations];
     for (int i = 0; i < maxLocations; i++)
     temp[i] = locations[i];
     maxLocations = 2*maxLocations;
     locations = temp;
   }
}
}
}
```

The code uses arrays for the storage of words and locations when a Vector would do a better job. The aim of this section is to modify the code so that instead of using arrays the Vector class is employed. Before doing this it is worth making a point about the progression of the running example through the book. The way we handle the example is based on pedagogic principles, not on design principles. Normally this example would have been implemented as a Vector from the beginning. However, because we had not covered vectors in the early chapters we had to use arrays for the implementation and we are now rectifying that decision.

How would you modify the Links class so that it uses vectors?

The instance variable locations will be declared as a Vector and all the methods which access locations will need to be modified. This means that since vectors are adaptable data structures which carry information within themselves about the data they contain there is no need for the two int instance variables noOfLocations and maxLocations.

The code for the class Links is shown below.

```
class Links{
private String word;
private Vector locations;

public Links(String wordToBeCreated){
this (20, wordToBeCreated);
}

public Links (int size,  String wordToBeCreated){
locations = new Vector(size);
word = wordToBeCreated;
}

public int getnoOfLocations(){
return locations.size();
}

public String getWord(){
return word;
}

public Vector getLocations(){
return locations;
}

public void addLocation(String locationToBeAdded)throws
IllegalArgumentException{
```

```
if (locations.contains(locationToBeAdded))
  throw new IllegalArgumentException(
    "Duplicate location " + locationToBeAdded +
    " tried to be added");
else locations.addElement(locationToBeAdded);
}

}
```

The major effect of this change has been to shorten considerably the code associated with `addLocation`. This shortening has occurred because `Vector` objects automatically carry out the reallocation of space when they reach their maximum size.

The code for the class `LinksData` is shown below. An important point to make is that the code has not been substantially decreased since we have still needed to access individual elements of `wordInfo` because the search method for `Vector` objects is that of a linear search rather than a fast binary search. So for efficiency's sake we have not used the `Vector` method `contains` and have had to program our own search method `findWordIndex`. It is also worth pointing out the extensive use of casting since the `Vector` class contains objects defined by `Object`.

```
public class LinksData{
Vector  wordInfo;

public LinksData(){
this(100);
}

public LinksData(int size){
wordInfo = new  Vector(size);
}

public int getNoOfWords(){
return wordInfo.size();
}

public void addWord (String word)
throws IllegalArgumentException{
  if (checkWordIn(word))
  throw new IllegalArgumentException
    ("Duplicate word " + word +
      " attempted to be added");
  else{
    int i = 0;
    while (i < wordInfo.size() &&
```

```
        (word.compareTo(((Links)wordInfo.elementAt(i))
        .getWord()) > 0))
           i++;
      for(int j = wordInfo.size(); j > i; j--)
         wordInfo.insertElementAt
            (wordInfo.elementAt(j-1),j);
      wordInfo.insertElementAt(new Links(20, word),i);
      }
}


public boolean checkWordIn(String word){
int val = findWordIndex(word);
return val != -1;}


private int findWordIndex(String word){
int first = 0, last = wordInfo.size() - 1, middle = 0;
boolean found = false;
while (!found && (first <= last)){
middle = (first+last) / 2;
if(word.compareTo((((Links)wordInfo.elementAt(middle)).ge
tWord())) == 0)
   found = true;
else{
  if
(word.compareTo((((Links)wordInfo.elementAt(middle)).getW
ord())) < 0)
    last = middle - 1;
  else first = middle + 1;
  }
}
if (!found) return -1;
else return middle;}


public void addLocation(String loc, String word) throws
IllegalArgumentException{
int pos = findWordIndex(word);
((Links) wordInfo.elementAt(pos)).addLocation(loc);}

public Vector getLocations(String word){
int pos = findWordIndex(word);
return ((Links)wordInfo.elementAt(pos)).getLocations();
}

}
```

7.8 SUMMARY

This chapter has contained our first look at libraries. In it we have used the util library to give you a flavour of what you should do to access and use the classes which are in the Java class library. You have also had your first peek at the Java documentation; if you are going to carry out a large amount of Java programming, then this certainly will not be your last exposure to it: you will find it a continuous companion.

To conclude the chapter we examined two very useful data structures which you will find yourself using time and time again and looked at the flexibility that Java allows the user in that any type of object can be stored in its data structure classes. This led to a discussion of the use of object wrappers.

CHAPTER EIGHT

Abstraction Mechanisms

- To show how abstract classes implement the natural hierarchy of abstraction within an object-oriented system.
- To show how interfaces allow a form of multiple inheritance to be implemented in Java.
- To demonstrate how packages allow Java developers to build their own libraries.

8.1 Introduction

One of the features of any class hierarchy is the fact that as you progress towards the bottom of a class hierarchy the classes that you encounter become more and more specialized versions of the classes which lie above: that is, they become less abstract. As an example consider Figure 8.1.

This represents the classes in a database used for a personnel application. The top class contains information needed for all the employees in an organization: it will, for example, contain instance variables for the name of an employee, their address and their tax information. Below this class are two further classes: one represents those employees who are paid monthly, who often will receive special payments such as travelling expenses and commissions; the other class WeeklyEmployee represents other workers who are paid weekly and whose pay is calculated in a different way from monthly paid employees, for example they may receive overtime payments.

At the lowest level of the hierarchy are monthly paid staff who are given a car by the company. These would be staff for whom car travel is seen as essential, for example sales staff. Inside this class there would be methods and instance variables which would not be found within the normal monthly paid employees class since they would be too specific.

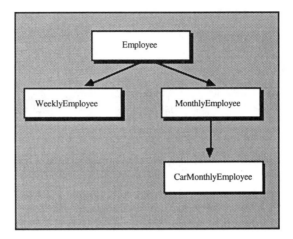

Figure 8.1 An example of a class hierarchy.

These extra variables and methods would involve the cars that the employee was given to drive, for example there would be a string instance variable which described the make of car and methods to retrieve and set this string variable.

The classes in the hierarchy represent an increasingly less abstract view of the notion of an employee: the topmost class represents the most general concept of an employee and will contain instance variables and methods which will be shared across all employees; as you proceed down the hierarchy, the category of employee will become more specialized and will carry out seemingly similar functions in a different way. For example, assume that the notion of a monthly paid employee does not include that of overtime, but that some bonus is paid depending on company performance; this means that the methods which calculate the employee's pay will be functionally similar – they calculate the pay – but will be carried out in different ways.

8.2 Abstract methods

Abstract methods are a concept in Java which enable this idea of abstraction to be implemented. The keyword `abstract` in front of a class indicates that the class that is to be defined is going to contain methods which are in effect blank, but will be filled in when classes are defined which inherit from the class.

For example, the `Employee` class described above would be defined as:

```
abstract class Employee{
```

What the keyword `abstract` indicates is that when you look inside the class you will find a number of methods (at least one) which will be defined in terms of their visibility, name and arguments, but they will contain no code.

These methods will be headed by the keyword abstract. As an example consider the Employee class defined above. The skeleton code for this is shown below:

```
abstract class Employee{

//   instance variables, constructors and common methods
//   for Employee

public abstract int calculatePay();

}
```

Here the method calculatePay which returns a dollar or pound amount is declared as abstract, but no code is provided. This code will be provided by any class that inherits from Employee. The definition of MonthlyEmployee is:

```
class MonthlyEmployee extends Employee{
//new instance variables for MonthlyEmployee

//constructors for MonthlyEmployee

//any new methods for MonthlyEmployeee

public int calculatePay(){
//code which calculates the pay of a monthly employee
}

}
```

The important point to make about abstract classes is that they force the programmer to implement certain methods; they form a type of certification where the programmer who extends the inheritance class promises the implementation of these methods.

Programmers have to promise this implementation because Java forbids the creation of an object defined by an abstract class. It is worth looking at another example as abstraction is an important principle in object-oriented design. This example concerns a security facility known as a log file.

Log Files

One of the most useful tools that a system administrator can use to detect unauthorized users accessing a computer is a log file. Many operating systems allow the system administrator to set up flags which allow certain system activities to be logged to a file. Logging data is often sent to a files on another computer – often an obsolete one – which is in a secure physical location. The log files that are produced are immensely useful as they contain information that can be processed which could indicate a break-in has occurred; they can also be used to track down the specific events which lead to an intrusion. In the UNIX operating system a whole series of log files can be created; some examples are shown below:

* A file containing a record of every command run by users.

* A file containing a record of the use of dial-out modems.

* A file containing a record of attempts to log in to the computer which failed.

* A file containing all FTP accesses.

These files are one of the components used in a particularly severe form of security auditing known as a **C2 audit**. This conforms to a series of standards laid down by the US Department of Defense which require the extensive writing of logging data to secure files. Computer systems which carry out this form of auditing are regarded by the Department of Defense to be secure to the C2 level of security specified in their Trusted Computer System Evaluation Criteria, often referred to as the 'Orange Book'.

Log files in an operating system can be regarded as forming an inheritance hierarchy shown in Figure 8.2.

The topmost class is a general class which contains instance variables and methods which are common to all log files, for example it would hold an instance variable which contained the date of creation of the log file and a method to set and access this instance variable. The topmost abstract class LogFile would also contain a blank method which returned an indicator that reflected the degree of worry that the system administrator has about the activities that were logged.

Underneath the topmost class are three log file classes which contain data on the use of modems, the use of system commands and a record of logins which were attempted but which did not work. These classes would be more specialized and, hence, less abstract versions of LogFile.

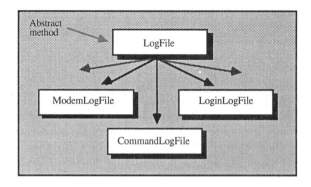

Figure 8.2 A class hierarchy showing log files.

They would contain methods which manipulated the information held in their instance variables, for example in the `LoginLogFile` class there would be arrays containing the date on which an unsuccessful login occurred and details about the login such as the user identity that the intruder tried to use. These classes would also include the full code of a method which indicated the degree of suspicious activities which the file currently contained. For example, the `LoginLogFile` class might calculate a value which depended on the number of incorrect logins every day.

8.3 Interfaces

Java has a form of class inheritance known as **single inheritance**. This means that a class is only allowed to inherit from *one* other class, that the situation shown in Figure 8.3 is not allowed to happen.

Figure 8.3 shows a form of inheritance known as **multiple inheritance**. At the present time multiple inheritance is difficult to implement in a compiler, leads to major inefficiencies and requires a language designer to include facilities which enable problems to be resolved such as the same method name being used in the classes which are inherited from. For these reasons Java has single inheritance.

However, since multiple inheritance can be useful there is a facility which mimics it without having the disadvantages. This facility is known as an **interface**.

An interface is a class definition in which *all* the methods contain no code. A schematic of an interface is shown below:

```
public interface ClassName{

public int methodA();

public void methodB(int a, int b);

public boolean methodC(int a);

}
```

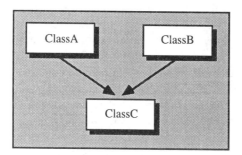

Figure 8.3 Inheritance not allowed in Java.

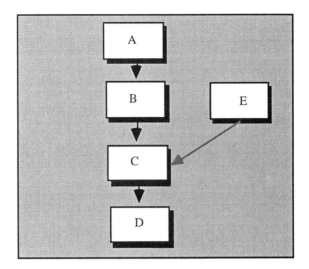

Figure 8.4 An inheritance hierarchy showing the use of an interface E.

Here the class `ClassName` contains three methods where the code is not defined. Any class which uses this class must use the keyword `implements`. Thus, if the class `UseClass` wishes to implement the methods within `ClassName` then the heading of the class must look like:

```
class UseClass implements ClassName{
```

This class must then provide definitions for the three methods `methodA`, `methodB` and `methodC`.

Interfaces allow inheritance hierarchies to be built up where a class can inherit from another class via the interface facility, but where the superclasses of that class do not inherit. This is shown in Figure 8.4.

Here D extends C which, in turn, extends B which again extends A. E is an interface which C promises to implement so that the methods defined in E have to be implemented in C. The important idea here is that when a class implements an interface the programmer of the class makes a promise to implement the methods in that class.

There are two facilities within Java which make extensive use of interfaces. The first is that of Threads, the way that Java implements concurrent processing – a topic dealt with in depth in the next chapter. The second is that of **enumerators**. This is a very clever way of enabling a programmer to travel over the elements of a collection data structure without making use of knowledge of how the data structure is implemented. In order to illustrate this we shall develop a linked list queue which contains Internet entities known as datagrams.

SAQ

If in Figure 8.4 the class A has associated with it the methods a, b and c; class B has methods a, d, and e; class C has methods d, g and h; class D has methods i, j and k; and interface E has three blank or dummy methods p, q and r, which methods are executed when the following occurs?

(i)   class A uses a;

(ii)   class B uses a;

(iii)   class C uses d;

(iv)   class C uses h;

(v)   class D uses p;

(vi)   class D uses j;

(vii)   class B uses r.

Solution

(i) The method a defined in A is executed. (ii) The method a defined in B is executed since it overrides the definition in A. (iii) The method d defined in C is executed. (iv) The method h defined in C is executed. (v) The method that C contains which provides code for the method p which it implements is executed. (vi) The method j defined in class D is executed. (vii) An error occurs since r cannot be found within B or the class A from which it inherits. Only those classes lower than C, or C itself, can execute this method.

Within the Internet there will be computers continually sending or receiving datagrams. Since the datagram traffic in a network can be very high there will be times when datagrams need to be queued up awaiting processing. We could queue these datagrams in an array or a vector. However, there is a problem here in that to cater for a peak number of datagrams awaiting processing we would need to allocate a size of array or a large increment for a vector which would waste memory.

One way of coping with this problem is to store the datagrams in a **dynamic data structure.** Such a structure changes its size – shrinking or expanding according to demand. The defining property of such a data structure is that it only contains enough memory for the current data that it is called on to store. A simple example of a dynamic data structure which contains datagrams is shown in Figure 8.5.

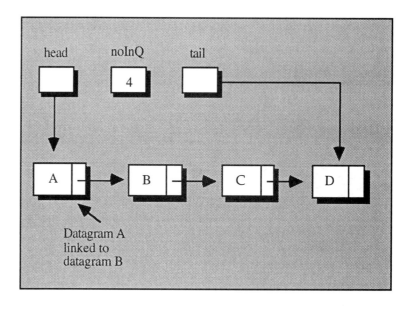

Figure 8.5   A dynamic data structure holding datagrams.

Datagrams

The **datagram** is the basic transfer unit used by the Internet. Each datagram contains data that is to be transferred from one computer to another. It contains a header which provides data that is necessary for both the computer that is sending the datagram and the computers that are receiving the datagram. The header contains information such as:

• The Internet protocol version number of the software that produced the datagram. Internet protocol standards do change and this number gives the receiving computer enough information to enable it to split up the datagram into its constituent elements according to the standard that the sending software is using.

• The length of the datagram in bytes.

• A checksum which is used by the receiving computer to determine whether the datagram has been corrupted.

• The sending address of the computer that originated the datagram.

• The receiving address of the computer to which the datagram has been sent.

Needless to say Java has excellent facilities for processing datagrams.

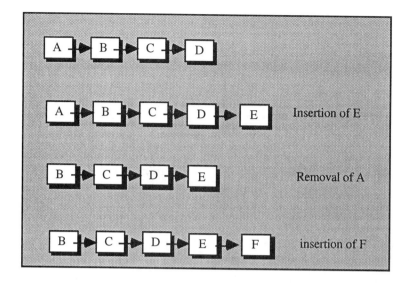

Figure 8.6   The behaviour of a queue under the operations of insertion and removal.

Here, four datagrams are stored. Each item in the queue contains a datagram together with a pointer to the next datagram in the queue. As the queue extends, a new datagram entry is created and linked to the queue.

This position would normally be at the end of the queue. The queue will also have items removed. This will occur at the head of the queue. Associated with the queue are three variables: head contains the address of the first item in the queue, tail contains the address of the last element in the queue and noInQ will contain the number of items in the queue; the last variable will be useful for software which wants to find out the level of transmission of traffic.

We shall assume that four methods are required: addDataGram which adds a datagram to the end of the queue, removeDatagram which removes the first datagram in the queue, dataGramsInQ which returns with the number of items in the queue and emptyQ which returns a Boolean value true if the queue is empty and false otherwise.

The effect of the insertion and removal operation is shown in Figure 8.6; in this figure we do not show the values of the three instance variables. We shall assume the existence of a class DataGramHolder which contains instance variables holding a datagram together with an instance variable which links to the next datagram in the queue by means of holding its address. The definition of the class, together with some of its methods, is shown below:

```
public DataGramHolder(Datagram d){
link = null;
contents = d;}
```

```
public Datagram getContents(){
return contents;
}

public DataGramHolder getLink(){
return link;
}

}
```

The class contains one constructor and two methods which access the values of the two instance variables which make up each `DataGramHolder` object.

The code for the header of the class is shown below together with its constructor.

```
class DataGramQ{
private DataGramHolder head, tail;
private int noInQ;

public DataGramQ(){
head = null;
tail = null;
noInQ = 0;
}
```

SAQ

Write down the definitions of the methods `dataGramsInQ()` and `emptyQ()`.

Solution

The code is shown below:

```
public boolean emptyQ(){
return noInQ == 0;
}

public int dataGramsInQ(){
return noInQ;
}
```

The remaining methods are those which add a datagram to the queue and remove a datagram. The method which carries out the addition is shown below.

```
public void addDataGram(Datagram a){
```

```
DataGramHolder di = new   DataGramHolder(a);
if (noInQ == 0){
  head = di;
tail = di;
}
else{
  tail.link = di;
  tail = di;
}
noInQ++;
}
```

All that is required here is for a new `DataGramHolder` to be created and its address placed in the instance variable `tail` which stores the end of the queue. If the queue was empty, then this newly inserted element also becomes the tail of the queue.

SAQ

Write down the code for the method `removeDataGram`. Don't forget that the method throws an exception when the queue is empty. Assume that this exception is defined elsewhere. Assume that the value of the removed `DataGram` is returned.

Solution

The code for this method is shown below:

```
public Datagram removeDataGram()
throws EmptyQueueException{
if (noInQ == 0)
  throw new EmptyQueueException();
else{
  noInQ--;
  Datagram h = head.getContents();
  head = head.getLink(); return h;}
}
```

If the queue is empty an `EmptyQueueException` exception object is created; if it isn't then the count of the number of items in the queue is decremented, the head is pointed at the next element in the queue and the `DataGram` is returned.

These, then, are the methods which are defined for this class. In order to introduce the use of an interface as an iterator let us assume that we also need to implement a facility whereby we can travel down a queue carrying out some processing.

The Enumeration interface has just two methods associated with it. These are hasMoreElements which returns true if there are more elements to be processed and false otherwise, and nextElement() which returns with the next element that is to be processed as an object described by Object and then moves to the next element. The code for these two methods has to be written for each collection that implements an Enumeration interface. For our example this code is shown below:

```
class QueueEnumeration implements Enumeration{
private DataGramHolder cursor;

public QueueEnumeration(DataGramHolder d){
cursor = d;
}

public boolean hasMoreElements(){
return cursor != null;
}

public Object nextElement(){
Object o = cursor.getContents();
cursor = cursor.getLink();
return o;
}

}
```

The first line states that the Enumeration interface is to be implemented. The second line declares that a private variable cursor is to be used within this class. This variable will track through the elements of the queue as it is processed. The constructor for the enumerator sets this variable to be the argument of the constructor. The definition of the two methods within the enumeration interface follows. The method hasMoreElements checks whether any more elements remain in the collection that is to be processed. Since we are using cursor to track progress, all that is required is to compare the value of cursor to the null object. The second method returns the current object in the collection that cursor points at. It then moves cursor to the next element. In order to allow processing of elements of our DataGramQ we need to make one more change to the class we have defined: we need to add a method which returns a QueueEnumeration which can then be used to carry out the processing. The code for this method is shown below:

```
public QueueEnumeration elements (){
return new QueueEnumeration(head); }
```

This class returns an iterator which has its cursor initialized to the head of the queue. This gives the final code for our classes shown below. Notice that the class now advertises the fact that it throws an EmptyQueueException object and that since we are using the Enumeration interface we need to inform the Java system via an import statement.

```java
import java.util.Enumeration;
//
//
// Class describing each element of a Datagram queue
//
//

class DataGramHolder{
Datagram contents;
DataGramHolder link;

public DataGramHolder(Datagram d){
link = null;
contents = d;
}

public Datagram getContents(){
return contents;
}

public DataGramHolder getLink(){
return link;
}

}

//
//
// Class describing a DataGram queue
//
//

class DataGramQ{
private DataGramHolder head, tail;
private int noInQ;

public DataGramQ(){
head = null;
tail = null;
noInQ = 0;
}

public boolean emptyQ(){
```

```
return noInQ == 0;
}

public int dataGramsInQ(){
return noInQ;
}

public void addDataGram(Datagram a){
DataGramHolder di = new  DataGramHolder(a);
if (noInQ == 0){
   head = di;
   tail = di;
}
else{
   tail.link = di;
   tail = di;
}
noInQ++;
}

public Datagram removeDataGram()
throws EmptyQueueException{
if (noInQ == 0)
   throw new EmptyQueueException();
else{
   noInQ--;
   Datagram h = head.getContents();
   head = head.getLink();
   return h;}
}

public QueueEnumeration elements (){
return new QueueEnumeration(head);
}
//
//
// Class describing the iterator for a DataGram queue
//
//
class QueueEnumeration implements Enumeration{
private DataGramHolder cursor;

public QueueEnumeration(DataGramHolder d){
cursor = d;}
```

```
public boolean hasMoreElements(){
return cursor != null;
}


public Object nextElement(){
Object o = cursor.getContents();
cursor = cursor.getLink(); return o;
}

}
```

An example of a QueueEnumeration object being used is shown below:

```
DataGramQ dq;
Object dGram;
dq = new DataGramQ();
// code which adds elements to dq
QueueEnumeration qe = dq.elements();
while(qe.hasMoreElements()){
  dGram = qe.nextElement();
  System.out.println(" Element = " +
              ((Datagram) dGram).getDatagramValue());
}
```

The important point about this example is that by using an Enumeration we are effectively hiding the implementation of the DataGramQ from the user: no programmer looking at the specification of the methods within the class DataGramQ would know how it was implemented.

8.4 Packages

So far you have seen how packages are provided as part of the Java class library; however, it is perfectly possible for you to create your own packages. In large projects where a considerable number of classes are developed this would be mandatory since nobody wants to carry out long compilations of the huge number of Java source lines that such packages would contain.

When you want to inform the Java system that a collection of classes is to be treated as a package then all you need do is to precede the source code of the classes with the keyword package followed by the name of the package. So, for example, the line:

```
package telNetCommsPackage;
```

would introduce a series of classes which could be treated as a package. The question that this poses is that given such a definition, how do you refer to a package in order to use it in a program?

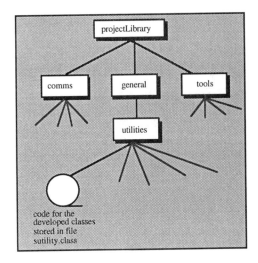

Figure 8.7 A directory hierarchy.

The answer is, of course, to use the import facility. But what do we write after the import keyword? Consider Figure 8.7.

This shows the structure of a typical file directory for a project. Let us focus on the file sutility.class which contains some classes which we want to use as a library (all class source code is stored in files with the *class* extension). If we have declared this class collection in a package defined as:

```
package sutility;
//code for the package
```

then when we want to import the package we quote the directory names and file names separated by dots. So, if we want to use the library contained in the file sutility.class which is contained in the directory utilities which, in turn, is held in the directory general, which forms part of the directory projectLibrary, then we would write:

```
import projectLibrary.general.utilities.sutility;
```

8.5 A further extension to the running example

At this point we shall make a small extension to our running example so that the user of the classes we have developed can iterate through both the Links and LinkData classes. You will remember that the code for the former was:

```
class Links{
private String word;
```

```
private Vector locations;

public Links(String wordToBeCreated){
this (20, wordToBeCreated);
}


public Links (int  size,  String wordToBeCreated){
locations = new Vector(size);
word = wordToBeCreated;
}


public int getnoOfLocations(){
return locations.size();
}


public String getWord(){
return word;
}


public Vector getLocations(){
return locations;
}


public void addLocation(String locationToBeAdded)throws
IllegalArgumentException{
if (locations.contains(locationToBeAdded))
   throw new IllegalArgumentException(
     "Duplicate location " + locationToBeAdded +
     " tried to be added");
else locations.addElement(locationToBeAdded);
}

}
```

Let us assume that we need to be able to iterate over the locations. How can we do this by employing an emumeration? The answer is to add a method which delivers an Enumeration object for the Vector object locations. The code for this is shown below:

```
public Enumeration locationElements(){
return locations.elements();
}
```

This code uses the Vector method elements which itself delivers the enumeration of the objects contained in a Vector object. Again it is important to point out that this method will allow us to return an enumeration of objects described by Object and so, if it was used, casting would have to be employed.

The modification to the code for the class LinksData is similar. We need to iterate over the Links objects contained in the instance variable wordInfo. The code for the method which does this is shown below:

```
public Enumeration linksElements(){
return wordInfo.elements();
}
```

Again it uses the method elements contained in the class Vector. The code for the two classes is now:

```
//
// LinksData class
//

public class LinksData{
Vector   wordInfo;

public LinksData(){
this(100);
}

public LinksData(int size){
wordInfo = new   Vector(size);
}

public int getNoOfWords(){
return wordInfo.size();
}

public void addWord (String word)
throws IllegalArgumentException{
  if (checkWordIn(word))
  throw new IllegalArgumentException
    ("Duplicate word " + word +
      " attempted to be added");
  else{
    int i = 0;
    while (i < wordInfo.size() &&
  (word.compareTo(((Links)wordInfo.elementAt(i)).getWord
  ()) > 0))
      i++;
    for(int j = wordInfo.size(); j > i; j--)
      wordInfo.insertElementAt
          (wordInfo.elementAt(j-1),j);
  wordInfo.insertElementAt(new Links(20, word),i);
```

```
    }
}

public boolean checkWordIn(String word){
int val = findWordIndex(word);
return val != -1;
}

public Enumeration linksElements(){
return wordInfo.elements();
}

private int findWordIndex(String word){
int first = 0, last = wordInfo.size() - 1, middle = 0;
boolean found = false;
while (!found && (first <= last)){
middle = (first+last) / 2;
if(word.compareTo((((Links)wordInfo.elementAt(middle)).
  getWord())) == 0)
  found = true;
else{
  if(word.compareTo((((Links)wordInfo.elementAt(middle))
    .getWord())) < 0)
    last = middle - 1;
  else first = middle + 1;
  }
}
if (!found) return -1;
else return middle;
}

public void addLocation(String loc, String word) throws
IllegalArgumentException{
int pos = findWordIndex(word);
((Links) wordInfo.elementAt(pos)).addLocation(loc);
}
public Vector getLocations(String word){
int pos = findWordIndex(word);
return ((Links)wordInfo.elementAt(pos)).getLocations();
}
//
// Links class
//

class Links{
```

```
private String word;
private Vector locations;

public Links(String wordToBeCreated){
this (20, wordToBeCreated);}

public Links (int  size,  String wordToBeCreated){
locations = new Vector(size);
word = wordToBeCreated;}

public int getnoOfLocations(){
return locations.size();}

public String getWord(){
return word;}

public Vector getLocations(){
return locations;}

public void addLocation(String locationToBeAdded)throws
IllegalArgumentException{
if (locations.contains(locationToBeAdded))
   throw new IllegalArgumentException(
   "Duplicate location " + locationToBeAdded + " found");
else locations.addElement(locationToBeAdded);}

public Enumeration locationElements(){
return locations.elements();}

}
```

8.6 SUMMARY

This chapter has described a number of topics which are concerned with the large-scale development of Java code. We have shown how abstract classes mirror the abstraction levels in an inheritance hierarchy. We have demonstrated that interfaces enable us to have a form of multiple inheritance within Java, without the normal problems which accompany this facility within other languages such as Eiffel. We concluded by showing how you can develop packages and how they are identified.

CHAPTER NINE

Threads

- To outline the reasons for having thread support in Java.
- To describe how threads are created.
- To describe many of the facilities which are provided by the Thread class.
- To show how the use of the synchronized modifier leads to a secure implementation of multi-threading.

9.1 Introduction

A millisecond may not seem very long; however, in computer terms a lot can happen in such a small moment in time, for example hundreds of thousands of programming instructions could be executed. During the execution of a simple program there will often be times when a program will be idle for many milliseconds waiting for something to happen. Examples of this are:

- A program awaiting the response of a user who is to key in some characters from a keyboard.

- A program awaiting the retrieval of data from a disk drive, a mechanical device which can take many milliseconds to carry out its work.

- The wait that occurs when the frames of an animation are being loaded.

These are just a few of the events that can occur during the execution of a computer program which can waste an appreciable amount of the resources. In highly interactive programs as much as 99% of the processor time of the program might be idle.

Threading is an approach to sharing the resources of a computer in such a way that when a sequence of program code can proceed no further another sequence of code is executed. When this sequence is held up, another sequence of code – perhaps even the one which was originally held up - can be executed.

The name given to these collections of code is a **thread**. A thread is treated as an object in Java. The Thread class within the java.lang library contains this class; it has within it a number of methods for creating, destroying and modifying threads.

Threads can be created in two ways: by inheriting from the Thread class or by implementing a Java interface known as Runnable.

Exercise

Why do you think Java has this facility? Surely inheriting from Thread would be good enough?

Solution

The problem is that a class may already have inherited from another class and you may want to make it a thread by inheriting from Thread as well. As you will already have seen Java explicitly forbids this form of multiple inheritance; however, an interface can be used and hence Java provides one known as Runnable which implements threads.

9.2 Creating threads

As the previous section has described there are two methods of creating threads: via inheritance from the class Thread and by using the Runnable interface. This section describes these two methods.

An example of thread creation using the former is shown below:

```
Class ArrayInit extends Thread{
// any instance variables

public void run(){
(int i = 0; i < aArrLength; i++)
   a[i] = 0;
(int i = 0; i < bArrLength; i++)
   b[i] = 0;
}

}
```

This creates a chunk of code which is treated as an executable whole. Part of the Thread class is a method called run() which needs to be overriden by the code that you are going to nominate as a thread: in the case above this code initializes the first aArrLength items of an array a to zero and the first bArrLength items in b to zero.

So far all we have done is to create a class which describes a certain type of thread. To execute the code associated with this thread we need to create the thread and then execute an instruction for it to run. This is achieved by the code below:

```
ArrayInit a = new ArrayInit();
...
a.start();
...
```

What this does is to create a new thread object and then use the method start() defined in the class Thread to start the execution of the code defined in run(). This code will execute to termination.

So far we have started the thread; there is also a method within the class Thread which carries out the process of stopping a thread. This is the method stop(). If you wish to stop a thread a from executing all you need write is:

```
a.stop()
```

So far we have not really described anything that is particularly useful: we could have achieved the effect of starting and stopping the code in a thread object just by executing it in the normal way. In order to be useful we first need some facility whereby a thread could suspend itself so that control can be passed to another thread. This is the function of the sleep() method found in the class Thread. Let us assume that in the code we presented above we wanted to suspend the code within the thread for a specified time of 1 millisecond after the array a has been executed so that another thread can execute; we would write the definition of the thread as:

```
Class ArrayInit extends Thread{
// any instance variables

public void run(){
for (int i = 0; i < aArrLength; i++)
  a[i] = 0;
try{Thread.sleep(10);
} catch(InterruptedException e) {};
for (int i = 0; i < bArrLength; i++)
  b[i] = 0;
}

}
```

sleep(10) is a call on the method sleep() defined within the Thread class. Since it does not have a receiver object it is applied to any ArrayInit object.

What it does is to block the progress of the thread for 10 milliseconds (the argument to sleep()).

You will notice that we have monitored whether an Interrupted-Exception exception has been thrown. The reason for this is that sleep (and a number of other Thread methods) throw this exception when another thread has attempted to interrupt the progress of a thread. This is a drastic way of accessing a thread; in this example there is little likelihood that this would happen and hence we shall assume that no method will interrupt and hence we will have an empty interrupt handler.

The action of the code above is then to initialize the array a, block the progress of the thread for 10 millisecond and then carry on the final processing of the initialization of the array b. Once this code has been completed the thread dies. Another way that the code can be blocked is if the code between the two array initializations contained some task which was to take a considerable time to carry out with execution waiting until the task has been completed, for example the retrieval of a considerable amount of data from a slow input device. This is shown below:

```
Class ArrayInit extends Thread{
// any instance variables

public void run(){
for (int i = 0; i < aArrLength; i++)
  a[i] = 0;
//code which carries out some activity which requires
//a long time to complete
for (int i = 0; i < bArrLength; i++)
  b[i] = 0;
}

}
```

Here the thread is executed and the following happens:

- The array a is initialized.

- The thread is blocked while waiting for a long input operation to terminate. Other threads can then execute.

- Other thread(s) are run; eventually the thread that has blocked will be able to start up again and the Java system will eventually execute the code from the point where it was blocked.

- The array b is initialized.

The blocking of the thread is achieved by the Java system when it realizes that some lengthy task is to be carried out such as an input/output task.

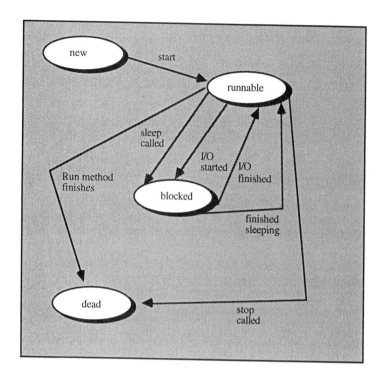

Figure 9.1 The states that a thread can exist in.

When a thread is blocked – either because it has called sleep, other code has sent a sleep message to the thread or it is awaiting a lengthy task to be completed – the Java system looks for another thread to be executed which can be run. The states that a thread can progress through are shown in Figure 9.1.

A thread is made runnable by means of it being created using new. It is not immediately run (there may be another thread which is being run by the computer processor). At certain times during the execution of a program that contains threads the Java system will have a look at all the runnable threads and will execute one of these (which one it picks will be described later). This decision may be prompted by the fact that the current thread that is running may have become blocked by virtue of the fact that it is waiting for an I/O transfer or by the use of sleep.

When a thread is blocked it can be made runnable by two events: first, the I/O task which was blocking it could have finished or the time for which it was asked to sleep could have finished. Finally a thread becomes dead when the run() method code terminates or when another thread sends a stop() message to the thread.

There are other ways of changing the state of a thread, and later in this chapter we will describe them. The important concept that you should be happy with at this stage is that a Java program consists of a series of threads, some of which are runnable and ready to be executed by a processor and others which are unable to proceed and are blocked. Above all this is a component of the Java system known as the **scheduler** which makes decisions about which thread to run next.

Exercise

The following actions occur in a Java program which has created four threads:

> Threads a and b are runnable, thread c is currently running and thread d is blocked awaiting an I/O transfer.

> Thread c sends itself to sleep for 3 milliseconds.

(i) Which threads can the Java system choose to run at this stage?

> Assume that thread a is chosen. It is run and makes an I/O request after 1 millisecond.

(ii)   Which threads can the system choose to run at this stage?

> Assume that b is chosen. After 1 millisecond this thread sends itself to sleep for 5 milliseconds.

(iii)   Which threads can the system choose to run at this stage?

Solution

The answers are:

(i)   Since thread d is blocked and thread c is blocked because it has sent itself to sleep for 3 ms, then either a or b, both of which are runnable, can be executed.

(ii)   The only thread capable of being run is b since all the others have been blocked.

(iii)   The system is unable to choose any thread to execute. Thread a is blocked because of an I/O transfer, c and d are still blocked and thread b is blocked since it sent itself to sleep for 5 milliseconds and this time is not yet up. The processor will idle until a thread becomes runnable. (In reality the processor will occupy itself with system-level activities such as running the garbage collector.)

Before looking at more aspects of the change of state of threads it is worth looking at the other way of creating them: via the Runnable interface. This is an interface which just contains one method, run(). To create the `ArrayInit` thread that we created using inheritance all we need do is write:

```
Class ArrayInit implements Runnable{
// any instance variables

public void run(){
(int i = 0; i < aArrLength; i++)
  a[i] = 0;
try{
  sleep(10);
} catch(InterruptedExecution e) {};
(int i = 0; i < bArrLength; i++)
  b[i] = 0;
}

}
```

Here the run() method code which forms part of the Runnable interface is provided within `ArrayInit`.

It is important to point out that you can create threads which have local instance variables. For example, the code below shows a thread which has two instance variables which are ints and two constructors which set these values:

```
Class TwoIntThread implements Runnable{
int first, second;

public TwoIntThread(){
this(0,0);}

public TwoIntThread(int a, b){
{first = a;
second = b;}

public void run(){
// code for TwoIntThread
}

}
```

The no-argument constructor initializes the instance variables to zero, while the two-argument constructor initializes the variables to its arguments.

It is important to point out that these two instance variables are not shared between threads; that is, if you wrote the code:

```
TwoIntThread a, b, c, d;

...
a = new TwoIntThread (10, 34);
```

```
b = new TwoIntThread (16, 32);
c = new TwoIntThread (15, 100);
d = new TwoIntThread (11, 100);
...
```

then each of the instance variables associated with a, b, c and d are separate: there are not just two instance variables but each object is associated with its own two instance variables. Consequently, the constructor in the second line will not overwrite the instance variables within the thread a. This may not seem an important point to make now. However, when the instance variables refer to common objects a serious problem occurs. We will discuss this problem later and describe its solution.

9.3 Suspend and resume methods

So far we have described ways in which a thread can be blocked and eventually become unblocked: the sleep method only makes a thread blocked for a finite amount of time and the blocking of a thread by an I/O transfer will stop after the transfer has ceased. There is a need in thread programming for a method which blocks a thread until it is explicitly unblocked. This is the role of the suspend() and resume() methods found in the thread library.

suspend() blocks a thread from running. A thread to which a suspend message has been sent will remain permanently blocked until a resume() message is sent to it. Figure 9.2 shows the modification of Figure 9.1 which demonstrates this.

9.4 Thread priorities

One question which you would be forgiven for asking at this stage is: how does the scheduler in the Java system make a decision about which thread to run? The answer is that threads are given a priority between 1 and 10. These are contained in the Thread class as static constants MIN_PRIORITY and MAX_PRIORITY with the former having the value 1 and the latter having the value 10. When a thread is created it will have a value of 5; this is implemented in the Thread class as the constant NORM_PRIORITY.

The decision that the scheduler makes about running a thread which is runnable is simple: it finds the thread with the highest priority and then runs it. The scheduler is invoked whenever a thread which is running becomes blocked or when a thread which has a higher priority than the current running thread becomes unblocked.

The priority of threads can be dynamically changed by sending a setPriority message to the thread. For example, the code:

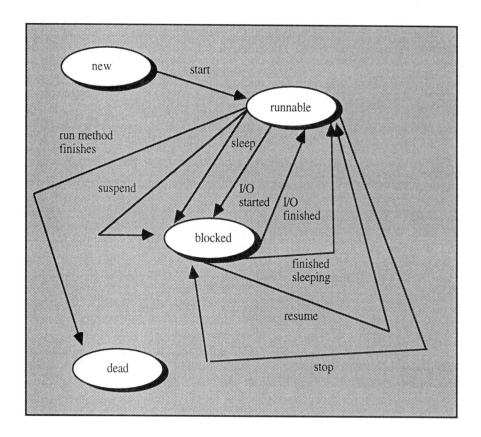

Figure 9.2 The states of a thread showing the effect of suspend() and resume().

```
ExThread a, b, c, d;
...
a.ExThread.start();
b.ExThread.start();
c.ExThread.start();
d.ExThread.start();
...
a.setPriority(Thread.MAX_PRIORITY);
b.setPriority(Thread.MIN_PRIORITY);
c.setPriority(6);
d.setPriority(9);
```

resets the priorities of the four threads a, b, c and d to be 10, 1, 6 and 9 respectively since when threads are initially created they are given a priority value of 5.

Exercise

Assume that four threads are currently capable of being run. These threads are called a, b, c and d; a has a priority of 3, b has a priority of 2, c has a priority of 9 and d has a priority of 8. At one point in the execution of the Java program that runs these threads a and b have been blocked awaiting an I/O transfer. Currently c is running and d is runnable.

The following events occur:

> c is blocked awaiting an I/O transfer.

(i) Which thread is executed by the processor?

> The I/O transfer associated with threads a and b are completed and they both become runnable.

(ii) What happens now?

> Thread c is unblocked because its I/O transfer is completed.

(iii) Now what happens?

Solution

The solutions are:

(i)   Since d is the only thread capable of being run it is executed by the processor.

(ii)   Nothing happens since both a and b have a lower priority than the current running thread (d). Thread d continues running.

(iii)   Since thread c has a higher priority than the current running thread (thread d) the scheduler picks it for execution and it runs.

9.5 The problem with shared objects

We now seem to have quite a nice toolkit for the manipulation of threads. Unfortunately, our discussion of this toolkit has not mentioned one problem which occurs with threads. It is connected with the topic of shared objects. This is not just a problem that occurs in Java or any other object-oriented programming language; it has occurred in programming languages ever since computer hardware first enabled us to share processing between code.

This is the problem of access to shared resources. Consider the code for the thread SharedThread shown below:

```
class SharedThread implements Runnable{
Employee curr;
Int salaryIncrement;

sharedThread(Employee e, int i){
curr = e;
salaryIncrement = i;
}

public void run(){
curr.increment(i);
}

}
```

This thread implements the process of adding an amount to the current month's salary of employees when, for example, they have achieved a higher level of sales than their target.

This thread works by sending an `increment` message to an `Employee` object, where this method is defined in the class `Employee`. Let us assume that the increment method will do something like:

```
public void increment(int i){
currentMonthSalary = currentMonthSalary + i;
}
```

where `currentMonthSalary` is an instance variable defined in the class `Employee`.

Let us assume that in a section of program we have the code:

```
s1 = new SharedThread(jones, 12);
...
s2 = new SharedThread(jones, 18);
...
s2.start();
s1.start();
...
```

We would expect that the employee Jones's salary would have increased by 30 dollars or pounds. Often this would be true. However, sometimes this does not happen. What is the reason for this?

The reason is that two threads are attempting to access and update the same object (the object represented by the employee Jones). In order to explain what has happened we shall assume that the memory location which holds the instance variable of the employee Jones is location 56678, and that the process of updating this location by adding a salary increment is achieved by the following atomic machine instructions:

- Get the monthly salary amount from location 56678 and place it in a register A.

- Add the increment to it in the register.

- Write the new monthly salary amount back to the location 56678 from the register.

Let us assume that the threads s2 and s1 are runnable and that s2 is chosen to start this process going. We shall also assume that the current monthly salary of Jones is 1500. The first thing that happens is:

(1) Thread s2 gets the monthly salary amount from location 56678 and places it in a register A. A now contains 1500.

(2) Thread s2 then adds 18 to the register which now contains 1518.

Assume at this point that the execution of the thread is interrupted, for example a higher priority thread has been unblocked and is then run. Once this higher priority thread has finished the scheduler picks another thread to execute. Let us assume that this is thread s1. If we assume that s1 completely executes its code and then dies what will happen is:

(3) Thread s1 gets the monthly salary amount from location 56678 and places it in a register A. A now contains 1500.

(4) Thread s1 then adds 12 to the register which now contains 1512.

(5) Thread s1 then writes the contents of register A to location 56678, which now contains 1512.

The thread s1 now dies since it has completed its processing. The Java scheduler now chooses another thread. Assume that some time in the future it picks thread s2 which is runnable and which has carried out its first two tasks. Thread s2 will finish its execution and will:

(6) Write the contents of register A to location 56678. The register will contain the value 1512 from the code which s1 has executed. This is written back to location 56678 and the location will still contain 1512.

Thus, instead of containing 1530 the location contains an erroneous value. This has occurred because of the interruption of processing by the thread s2 of the processing of thread s1. This problem will occur in any context where threads access some data which is shared between them. The solution adopted by Java and a number of other programming languages is to designate certain methods which access shared data as synchronized. This is achieved by prefacing the method with the keyword synchronized. Thus the code above for increment would be written as:

```
public synchronized void increment(int i){
currentMonthSalary = currentMonthSalary + i;
}
```

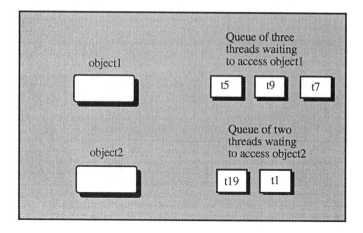

Figure 9.3 Threads waiting to enter a synchronized method.

When a thread enters the code of a synchronized method, the rule is that no other thread can interrupt its processing by gaining access to the shared data: the thread that has entered completes the processing.

Now during the processing there may be a number of threads trying to access an object. What happens to them? Well, the answer is that the Java system maintains, for each created object which is associated with a class that has synchronized methods, a queue of processes awaiting permission to access this object. This is shown in Figure 9.3.

Such objects which are associated with thread queues are known as **monitors.** Does this solve the problem? Almost, but not quite. In order to put the last pieces of the jigsaw in place we will need to consider another example.

9.6 The circular buffer

A **buffer** is a set of memory locations used to store data which is produced and consumed by a number of programs. For example, a buffer is used when data is transferred from a user program to a printer: the user program deposits data that is required to be printed into a buffer and the program operating the printer takes the data out of the buffer. One popular way of implementing a buffer is as a circular queue. An example of such a queue is shown in Figure 9.4.

This shows that a circular buffer is represented as a fixed length array with two instance variables which point at the beginning and end of the array. One variable contains the first location in the buffer and the second variable contains the final location in the array.

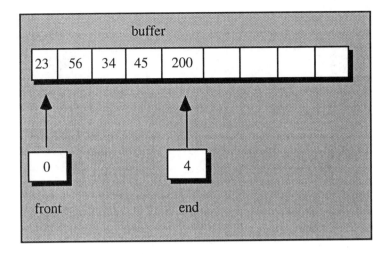

Figure 9.4 An example of a circular buffer.

When an item is removed from the array the element pointed at is taken off and the front pointer incremented by one. When an item is added to the array the end pointer is incremented and the item is written to the location it now points at. If the item to be added overflows the end of the buffer it is added to the front of the buffer.

A class describing a circular buffer is shown below. As well as having two pointers as instance variables, it also has an instance variable noInBuffer which contains the current number of items in the buffer and an instance variable bufferLength which contains the maximum number of items in the buffer. For the sake of simplicity we shall assume that the buffer contains integers.

```
class CircBuffer{
private int front, end, noInBuffer, bufferLength;
private int [] buffer;

CircBuffer(int length){
buffer = new int [length];
front = 0;
bufferLength = length;
end = -1;
noInBuffer = 0;
}

CircBuffer(){
this(100);
}
```

```
public void addItemToBuffer(int i)
throws BufferFullException{
if (noInBuffer < bufferLength){
  if (end == bufferLength)
    end = 0;
  else
    end++;
  buffer[end] = i;
  noInBuffer++;
}
else
  throw new BufferFullException();
}


public int removeItemFromBuffer()
throws BufferEmptyException{
int value;
if (noInBuffer > 0){
  value = buffer[front];
  if (front == bufferLength)
    front = 0;
  else
    front++;
  noInBuffer--;
  return value;
}
else
  throw new BufferEmptyException();
}


public int noInBuffer(){
return noInBuffer;
}

}
```

The class contains two constructors, one of which defaults the buffer to 100 locations. It also throws two exceptions – one when the buffer is full and one when the buffer is empty – which we shall assume are defined elsewhere.

This is a good implementation of a buffer in a non-threaded application. However, it is not so good when there might be a large number of threads adding and removing data from the buffer. For example, the buffer might contain datagrams which are being deposited in it by a number of computers which are connected to the computer running the buffer application.

| Exercise |

Why do you not think this is such a good implementation for a threaded environment?

| Solution |

The reason is that if the buffer is empty then the method which retrieves a value from the buffer exits since an exception is thrown. In a threaded environment there may be a number of processes just about to write data to the buffer and what is needed is for this method to wait for this to happen. Similarly the method which adds an item to the buffer exits if the buffer is full, even when there may be some threads about to write data to the buffer.

Another problem, of course, is that the buffer becomes a shared resource and some of the methods within the circular buffer class need to be declared as synchronized.

An alternative solution which programs the two methods to wait is shown below.

```
class CircBuffer {
private int front, end, noInBuffer, bufferLength;
private int [] buffer;

CircBuffer(int length){
buffer = new int [length];
front = 0;
bufferLength = length;
end = -1;
noInBuffer = 0;
}

CircBuffer(){
this(100);
}

public synchronized void addItemToBuffer(int i)
{
while (noInBuffer == bufferLength)
try{
  Thread.sleep(20);}
catch (InterruptedException e){};
if (end == bufferLength)
  end = 0;
else
```

```
  end++;
buffer[end] = i;
noInBuffer++;
}

public synchronized int removeItemFromBuffer()
{
int value;
while (noInBuffer == 0)
try{
   Thread.sleep(20);}
catch (InterruptedException e){};
value = buffer[front];
if (front == bufferLength)
   front = 0;
else
   front++;
noInBuffer--;
return value;
}

public int noInBuffer(){
return noInBuffer;
}

}
```

Here, the code:

```
while (noInBuffer == bufferLength)
try{
   Thread.sleep(20);}
catch (InterruptedException e){};
```

in the method which adds items to the buffer sends the thread to sleep for 20 ms while the value of noInBuffer remains equal to length; that is, the buffer is full. Also, the code:

```
while (noInBuffer == 0)
try{
   Thread.sleep(20);}
catch (InterruptedException e){};
```

within the method that removes items from the buffer puts the thread to sleep until the buffer contains at least one item. This looks quite a nice solution to the problem. However, you may remember that at the end of the last section we said that there is still an open problem left to solve with regard to synchronized methods.

In order to focus in on this problem let us concentrate on the method which adds items to the buffer. When the code which sends the current thread to sleep is executed we would hope that another thread would add at least one item to the buffer. When this happens and the current thread awakes from its sleep it can continue executing. Unfortunately, no thread can do anything to the buffer object since its methods are synchronized: only one thread – the current one which is sleeping – is allowed access at a time. We get over this problem by using a technique which uses two more methods, wait and notify.

The wait method is defined in the Object class and when it is called during an object access by a thread it deactivates the thread and places it on the queue of threads waiting to access the object. This, for example, gives another thread the chance to add an item to the buffer and when the read thread is activated again there would be data there. The wait method is associated with another method known as notify. This method is called when the state of an object has changed and the threads in the queue for that object can be given a chance to access it. Sending a notify message informs the queue that another thread can now access the object. Our code will now become:

```
class CircBuffer {
private int front, end, noInBuffer, bufferLength;
private int [] buffer;

CircBuffer(int length){
buffer = new int [length];
front = 0;
bufferLength = length;
end = -1;
noInBuffer = 0;
}

CircBuffer(){
this(100);
}

public synchronized void addItemToBuffer(int i){
while (noInBuffer == bufferLength)
try{
  wait();}
catch (InterruptedException e){};
if (end == bufferLength)
  end = 0;
else
  end++;
buffer[end] = i;
noInBuffer++;
notify();}
```

```
public synchronized int removeItemFromBuffer(){
int value;
while (noInBuffer == 0)
try{
  wait();}
catch (InterruptedException e){};
value = buffer[front];
if (front == bufferLength)
  front = 0;
else
  front++;
noInBuffer--; notify();
return value;
}

public int noInBuffer(){
return noInBuffer;
}

}
```

This seems a complicated idea. However, it translates into a simple set of rules:

(1) If two or more threads modify a common object then declare the methods that do the modifying as being synchronized.

(2) If a thread needs to wait for an object to change make sure that it waits inside the thread. It does this by entering a synchronized method and calling wait().

(3) When a method has changed an object it should call the notify method before terminating. This gives other methods a chance to access the object.

9.7 SUMMARY

We have described some of the facilities of the Thread library and how the one problem that arises with threads – that of shared access to objects – can be overcome by means of the synchronized facility. Later in this book, in Chapter 13 which deals with communication system programming in Java and Chapter 12 which deals with the programming of applets, you will see threads being put extensively to work.

CHAPTER TEN

Input and Output

- To describe the general features of the I/O library in Java.
- To describe some of the more useful facilities for I/O in Java.

10.1 Introduction

So far we have ignored the question of how data is communicated to a Java program. There are effectively two ways: via some sequential source such as a file or another computer, or via some human-computer interface. The aim of this chapter is to look at the former. The next chapter will deal with the latter. The facilities that we discuss in this chapter will be useful whatever the source of data that your Java programs will process: whether it is a file, your keyboard or another computer.

10.2 Streams

Java relies on the concept of a stream for providing its input/output facilities. A **stream**, sometimes referred to as a **byte stream**, contains a sequence of bytes. In Java there are 22 different stream types. These include streams which allow random access, which provide line numbers as well as the data that is to be read or written, and streams which just process bytes. All the streams which are provided in Java can be found in the `java.io` package, so that any program that uses streams needs to include the statement:

```
import java.io.*;
```

at its head.

The `System` class found in `java.io` provides three existing streams, `System.in`, `System.out` and `System.error`. `System.in` is the standard input stream and will normally be taken from the keyboard of your computer.

System.out is the standard output stream and is normally directed to the screen of your computer. System.error is the stream that will contain error information when an I/O error occurs.

In order to give you an idea of the processing that occurs with streams, consider the code shown below. This processes a useful type of stream known as a DataInputStream. This is a stream which reads individual scalar values such as ints, chars and strings. In the example the DataInputStream is formed from System.In. The output from the program is placed on System.out.

```
DataInputStream inputVal =
     new DataInputStream(System.in);
String readString;
try{
  while ((readString = inputVal.readLine())!= null)
    System.out.println(readString);
}
catch(IOException i)
   {System.out.println("An I/O Error has occurred");}
```

This program will read lines from a keyboard until a null line has occurred (this is usually when the person providing the data types the Ctrl-Z character). Each line is read and then sent to the System.out stream which is normally attached to the screen of the originating computer.

An important point to notice is that the code for reading data in is enclosed within a try-catch block. This is because I/O operations are quite capable of generating errors such as an attempt at reading past the end of a file. The exception IOException is a Java exception which is thrown when an I/O error occurs.

This, then, gives you a flavour of what input/output looks like in Java. The remainder of this chapter will look at some of the more important streams and provide a summary of the capabilities of the remainder of the streams.

10.3 Some important streams

10.3.1 The class PrintStream

Print streams allow you to carry out text output. Already you have seen one example of a print stream: the System.out object. A print stream can print any string or number in a text format. It is quite easy to create a print stream object: its constructor takes as its single argument any output stream object. An example of its use is shown below:

```
FileOutputStream f =
  new FileOutputStream("compData.dat");
PrintStream p = new PrintStream(f);
```

Table 10.1 Some print methods.

Method	Meaning
print(String s)	Prints a string in ASCII
print(double d)	Prints a double length integer
print (char[] s)	Prints an array of characters
print(char c)	Prints a character in ASCII
print (int i)	Prints an integer
print(long l)	Prints a long integer
print(float f)	Prints a floating point number
print(Object o)	Prints an object
print (boolean b)	Prints a Boolean

Here, we have created another stream called a `FileOutputStream` which is connected to a file which will contain output data (we will describe this type of stream in Section 10.4). We then use this stream as an argument to the constructor which creates the `PrintStream p`. This has the effect of creating a new empty file with the name `compData.dat` which is initially empty.

The `PrintStream` class supports a number of print methods. These print data values (print) or data values followed by a new line (println). So, for example, the code below shows the creation of a file to which three integers are written, with the final integer followed by a new line.

```
try{FileOutputStream fos =
  new FileOutputStream("salData.txt");
int a, b, c;
PrintStream ps = new PrintStream(fos);
// a, b and c gain values here
ps.print(a); ps.print(b);
ps.println(c);
}
catch(IOException e){
  System.out.println("Problem occurred in I/O");}
}
```

Again note the use of the `try-catch` since an I/O problem such as the file `salData.txt` not being found might occur. It is easy to remember the print messages that are associated with the `PrintStream` class: most of them are called either `print` or `println`, irrespective of the data that is to be printed. Remember that `System.out` is already a `PrintStream` object, so that there is no need for the first few lines of the code above. All that you need do is to write:

```
System.out.print(a); System.out.print(b);
System.out.println(c);
```

A list of useful print methods associated with the `PrintStream` class is shown in Table 10.1. Each is also associated with a corresponding `println` method which issues a new line just after printing the argument.

10.3.2 DataStreams

These streams allow you to write scalar data. There are two types of stream represented by the `DataStream` class; these are the classes `DataInputStream` and `DataOuputStream`. DataInputStreams are associated with methods which are of the form:

```
readBasicType()
```

so, for example, if you wish to read an integer from an InputDataStream `i` and assign it to the int variable `hVal` then you would write:

```
hVal = i.readInt();
```

and if you wish to read a Boolean value from the InputDataStream `i` and assign it to the variable `setNext` then you would write:

```
setNext = i.readBoolean();
```

The way that you set up data streams is similar to that shown for print streams. For example, the code:

```
FileInputStream fis =
   new FileInputStream("salData.txt");
DataInputStream ds = new DataInputStream(fis);
```

sets up a `DataInputStream` associated with the file `salData.txt`. A selection of methods associated with this stream is shown as Table 10.2.

Table 10.2 Some methods associated with the class `DataInputStream`.

Method	Meaning
read(byte[])	Reads data into an array of bytes
readBoolean()	Reads a Boolean value
readChar()	Reads a character
readDouble()	Reads a double length floating point value
readFloat()	Reads a floating point value
readLine()	Reads the end of a line
readLong()	Reads a long integer
readInt()	Reads an integer

Table 10.3 Some methods associated with the `DataOutputStream` class.

Method	Meaning
`write(int i)`	Writes a byte
`writeBoolean(boolean b)`	Writes a Boolean value
`writeBytes(String s)`	Writes a string
`writeChar(char c)`	Writes a character
`writeDouble(double d)`	Writes a double length floating point number
`writeFloat(float f)`	Writes a floating point number
`writeInt(int i)`	Writes an integer
`writeLong(long l)`	Writes a long integer

The second type of stream is the `DataOutputStream`. This is the output analogue of the `DataInputStream`. It allows writing data to a stream which can be reprocessed using a `DataInputStream` object.

The majority of methods associated with this stream are of the form:

```
writeBasicType()
```

so, for example, if you wish to write a Boolean b to an OutputDataStream o, then this would be achieved by the code:

```
o.writeBoolean(b)
```

and if you wanted to write a long integer `lk` to the same output stream then you would write:

```
o.writeLong(lk)
```

Again such streams are set up by using an existing `Stream` class. An example is shown below:

```
FileOutputStream fos =
  new FileOutputStream("salData.txt");
DataOutputStream ds = new DataOutputStream(fos);
```

This creates a file `salData.txt` and prepares it for writing by methods such as `writeBoolean` and `writeLong`.

A list of useful methods associated with this class is shown in Table 10.3.

10.4 Other classes

You will find yourself using the classes described in Section 10.3 most of the time. However, there are a number of other classes which Java provides that are worth mentioning. We will not describe them in much detail: you will find the details of the methods in the class documentation that comes with the Java system.

RandomAccessFile. This class implements a stream which is associated with a file that can be processed randomly. The classes described in the previous section were sequential: you had to read the items in a stream in the order in which they were written. The RandomAccessFile class removes this restriction. It allows you to set a pointer anywhere in a file and then read the data after that pointer. This class is ideal for an application based on some form of query processing. For example, if you had a file containing statistical information about a large number of computers and you wanted to retrieve information about a single computer, then this class would be the one to use.

BufferedInputStream. This stream is used in applications where a source provides data slower than the Java program can cope with. The data that is waiting to be processed by the methods of BufferedInputStream is then stored in an area of memory known as a buffer.

BufferedOutputStream. Similar to BufferedInputStream except that data is transferred *from* the Java program.

FileInputStream. You have seen this stream in action in the previous sections. It creates an input stream which is associated with a file.

FileOutputStream. The output analogue of InputStream. It creates a stream associated with an output file.

LineNumberInputStream. This stream is associated with an Inputstream and provides a line number for each line that is processed.

10.5 The StringTokenizer class

The example which we are going to describe processes a string and splits it up into individual tokens. In many programming languages such a process is often very fiddly to program. However, in Java there is a facility which enables this splitting to be programmed very easily. This facility is provided by the StringTokenizer class which can be found in java.util. A StringTokenizer object is very much like an enumeration object in that it enables the programmer to travel down a string extracting all the substrings terminated by particular characters in a painless way. A sample declaration of a StringTokenizer is shown below:

```
StringTokenizer st =
  new StringTokenizer(strToBeProcessed, " \n\t\r");
```

This sets up a tokenizer which is to examine and extract all the substrings within the string strToBeProcessed that are terminated by the stop characters held in the second argument: a tab, a space, an end of string or a return. Thus it picks up any substring which is terminated by white space and, of course, the final substring.

Associated with the `StringTokenizer` class are a number of methods which carry out the traversal of the string and the checking that the final substring has been extracted. The two most important are:

`String nextToken()`. This extracts out the next string delimited by the stop characters and moves a pointer to the next string.

`boolean hasMoreTokens()`. This returns true if there are more tokens to be processed in the string that is being traversed.

An example of this class being used is shown below. It shows code which finds the first three substrings within `eMailAddress` which are terminated by a period.

```
StringTokenizer tt =
    new StringTokenizer(eMailAddress, ".");

String    first = nextToken(tt),
          second = nextToken(tt),
          third = nextToken(tt);
```

Exercise

The string `nameSpace` contains a number of substrings which are separated by either '|' or ',' characters. Write code which places all these substrings in a string array `collArr` and places a count of the number of substrings processed in the variable `count`. Do not worry about declaring it as a method, just write the code.

Solution

```
int count = 0;
String nameSpace;
String[] collArr;

// code which gives nameSpace a value

StringTokenizer st =
    new StringTokenizer(nameSpace, "|,");
while(st.hasMoreTokens()){
    collArr[count] = (String) st.nextToken(); count++;
}
```

10.6 An example

In order to reinforce the teaching of this chapter we will describe two examples. The second is an extension of our running example and will be presented at the end of the chapter. The one described here concerns the output from a utility program used by network system administrators.

Routing Tables

A routing table is a data structure which contains the names of the computers in a network and the connections between each computer. Such a table is used by the network system software to determine the route that a data package to be sent from one computer to another computer will take. In large networks the number of routes is almost infinite and to determine an optimal route the communications software will consult the routing table. There are a number of utilities which enable a system administrator to examine data connected with routing tables. One of the most popular is Netstat. A typical output from Netstat is shown below:

Destination	Gateway	Flags	Refs	Use	Interface
Ihj	rpcw	U	7	12	Ik0
Camelot	rpcw	UH	0	22	Ilu0
Mirian	Mirian	UH	99	200	jj0
Merlin	Mirian	UH	200	12	kk0

Each line shows the name of a destination computer; the name of the gateway to be used; a flag which indicates whether the route is active (U) and whether it is connected to a gateway (G) or a host (H); a reference counter which describes how many connections can be made simultaneously; a count of the number of packets of data that have been sent over the route; and the name of the interface.

The section of code that is associated with this example will take a file of data which conforms to the format shown above and produces: the number of routes, the total number of packets of data sent, and the number of computers which are both destinations and gateways.

Assume that the data has been placed in the file nestatef.dat and that each line consists of a string into which the data is embedded as substrings. Also assume that we are sending the results to a file nestater.res.

The code which establishes the input stream is shown below:

```
FileInputStream ni =
  new FileInputStream("nestatef.dat");
DataInputStream di = new DataInputStream(ni);
```

The code for the DataOutputStream is shown below:

```
FileOutputStream no =
  new FileOutputStream("nestater.res");
DataOutputStream dou = new DataOutputStream(no);
```

Exercise

Write down the code that carries out the processing. Read each line as a string and then use any method(s) in the class java.lang.Integer to carry out the conversion to the two integers that are needed. You will need to split up each line using the StringTokenizer class described earlier in this chapter. Assume that the file contains correct data.

Solution

The code is shown below:

```
int totalPackets = 0, totalRoutes = 0,
totalHostAndGate = 0, refs, use;
String destination, gateway, flags, readString;
StringTokenizer st;
try{ FileInputStream ni =
  new FileInputStream("nestatef.dat");
DataInputStream di = new DataInputStream(ni);
FileOutputStream no =
  new FileOutputStream("nestater.res");
DataOutputStream dou = new DataOutputStream(no);
  while ((readString = di.readLine()) != null){
    st = new StringTokenizer(readString," \t\n\r");
    destination = (String)st.nextElement();
    gateway = (String)st.nextElement();
    flags = (String)st.nextElement();
    refs = Integer.parseInt((String)st.nextElement());
    use = Integer.parseInt((String)st.nextElement());
    totalRoutes++; totalPackets+=use;
    if (destination.equals(gateway)) totalHostAndGate++;
    }
}catch(IOException i)
{System.out.println("An I/O Error has occurred");}
catch(NumberFormatException n)
{System.out.println("Illegal integer encountered");}
```

Here the StringTokenizer is used to split up the five strings within each line with the final string being ignored, and the static method parseInt, contained in the Integer class, is used to convert the two integer strings to their integer values.

Notice the use of the catch clauses to monitor the generation of I/O exceptions and the possibility that `parseInt` will encounter a string which is not an integer.

10.7 StreamTokenizers

Another useful class which is similar to the `StringTokenizer` class is the `StreamTokenizer` class. This splits up characters which are read by an `InputStream`. The constructor for this class has one argument which is an `InputStream` object. Thus,

```
StreamTokenizer st = new InputStream (is);
```

sets up a `StreamTokenizer` object `st` based on the `InputStream` object `is`. This means that tokens can be read from this stream, with tokens being delineated by white space. The main method used to extract tokens from a `Stream-Tokenizer` object is `nextToken`. This returns an integer which describes what token has been read. This will have one of a number of constant values. There are four values which it can deliver: these are represented by the constants `TT_EOF`, `TT_EOL`, `TT_NUMBER` and `TT_WORD` which can all be found within the `StreamTokenizer` class. `TT_EOF` indicates that an end of file token has been read, `TT_EOL` indicates that an end of line token has been read, `TT_NUMBER` indicates that a number has been read and `TT_WORD` indicates that a word has been read. When `nextToken` has been executed the token is either stored in the public instance variable `nval` (if it is a number) or in the public instance variable `sval` (if it is a string). The next section describes the use of this class in creating the data structure used in the running example.

10.8 Revisiting the running example

At the heart of our running example is a data structure which stores words that can be found in a Web document and the list of locations where this word can be found. In order to add data to this data structure we have written two methods: the first is `addWord` which adds a word, the second is `addLocation` which adds a location associated with a particular word.

We shall assume that we have already written a program which wanders through cyberspace forming files which contain the locations and words which are to be added. We shall assume that the format of individual chunks of these files is:

```
Word   Location 1   Location2    Location3 ... ****
```

where a word written as a string is followed by a sequence of the locations where it can be found, also expressed as strings. The locations are terminated by the string "****".

The code which processes a single word/locations chunk is shown below. It assumes that an `InputStream` object `is` has already been initialized.

```
...
try{
  InputStream is =
    new FileInputStream("Data.txt");
  StreamTokenizer st = new StreamTokenizer(is);
  int i;
//
//
// Start of loop processing each word/locations pair
//
//

  try{i = st.nextToken();
    String word = st.sval;
    l.addWord(word);
    i = st.nextToken();
    while(!(st.sval).equals("****")){
    // Body of loop
      l.addLocation(st.sval,word);
      i = st.nextToken();
    }
  }
  catch(IOException io)
    {System.out.println("Error in file");}
}
catch(FileNotFoundException fe){
  System.out.println("Problem with file " +
                     "does not exist");
}
}
//
//
//End of loop
//
//
...
```

An `InputStream` is first created using the file `Data.txt`. The `StreamTokenizer` object is then created based on the `InputStream` object. The word is first extracted and then added to the data structure using `addWord`. A loop then extracts out each location associated with the word and adds them to the data structure. This loop terminates when a **** string is encountered.

10.9 SUMMARY

This chapter has described a number of ways in which sequential data can be processed by Java programs. The essential concept described in this chapter was a stream: an object which is used to read data from and write data to files and I/O devices. We also looked at a useful way of extracting substrings from a string or file using `StringTokenizer` and `StreamTokenizer` classes.

CHAPTER ELEVEN

HCI and Java

- To outline the general functions of the AWT library.
- To describe some of the graphics elements of the library.
- To introduce the event handling system.
- To introduce graphics contexts.
- To describe font and colour support in Java.

11.1 Introduction

The previous chapter described how data of a sequential nature could be communicated to a Java program. There is also a need to handle data which is communicated in a much more random way: from a human–computer interface (HCI). The part of the Java system which contains classes that enable this form of input/output is known as the Abstract Window Toolkit library (AWT). It contains pre-built classes of graphical interface elements. While it is possible to build an interface from scratch using the basic drawing primitives (rectangle, line, text), you will, for simplicity and consistency, mainly rely on the tools that the Java language provides.

11.2 Overview of the AWT

The AWT can be broken down into groups of related classes. In this section we will make a quick tour of each group and then return to them later by describing some small examples which illustrate them.

- *Containers.* The AWT provides a number of types of containers: Windows and Panels. Both classes are subclasses of the Java Container class. The Window subclasses include Dialog, FileDialog and Frame.

Containers are generally used to hold other elements such as buttons. Panels are used to group elements together in an existing area of a window or applet. An applet is a container which is embedded within an HTML page in a Web document.

- *Layout managers.* These are used by containers to arrange embedded elements into a particular layout style, for example laying the elements out in a grid. The various models are used to ensure spacing or alignment, and include `BorderLayout`, `CardLayout`, `FlowLayout` and `GridLayout`. You will meet a number of these in this chapter. Since the container classes implement the `LayoutManager` interface it is possible to write new classes to meet particular problems when the supplied classes are deficient.

- *Control elements.* This group of elements provide the means by which users will usually interact with your applications or applets. They include controls such as buttons, menus, choice selectors, text areas and lines, canvases, simple labels, scroll bars and lists. They form the backbone of the AWT library and will be the building blocks of most Java applications that require user interfaces.

An important part of the AWT hierarchy is shown in Figure 11.1. This inheritance hierarchy has containers as its central spine; these contain elements such as buttons, sliders and checkboxes. A panel is a container which can contain other containers and also HCI control elements such as buttons.

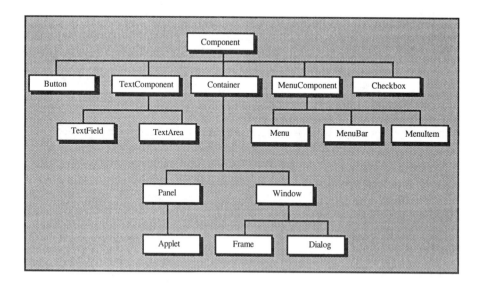

Figure 11.1 Part of the AWT hierarchy.

As you will see later, panels allow you to modularize the layout of the HCI. A frame is a window in which containers such as panels and control elements such as buttons can be embedded. These correspond to the normal windows you see when using an operating system such as Windows 95 or the Macintosh System 7. A dialog is a window that appears when the user of a program is asked a question or is prompted for information, for example a dialog might be produced in an application program when you are about to carry out some serious action such as deleting a file and the dialog asks you whether you are sure that this is what you want to do.

An **applet** is a particular form of panel. It is a container which can be embedded within a Web document. Like many other containers it can contain not only other containers such as panels, but also HCI elements such as checkboxes and radio buttons.

There are a number of aspects to programming an interface:

- The control elements that you use.

- The way that these control elements are laid out on a screen.

- The way that the program which uses the interfaces responds to events that occur with an interface such as a mouse being clicked or text being entered into a field.

These aspects will all be dealt with in the next three sections.

11.3 HCI elements

The aim of this section is to examine many of the HCI control elements which you can place in containers. The next section will describe how you can arrange them using layout objects.

11.3.1 Buttons

Buttons are normally used in interfaces to signify that some form of processing is to occur. For example, a button might be used to change the error messages displayed by an application so that they become terser than normal. A button, like every other Java element, is an object and is defined by a class within the AWT. To create an unlabelled or labelled button you should use new. For example, the statement:

```
Button offButton = new Button();
```

creates an unlabelled button and:

```
Button onButton = new Button("TerseOutput");
```

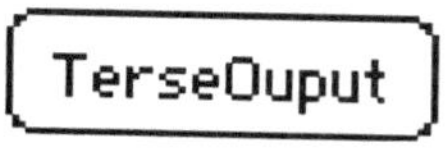

```
TerseOuput
```

Figure 11.2   An example of a button.

creates a button with the label given by the string which is its argument. Figure 11.2 shows the second button generated with the Java system developed for the Macintosh.

An important point that is worth making about the AWT is that the appearance of the control elements and containers will depend on the underlying operating system. Java is implemented in such a way that it uses the standard primitives for drawing elements such as buttons that are provided by the underlying operating system. The button in Figure 11.2 was generated by the Macintosh System 7 operating system. A button generated by Windows 95 would resemble those associated with that operating system.

A second point worth making is that the code above has not yet displayed the button on a screen, it has just created a button object. The next section will show you how to display control elements.

If you want to change the label on a button then you would send a `setLabel` message to a button. For example,

```
lb.setLabel("Press Me")
```

would associate the label `"Press Me"` with the button `lb`. To find the label associated with a button use `getLabel` method. Thus

```
String lbAttach = lb.getLabel()
```

sets the string variable `lbAttach` to `"Press Me"`.

11.3.2 Labels

Labels are just strings which can be placed within a container. To create a label use new. For example,

```
Label headLb = new Label("Verbose Interface Cluster");
```

associates the label `headLb` with the string `"Verbose Interface Cluster"`. You can change the text associated with a label by using the method `setText` and you can retrieve the text associated with a label by using the method `getText`.

For example,

```
Label lb = new Label("Hello there");
...
lb.setText("Good Bye");
```

```
. . .
String currentLabelStr = lb.getText();
```

...

sets a label, then overwrites it with a new string and, finally, sets the string `currentLabelStr` to the current string associated with the label.

11.3.3 Checkboxes

A checkbox is used to indicate some change in state of a system. For example, a checkbox might be used to indicate that the user is either a novice or an experienced user.

As with all other control elements checkboxes are created using new. Two examples of this are shown below:

```
Checkbox noviceUserType = new CheckBox("Novice"),
         expeUserType = new
             Checkbox("Experienced user");
```

Figure 11.3 shows these two checkboxes.

Checkboxes can be either on or off depending on whether they have been clicked or not. The two boxes shown in Figure 11.3 are off. The two boxes shown in Figure 11.4 are on.

The state of a checkbox - whether it has been clicked or not - can be discovered by means of the method `getState()` which returns with a Boolean result if the box has been clicked. Thus,

```
boolean b = expeUserType.getState();
```

will place true or false in b depending on whether a user has clicked the button.

Figure 11.3 An example of two checkboxes.

Figure 11.4 Two clicked checkboxes.

Figure 11.5   A set of radio buttons.

11.3.4 Radio buttons

Radio buttons are a special case of checkboxes. Radio buttons are grouped together and have the property that only one of the boxes is checked at a time. Clicking on one radio button means that the radio button which is currently checked will become unchecked.

Radio buttons are created from checkboxes by means of a constructor which connects them to a checkbox group. Code which illustrates this is shown below:

```
CheckboxGroup language = new CheckboxGroup();
...
Checkbox frenchBox =
  new Checkbox("French", language, true);
Checkbox germanBox =
  new Checkbox("German", language, false);
Checkbox englishBox =
  new Checkbox("English", language, false);
...
```

This set of radio buttons is displayed in Figure 11.5.

In the code a `CheckboxGroup` object is first created and then three checkboxes are created using the three argument constructor for that class. The first argument is the string that is to label the checkbox, the second argument is the name of the group of checkboxes which are to be treated as radio buttons and the final argument is a Boolean which indicates that the checkbox is to be initially set.

11.3.5 Choices

A choice is a pop-up menu which allows the user to specify a number of strings which can be selected. The code for creating a choice is shown below:

```
Choice computerChoice = new Choice();
computerChoice.addItem("VAX");
computerChoice.addItem("PC");
computerChoice.addItem("Mac");
computerChoice.select("VAX");
```

The pop-up menus produced by this code are shown in Figure 11.6.

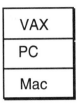

Figure 11.6 A pop-up menu.

The first line creates the pop-up menu. The next three lines add three strings to the menu and the final line sets the last string to the one to be displayed. When the user clicks on the menu all three strings will be displayed and one can be selected.

There are a number of methods associated with this class. The most important one is `paramString` which returns with the string of the currently selected item. So, for example, the code:

```
Choice computerChoice = new Choice();
computerChoice.addItem("VAX");
computerChoice.addItem("PC");
computerChoice.addItem("Macintosh");
computerChoice.select("PC");
String currentChoice = computerChoice.paramString();
```

will result in the string `currentChoice` being set to the string `"PC"`.

11.3.6 Lists

The `List` class allows you to create a scrolling collection of strings. The user can select a single string or a number of strings.

The no-argument constructor produces a scrolling list for which only one item can be selected. The code:

```
List nameList = new List();
```

creates the object `nameList` for which no item in the list is displayed and only one can be selected. A more useful constructor for lists is the two-argument selector. This has an `int` argument which gives the current number of items in the list which can be displayed and a Boolean which indicates whether multiple selection is allowed. The code:

```
List nameList = new List(5,true);
```

creates a list which displays five values and will allow multiple selection.

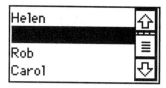

Figure 11.7 A scrolling list.

Items are added to a list by means of the addItem() method. The code below creates a list which allows multiple selections and displays four items at a time – six items are added to the list.

```
List nameList = new List(4,true);
nameList.addItem("Pat");
nameList.addItem("Darrel");
nameList.addItem("Helen");
nameList.addItem("Linda");
nameList.addItem("Rob");
nameList.addItem("Carol");
```

The list is displayed in Figure 11.7.

This shows the fact that the item Linda has been selected; it has been hidden by the black box in the screen dump. As well as addItem there are a number of methods which can be used to modify items in a list and select the items that have been clicked. Some of the more important ones are described below:

public String[] getSelectedItems() returns with a string array which contains the names of the items that have been selected. For example, the code:

```
String[] selectedNames =
    nameList.getSelectedItems();
```

will place in the string array selectedNames the strings which represent the names that have been selected by the user.

public boolean allowsMultipleSelections(). This will return true if the receiver object allows multiple selections.

public int countItems(). This returns with the number of items in a list.

public String getItem(int index). This returns with the string which can be found at the specified index. So, for example, if the first string in your list is "Diana" then a call to this method with the argument equal to zero will return this string.

Figure 11.8 Two examples of objects described by the TextField class.

11.3.7 Text felds

A text field is part of an interface into which text can be typed by a user. TextField objects are described by the class TextField. These can be created using new. There are a number of constructors for text fields. Examples of their use are shown below:

```
TextField txfA = new TextField();
TextField txfB = new TextField(24);
TextField txfC = new TextField("Type here");
TextField txfD =
  new TextField("This is for typing", 20);
```

The first line creates an empty text field. The second line creates a text field which has 24 columns. The third creates a text field which contains the string "Type here". The fourth line creates a text field with 20 columns with the text "This is for typing" contained in the field. Figure 11.8 shows the text fields generated by the second and fourth lines above.

There are a number of methods associated with the TextField class. The method getText() retrieves the text which has been placed into a text field. Thus,

```
TextField txfC = new TextField("Type here");
String text = txfC.getText();
```

will place the string "Type here" into the string variable text. The TextField class also contains methods which carry out actions such as retrieving text that has been highlighted by the user, selects text depending on the start and end position of the text to be highlighted and returns with the current length of the text field.

11.3.8 Text areas

These are very similar to text fields. The main difference is that a text area is capable of containing a number of lines of text, rather than the single line found in a text field. Both the class TextArea and the class TextField inherit from a class known as TextComponent which provides many of the methods that are used for manipulating objects described by these classes. Hence you will find quite a lot of commonality between the methods used for accessing and manipulating objects described by both these classes.

This is some text to start off ⬆
with. Do you like it? yes or
no? ⬇

Figure 11.9   An example of a `TextArea` object.

The code below creates a `TextArea` object.

```
TextArea ta = new TextArea (4, 20);
```

It creates an empty text area which will have four rows and 20 columns for text to be typed into. The code:

```
TextArea ta = new
TextArea (" This is some text to start off with." +
"Do you like it? yes or no?", 4, 20);
```

creates a text area which is already initialized with some text. We have used the string concatenation operator + to form the string since the Java compiler does not accept strings which have a physical new line within them. This is shown in Figure 11.9. It is important to point out that the text area is equipped with a scroll bar that allows the text to be scrolled up or down when it occupies more space than is available in the text area.

11.3.9 Scroll bars

A scroll bar is an input control element which enables a slider to be moved; the scroll bar transmitting a value from some minimum value to a maximum value. There are a number of constructors associated with the `Scrollbar` class. The no-argument constructor creates a simple scroll bar. The one-argument constructor is used to specify whether a scroll bar is to be displayed horizontally or vertically. For example:

```
Scrollbar scbV = new Scrollbar(Scrollbar.VERTICAL);
          scbH = new Scrollbar(Scrollbar.HORIZONTAL);
```

The single argument to this constructor is one of two constants which can be found in the `Scrollbar` class. You will find yourself using the five-argument constructor most. Its first argument is the constant which indicates the orientation, the second argument is the starting position of the scroll bar, the third argument is the size of the visible portion of the bar, the fourth argument is the minimum value to be communicated by the scroll bar and the final argument is the maximum value. So, for example, the statement:

```
Scrollbar scbV =
  new Scrollbar(Scrollbar.VERTICAL, 20, 5, 0, 80)
```

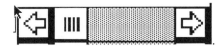

Figure 11.10 An example of a scroll bar.

creates a vertical scroll bar which has a starting position for the scroll as 20, an increment of 5, a minimum value of 0 and a maximum value of 80. When this scroll bar is moved it is incremented in steps of 5. An example of such a scroll bar is shown in Figure 11.10.

Values generated by scroll bars can be accessed with a variety of methods associated with the `Scrollbar` class. For example, the method `getValue` returns with the current value of the scroll bar, `getMinimum` returns with the integer which represents the minimum value of the scroll bar and `get-Orientation` returns with the orientation of the scroll bar. There are also a variety of methods which allow the user to alter the parameters of a scroll bar, for example methods which allow you to alter the maximum and minimum values. An example of the use of the `getValue()` method is shown below:

```
Scrollbar   scbV =
    new Scrollbar(Scrollbar.VERTICAL, 20, 5, 0, 80)
...
int currValue = scbV.getValue();
...
```

Here `currValue` is updated to contain the current value of the scroll bar `scbV`.

11.4 Containers and layouts

The previous section discussed the control elements that make up the HCI for Java. The aim of this section is to describe how they are arranged on the screen.

The control elements are deposited in a component known as a **container**. In this book you will meet three containers:

Frame. This is a window used in Java applications.

Applet. This is a container which can be embedded in a Web page.

Panel. This is a container which can be used in both applications and applets. Panels are containers which can contain both control elements and containers. You will find yourself using objects described by the `Panel` class very frequently as they provide a large amount of flexibility in laying out control elements.

Both frames and panels are created using new. For example,

```
Frame fr = new Frame("Frame Title");
```

creates a window with the title "Frame Title".

The way in which control elements are laid out inside a container depends on the way you specify this layout. In order for you to communicate your requirements there is an object described by class Layout which provides a number of patterns that you can adopt.

Each container is associated with a method called setLayout() which allows you to specify the pattern of layout for the control objects within a container. So, for example, if you had a frame object f and you wanted to insist that the objects laid out within f are going to follow a BorderLayout, then you would write:

```
f.setLayout(new BorderLayout())
```

At this stage do not worry about what the BorderLayout object does; all you need to know is that the code says that when you add objects to f they are going to obey the BorderLayout rules. We will be discussing the various layout classes later in this chapter.

To cover this topic we will give a series of code fragments or small applications to cover specific topics. We won't cover every element in the AWT, but there should be enough to give you a solid foundation and allow you to access the AWT library without fear. When you start to use the AWT you will almost certainly begin to develop your own personal style of writing interfaces but, until that happens, the most effective way to progress is to experiment liberally with the classes until you find something that you like the look of which solves the particular problem in hand.

The two groups of classes can be logically described together, since they are closely related in practical use. We'll start by showing you how to create containers and then demonstrate some layout techniques.

11.4.1 Using containers

An AWT window is a top-level window without borders or a title bar. As it stands, it is not entirely useful, except for implementing a pop-up window, but it forms the basic building unit for the window subclasses. The Frame subclass, for example, has borders and a title bar and is normally used as the root window for building standalone Java applications. Each of the subclasses is associated with a default LayoutManager - for example, Dialog uses BorderLayout.

The following code is a very simple application which displays a frame and sets the title of the window:

```
import java.awt.*;

public class FrameDemo {
  public static void main(String args[]) {
    Frame fr = new Frame("We Love Java");
```

Figure 11.11 Screen shot of a simple frame.

```
    fr.resize(200,200);
    fr.show();
  }
}
```

Remember that a Frame object is normally associated with applications. This class just creates a frame, sets the title, sizes the frame (to 200 by 200 pixels) and then maps it to the screen using the method show(). Once you have an object which is described by a class which is subclassed from the Container class (for example, Frame) then you can add other user interface elements quite easily. It is worth pointing out that show and resize are only connected with window components such as Frame, and not with other containers such as Panel.

To make things even simpler, when you write an applet, the applet itself is subclassed from the Container class so you can just add elements with any container. The screen shot corresponding to the code above is shown as Figure 11.11.

Once you have created a top-level window (which is implicit in the case of an applet) you can use the Panel class to divide up the larger interface into manageable sections.

11.4.2 Placing elements using LayoutManager

We will follow the model of extending our simple class to include more features. In this part of the book, we will demonstrate some of the ways that the LayoutManager object can be used to place elements automatically. Each class that implements LayoutManager will place elements according to some algorithm; for example, BorderLayout will use the points of the compass.

We will start with the `BorderLayout` class. Our example code looks like this:

```java
import java.awt.*;

public class FrameDemo {
  public static void main(String args[]) {
    Button buttons[] = new Button[6];
    Frame fr = new Frame("We Love Java");
    /* Set the layout manager of the frame */
    fr.setLayout(new BorderLayout());
    /* Add some buttons */
    for (int i = 1; i < 6; i++) {
      buttons[i] = new Button("Button " + i);
    }
    /* Place the buttons */
    fr.add("North",  buttons[1]);
    fr.add("South",  buttons[2]);
    fr.add("East",   buttons[3]);
    fr.add("West",   buttons[4]);
    fr.add("Center", buttons[5]);
    fr.pack();
    fr.show();
  }
}
```

The code simply pads out the example for frames that we described in the previous section. We define an array of buttons each of which is created with a numbered string. We also explicitly set the layout model for the frame to `BorderLayout` by means of the method `setLayout` associated with frames. We then place each button into the frame.

When using the `BorderLayout` model each element is placed using a string `North`, `East`, `South`, `West` and `Center`. These strings define where in the frame the objects are placed, following the rough basis of a compass (Figure 11.12). When you add items to a container you always use an `add()` method, either with a string argument as shown above or an empty argument; which `add` you use depends on the layout chosen. In the case of the one above you use a string.

The element which is placed at the `Center` location is allocated as much space as has been left over by the other elements. Finally we call the `pack()` method to shape the frame around the elements and then call `show()` to display the frame on the screen. It is important to point out that `pack` is only associated with windows and is not, for example, associated with applets.

You can see how the elements are placed on the points of a compass. Notice that the first two buttons placed into the frame are expanded to fill the whole of the frame, while the others remain smaller.

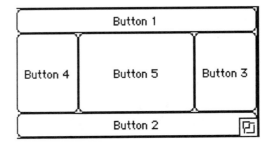

Figure 11.12   A more complex frame.

As an example, consider the code which creates a panel `pf` and then adds three buttons to its North, South and East areas. The first button is labelled `"Hello"`, the second `"Good-Bye"` and the third `"Return"`. A `TextArea` has been placed in the West area with no text in it but initialized to 30 rows and 4 columns. A label `"This label"` has been placed in the remaining area.

The code is shown below:

```
Panel pf = new Panel();
pf.setLayout(new BorderLayout());
pf.add("North", new Button("Hello"));
pf.add("South", new Button("Good-Bye"));
pf.add("East", new Button("Return"));
pf.add("West", new TextArea(30,4));
pf.add("center", new Label(This label"));
```

The next layout we'll examine is `FlowLayout`. This layout places the items in the order in which they are added. Notice that you still use the `add` method; however, there is not a string argument. The new code example is:

```
import java.awt.*;

public class FrameDemo {
  public static void main(String args[]) {
    Button buttons[] = new Button[6];
    Frame fr = new Frame("We Love Java");
    /* Set the layout manager of the frame */
    fr.setLayout(new FlowLayout(FlowLayout.LEFT));
    /* Add some buttons                        */
    /* Each executed statement in the for      */
    /* loop forms a string "button i"          */
    for (int i = 1; i < 6; i++) {
      buttons[i] = new Button("Button " + i);
    }
    /* Place the buttons */
```

```
    fr.add(buttons[1]); fr.add(buttons[2]);
    fr.add(buttons[3]); fr.add(buttons[4]);
    fr.add(buttons[5]); fr.pack(); fr.show();
  }
}
```

This time when we define the layout for the frame we call `FlowLayout`, with the argument set to align the buttons to the left (LEFT is a static constant associated with the `FlowLayout` class). When we place the buttons we don't need to specify any strings to position them as in `BorderLayout`, since the class maps them automatically. The display is shown as Figure 11.13.

You can see that the buttons have been laid out in a line. This is not only one of the simplest ways of arranging items, but it is also one of the most useful.

SAQ

Write down code which creates a panel object `pf` and then specifies the layout, which will be `FlowLayout`. Then place a button `b` with a label `"Here button"` in the panel followed by a `TextField t` which is initialized to contain the string `"Hello again"` and a `Scrollbar` object `s` which will be horizontal, have an initial value of 10, paging value of 10, a maximum of 100 and a minimum of 0.

Solution

The code is shown below:

```
Panel pf = new Panel();
Button b = new Button("Here button");
TextField t = new TextField("Hello again");
Scrollbar s =
  new Scrollbar(Scrollbar.HORIZONTAL, 10, 10, 100, 0);
pf.setLayout(new FlowLayout());
pf.add(b); pf.add(s); pf.add(t);
```

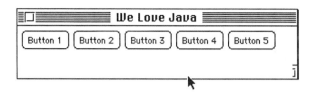

Figure 11.13 An example of flow layout.

An alternative to the above solution would be:

```
Panel pf = new Panel();
pf.setLayout(new FlowLayout());
pf.add(b = new Button("Here button"));
pf.add(t = new TextField("Hello again"));
pf.add(s = new
   Scrollbar(Scrollbar.HORIZONTAL, 10, 10, 100, 0));
```

since you will remember from Chapter 4 that an assignment statement will deliver the result assigned.

The final layout we will describe here is the GridLayout method. What this layout does is to place the elements to be added according to a grid of row and columns. When you define a GridLayout object it will have two arguments: the first is the number of rows and the second is the number of columns.

The code to demonstrate this is shown below; it uses three rows and two columns. The display of the frame is shown in Figure 11.14.

```
import java.awt.*;

public class FrameDemo {
  public static void main(String args[]) {
    Button buttons[] = new Button[6];
    Frame fr = new Frame("We Love Java");
    /* Set the layout manager of the frame */
    fr.setLayout(new GridLayout(3,2));
    /* Add some buttons */
    for (int i = 1; i < 6; i++) {
      buttons[i] = new Button("Button " + i);
    }
    /* Place the buttons */
    fr.add(buttons[1]);fr.add(buttons[2]);
    fr.add(buttons[3]); fr.add(buttons[4]);
    fr.add(buttons[5]);
    fr.pack();
    fr.show();
  }
}
```

Here five buttons have been added with the remaining part of the grid being empty. The only change in this example is the call to set the layout of the frame. The call to the GridLayout method with arguments (3 and 2) specifies the number of rows and columns in the grid.

As you might expect, in the GridLayout model the elements are arranged into a grid. The display corresponding to the code is shown in Figure 11.14.

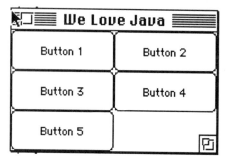

Figure 11.14   A frame using `GridLayout`.

| SAQ |

Write down the code which creates a frame fb and places four control elements in it according to a grid which has three rows and one column. The three items are a checkbox c which is associated with a label "Press Here", a text field t f which initially has 50 columns and no text associated with it and a button b which is labelled with the string "Verbose". Do not worry about using `pack()` and `resize()` in your answer.

| Solution |

The solution is shown below:

```
Frame fb = new Frame();
Checkbox c;
TextField tf;
Button b;
fb.setLayout(new GridLayout(3, 1));
fb.add(c = new Checkbox("Press Here"));
fb.add(tf = new TextField(50));
fb.add(b = new Button("Verbose"));
```

We have covered three of the layout models which are supported as a default in Java. The models are simple and easy to work with; however, they tend to suffer from a lack of flexibility and extensibility. In cases where the default models do not meet your requirements, you can write some bespoke classes which implement the `LayoutManager`; however, the details of this are outside the scope of this introductory book.

As an aside it is worth mentioning that it also possible not to use any layout manager and to place components manually. This is done by specifying the layout manager to be `null`, adding the component to the holder in the normal way and then using the reshape() method to place and size the component in the holder. For example:

```
. . .
holder.setLayout(null); Button b1 = new Button("Java!");
holder.add(b1); b1.reshape(10,10,20,20);
. . .
```

The advantage of this is that you get greater control over placement. The disadvantage is that every element has to be placed manually, rather than relying on a layout manager. This has major ramifications when you have to change the user interface; for example, inserting a new element will mean that many of the existing elements will need to be moved and individually recoded.

Exercise

Write down what you think the code below does.

```
Panel over, top, bottom;
Checkbox c, cu;
TextField tf;
TextArea ta;
label l;
over = new Panel();
over.setLayout(new GridLayout(2,1));
top = new Panel(new FlowLayout());
bottom = new Panel(new FlowLayout());
top.add(c = new Checkbox("Press Here"));
top.add(cu = new Checkbox("Press Again"));
bottom.add(tf = new TextField("To be typed in", 50));
bottom.add(l = new Label("Typing area"));
bottom.add
   (ta = new TextArea("Initial typing area",4, 30));
over.add(top);over.add(bottom);
```

Solution

The code constructs three panels. The panel top has a FlowLayout object associated with it, and the panel bottom also has a FlowLayout associated with it. The panel over has a GridLayout associated with it. The panel top has two control elements added, while the panel bottom has three added. Each of these panels is then added to the panel over. Thus over consists of two panels each of which has the same layout associated with it. This is an example of a container which has two elements contained within it – both of which are containers.

11.5 Control elements

Once you have created a holder for your interface and, optionally, selected a layout method you can begin to add the control elements which will do the real work. In this section we will illustrate some of the elements in sample code. We also have a subsidiary aim in this section: that of showing you how inheritance can be used to build up interfaces from existing classes which implement interface objects.

11.5.1 A simple class to build on

To begin with we will introduce a class which will provide the basis for adding the control elements. This class simply defines a top-level window with a number of panels which we will use to hold examples of control elements. Remember that panels are used to group elements such as buttons together. Our base class for this section looks like this:

```
import java.awt.*;
public class awtclass {
  Panel topPanel, botPanel;

  public static void main(String args[]) {
    awtclass thisclass = new awtclass();
    // Define the top-level frame
    Frame fr = new Frame("AWT Chapter");
    // Call our method to display the UI elements
    thisclass.doUI(fr);
    // Pack and display the frame
    fr.pack();
    fr.show();
  }

  public void doUI(Frame fr) {
    fr.setLayout(new BorderLayout());
    // Create the panels to hold the UI elements
    topPanel = new Panel();
    botPanel = new Panel();
    // Add the elements to the frame
    fr.add("North",topPanel);
    fr.add("South",botPanel);
  }
}
```

The class contains two methods: doUI which carries out the layout of the HCI elements and the main method which is executed. Before continuing it is worth your reading through this code in order to make sure you understand what it does. We create a new frame, then create an instance of this class and pass the frame as an argument to the method doUI which carries out the process of building up the interface elements. Inside the doUI method two panels are created and then added to the frame using the add method. We have used this method before and glossed over the details so it is worth providing a little more detail. Whenever you want to insert an object into a frame (or related container), you will use the add() method. There are two ways that the method can be called. The first:

```
add(Component)
```

is the most common, but the second way is:

```
add(String, Component)
```

which is required by layout managers that use the string to locate the component, for example the BorderLayout class.

The add() method you use is determined by the layout method your holder is using. If you are writing code and your calls to add() don't seem to be working, one of the first things that you should check is whether the layout manager you are using requires the string argument. This is especially likely to happen with certain classes which use the BorderLayout class - your code will compile and run, but if you call the wrong version of add() then the components will not appear.

If you build and run this class you won't see much at all. Depending on your development platform you will just see a very small window title. The reason for this is the occurrence of the pack() call near the end of the code which instructs the frame to resize around its components. Since all we have at the moment is the set of panels which will also shrink to nothing, the whole of the application disappears.

11.5.2 Adding a menu

The first thing that we will add is a menu bar. This HCI element has not been described before: it is just a bar which contains menus; these, in turn, contain individual menu items. The procedure for creating menus is somewhat convoluted. First you must create a MenuBar:

```
MenuBar mb = new MenuBar();
```

Then you must create a new item for each menu that you want to appear in the menu bar, for example:

```
Menu m = new Menu("Menu 1");
```

After this you must create MenuItems for each selectable item that you want to appear in the menu and tell the menu to hold the item:

```
m.add(new MenuItem("MenuItem 1");
m.add(new MenuItem("MenuItem 2");
```

Once you have completed adding items to the menu you must add the menu to the menu bar:

```
mb.add(m);
```

Finally, when all of this has been done, you must tell the frame that you want it to use the MenuBar that you have prepared:

```
fr.setMenuBar(mb);
```

This approach is very flexible, but at the cost of extensive coding and very little satisfaction.

The code now becomes:

```
import java.awt.*;

public class awtclass2 extends awtclass {
  public static void main(String args[]) {
    awtclass thisclass = new awtclass2();
    // Define the top-level frame
    Frame fr = new Frame("AWT Chapter");
    // Call our method to add the HCI control elements
    thisclass.doUI(fr);
    // Pack and display the frame
    fr.pack();
    fr.show();
  }

  public void doUI(Frame fr) {
    super.doUI(fr);
    MenuBar mb = new MenuBar();
    Menu m = new Menu("Menu 1");
    m.add(new MenuItem("MenuItem 1"));
    m.add(new MenuItem("MenuItem 2"));
    mb.add(m);
    fr.setMenuBar(mb);
  }
}
```

There are a number of things to notice about this code. First, awtclass2 extends awtclass which we defined previously, so all the methods and instance variables in this class become available to awtclass2. Second, the method doUI in awtclass2 calls the doUI method in awtclass by using the super facility that we discussed earlier. This sets the frame and the panels previously defined.

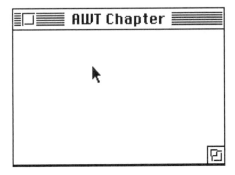

Figure 11.15   The display from `awtclass2`.

If you build and view this code, you still won't see very much. It is shown in Figure 11.15. In fact, it is not until the addition of more 'normal' components that the `pack()` command picks up the minimum sizes of the elements.

11.5.3 Adding a `TextArea` and a `Canvas`

We will now continue to add some useful elements to the top panel. We will add a `TextArea` and a `Canvas`. As you will remember a `TextArea` is a general-purpose text control element which can be used to hold arbitrary text strings. A `TextArea` comes complete with scroll bars which are linked to the text area. You will also remember that a `Canvas` is a general-purpose HCI element which can be used for a whole range of tasks. In this example, we have subclassed `Canvas` to produce `myCanvas`.

The code to add these two elements to the display looks like this:

```
import java.awt.*;
public class awtclass3 extends awtclass2 {
  public static void main(String args[]) {
    awtclass thisclass = new awtclass3();
    // Define the top-level frame
    Frame fr = new Frame("AWT Chapter");
    // Call our method to display the UI elements
    thisclass.doUI(fr);
    // Pack and display the frame
    fr.pack();
    fr.show();
  }

  public void doUI(Frame fr) {
    super.doUI(fr);
    // Set the layout model for the topPanel
    topPanel.setLayout(new GridLayout(1,2));
```

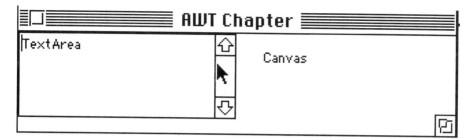

Figure 11.16   The display from class `awtclass3`.

```
    // Add the text area
    topPanel.add(new TextArea("TextArea",5,20));
    // Add the mycanvas item
    topPanel.add(new myCanvas());
  }
}
```

The display from this class is shown in Figure 11.16. As before, we have extended the class from the previous example. In the doUI method we begin by setting the layout for the panel we are going to use. In this case, we initially want a grid with one row and two columns. We then employ the add() method to insert a TextArea (with initial text set to the string "TextArea") and a myCanvas. The code for the myCanvas class is included below:

```
class myCanvas extends Canvas {
  public void paint(Graphics g) {
  g.drawString("Canvas",20,20);
  }
}
```

It is worth saying something important about this class. All container classes are provided with a class known as paint() which enables drawing to take place using a Graphics object. This object is the argument to paint. All the code above does is to create a new class which inherits from Canvas and overwrites the paint method of Canvas with a simple instruction to display the string "Canvas" at pixel (20,20) on the canvas. Later in this chapter we will be describing how to carry out drawing using objects defined by the Graphics class. For the time being just assume that the object myCanvas is an object with a simple string "Canvas" displayed on it.

11.5.4 Adding a Button, a TextField, a Choice and a CheckBox

The last set of additions to the interface will be some small user interface items: a Button, a Choice, a TextField and a CheckBox. This is shown below:

```
import java.awt.*;

public class awtclass4 extends awtclass3 {
  public static void main(String args[]) {
    awtclass thisclass = new awtclass4();
    // Define the top-level frame
    Frame fr = new Frame("AWT Chapter");
    // Call our method to display the UI elements
    thisclass.doUI(fr);
    // Pack and display the frame
    fr.pack(); fr.show();
  }

  public void doUI(Frame fr) {
    super.doUI(fr);
    // Add small things at the bottom.
    botPanel.add(new TextField("TextField"));
    botPanel.add(new Button("Button"));
    botPanel.add(new Checkbox("Checkbox"));
    Choice c = new Choice();
    c.addItem("Choice Item 1");
    c.addItem("Choice Item 2");
    c.addItem("Choice Item 3");
    botPanel.add(c);
  }
}
```

In the doUI method, we simply employ the add method to insert elements into
the panel. Starting with the TextField we create an instance with the default
text value of "TextField". We then proceed to add a Button, with the label
on the button set to be the string "Button". We also add a CheckBox in the
same manner and then create a Choice. Once the Choice is created, we use
the addItem() method to create the items that will appear in the pop-up menu.
Finally, the Choice is added to the Panel. At this point, the interface is as
shown in Figure 11.17.

11.6 The event system

You may have noticed that while we have created several interface elements none
of them carry out any processing. In Java the mechanism for handling events from
interface elements is handled separately from creating and displaying the elements.
This processing requires the trapping of events.

An **event** in Java is some action which is carried out by the user. Some
examples of events are shown below:

- A mouse is moved.

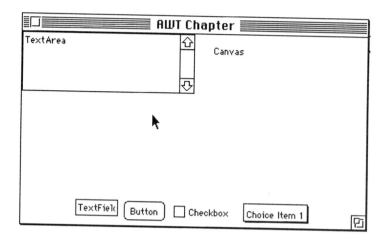

Figure 11.17 A screen with a wide variety of control elements.

- A mouse is clicked.

- An item on a scrollable list is selected.

- A button is pressed.

- Some text is entered into a text field or text area.

Events are described by the class Event. An event object contains information about what event has just occurred and data associated with the event. For example, if a mouse has been clicked then you will find the *x* and *y* coordinates of the position where the click occurred inside the event. Events also contain information about what HCI element caused the event. This information is held in an instance variable target which is an object defined by the class Object. For the majority of events generated by control elements you will find yourself accessing this variable in order to determine what the user has done.

11.6.1 Handling events

If you look in the Component class in java.awt - a class which describes the HCI components that you can use in Java - you will find a method called action. Since every HCI entity inherits from the class Component this method will be available for each of them to use or to override. For many HCI containers you will find yourself writing a new version of action which overrides the version in any superclass.

The method action handles the events from a wide variety of HCI elements. However, there are some events which it does not handle. The major class of event which is not handled by action is that concerned with the manipulation of the mouse and keyboard. There are, however, a whole series of mouse event handling methods which can be found in the `Component` class and can be overridden within a container. Some of these are shown below.

- `mouseDown`. Called when the mouse button is pressed over a component.

- `mouseDrag`. Called when the mouse is moved over a component while the mouse button is pressed.

- `mouseEnter`. Called when the pointer enters a component.

- `mouseExit`. Called when the pointer leaves a component.

- `mouseUp`. Called when the mouse button is released.

This is not the only collection of events not handled by `action`; for example, the event of pressing a key is processed by methods similar to the mouse methods above. However, in such an introductory text we will concentrate on `action` and the mouse methods since the former is the most important way of dealing with events and the mouse methods are representative of the whole non-`action` method approach.

11.6.2 Using `action()`

Whenever you have a container in which you have embedded control elements you will normally have to override the code of `action` inside the class which describes the container in which the elements have been embedded. For example, assume that we have a frame in which we have embedded elements such as buttons and pop-up menus. The definition of the class will look like:

```
Class NewPanel extends Panel{
//instance variables
//methods which carry out processing and placement of
//the control elements
...
public boolean action(Event e, Object o){
//code to handle all the actions that
//could have occurred in the panel
}
}
```

There are two things of note about `action`. The first is the parameters. The `Event` parameter contains all the information needed to discover the source of the event. The second parameter is an object that is returned which contains information that is specific to the HCI control element which has caused the event. For example, if an object described by the `Choice` class generated the action then the `Object` argument will contain a string that matches the choice made, or if the object that caused the event was a checkbox then the second argument would be a Boolean which indicated whether the box was clicked on or off. Since the second argument is an object you will need to use casting to convert the object to a form where it can be manipulated.

If you look in the code for `action` within sophisticated Java applications or applets, then you will find the code follows the same pattern: there will be a set of `if` statements which examine the target instance variable of the first argument of `action` in order to determine which control element caused the event to occur and inside each `if` branch there will be code which usually examines the second argument to determine the nature of the event or what data has been passed by the event.

The second thing to notice about `action` is that it returns a Boolean result. Whenever an event has been handled within `action` you should return true. If the event cannot be handled within the container within which it has been trapped, then the next alternative is to pass the event back to the superclass of the container. For example, you may have embedded an HCl element within a container class C1 which is formed by extending another container class C2; if you were unable to handle the event that was generated, perhaps because all the processing that was to occur was defined within C1, then you would write:

```
return super.action(e,o);
```

This calls the `action` method of the superclass and will usually return true after this method has carried out its processing. The only other action that you can carry out is to return false.

The only other thing worth saying about `action` is that sometimes you will not need to process the second argument. For example, for button events the second argument will contain a string which identifies which button has been pressed. If you only have one button within your container, then there is no need to use this argument to determine the button string. Even if there is no need to process the second argument, you still have to use `action` with two arguments: there is no one-argument method within the Java library that you could use.

We have written a simple applet with an interface similar to the one in the examples so far in this section in order to illustrate the use of the `action` method. The first chunk of code of the applet is shown below:

```
import java.applet.Applet;
import java.awt.*;

public class evui extends Applet {
  Panel botPanel;
  public void init() {
    setLayout(new FlowLayout());
    botPanel = new Panel();
    add(botPanel);
    botPanel.add(new TextField("TextField"));
    botPanel.add(new Button("Button 1"));
    botPanel.add(new Button("Button 2"));
```

```
botPanel.add(new CheckBox("Checkbox"));
Choice c = new Choice();
c.addItem("Choice Item 1");
c.addItem("Choice Item 2");
c.addItem("Choice Item 3");
botPanel.add(c);
}
```

The code above describes a simple applet. At this stage in the book just regard an applet as an example of a special-purpose container into which control elements can be placed. We are extending the class `Applet` since it contains a number of methods which we need to override. One of these is the method `init`. This is the part of the applet which is executed when it is first initialized. This code which constructs the applet contains instructions for adding two buttons, a text field, a choice and a checkbox to a panel which is embedded inside an applet. Notice that we do not need to use `resize`, `pack` and `show` since they are only connected with window components.

The `action` code is shown below:

```
public boolean action(Event evt, Object arg) {
  if (evt.target instanceof Button) {
    String str = (String) arg;
    if (str.equals("Button 1")) {
      showStatus("First Button!!");
    } else {
    if (str.equals("Button 2")) {
      showStatus("Second Button!!");
    } else {
      return false;
    }
  }
  }
  return true;
  } else {
    if (evt.target instanceof CheckBox) {
      showStatus("CheckBox: " + (Boolean) arg);
    } else {
      if (evt.target instanceof TextField) {
        showStatus("TextArea: " + (String) arg);
      } else {
        return false;
      }
    }
  }
  return true;
  }
}
}
```

When an event is sent to this method the code tries to establish what type of object has caused the event to be sent by applying the `instanceof` operator against the `target` instance variable of the event. This variable contains a reference to the object which sent the event. Once the type of object has been determined the code then handles the individual objects.

The `arg` parameter is of type `Object` and what it contains will depend on the type of element that has been executed. For example, if a button has been pressed it will contain a string which identifies the button; if a checkbox has been manipulated it will contain a Boolean value which will be true or false depending on whether the checkbox has been set or not. Once the type of user interface element has been determined a cast is needed to extract the value of `arg`.

Notice that we use the operator `instanceof` to determine what sort of object has caused the event. We do this by examining the target instance variable contained within the event; you may remember from the last section that this variable contains the object which caused the event.

The `arg` parameter is used to see which button has been pressed. The `arg` parameter is an arbitrary one. This means that it is set according to the object that caused the event. You can see how this operates when the `CheckBox` is altered. The parameter which was cast to a `String` for the `Buttons` must be regarded as a Boolean for the `CheckBox`. Similarly, the `TextField` uses the `arg` parameter to pass the text it holds.

If a button has been pressed then a string is displayed which identifies the button. Which button has been pressed is determined by the value of the second argument of `action`. As you will see in the code the string is extracted by casting. The code uses the method `showStatus`. This method displays its argument in the status field of the browser which is currently reading the HTML document that has the applet embedded in it. So, if you were using Netscape Navigator, you would see the message displayed in the lowest part of the Navigator window.

The second part of the code determines whether the event was caused by a checkbox being clicked. If it was, then the status line will contain the concatenation of the string `"Checkbox:    "` and the string version of the Boolean value which is passed as the second argument to the action method (+ automatically converts any scalar argument into a string representation of it). Thus if the button had been checked what you would see on the status line of the browser would be:

```
CheckBox: True
```

and:

```
CheckBox: False
```

if it had been unchecked.

The final part of the code is executed if the text field had caused the event, for example if the user had typed some new text into it. In this case the second argument processed by action would be the text that is in the text field.

This, then, is the general pattern of using an action method: use an if statement to discover what element generated the action (this normally requires the use of the instanceof operator). Once you have determined what caused the event then the processing takes place. This will often mean extracting subsidiary information from the second argument of action. If you have processed the action correctly then return true; if not then either pass the event and argument to an action method within the superclass of the container in which you have embedded the action method or pass false.

The only remaining remark that we would make concerns programming style. The action method can be rather difficult to read as it will contain lots of code embedded in a number of large if statements. If the action method is large then it is worth placing the code that handles particular events within separate methods and then use these methods within the if statement. For example, the code:

```
public boolean(Event e, Object 0){
if(e.target instanceof Button)
   handleButtonEvent(e,o);
else if (e.target instanceof TextField)
   handleTextEvent(e,o);
```

uses two methods handleTextEvent and handleButtonEvent to carry out the processing associated with their corresponding control elements.

SAQ

Assume that three buttons have been added to a panel - with the labels being associated with the strings "Beginner", "Advanced" and "Intermediate". When one of the buttons has been pressed a string variable sVar will be set to the string "Begin", "Interm" or "Advanced" depending on the button pressed. Also assume that there will be some other control elements within the panel. Write down the code which processes buttons within the action method. There is no need to write down the header of the action method.

Solution

The code is shown below.

```
if(evt.target instanceof Button){
   String label = (String) o;
   if (label.equals("Beginner")) sVar = "Begin"
   else if (label.equals("Advanced")) sVar = "Advanced"
   else if (label.equals("Intermediate")) svar = "Interm";}
```

SAQ

Assume that you have added a `TextField` object to a pane. Write down code which places in the `int` variable `asteriskCount` the count of the number of asterisks in the field whenever the user places new text within it (this will be just after the user has typed return). Assume that this is the only `TextField` object.

Solution

The code is shown below:

```
if(evt.target instanceof TextField){
    String textTyped = (String) o;
    asteriskCount = 0;
    for(int i = 0; i < textTyped.size(); i++)
        if (textTyped[i] == '*') asteriskCount++;
}
```

11.6.3 Other events

The previous section looked at how to handle events which have been generated by many of the control elements which you met in the first part of this chapter. There are, however, a number of events which you cannot trap and process using the action method approach described above. We are not going to look at all those events but concentrate on those associated with mouse movements and clicking. We do this for two reasons: first, mouse events will be generated by virtually all your applications or applets and second, the techniques we outline will serve as an excellent exemplar for all the other types of events which we cannot deal with in this book.

Each element in the AWT inherits from the class `Component`. This class contains a number of methods which are executed when a mouse event occurs:

`mouseDown(Event, int, int)`. Called if the mouse is clicked down.

`mouseDrag(Event, int, int)`. Called if the mouse is dragged.

`mouseEnter(Event, int, int)`. Called when the mouse enters the component.

`mouseExit(Event, int, int)`. Called when the mouse exits the component.

`mouseMove(Event, int, int)`. Called if the mouse moves (the mouse button is up).

`mouseUp(Event, int, int)`. Called if the mouse is unclicked.

Each method is associated with an event and two integer arguments which represent the *x* and *y* coordinates of the mouse when the event was generated. If the mouse was clicked when it was in an applet then these arguments would be the *x* and *y* pixel values of the applet window. Like action the methods return a Boolean value.

If a container has mouse actions associated with it then the class which defines the container will need to have methods which override the above methods written. For example, if the only event that you are interested is a mouse click down then you will only need to override the mouseDown method.

The code below which forms part of an applet shows how this is done.

```
public boolean mouseDown(Event e, int x, int y){
showStatus("Mouse at position: " + x + y);
}
```

Here, when the user clicks the mouse the method will execute and display the values of the *x* and *y* positions of the mouse on the status line of the browser.

SAQ

Write down code which stores each position of a mouse when it is clicked down in two arrays xPos and yPos. Assume that a count noOfClicks is used to index these arrays. When the first click occurs display the message "Collection started" on the status bar of the browser that is being used.

Solution

The code is shown below:

```
public boolean mouseDown(Event e, int x, int y){
if (noOfClicks == 0) showStatus("Collection started");
xPos[noOfClicks] = x; yPos[noOfClicks] = y; noOfClicks++;}
```

SAQ

Assume that we need to keep track of the number of times that a mouse enters or leaves a container such as an applet. How would you do this? Write the code which overrides some of the mouse method(s) to do this.

Solution

You would need to override the methods which are executed when the event of the mouse entering or leaving a component is executed. Two counts will need to be kept which will be held in instance variables. These would be initialized when the component is created using a constructor. We shall assume that the counts are represented by the two instance variables inCount and outCount. The code for the methods is shown below:

```
public boolean mouseEnter(Event e, int x, int y){
inCount++;
}
```

```
public boolean mouseExit(Event e, int x, int y){
outCount++;
}
```

Notice that even though we have two arguments which represent the mouse positions they are not used in the body of the code. This is the analogue to the non-use of the Object argument in some uses of the action method.

11.7 Graphics

11.7.1 Drawing methods

Many applications and applets require drawing. For example, if you were developing an applet which carried out the graphical display of data, say in a pie chart, then you would need to draw a circle, some lines and also fill in areas with some colour.

Normally you will only want to carry out drawing operations on applets or Canvases. The latter are special sort of container which can be used to display drawings. It is perfectly possible to draw on other components such as objects described by the Panel class. However, these objects will also contain HCI control elements such as buttons and text fields which should not really be drawn over.

There is a special class known as Graphics which enables drawing to take place. The Graphics class is an abstract graphics device which is used in the Applet class. Rather than define a graphics class for every type of client machine, Java defines an abstract class which the local Java system translates to the real graphics device when graphics operations occur.

The drawing process is achieved by means of a method called paint. This takes a Graphics object as its argument and carries out drawing actions on that object which will be displayed on a screen. If you look in the Java class library you will find that the class Component which forms the basis of all the HCI objects you require has this method in it and hence all the elements of the AWT toolkit inherit this method including Applet.

The paint method is invoked whenever an HCI object is created or some external action which requires redrawing occurs such as a window being moved. It can also be called by other methods. This is achieved by calling the method repaint. An example of the use of paint is shown below:

```
import java.applet.Applet;
```

```
import java.awt.Graphics;
public class simpleApplet extends Applet {
  public void paint(Graphics g) {
    g.drawRect(10,10,100,75);
  }
}
```

In this example a rectangle is drawn at an offset (10,10) from the origin. The origin of an applet is at the topmost left-hand position in the applet window. This will occur when the browser document which contains the applet is moved or resized or scrolled into.

There are a number of methods available which allow us to draw closed figures and lines. A selection of these are described below:

drawRect(int, int, int, int). Draws the outline of the specified rectangle using the current colour. The rectangle is defined by a pair of *x* and *y* coordinates. The final two arguments give the width and height.

drawRoundRect(int, int, int, int, int, int). Draws an outlined rounded corner rectangle using the current colour. The rectangle is defined by *x* and *y* coordinates which are its first two arguments, a width which is its third argument and height which is its final argument. The final two arguments give the width and height of the arcs used.

drawString(String, int, int). Draws the specified String using the current font and colour. The starting position of the string is defined by an *x* coordinate and a *y* coordinate.

fill3DRect(int, int, int, int, boolean). Paints a highlighted 3-D rectangle using the current colour. The first two arguments are the *x* and *y* coordinates of the rectangle, the next two are the width and height and the final argument is a Boolean which if true will draw a raised rectangle.

fillArc(int, int, int, int, int, int). Fills an arc using the current colour. The first two arguments are the *x* and *y* starting coordinates, the next two arguments are the width and height of the arc, the fifth argument is the starting angle of the arc and the last argument is the final angle.

fillOval(int, int, int, int). Fills an oval inside the specified rectangle using the current colour. The final two arguments give the width and height.

fillPolygon(int[], int[], int). Fills a polygon with the current colour. The polygon *x* values are held in the first argument with its *y* values held in the second argument. The third argument is the number of sides to the polygon.

These are just a selection of the methods you can use for drawing. These and a number of other drawing methods can be found in the class `java.awt.Graphics`.

11.7.2   Fonts and colour

The AWT also provides support for fonts and colours. The model adopted by Java to communicate colours to drawing methods and fonts to methods which display strings and characters is to set a current colour and current font. These will be used by all the Graphics methods until such time as they are reset to other values.

In Java there are two classes which relate directly to font support, the `Font` and `FontMetric` classes. The `Font()` method is usually the most frequently used, while `FontMetric` is required when information about an existing instance of `Font` is needed.

The `Font` class defines the font itself, including the font family, size and style. For example, to create a font in Courier at 12 point and in Bold you would use:

```
someFont = new Font("Courier", Font.BOLD, 12);
```

The first parameter to the constructor is a string which defines the font family. The next parameter is a static variable from the `Font` class which defines the font as being bold. Finally, the last integer is the size of the type.

By default, the Java system guarantees that the *Helvetica, TimesRoman, ZapfDingBats, Dialog, DialogInput* and *Courier* families are always available. The *Dialog* family relates to a native font on the client system which is the standard for the system to use in dialog with the user. For each of the default families the sizes 8, 10, 12, 14, 24 and 36 points are always available. It is possible to specify other sizes than the default and, if the client system supports font scaling, then this will be used to generate the type. However, if the client system does not implement a method for font scaling, then the nearest available size will be used instead of the size that has been specified. This means that if an interface has been designed expecting type to take a certain amount of screen space, then changes in font size at the client system can make applications and applets look very strange and not at all as intended.

Once an instance of `Font` has been created, it can be used to define the appearance of text in a display. For example, in an applet the following would be possible:

```
public void paint(Graphics g) {
    Font someFont = new Font("Courier", Font.BOLD, 12);
    g.setFont(someFont);
    g.drawString("Some Text!",10,10);
}
```

In this example, the `paint()` method defines a new font and then asks the Graphics context to use the font for further graphics operations. The next operation uses text and displays a string in the context. Because the font for the context was set prior to the call to drawString using the setFont method the text will be drawn using the font that was created.

The FontMetric class can be used to obtain information about a particular font. This information is most useful when the display of an application or applet requires the accurate positioning of components or when text needs to be formatted in a particular manner. The FontMetric constructor requires an instance of Font as a parameter. For example:

```
Font someFont = new Font("Courier", Font.BOLD, 12);
FontMetric someFontMetric = new FontMetric(someFont);
```

Once an instance of FontMetric exists, it is possible to use the methods of the class to return information about the font. Some of the methods in the class include stringWidth(String) and charWidth(char) which return the pixel widths of strings and characters in the font that was used to create the instance. For example, the code:

```
int    wordLength =
          someFontmetric.stringWidth("Hello there"),
       charLength =
          someFontmetric.charWidth('h');
```

places in wordLength the width of the string "Hello there" and in charLength the width of the character 'h'.

As an example of using these methods imagine that you require the title of a file to be centred in a window. If the user loads the file from a dialog, there is no way of knowing the file name in advance and therefore no way of knowing what the required offset is to ensure that the name of the file is centred as expected. However, by creating an instance of FontMetric, it is a simple matter to determine the width of the filename using stringWidth() and then centre the string based on the width of the parent window. Other related methods return the height of a font and the ascent and descent of a font.

The Color class encapsulates RGB colours. The colours are used to define the appearance of text, graphics primitives and user interface (UI) components. To create a Color, there are several constructors which are supported.

Color(int, int, int). This creates a Color with each of the ints representing a value for one of the red, green and blue channels.

Color(int). This creates a Color with the bits of the integer representing the values of the channels.

Color(float, float, float). This creates a Color with the channels being defined by the floats in the range 0.0 to 1.0.

So, for example, to create a colour where all three channels are set to 100:

```
Color myColor = new Color(100,100,100);
```

However, most of the time there will not be a need to define colours with such precision, and so the `Color` class defines a number of standard colours for general use. The range of colours is `black`, `blue`, `cyan`, `darkGray`, `gray`, `green`, `lightGray`, `magenta`, `orange`, `pink`, `red`, `white` and `yellow`. To use one of these predefined colours, for example green, use the following constructor:

```
Color myColor = new Color(Color.green);
```

These predefined colours can be found in the package `java.awt.Color`. Once you have defined a colour, you can use it in your interface code. For example:

```
public void paint(Graphics g) {
        Color myColor = new Color(Color,green);
        g.setColor(myColor);
        g.fillRect(10,10,100,100);
}
```

Once a colour has been set, any subsequent operations will be performed using this colour. Consequently, it makes sense to group operations that require the same colours and fonts together in your code to avoid switching more than you really need to.

When using colour in your interface, remember that the Java colour support is not device independent, and some colours will look radically different on a range of client machines. If colour accuracy is important to you then you should either select a set of colours which vary from machine to machine, catering for the differences between the hardware, or consider implementing a device-independent imaging method.

11.8 Some examples

In order to conclude this chapter we shall describe three examples. Each of these covers the techniques which we have described in the previous sections. All the examples are of applets: containers which can be embedded within an HTML document. In all the examples we will extend the class `Applet`. This, as you will see in the next chapter, is the standard way of programming applets. We do it because we will need to overwrite a number of methods which are supplied with this class. The main two we overwrite are `init` which is called when an applet is initialized and `paint` which is called when an external event such as the browser window being moved necessitates redrawing.

11.8.1 Example 1

The first example displays a canvas. When the user clicks at a point in the canvas a message is displayed. The user can switch the colour in which the message is displayed by clicking a radio button.

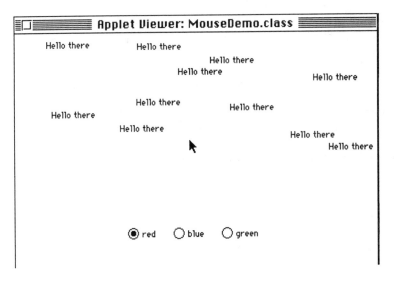

Figure 11.18   The first example.

The applet is shown in Figure 11.18. Here we see the radio buttons with the red button having been clicked and the result of a number of clicks on a canvas which forms the top half of the applet. The text to be displayed is the string "Hello there". The first part of the code for the applet is shown below:

```
import java.applet.*;
import java.awt.*;

public class MouseDemo extends Applet{
ClickableCanvas top;
Panel bottom;
Checkbox redButton, blueButton, greenButton;
Color currentColour;

public void init(){
bottom = new Panel(); top = new ClickableCanvas();
bottom.setLayout(new FlowLayout());
CheckboxGroup radioGroup = new CheckboxGroup();
```

This first makes the required libraries available, declares a panel bottom which is going to contain the radio buttons, a canvas which is to be drawn on and three radio buttons corresponding to the three colours. The final line declares an object currentColour which will contain the current colour for displaying the text on the canvas.

The next line declares a method init. As you will learn in the next chapter this is a method which is executed when an applet is first started up: for example, when it comes into view in an HTML document. This creates the panel bottom and a clickable canvas `top` (the definition of a `ClickableCanvas` follows later). The next line of code specifies that a flow layout is to be adopted for the panel containing the radio buttons and then declares a radio button checkgroup `radioGroup`.

Exercise

Write down the next section of code which terminates the `init` method: it should add the three buttons to `radioGroup`, adopt a grid layout with two rows and one column for the applet and then add `top` and `bottom` to the applet.

Solution

The code is shown below:

```
bottom.add(redButton =
  new Checkbox("red", radioGroup , true));
bottom.add(blueButton =
  new Checkbox("blue", radioGroup , false));
bottom.add(greenButton =
  new Checkbox("green", radioGroup , false));
setLayout(new GridLayout(2,1));
add(top);
add(bottom);
}
```

An alternative to the above solution is:

```
redButton = new Checkbox("red", radioGroup , true);
blueButton = new Checkbox("blue", radioGroup , false);
greenButton = new Checkbox("green", radioGroup , false);
bottom.add(redButton);
bottom.add(blueButton);
bottom.add(greenButton);
setLayout(new GridLayout(2,1));
add(top);
add(bottom); }
```

The next code segment is that for handling the event of a radio button being checked. The code is shown below:

```
public boolean action(Event e, Object obj){
Checkbox currentCheckbox = (Checkbox) e.target;
if (redButton.getState()) {
  currentColour = Color.red;};
if (blueButton.getState()) {
```

```
  currentColour = Color.blue;};
if (greenButton.getState()) {
  currentColour = Color.green;};
top.setClickColour(currentColour);
return true;
}
```

This follows the pattern that we described for event handlers. It checks the state of each button using the method getState found in the class Button; this returns true if the button has been checked. If a button has been checked a message is sent to the ClickableCanvas top that the current colour has been changed. This uses the method setClickColour which you will see coded soon. Colours can be found in the java.awt library in the class Color. There are a number of colour variables associated with this class and we use three of them in the code above.

All that is now needed is to program the ClickableCanvas class. The first lines of this class are shown below:

```
class ClickableCanvas extends Canvas{
Color cColour;
int noOfClicks;
int[] xVals, yVals;
```

This class inherits from Canvas. It contains instance variables which hold the current colour used for writing the strings, the number of clicks that have occurred with this component and two arrays which hold the corresponding *x* and *y* values of each click that has occurred.

The constructor of the ClickableCanvas class is shown below. It must initialize the number of clicks, set the first colour to red (Color.red) and allocate memory for the arrays.

```
ClickableCanvas(){
super();
cColour = Color.red;
xVals = new int[100];
yVals = new int[100];
noOfClicks = 0;
}
```

This sets up a Canvas object and sets the first colour to red since that corresponds to the radio button which will initially be clicked.

Two further methods of the ClickableCanvas class are shown below:

```
public void setClickColour(Color c){
cColour = c;
}

public void paint(Graphics g){
```

```
g.setColor(cColour);
for(int i = 0; i < noOfClicks; i++)
g.drawString("Hello there", xVals[i], yVals[i]);
}
```

The first method is simple, all it does is to set the current colour. You will remember that it was used by the applet when a radio button was clicked. The next method overrides the `paint` method supplied with the class `Canvas`. All this does is to set the current colour for drawing for the canvas to the current colour and then draw all the instances of the string on the canvas. The code uses the methods `drawString` and `setColor` provided as part of the `Color` class in the `java.awt` library.

The final method is shown below:

```
public boolean mouseDown(Event e, int x, int y){
xVals[noOfClicks] = x; yVals[noOfClicks] = y;
noOfClicks++;
repaint();
return true;
}
```

This overwrites the `mouseDown` method supplied with the class `Canvas`. When the user clicks the mouse this will store the *x* and *y* positions in the two arrays, increment the number of clicks and repaint the canvas. You will remember that `paint` can be called by other methods by calling the method `repaint`.

This, then, is the code for our applet. The full code is shown below:

```
import java.applet.*;
import java.awt.*;

public class MouseDemo extends Applet{
ClickableCanvas top;
Panel bottom;
Checkbox redButton, blueButton, greenButton;
Color currentColour;

public void init(){
bottom = new Panel();
top = new ClickableCanvas();
bottom.setLayout(new FlowLayout());
CheckboxGroup radioGroup = new CheckboxGroup();
bottom.add(redButton = new Checkbox
   ("red", radioGroup , true));
bottom.add(blueButton = new Checkbox
   ("blue", radioGroup , false));
bottom.add(greenButton = new Checkbox
   ("green", radioGroup , false));
```

```
setLayout(new GridLayout(2,1));
add(top);
add(bottom);
}

public boolean action(Event e, Object obj){
Checkbox currentCheckbox = (Checkbox) e.target;
if (redButton.getState()) {
  currentColour = Color.red;};
if (blueButton.getState()) {
  currentColour = Color.blue;};
if (greenButton.getState()) {
  currentColour = Color.green;};
top.setClickColour(currentColour);
return true;
}

}

class ClickableCanvas extends Canvas{
Color cColour;
int noOfClicks;
int[] xVals, yVals;

ClickableCanvas(){
super();
cColour = Color.red;
xVals = new int[100]; yVals = new int[100];
noOfClicks = 0;
}

public boolean mouseDown(Event e, int x, int y){
xVals[noOfClicks] = x; yVals[noOfClicks] = y;
noOfClicks++; repaint();
return true;}

public void setClickColour(Color c){
cColour = c;}

public void paint(Graphics g){
g.setColor(cColour);
for(int i = 0; i < noOfClicks; i++)
g.drawString("Hello there", xVals[i], yVals[i]);

}}
```

The code for `MouseDemo` consists of code which initializes the applet and monitors any event which occurs with the buttons. The code for `ClickableCanvas` keeps track of the past mouse clicks and refreshes the screen with all the text that needs to be displayed. It does this by continually calling `paint` via the method `repaint`.

11.8.2 Example 2

The second example demonstrates the use of some of the control elements we discussed in the earlier part of this chapter. What it does is to use three sliders to adjust the red, green and blue colour components of a colour and display the resulting colour which is formed by adjusting the components. Four canvases are used: one will display the current red colour, another the current blue colour, another the green colour and the final canvas will display the colour made up of combining the red, green and blue.

Again we will develop an applet. The display for this applet is shown in Figure 11.19. The topmost left canvas contains the mixed colour, the topmost right the red colour, the bottommost left the blue and the bottommost right the green. The sliders adjust the colour values and the value of each colour is shown on the left. The first lines of the applet are shown below:

```
import java.applet.*; import java.awt.*;

public class ColourAdjust extends Applet{
Scrollbar redSlider;
Scrollbar blueSlider;
Scrollbar greenSlider;
TextField redText;
TextField blueText;
TextField greenText;
ColourCanvas colCanvas;
ColourCanvas blueCanvas;
ColourCanvas redCanvas;
ColourCanvas greenCanvas;
int blueValue, redValue, greenValue;
```

This declares the various sliders, text fields and canvases necessary for the operation. The integer values are the colour values that are to be made to construct the composite colour.

The code for the `init` method of the applet is shown below:

```
public void init(){
Panel top = new Panel(), bottom = new Panel();
colCanvas = new ColourCanvas();
redCanvas = new ColourCanvas();
blueCanvas = new ColourCanvas();
```

```
greenCanvas = new ColourCanvas();
bottom.setLayout(new GridLayout(4,2));
redSlider =
  new Scrollbar(Scrollbar.HORIZONTAL, 0,10, 0, 256);
blueSlider =
  new Scrollbar(Scrollbar.HORIZONTAL,0,10, 0, 256);
greenSlider =
  new Scrollbar(Scrollbar.HORIZONTAL, 0,10, 0, 256);
redText = new TextField("000", 4);
blueText = new TextField("000", 4);
greenText = new TextField("000", 4);
bottom.add(redText);bottom.add(redSlider);
bottom.add(blueText);bottom.add(blueSlider);
bottom.add(greenText);bottom.add(greenSlider);
top.setLayout(new GridLayout(2, 2, 10,10));
top.add(colCanvas);
top.add(redCanvas);
top.add(blueCanvas);
top.add(greenCanvas);
setLayout(new GridLayout(2,1));
add(top);
add(bottom);
}
```

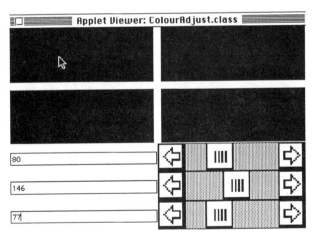

Figure 11.19 The colour applet.

This declares and allocates the various objects that are needed for the applet. It collects the canvases that are required into a panel which has a grid layout of two rows and two columns. The extra two parameters to GridLayout are spacing values which separate the panels. It then adds the top panel containing the colours and the bottom panels containing the sliders and text fields to the applet. The sliders and text field panel has a default layout associated with it which is a flow layout.

The class defining a ColourCanvas object is shown below:

```
class ColourCanvas extends Canvas{
Color currColour;

ColourCanvas(){
currColour = new Color(0,0,0);
}

public void paint (Graphics g){
Dimension d = size();
g.setColor(currColour);
g.fillRect(0,0, d.width, d.height);
}

public void changeColour(int r, int g, int b){
currColour = new Color(r,g,b);}

public Color getColour(){
return currColour;}
}
```

This is fairly unremarkable code. There are two things to note. First, that it uses the constructor of Color which takes three integer values that represent the red, green and blue components of a colour. The second thing to note is that the paint method associated with ColourCanvas objects finds the size of the canvas by applying the size method which is associated with the Component class. This method delivers a Dimension object which has two public instance variables width and length. These are used to draw a filled rectangle on a canvas using the current colour of the canvas.

The only remaining part of the code is the code which handles the event of a slider being moved. This is shown below:

```
public boolean handleEvent(Event evt){
if (evt.target == redSlider){
  redValue = redSlider.getValue();
  redText.setText(""+redValue);
  redCanvas.changeColour(redValue,0,0);
  redCanvas.repaint();
```

```
};
if(evt.target == blueSlider){
   blueValue = blueSlider.getValue();
   blueText.setText(""+blueValue);
   blueCanvas.changeColour(0,0,blueValue);
   blueCanvas.repaint();
};
if(evt.target == greenSlider ){
   greenValue = greenSlider.getValue();
   greenText.setText(""+greenValue);
   greenCanvas.changeColour(0,greenValue,0);
   greenCanvas.repaint();
};
colCanvas.changeColour(redValue, greenValue, blueValue);
colCanvas.repaint();
return true;
}
```

The main thing to note here is that the scroll bar does not use the `action` method. It is one of the few control elements which does not use `action`. It uses a method known as `handleEvent`. The code is simple: if it detects an event generated by the movement of a scroll bar, then it gets the value of the scroll bar using the method `getValue` defined in the class `Scrollbar`. It then sets the text in the three text fields to the new values, using the method `setText` defined in the class `TextField`. The message `changeColour` is then sent to the canvas containing the composite colour. After a canvas has had its colour updated it is painted by calling the method `repaint`. You will remember that `repaint` is the way that other classes instruct an AWT component to draw itself.

The whole code for the applet is shown below:

```
import java.applet.*;
import java.awt.*;

public class ColourAdjust extends Applet{
Scrollbar redSlider;
Scrollbar blueSlider;
Scrollbar greenSlider;
TextField redText;
TextField blueText;
TextField greenText;
ColourCanvas colCanvas;
ColourCanvas blueCanvas;
ColourCanvas redCanvas;
ColourCanvas greenCanvas;
int blueValue, redValue, greenValue;
```

```
public void init(){
Panel top = new Panel(), bottom = new Panel();
colCanvas = new ColourCanvas();
redCanvas = new ColourCanvas();
blueCanvas = new ColourCanvas();
greenCanvas = new ColourCanvas();
bottom.setLayout(new GridLayout(4,2));
redSlider = new Scrollbar(Scrollbar.HORIZONTAL, 0,10, 0,
256);
blueSlider = new Scrollbar(Scrollbar.HORIZONTAL,0,10, 0,
256);
greenSlider = new Scrollbar(Scrollbar.HORIZONTAL, 0,10,
0, 256);
redText = new TextField("000", 4);
blueText = new TextField("000", 4);
greenText = new TextField("000", 4);
bottom.add(redText);bottom.add(redSlider);
bottom.add(blueText);bottom.add(blueSlider);
bottom.add(greenText);bottom.add(greenSlider);
top.setLayout(new GridLayout(2, 2, 10,10));
top.add(colCanvas);
top.add(redCanvas);
top.add(blueCanvas);
top.add(greenCanvas);
setLayout(new GridLayout(2,1));
add(top);
add(bottom);
}

public boolean handleEvent(Event evt){
if (evt.target == redSlider){
  redValue = redSlider.getValue();
  redText.setText(""+redValue);
  redCanvas.changeColour(redValue,0,0);
  redCanvas.repaint();
};
if(evt.target == blueSlider){
  blueValue = blueSlider.getValue();
  blueText.setText(""+blueValue);
  blueCanvas.changeColour(0,0,blueValue);
  blueCanvas.repaint();
};
if(evt.target == greenSlider ){
  greenValue = greenSlider.getValue();
  greenText.setText(""+greenValue);
```

```
    greenCanvas.changeColour(0,greenValue,0);
    greenCanvas.repaint();};
colCanvas.changeColour(redValue, greenValue, blueValue);
colCanvas.repaint();
return true;}
}

class ColourCanvas extends Canvas{
Color currColour;

ColourCanvas(){
currColour = new Color(0,0,0);}

public void paint (Graphics g){
Dimension d = size();
g.setColor(currColour);g.fillRect(0,0,d.width,d.height);}

public void changeColour(int r, int g, int b){
currColour = new Color(r,g,b);}

public Color getColour(){
return currColour;}
```

Exercise

The display of the applet shown in Figure 11.19 is a little defective in that the text fields are quite large. They should also be labelled with the name of the colour that they represent. Can you think of any way that you can reduce them and carry out the labelling at the same time?

Solution

This can be done by making the grid contain more squares. This forces the size of each element in a square down:

```
bottom.setLayout(new GridLayout(4,3));
```

and the new code which adds the items, including the labels, will be:

```
bottom.add(new Label("Red"));bottom.add(redText);
bottom.add(redSlider); bottom.add(new Label("Blue"));
bottom.add(blueText); bottom.add(blueSlider);
bottom.add(new Label("Green"));bottom.add(greenText);
bottom.add(greenSlider);
```

This gives the display shown in Figure 11.20.

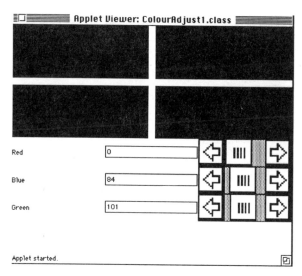

Figure 11.20   An improved applet.

11.8.3 Example 3

The final code is for an applet which carries out the drawing of many-sided figures and the filling in of these figures using a pre-selected colour.

The display for the applet is shown in Figure 11.21. A canvas is used to draw n-sided figures using a mouse. The user will click the mouse when he or she has reached the end of a line and wishes to draw another line.

When the polygon that is being drawn is eventually clicked at its first position it will be filled with the current colour. The first lines of the applet are shown below:

```
import java.applet.*;
import java.awt.*;

public class ShapeDrawer extends Applet{
PaintCanvas c;
CheckboxGroup colGroup;
```

All this does is to set up a Canvas object and a radio button group.

Exercise

Write down the code for the init method of the applet. This init method should set up a grid layout, then add the canvas and the individual checkboxes. It should use the method setBackground which is found in the Canvas class.

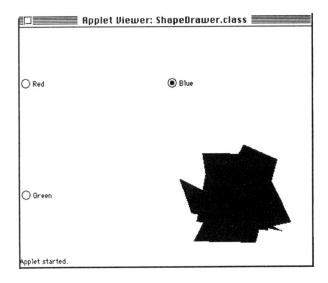

Figure 11.21 The drawing applet.

This has one argument that is the background colour that the canvas starts off with. In this case choose white.

Solution

The code is shown below:

```
public void init(){

c = new PaintCanvas(Color.red);
c.setBackground(Color.white);
colGroup = new  CheckboxGroup();
setLayout(new GridLayout(2,2));
add(new Checkbox("Red", colGroup, true));
add(new Checkbox("Blue", colGroup, false));
add(new Checkbox("Green", colGroup, false));
add( c);
}
```

The next method within the applet is the one which senses that a checkbox has been checked. It should discover which one has been checked and set a drawing colour according to the choice made. The code is shown below:

```
public boolean action(Event evt, Object o){
if (evt.target instanceof Checkbox){
```

```
Checkbox current = (Checkbox) evt.target;
if (current.getLabel() == "Red")
  c.setColour(Color.red);
else
if (current.getLabel() == "Blue")
  c.setColour(Color.blue);
else
if (current.getLabel() == "Green")
  c.setColour(Color.green);
};
return true;
}
```

Since the checkboxes have not been associated with variable names the action method looks at the label. This is the string of the checkbox that has been clicked. Once the box has been identified the drawing colour can be adjusted. This is done by sending a setColour message to the PaintCanvas c. This method is defined in the class PaintCanvas which is shown below:

The first lines of this class are:

```
class PaintCanvas extends Canvas{
private int[] xPoints, yPoints;
private Color currentColour;
private int polyCount, noOfPoints;
private Polygon[] polyStore;
private Color[] polyColours;
```

It contains two arrays xPoints and yPoints which contain the *x* and *y* coordinates of the polygon which is currently being drawn; an instance variable which contains the current colour used to fill the polygons; a count of the number of polygons which have been drawn and the number of points currently drawn for the polygon which is being drawn at the current time; an array of polygons which contains each polygon that has been drawn (Polygon is a Java class found in java.awt); and an array which contains the colour of each polygon that has been drawn.

The constructor shown below initializes all the values for these instance variables:

```
PaintCanvas(Color c){
super();
currentColour = c;
polyCount = 0; noOfPoints = 0;
polyColours = new Color [100];
polyStore = new Polygon[100];
xPoints = new int [50];
yPoints = new int [50];
}
```

The most complex method within the applet is the one that deals with the action of mouse clicking. When this happens the code should check that the click is near to the first element of the current polygon being drawn, that is, within 20 pixels. If this is so, then a new polygon has been formed. After the click the code should display all the stored polygons using their colours to fill them and also display all the black lines of the polygon that is being drawn. The code is shown below:

```
public boolean mouseDown(Event e, int x, int y){
xPoints[noOfPoints] = x;
yPoints[noOfPoints] = y;
noOfPoints++;
if (noOfPoints > 1)
   repaint();
if (noOfPoints > 2
   && Math.sqrt((double) Math.pow((double) xPoints[0]-
   xPoints[noOfPoints-1], 2.0) + Math.pow
((double) yPoints[0]-yPoints[noOfPoints-1], 2.0)) < 20){
   polyStore[polyCount] = new
     Polygon(xPoints, yPoints, noOfPoints);
   polyColours[polyCount] = currentColour;
   polyCount++; noOfPoints = 0;
   repaint();
   }
return true;
}
```

This code uses the methods power and sqrt found as static methods within the Math class found within the java.lang library. The method power has two arguments, a double length value which is raised to the power indicated by the second argument (for squaring this is 2.0). The sqrt method just takes the square root of the double length value which is its argument. Notice the use of the (double) cast which makes sure that the integer values within the arrays holding the polygon points are of the right type for these two methods.

The only other code of note is:

```
polyStore[polyCount]= new
    Polygon(xPoints, yPoints, noOfPoints);
```

which forms a polygon from the contents of the x and y coordinate arrays and the number of sides contained in noOfPoints. This method can be found in java.awt.

The final component of our code is that dealing with the setting of colours and painting. The methods which carry out these processes are shown below:

```
public void setColour(Color c){
currentColour = c;
}
```

```
public void paint(Graphics g){
for(int i = 0; i < polyCount; i++){
  g.setColor(polyColours[i]);
  g.fillPolygon(polyStore[i]);
};
g.setColor(Color.black);
for(int j = 0; j < noOfPoints-1; j++)
  g.drawLine   (xPoints[j],yPoints[j],
           xPoints[j+1],yPoints[j+1]);
}
```

First the polygons in the array `polyStore` are displayed using the method `fillPolygon` found in `java.awt`, then the lines of the polygon which is currently being built up are displayed using black as the colour for the outline.

The full code for this applet is shown below:

```
import java.applet.*;
import java.awt.*;

public class ShapeDrawer extends Applet{
PaintCanvas c;
CheckboxGroup colGroup;

public void init(){
colGroup = new   CheckboxGroup();
c= new PaintCanvas(Color.red);
c.setBackground(Color.white);
setLayout(new GridLayout(2,2));
add(new  Checkbox("Red", colGroup, true));
add(new  Checkbox("Blue", colGroup, false));
add(new  Checkbox("Green", colGroup, false));
add( c);
}

public boolean action(Event evt, Object o){
if (evt.target instanceof Checkbox){
Checkbox current = (Checkbox) evt.target;
if (current.getLabel() == "Red")
  c.setColour(Color.red);
else
if (current.getLabel() == "Blue")
  c.setColour(Color.blue);
else
if (current.getLabel() == "Green")
  c.setColour(Color.green);
};
```

```
return true;
}

}

class PaintCanvas extends Canvas{
private int [] xPoints, yPoints;
private Color currentColour;
private int polyCount, noOfPoints;
private Polygon [] polyStore;
private Color [] polyColours;


PaintCanvas(Color c){
super();
currentColour = c; polyCount = 0; noOfPoints = 0;
polyColours = new Color [100];
polyStore = new Polygon[100];
xPoints = new int [50]; yPoints = new int [50]; }

public boolean mouseDown(Event e, int x, int y){
xPoints[noOfPoints] = x;
yPoints[noOfPoints] = y;
noOfPoints++;
if (noOfPoints > 1)
  repaint();
if  (noOfPoints > 2 &&
    Math.sqrt((double) Math.pow((double) xPoints[0]-
    xPoints[noOfPoints-1], 2.0)+ Math.pow((double)
    yPoints[0]-yPoints[noOfPoints-1], 2.0)) < 20){
      polyStore[polyCount] = new
        Polygon(xPoints, yPoints, noOfPoints);
      polyColours[polyCount] = currentColour;
      polyCount++; noOfPoints = 0; repaint();
  }
return true; }

public void setColour(Color c){
currentColour = c; }

public void paint(Graphics g){
for(int i = 0; i < polyCount; i++){
  g.setColor(polyColours[i]);
  g.fillPolygon(polyStore[i]);
  }
```

```
g.setColor(Color.black);
for(int j = 0; j < noOfPoints-1; j++)
   g.drawLine(xPoints[j],yPoints[j],
     xPoints[j+1],yPoints[j+1]); }
}
```

11.9 SUMMARY

This has been a very substantial chapter. In it we have described how you can build up interfaces and also shown how certain types of container such as applets and canvases can be drawn on. The last part of the chapter described three examples of control elements being used in conjunction with drawing methods to produce applets. As we proceeded through this chapter we also introduced, on the fly, a number of the methods which form part of the `java.awt` library. Again it is worth stressing that the only way to program in Java – and any other object-oriented language, come to that – is to have the class library documentation next to you.

CHAPTER TWELVE

Applets

- To describe the major events in the life cycle of an applet.
- To reinforce the concepts of event handling and drawing.
- To outline the basic use of threads within applets.
- To introduce the basics of applet user interface support.
- To build a sample applet to demonstrate some of these new topics.

12.1 Introduction

At this point you should understand the differences between an applet and an application. In short, applications are standalone while applets conform to rules which allow them to be 'hosted' in a Java-compatible browser. You will already have met some applet code. This chapter focuses in on applets in a lot more detail and the differences that arise from requiring a host. There are some subtle differences between writing an applet and writing an application. When working with a standalone application you can make arbitrary decisions about pretty much any aspect of your code. When writing an applet it is essential that your code conforms to the applet standard so that your work can be executed within a Java-compatible browser. Of course, it is possible to write an applet which conforms to the letter of the applet class while still being a 'bad' example of coding because it fails to operate within the spirit of the hosted system. To help you write code that will cooperate with the Java system, we will describe some pointers during the chapter that should assist you in writing better applets.

12.1.1 'Hello World' revisited again

As with the previous chapter, we will use the standard issue 'Hello World' building block and extend the code to introduce new concepts. For an applet, the code looks like this:

```
import java.awt.Graphics;

public class HelloWorld extends java.applet.Applet {
   public void init() {
      resize(100,100);
   }

   public void paint(Graphics g) {
      g.drawString("Hello World!",5,20);
   }
}
```

The first line in the applet 'imports' the awt.Graphics library into the applet file. Chapter 11 described the AWT library in more detail.

You can see from the declaration of the class that the HelloWorld class inherits from the Applet class. The Applet class itself inherits from classes within the AWT library which means that applets can make use of interface components when constructing interfaces. We'll cover this in more detail later in the chapter.

Because this is a very simple applet there are only two methods. Both are contained in the class Applet and can hence be overridden by any subclass. The first method in the code, init, is always called by the system to allow the applet to prepare for execution. In this example, our applet just increases the amount of browser page space from the system default that it occupies. The paint method is called by the system when the applet is asked to display itself on the screen. This could be because the applet has just been loaded or because the browser has been uncovered from under another window. In this applet, all we do is draw our string into the Graphics context at the specified pixel coordinates.

12.2 Introducing some essential applet methods

Real applets won't be as simple as the 'Hello World' example above. An applet can perform a whole range of tasks including games, advertising, spicing up a home page and simulating a real-world situation. Clearly the limits of an applet's functionality are the limits of the developer's imagination. Because applets are typically embedded in pages of HTML, there is a need for them to coexist in a peaceful manner. To this end the Applet class defines a set of methods which applets can override to allow code to be hosted happily in a browser. To start off, we will look at a group of methods which control the 'life cycle' of an applet.

12.2.1 Methods to control the life of an applet

The Java system needs a way to control the execution of an applet. The system needs to tell an applet when it has been loaded into the page or when it has been unloaded. The core set of such methods is described briefly below. Again it is worth pointing out that these methods are contained in the class `Applet` and will need to be overridden if you wish to do any processing in an applet.

- `init`. This method is called by the Java system to initialize the applet each time that it is loaded or reloaded.

- `start`. The Java system calls this method when the applet is loaded and the applet can begin executing its main task.

- `stop`. When the user leaves the page or exits from the browser the system will call this method. The applet should suspend any outstanding tasks and threads.

- `destroy`. This method is the last chance that an applet will have to clean up before it is unloaded from the browser. All tasks should be stopped and any threads halted.

The `HelloWorld` class doesn't need to override all of the methods. Typically, the `init` method should be used to prepare the applet for the main task ahead by performing work which only needs to be done once in the lifetime of the applet, for example allocating storage for arrays.

The `start` method performs the applet's work or establishes other objects to do the work. Most applets that override `start` will also need to override `stop`. The `stop` method should be used to prevent the applet consuming system resources when the applet is not active – for example, halting a demanding graphics routine when the user moves on to a different browser page.

One of the most common ways of redefining `start` is to create a thread which runs as a background process and then uses a call to `stop` to halt the thread at the start of the next loop. This means that the thread doesn't die immediately after `stop` is called; however, for most applets this won't be a big issue. If your applet uses a thread with a very time-consuming main loop you should consider breaking up the code so that the thread checks for `stop()` being called more frequently. The effect of letting a thread (or any other similar object) live long after the user has moved on is to slow down the client machine. If the user encounters several such ill-behaved applets then the client can be ground to a halt.

Many applets don't bother to override the `destroy()` method, because their `stop` method puts the applet into a state suitable for being unloaded. This is an acceptable approach because the Java system guarantees to call `stop()` prior to calling `destroy`.

12.2.2 Adding life-cycle methods to the `HelloWorld` class

So, let us build on the `HelloWorld` class to include examples of the life-cycle methods. To keep things simple, we will just have the class print a line to the standard output when each of the methods is invoked. You should spend some time loading, reloading, and unloading the applet until you are happy that all of the methods are called and, more importantly, the methods are called in the correct order. The first part of the revised class is shown below:

```
import java.awt.Graphics;
public class HelloWorld extends java.applet.Applet {
  public void init() {
    System.out.println("Applet: system " +
                       "has called init()");
    resize(100,100);
  }

  public void paint(Graphics g) {
    g.drawString("Hello World!",5,20);
  }

  public void start() {
    System.out.println("Applet: system " +
                       "has called start()");
  }
```

Note that since the strings go over a line we need to use the concatenate operator +.

Exercise

Write down the code for the `stop` and `destroy` methods. All they should do is to display a similar message to that shown in `start` above.

Solution

The code is shown below.

```
  public void stop() {
    System.out.println("Applet: system" +
                       "has called stop()");
  }
  public void destroy() {
    System.out.println("Applet: system
                       has called destroy()");
  }
}
```

At this point you should compile the applet and view it in a browser. Play around with the page and watch the output as you load and unload the applet code. Each time one of the methods is invoked, the applet just prints out a line using the

System class library detailing the method. If all is well, the methods should be called in the following order when the applet is first loaded: init(), start(), stop(), destroy().

12.3 Drawing and handling events

So far our HelloWorld class has been simple: there has been no interaction with the user and we have only displayed a single string on the browser page. The rest of the information has been sent to the standard out. Real applets are going to want to change their appearance and receive input from the user. Happily, the Applet class supports both of these requirements.

12.3.1 Drawing to the screen

There are three main methods that you will need to know about to handle drawing to the browser page, paint, repaint and update. By default, the paint method is used by the applet to draw its representation onto the browser page, repaint will call paint from outside an applet class and the update method is used when part or all of the applet needs to be refreshed. If you don't override them using inheritance then the applet will inherit the following defaults:

```
public void update(Graphics g) {
    g.setColor(getBackGround());
    g.fillRect(0, 0, width, height);
    g.setColor(getForeground()); paint(g);
}

public void paint(Graphics g) {
}
```

The methods getBackGround and getForeGround are contained in java.awt.Component. The former gets the colour which is the current background colour of the applet, while the latter gets the colour which is the one which is currently used for drawing in the applet. The variables width and height contain the width and height of the applet and fillRect will paint a rectangle with the background colour. So you can see that the update method just paints a rectangle the size of the applet in the background colour which is typically the colour of the browser page; it then resets the applet screen to the colour it was before and calls paint, which by default does nothing. In the rest of this book we shall assume that most of your display code will go into a paint method.

12.3.2 Adding drawing methods to the HelloWorld class

To illustrate a simple example using these methods, we will extend the HelloWorld class to draw a filled 3-D rectangle into which we will place the "Hello World!" string.

The revised code is shown below:

```
import java.awt.Graphics;
import java.awt.Color;
import java.Applet.*

public class HelloWorld extends Applet {
  public void init() {
    System.out.println("Applet: system " +
                       "has called init");
    resize(100, 100);
  }

  public void paint(Graphics g) {
    g.setColor(Color.red);
    g.fill3DRect(5,5,95,95,true);
    g.setColor(Color.black);
    g.drawString("Hello World!",5,20);
    System.out.println("Applet: system" +
                       "has called paint");
  }

  public void update(Graphics g) {
    super.update(g);
    System.out.println("Applet: system " +
                       "has called update");
  }

  public void start() {
    System.out.println("Applet: system " +
                       "has called start");
  }

  public void stop() {
    System.out.println("Applet: system " +
                       "has called stop");
  }

  public void destroy() {
    System.out.println("Applet: system "+
                       "has called destroy");
  }
}
```

The code:

```
g.fill3DRect(5,5,95,95,true);
```

displays a three-dimensional rectangle at the pixel points specified with the fifth parameter with the rectangle casting a shadow. It uses `fill3DRect` which can be found in `java.awt.Graphics`.

So what have we added? Well, we have imported another class, `java.awt.Color`. We need this because our rectangle must be a different colour to our text in order for us to be able to read it. We have redefined the `paint()` method to:

(1)   set the colour to use to red (using the `Color` object);

(2)   draw a 3-D rectangle which is slightly smaller than the applet area;

(3)   set the colour to use back to black;

(4)   draw our string using the colour black;

(5)   print out a line saying that the method has been called.

We have also added an `update` method. You will recall from previous chapters that the `super` variable refers to the superclass, so we are invoking the `update` method contained in the `Applet` class which we listed earlier in this section. After invoking the superclass method, our `update` call goes on to write out a status line.

12.3.3 Improving drawing performance

We mentioned in Section 12.3.1 that you usually won't need to override the update method. One of the exceptions to this rule of thumb is when your applet requires improved graphics performance. By default, the `update()` and `paint()` methods affect the whole applet and cause the whole of the Graphics context to be redrawn. This approach becomes unacceptable when your applet only wants to update a small section of the screen.

As an example, consider a simple applet which draws a ball bouncing around inside a box. By default, every time the ball moves the whole of the applet must be redrawn. All that is really needed is for the area that the ball has moved out of and the area that the ball has moved into to be handled. This type of selective updating can be done with the judicious use of the `paint` and `update` methods.

12.3.4 Handling applet events

Previous chapters will have introduced you to the idea of events. In this section we will discuss some of the non-action events that are defined in the `Component` class and inherited by the `Applet` class and, therefore, by your applet as well. Already you have seen in Chapter 11 how `action` events such as a button being pressed are handled and have been introduced to non-action events.

As you might expect there is one method which handles all incoming events and acts in the manner of an exchange to route the event to the appropriate specialist method. This routing method is called `handleEvent()`. Although it is possible for you to override this method, for the moment it is more important for you to realize that the method exists.

Some other methods that you have already encountered include:

- mouseDown, mouseUp. These methods inform the applet that the mouse button has been pressed or released.

- mouseEnter, mouseExit. These methods inform the applet that the pointer has entered or left the browser page.

- mouseDrag, mouseMove. These methods inform the applet when the mouse is moved with either the button pressed (mouseDrag) or the button released (mouseMove).

- keyDown. This method notifies the applet that the user has pressed a key.

In general this set of seven methods will form the core of the events that you are interested in.

12.3.5 Adding event handling to HelloWorld

To demonstrate the use of non-action event methods, we will extend our HelloWorld class to have two extra features. When the mouse moves over the area of the applet, we will have the string move with the cursor, and when the user presses a key, we will append the key character to the string.

The code to do this is shown below without the code for handling the key down event:

```
import java.awt.Graphics;
import java.awt.Color;
import java.Applet.*;
import java.awt.Event;

public class HelloWorld extends Applet {
   int sx,sy;          // The coordinates of the string
   StringBuffer hw;    // The string to display
   public void init() {
     sx = 5;
     sy = 20;
     hw = new StringBuffer("Hello World!");
     System.out.println("Applet: system " +
                         "has called init");
     resize(100, 100);}


  public void paint(Graphics g) {
    g.setColor(Color.red);
    g.fill3DRect(5,5,95,95,true);
    g.setColor(Color.black);
```

```
      g.drawString(hw.toString(),sx,sy);
      System.out.println("Applet: system " +
                              "has called paint");}


   public void update(Graphics g) {
      super.update(g);
      System.out.println("Applet: system " +
                              "has called update");}


   public void start() {
      System.out.println("Applet: system " +
                              "has called start");}


   public void stop() {
      System.out.println("Applet: system " +
                              "has called stop");}


   public void destroy() {
      System.out.println("Applet: system " +
                              "has called destroy");}

   public boolean mouseMove(Event evt, int x, int y) {
      sx = x;
      sy = y;
      repaint();
      return true;}
```

Exercise

Write down the code for the keyDown event. This appends a character to the end of the string hw and repaints the screen. Use the method append defined in java.lang.StringBuffer. The method keyDown has two arguments: an event and the character that was pressed on the keyboard.

Solution

The code is shown below.

```
   public boolean keyDown(Event evt, int ch) {
      hw.append((char)ch);
      repaint();
      return true;
   } }
```

As you might expect by now we have had to import the `java.awt.Event` class so that we could override the event-based methods. We have used two ints to hold the coordinates of the string (the initial values are defined in the `init` method).

Because we are going to be appending characters to the `"Hello World!"` string, we have declared a `StringBuffer`, which is also initialized in the `init` method. Remember that the `String` class only generates constant strings which cannot be changed. The `paint()` method then converts the StringBuffer to a String and plots it at the coordinates held by the two integers (`sx` and `sy`). The method `toString` converts a `StringBuffer` to a `String` which is expected by `drawString`.

The `mouseMove` method simply takes two coordinates of the pointer as supplied by the system and sets the int values. The `repaint` method is called to have the applet redrawn. As an aside, this simple applet would benefit from overriding the `update` method. Currently, `update` calls `paint` and the whole of the applet is drawn. A more effective way to do this would be just to redraw the area that the string has left and then call `drawString` to place the text in the new position. Clearly, if such a simple applet can benefit from this technique, larger and more complex drawing operations should certainly be optimized.

The last remaining method we have added takes the `keyDown` event and appends the character to the `StringBuffer`. The method `keyDown` is an event method associated with the keyboard; it is the analogue to the `mouseDown` method. It is called when the user presses a key. Because the `keyDown` method receives the character in the form of an int, we have made an explicit cast to a char and then appended it to the StringBuffer. If we had not cast in this manner, `StringBuffer` would append the integer value directly.

It is worth pointing out that the call to `repaint()` in `mouseMove` and `keyDown` causes the system to call the `update()` method which, as you saw in Section 12.3.1, by default clears the graphics context and then calls the `paint` method.

In this simple applet, there is no support for handling special case characters, such as the delete key. We can extend our `keyDown` method quite simply:

```
public boolean keyDown(Event evt, int ch) {
  switch (ch) {
  case(8):  // This is the delete key

    if (hw.length() > 0) {
      hw.setLength(hw.length() - 1);
    }
    break;


    default:   hw.append((char)ch);

}
```

```
  repaint();
  return true;
}
```

In this example, if there are any elements in the StringBuffer when the delete key is pressed, then the StringBuffer is made smaller by one character. When any other key is pressed, the character matching the integer representation is appended to the StringBuffer as before. The method `setLength` can be found in `java.lang.StringBuffer`.

12.4 Using threads in applets

One of the most common problems introduced into applets is excessive code in the `init()` method. The reason that this causes a problem is because the browser waits for the `init()` method to run before continuing to the next applet. So, if an applet which executes all of its code in the `init()` method is at the top of the page, no other applets will be loaded until after the first applet has returned from the method.

12.4.1 Threads can be very useful

One solution to this issue is to create a thread and move as much of the code from the `init()` method to the thread as possible. This model forms a good general principle: if an applet performs an intensive task then you should arrange for the code to be placed in a thread and have the task executed in the background.

As stated previously there are two main approaches to adding threads to your applet or application. The first way is to subclass the `Thread` class and override the relevant method (usually you can just override `run()` and expect the default methods to do the right thing) and the second is to provide a runnable interface in your class. If you do this and provide a handle to your runnable interface then the threads you generate will use the `run()` method defined in your class.

12.4.2 Making sure your threads die with your applet

You should ensure that your applet can stop any running threads when the system calls `stop()` or `destroy()` (remember that if your `stop()` method prepares your applet for unloading then you can effectively ignore the `destroy()` method). If you let your threads run wild then the client machine will be slowed and, in the case of processor-intensive tasks, this could be a considerable problem. One simple way of making sure that your threads die is to use a variable known as a **sentinel** which is checked with each iteration of the thread. For example:

```
public class SomeThreadClass implements Runnable {
  Thread kicker = null;
```

```
public void start() {
  kicker = new Thread(this);
  kicker.start();
}

public void run() {
  while (kicker != null) {
    ...
  }
}

public void stop() {
  kicker = null;
}
}
```

In this simple example, the class SomeThreadClass implements the Runnable interface. When the system calls start, the thread is created and inherits the run method of SomeThreadClass. Each iteration of the thread checks to see that the Thread object is not null and continues to loop (remember that passing a handle which refers to an instance of the class implementing the Runnable interface means that the thread uses the run method we have defined).

When the applet is about to be unloaded the system calls the stop method and the thread is set to null. This halts the thread operation the next time that the while statement is encountered. This approach of stopping the thread at the next convenient moment is fine unless the main section of the thread takes a particularly long time to complete. If that is the case then you should consider either using multiple threads or checking the state of the thread more frequently. However, there is a point where checking the state of the thread too frequently will consume more system cycles than would be used by letting the thread complete a full iteration – so experiment with your code and find a balance that seems a reasonable trade-off.

12.4.3 Scheduling threads within applets

The Thread class contains a method setPriority which enables a programmer to give a thread a priority value; and it is sometimes tempting to use it to set the priority of threads to a maximum and never to yield the CPU. Sometimes, this is not a problem, but it will often affect the whole of the Java system and quite possibly the client machine as well.

Not only should you consider the effect of prioritizing the threads in your applet relative to other threads in the same applet, but you should also consider the impact of your threads on the system as a whole.

Threads running at high priority in tight code loops which never yield the CPU are irritating at best and can destroy any interactive elements of other applets

- or even of your own applet. So, try to select an appropriate priority value and use the scheduling system to your advantage.

One constructive way of using high priority threads is when you need a periodic display update of a code-intensive loop. By scheduling the thread at a higher priority for the display than for the calculations you can be sure that when the display thread wakes, the system will execute that thread in preference to the calculation thread(s) thus ensuring that the display is updated. When the display thread sleeps, the system will run the calculation threads and keep beavering away.

If you are running multiple threads, you should give some serious thought to your priority assignments. While it is possible to ignore the whole issue and let the system run with the default assignments, it is possible to streamline the operation of your applet considerably by careful selection of priorities and thread design. There is no benefit in running multiple related threads at the same priority, because the system will simply execute the peer threads in rotation, waiting for each thread to yield the CPU. Some systems will switch between equal priority threads, but since you can't rely on this feature to be available on all of the architectures which support Java you should not design code around its availability.

12.4.4 Adding thread support to the `HelloWorld` class

To illustrate the principles of threads and thread scheduling we will provide two examples. The first example shows the effect of running two threads at different priorities performing the same task. In addition, there is a third thread which periodically wakes up and displays the current values. We will use both methods of implementing threads, starting with subclassing the `Thread` class for the counting threads. The class is very simple and looks like this:

```
public class myThread extends Thread {
    int value = 0;

    public void run() {
    while (value < 1000000) {
      value++;
      }
    }

    public int getValue() {
      return value;
    }
}
```

The `myThread` class extends the `Thread` class and only needs to override the `run` method. In this method, the class simply increments a counter until it reaches a reasonably large number. If you are going to run this code on a particularly fast machine you might need to increase the ceiling for the counting if your system can reach the goal before the display thread wakes up.

Instead of extending the `HelloWorld` class any further, we have subclassed it to produce the `ThreadHelloWorld` class which is listed below:

```
import java.awt.Event;

public class ThreadHelloWorld extends HelloWorld
            implements Runnable {

  myThread counter[];    // The threads which will count
  Thread dispthread;     // The thread which will display
public void init() {
  sx = 5;
  sy = 20;
  hw = new StringBuffer("Hello World!");
  counter = new myThread[2];
  /* Start the counter threads */
  for (int i = 0; i < 2; i++) {
    counter[i] = new myThread();
    counter[i].setPriority(i+1);
  }
  /* Start the display thread */
  if (dispthread == null) {
    dispthread = new Thread(this);
    dispthread.setPriority(Thread.MAX_PRIORITY);
  }
  System.out.println("Applet: system has called init");
  resize(100, 100);
}

public void run() {
  while (dispthread != null) {
  printVals();
  try {
  dispthread.sleep(10);
  } catch (InterruptedException e) {
  /* Do nothing */
    }
  }
}

public void printVals() {
  int cval[] = new int[2];
  /* Get the current values from the threads */
  for (int i = 0; i < 2; i++) {
    cval[i] = counter[i].getValue();
  }
  /* Write out the values */
```

```
    System.out.println("Thread 1: " + cval[0] +
                        " Thread 2: " + cval[1]);
    /* See if we should stop the threads */
    if (cval[0] == 1000000 && cval[0] == 1000000) {
      stop();
    }
  }
}
public void stop() {
  /* Stop the counting threads */
  for (int i = 0; i < 2; i++) {
    if (counter[i].isAlive()) {
      counter[i].stop();
      counter[i] = null;
    }
  }
  /* Stop the display thread */
  if (dispthread.isAlive()) {
    dispthread.stop();
    dispthread = null;
  }
  System.out.println("Applet: system has called stop");
}


public boolean mouseDown(Event evt, int x, int y) {
  /* Start the counting threads */
  for (int i = 0; i < 2; i++) {
    if (!counter[i].isAlive()) {
      counter[i].start();
    }
  }
  /* Start the display thread */
  if (!dispthread.isAlive()) {
    dispthread.start();
  }
  return true;
}
}
```

We have just extended the HelloWorld class to include some basic threads and have altered the init() method to create the threads we require. Notice that the priority of the two counting threads is low and that one thread will have a higher priority than the other. Notice also that the display thread has been given maximum priority.

Because our class implements the `Runnable` interface we have to supply a `run` method. In this case we simply obtain and write out the current values of the counters and then sleep for a fraction of a second. When the counters reach the target value the threads are stopped. You will notice that the targets are defined both in the `myThread` class and in the `ThreadHelloWorld` class. This is somewhat redundant, because the display thread has a higher priority than the counting threads and the system will execute that thread whenever it wakes. However, while redundant, we always like to make sure that each of our threads is capable of yielding in case we get the scheduling wrong. In this case there is the additional reason for the `ThreadHelloWorld` class checking that both counters are at the target which requires some additional checking in the `myThread` class. The rule of thumb is that you can never be too careful with terminating threads.

We have also added another event method, which we use to start the threads off. When the mouse button is pressed within the applet area the threads are started and the whole thing is kicked off. The counter threads start up and the display thread starts the sleep/wake cycle.

So what happens? Well, as you might expect, the counter thread with the higher priority holds the CPU when the display thread is asleep. Periodically the display thread wakes up and is executed, displaying the current values of both threads. Only when the higher priority counting thread has finished counting will the system execute the other counter. So what you see is output which shows the first counter at zero until the second counter hits the target. At that point, the second thread is allowed to start counting.

So, we hear you asking, why bother with the priority at all? Why not just let everything run at the same level? Well, let us try it. If we change the line in the `ThreadHelloWorld` class from:

```
counter[i].setPriority(i+1);
```

to:

```
counter[i].setPriority(2);
```

and run the applet again, you should see one of two things. If you are on a UNIX system you will probably see both counters increasing together, although not always in equal amounts. If you are on some other system, then you won't see any difference from the first version of the code.

And this is the problem with not deliberately scheduling. For something as simple as a counter in the example it doesn't matter which of the threads reaches the target first. But in some situations where the completion of one thread prior to the start of another is critical it isn't possible to assume that the client system will divide up the time evenly between threads of the same priority: even systems which do slice up time are not required to do so evenly or consistently. So if thread sequencing is important to your code strategy then ensure that you make full use of the priority system.

12.4.5 Summary of thread use in applets

- Whenever an applet has a time-consuming task to perform, you should use threads. This is especially true when the tasks would be included in the init() method, because the browser may not be able to move on to the next applet until your method has returned.

- Make sure that your threads are able to stop when required. You should do this by writing checks at convenient points in your code to ensure that the thread is still required.

- Make sure that your threads are considerate. Your code will have to share a common set of resources on the client machine and the more compliant the applet code the better all of the applets will perform.

- Make proper use of the thread scheduling facilities. Do not assume that the end system will allocate time slices to threads of the same priority.

12.5 Adding an interface to the applet

In this section we will use classes from the AWT library to add a simple interface to our threaded HelloWorld class. In this case, we will display the progress of the counting threads in a TextField, add a start button to initiate the thread sequence, and add a selector which will allow the user to view the threads performing with the same priority or different priorities.

12.5.1 Adding a TextField

So, to start with let us add the TextField and some general support code. The class looks like this:

```
import java.awt.*;
public class UIHelloWorld extends ThreadHelloWorld {
  TextField textfield = new TextField(20);
  Panel topPanel,bottomPanel;
  public void init() {
    super.init();
    /* Create two new panels */
    bottomPanel = new Panel();
    topPanel = new Panel();
    /* Set the layout model for this element */
    setLayout(new BorderLayout());
    /* Add the two panels to this element */
    add("South", bottomPanel);
    add("North", topPanel);
```

```
    /* Set the layout model for the top panel */
    topPanel.setLayout(new BorderLayout());
    /* Add a label to the panel */
    topPanel.add("North", new Label("Results",
    Label.CENTER));
    /* Add the text area to the top panel */
    topPanel.add("South", textfield);
  }
  public void printVals() {
    int cval[] = new int[2];
    /* Get the current values from the threads */
    for (int i = 0; i < 2; i++) {
      cval[i] = counter[i].getValue();
    }
    /* Set the text in the field to the current values
    */
    textfield.setText("Thread 1: "+cval[0]+" Thread 2:
                      "+cval[1]);
    /* See if we should stop the threads */
    if (cval[0] == 1000000 && cval[0] == 1000000) {
      stop();
    }
  }
  public void paint(Graphics g) {
  /* Do nothing */
  }
}
```

We override the init method so that we can define the interface elements. We also make a call to the superclass init method to ensure that anything we might need to make use of later is ready.

We start the interface by creating two panels. The first will hold the TextField to display the progress of the counting threads and the second will hold the start button and the selector. We then set the layout style for this applet, and add the two panels to the applet display.

For the rest of this subsection, we will concentrate on topPanel for which we set the layout style, add a simple label and add a TextField. In order to have the progress displayed within the applet we have to override the printVals method. Instead of printing the string to the standard out, we set the text content of the TextField. The final change required for this stage is to override the paint() method to do nothing.

If you look at the final iteration of the ThreadHelloWorld class, you will see that the paint method places several things into the applet display. Since we no longer require these elements, we want the method to do nothing. At this first stage the applet should produce the display shown in Figure 12.1.

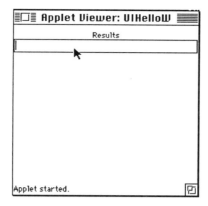

Figure 12.1 Screen shot of applet.

12.5.2 Adding the start button

We will now extend the code to have a start button. Instead of clicking on the applet area to start the threads we will have a button which has to be clicked on. The code for the extension class looks like this:

```java
import java.awt.Button;
import java.awt.Event;
public class UIHelloWorld2 extends UIHelloWorld {
  public void init() {
    super.init();
    // Add the button to the lower panel
    bottomPanel.add(new Button(" Start! "));

    public boolean action(Event evt, Object arg) {
    if (" Start! ".equals(arg)) {
      /* Start the counting threads */
      for (int i = 0; i < 2; i++) {
        if (!counter[i].isAlive()) {
          counter[i].start();
        }
      }
      /* Start the display thread */
      if (!dispthread.isAlive()) {
        dispthread.start();
      }
      return true;}
    return false;

}
```

In the `init` method of this class, we call the `init` method of the superclass and then insert a button into the lower pane that the superclass created. We also need to create a handler for the event that will be generated when the button is pressed. Although it is the only object which is likely to generate an event to be passed to the `action` method, it is still good programming practice to check that the event we are processing is in fact sent from the button. In this case if the event is from the button, then we start the threads using the same code that was previously used in the `mouseDown` method.

12.5.3 Adding the selector

The final element that we are going to add is a `Choice` that will allow the user to select the two models of thread priority that were discussed in Section 12.4.4. We just need a simple two-option `Choice` which we will use to set the priority of the threads prior to execution. The code for this is:

```
import java.awt.*;
import java.lang.Thread;
public class UIHelloWorld3 extends UIHelloWorld2 {
Choice c;
public void init() {
  super.init();
  // Set the layout of bottomPanel
  bottomPanel.setLayout(new BorderLayout());
  // Add the start button to p1
  bottomPanel.add("North",new Button(" Start! "));
  // Add the choice
  c = new Choice();
  // Add the two options to the choice
  c.addItem("Equal Priority");
  c.addItem("Unequal Priority");
  // Add the choice to the frame
  bottomPanel.add("South",c);
}
public boolean action(Event evt, Object arg) {
  String tmpstr;
  if (" Start! ".equals(arg)) {
    tmpstr = c.getSelectedItem();
    if (tmpstr.equals("Equal Priority")) {
      counter[0].setPriority(counter[1].getPriority());
    }

    /* Start the counting threads */
    for (int i = 0; i < 2; i++) {
      if (!counter[i].isAlive()) {
```

```
        counter[i].start();
      }
    }
    * Start the display thread */
    if (!dispthread.isAlive()) {
      dispthread.start();
    }
    return true;
  }
  return false;
  }

}
```

The interface is shown in Figure 12.2.

In this class we inherit from the original `UIHelloWorld2`. In the `init()` method we invoke the method from the superclass and then add the buttons as we did in the previous example. We then create the `Choice` and add the two elements that we want the user to pick from. The first element that we add to the choice will be the default that is displayed unless an explicit call is made to select another.

As you might have expected, we have overriden the `action()` class. There are two ways that the user selection can be handled. The first involves taking the event generated when the user selects from the `Choice` and setting the threads appropriately. The second way which we have adopted here is simply to check the value of the selected item prior to starting the threads.

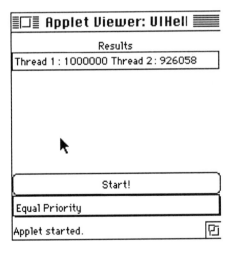

Figure 12.2 The final applet.

When adding interface elements to applets, make sure that the final interface is usable. One of the problems that plagues programming and seems particularly prevalent with applets is poor design. Your applet could be used by a huge number of people and it is worth paying serious consideration to the human factors involved in your system. If you are writing applets for commercial or large-scale deployments, you should engage in a serious human factors evaluation. Increasingly, the worth of your company will be judged by applets and Web pages, and the more usable and suitable your applets are the better the perception of your company will be.

12.6 Double buffering

It is also possible to create an offscreen Image and Graphics context and use them for screen buffering. Buffering the display is useful when you have a series of discrete operations to apply to the display which consume a long period of time. When applying a large number of operations the Java system will update periodically. This means that the user is presented with a partially complete display. Performing the operations on a display which is not shown to the user and then copying the final work to the main display leads to two positive things happening: first, it prevents the display updating before the tasks are complete and, second, stops the display flickering as the context is manipulated.

An applet which draws a large number of lines to a display is shown below:

```
import java.applet.Applet;
import java.awt.*;

public class singleBuffer extends Applet {
  public void init() {
  }

  public void paint(Graphics g) {
    for (int x = 0; x < size().width; x += 2) {
      g.drawLine(x,0,x,size().height);
    }
    for (int y = 0; y < size().height; y += 2) {
      g.drawLine(0,y,size().width,y);
    }
  }
}
```

The code in the first for loop draws vertical lines which are the height of the applet display until the end of the width of the display has been met. The drawLine method associated with the Graphics class has four arguments: the first two represent the start position of a line while the remaining two represent the end position of a line. The second loop draws horizontal lines.

In this code, the `paint` method draws a large number of lines directly to the display. On some machines (notably slower client machines) the amount of time that is taken to draw a large number of graphics operations will mean that the screen suffers from flicker as the system updates the screen. On faster machines, this may not happen; however, it is wise not to make assumptions about the hardware at the client end – even when you think you know who will be using the software.

The code for an applet which uses an offscreen Image and Graphics is displayed below:

```
import java.applet.Applet;
import java.awt.*;

public class doubleBuffer extends Applet {
   Image offScrImage;
   Graphics offScrGr;

   public void init() {
      offScrImage =
      createImage(size().width,size().height);
      offScrGr = offScrImage.getGraphics();
   }

   public void paint(Graphics g) {
   for (int x = 0; x < size().width; x += 2) {
      offScrGr.drawLine(x,0,x,size().height);
   }
   for (int y = 0; y < size().height; y += 2) {
      offScrGr.drawLine(0,y,size().width,y);
   }
   g.drawImage(offScrImage,0,0,this);
   }
}
```

In this version, the `Init()` method creates an Image and then gets the graphics context (also sometimes called a surface) associated with it. When the `paint` method is called the graphics operations are performed on the offscreen context which is not subject to being displayed on the screen and coinciding with system updates. When the lines have been drawn, the whole of the offscreen image is copied into the default Graphics context by the `drawImage` method (notice that the offscreen Graphics occupies the whole of the offscreen Image) and the display updates smoothly. This approach to screen management is especially useful with animation and with tasks which generally take a long time or require a large number of screen operations.

12.7 Another example applet

To conclude this section we will describe a more substantial applet. This one does not require any thread support. The applet implements a game known as Mastermind. In this game the computer selects four random colours, some of which are duplicated. The user then clicks a radio button in order to guess which colours have been selected. As each radio button is clicked the choice is built up in the fifth box on the top row of the applet. The computer will display four circles when the guess has been completed: a black circle means that the user has selected a colour in the right position, while a white circle means that the user has guessed a correct colour but has not guessed the right position. So, for example, if the computer had generated:

        green   red   green   white

and the user had guessed:

        green   white   black   yellow

then the computer would respond with a black circle and a white circle. The interface to the game is in Figure 12.3.

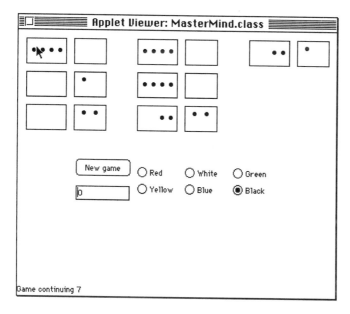

Figure 12.3 The Mastermind applet.

The applet consists of a canvas in which the boxes are embedded, six radio buttons which choose the colours, a button which starts a new game and a text field which displays the number of games so far played. The display shows the guesses drawn in a large box and a small box which contains the black and white circles.

The first lines of the applet are shown below:

```
import java.applet.*;
import java.awt.*;

//****Applet class
public class MasterMind extends Applet{
Color selectedColor;
int gameCount;
Box colBox, blackWhiteBox;
BoxCanvas c;
Button newGameButton;
Panel bottomPanel, leftBottomPanel, rightBottomPanel;
CheckboxGroup colChecks;
Checkbox redBox, whiteBox, blueBox, greenBox, blackBox,
yellowBox;
TextField noOfGamesfield;
Box toBeGuessed;
```

This just declares the various HCI control elements, the colour which has been selected at each click and the number of games played. The declaration uses a Box object which will contain guesses. The code for this will be developed later in this section. The code for the init class is shown below:

Exercise

Write down the code for init which initializes any variables and sets out the layout shown in Figure 12.3. Assume the existence of a method generateRandomBox which sets up a box with a random selection of colours in it.

Solution

The code is shown below.

```
public void init(){
gameCount = 0;
colBox = new Box();
toBeGuessed = Box.generateRandomBox();
blackWhiteBox = new Box();
```

```
c = new BoxCanvas();
c.noOfScreenBoxes = 0;
newGameButton = new Button("New game");
bottomPanel = new Panel();
leftBottomPanel = new Panel();
rightBottomPanel = new Panel();
colChecks = new CheckboxGroup();
redBox = new Checkbox("Red", colChecks , false);
whiteBox = new Checkbox("White", colChecks , false);
blueBox= new Checkbox("Blue", colChecks , false);
greenBox = new Checkbox("Green", colChecks , false);
blackBox = new Checkbox("Black", colChecks , false);
yellowBox = new Checkbox("Yellow", colChecks , false);
noOfGamesfield = new TextField("0",4);
bottomPanel.setLayout(new FlowLayout());
leftBottomPanel.setLayout(new GridLayout(2, 2, 10, 10));
rightBottomPanel.setLayout(new GridLayout(2, 1));
leftBottomPanel.add(newGameButton);
leftBottomPanel.add(noOfGamesfield);
rightBottomPanel.add(redBox);
rightBottomPanel.add(whiteBox);
rightBottomPanel.add(greenBox);
rightBottomPanel.add(yellowBox);
rightBottomPanel.add(blueBox);
rightBottomPanel.add(blackBox);
bottomPanel.add(leftBottomPanel);
bottomPanel.add(rightBottomPanel);
setLayout(new GridLayout(2,1));
add(c);
add(bottomPanel);
}
```

This just sets up the various layouts that are to be used and initialises any variables. The method `generateRandomBox` is a method in the class `Box` which generates a random set of colours; its code is shown later. The code for the action that is to occur when one of the radio buttons is clicked is shown below. The code makes use of a number of `Box` methods (`boxFull`, `addToBox`, `formsBWBox`) which are all defined later. The method `boxFull` returns true if the box containing colours is full, `addToBox` adds a colour to a box, and `formsBWBox` forms a box full of black and white colours depending on whether a guessed box is the same as the box which has been randomly selected.

```
public boolean action(Event e, Object o){
if (e.target instanceof Checkbox){
  Checkbox cb = (Checkbox) e.target;
  if (cb.getLabel() == "Red") selectedColor = Color.red;
```

```
  if (cb.getLabel() == "White")
    selectedColor = Color.white;
  if (cb.getLabel() == "Blue")
    selectedColor = Color.blue;
  if (cb.getLabel() == "Green")
    selectedColor = Color.green;
  if (cb.getLabel() == "Black")
    selectedColor = Color.black;
  if (cb.getLabel() == "Yellow")
    selectedColor = Color.yellow;
    if(!colBox.boxFull())
    colBox.addToBox(selectedColor);
    if (colBox.boxFull()) {
      c.screenBoxes[c.noOfScreenBoxes] = colBox.copy();
      c.bandWbox[c.noOfScreenBoxes] = (
      colBox.formBWBox(toBeGuessed));
      colBox.emptyBox();
      c.noOfScreenBoxes++;
      c.repaint();
      showStatus ("Game continuing "+c.noOfScreenBoxes);
      if(c.bandWbox[c.noOfScreenBoxes-
      1].allSameColour(Color.black)){
        showStatus("You win");
        toBeGuessed = Box.generateRandomBox();
        c.noOfScreenBoxes = 0;
        c.repaint();
      }
      if(c.noOfScreenBoxes == 9){
        c.repaint();showStatus("game over");
         c.noOfScreenBoxes = 0;
        toBeGuessed = Box.generateRandomBox();
      }
    }
  }
}
if (e.target instanceof Button){
  String name = (String) o;
  if (name == "New game"){gameCount++;
    noOfGamesfield.setText(""+gameCount); c.repaint();
    toBeGuessed = Box.generateRandomBox();
    c.noOfScreenBoxes = 0; showStatus("New game");
  }
};
return true;
}
}
```

The second `if` statement in the action method is executed if the user has clicked the button which asks for a new game. In this case the count of the number of games is incremented, the number of guessed boxes initialized to zero and a random set of colours chosen.

There is a need for a class which defines a canvas which will contain boxes. The code for this is shown below:

```
//**** BoxCanvas class

class BoxCanvas extends Canvas {
Box[] screenBoxes; Box[] bandWbox;
int noOfScreenBoxes;

public BoxCanvas(){
screenBoxes = new  Box[9];
noOfScreenBoxes = 0;
bandWbox = new Box [9];
}

public void paint(Graphics g){
drawBoxes(g, screenBoxes, noOfScreenBoxes);
}

public void drawBoxes
   (Graphics g, Box[] sb, int noBoxes){
int rectDrawn = 0;
int x = 10, y = 10;
while(rectDrawn < noBoxes){
  int pegCount = 0;
  g.setColor(Color.black);
  g.drawRect(x, y, 50, 30);
  for(int i = x+7; i < 51+x; i+=11){
    g.setColor(sb[rectDrawn].getPeg(pegCount));
    g.fillOval(i, y+12, 5,5); pegCount++;
  };
  g.setColor(Color.black);
  g.drawRect(x+60,y,40,30);
  g.setColor(bandWbox[rectDrawn].pegBox[0]);
  g.fillOval(x+70,y+7,5,5);
  g.setColor(bandWbox[rectDrawn].pegBox[1]);
  g.fillOval(x+85,y+7,5,5);
  g.setColor(bandWbox[rectDrawn].pegBox[2]);
  g.fillOval(x+70,y+19,5,5);
  g.setColor(bandWbox[rectDrawn].pegBox[3]);
  g.fillOval(x+85,y+19,5,5);
```

```
    rectDrawn++;
    if (rectDrawn % 3 == 0){
      x+=140; y = 10;
    }
    else
      y+=40;
};
}
```

There are a number of instance variables associated with this class which need to be drawn: a set of boxes containing colours that have been guessed, a collection of boxes containing the black and white circles and a count of the number of boxes. The constructor initializes these values.

The paint method for this class calls the method drawBoxes which carries out the drawing. The only method that you may not have met before is fillOval which draws an oval in the current colour at an x position and y position given by its first two arguments and a height and width given by its third and fourth arguments. Since these latter two arguments are the same, the oval drawn will be a circle.

The only code left to describe is that of the class Box:

```
public class Box{
int noInBox;
Color[] pegBox;

public Box(){
noInBox = 0;
pegBox = new Color[4];
}

public static Box generateRandomBox(){
int  val;
Box p = new Box();
for (int i = 0; i < 4; i++){
val = (int) (10*Math.random());
val = val % 6;
if (val==0) p.pegBox[i] = Color.red;
if (val==1) p.pegBox[i] = Color.black;
if (val==2) p.pegBox[i] = Color.green;
if (val==3) p.pegBox[i] = Color.white;
if (val==4) p.pegBox[i] = Color.yellow;
if (val==5) p.pegBox[i] = Color.blue;
};
p.noInBox = 4;
return p;
}
```

```
public Color getPeg(int pos){
return pegBox[pos];
}

public boolean boxFull(){
return noInBox == 4;
}

public Box copy(){
Box p = new Box();
p.noInBox = this.noInBox;
for (int i = 0; i < 4; i++)
  p.pegBox[i] = this.pegBox[i];
return p;
}

public void addToBox(Color c){
pegBox[noInBox++] = c;
}

public void emptyBox(){
noInBox = 0;
}
```

The class has two instance variables, pegBox which contains the colours in a box and noInBox which contains the number of colours contained in a box. Most of the methods are self-explanatory. However, it is worth describing the static method generateRandom. This makes a call on the method random found in java.lang.Math which generates a double length random number. This is converted to an int by using a cast and the remainder on dividing by 6 found. This value is then used to set the colours in the box p which is then returned.

The only method left to describe is formBWBox which compares two boxes and returns a box filled with black and white colours depending on whether the two box colours are in corresponding positions.

```
public Box formBWBox(Box b){
Color ext;

Box pass = new Box();
int exactMatch = 0;
int bRedCount = 0, bGreenCount = 0, bBlueCount = 0,
bWhiteCount = 0, bBlackCount = 0, bYellowCount = 0;
int tRedCount = 0, tGreenCount = 0, tBlueCount = 0,
tWhiteCount = 0, tBlackCount = 0, tYellowCount = 0;
int oRedCount = 0, oGreenCount = 0, oBlueCount = 0,
oWhiteCount = 0, oBlackCount = 0, oYellowCount = 0;
```

```
for (int i = 0; i < 4; i++){
  if (b.pegBox[i] == Color.red)   bRedCount ++;
  if (b.pegBox[i] == Color.white)  bWhiteCount ++;
  if (b.pegBox[i] == Color.blue)  bBlueCount ++;
  if (b.pegBox[i] == Color.green)   bGreenCount ++;
  if (b.pegBox[i] == Color.black)   bBlackCount ++;
  if (b.pegBox[i] == Color.yellow)  bYellowCount ++;
};
for (int i = 0; i < 4; i++){
  if (this.pegBox[i] == Color.red)   tRedCount ++;
  if (this.pegBox[i] == Color.white)   tWhiteCount ++;
  if (this.pegBox[i] == Color.blue)   tBlueCount ++;
  if (this.pegBox[i] == Color.green)   tGreenCount ++;
  if (this.pegBox[i] == Color.black)   tBlackCount ++;
  if (this.pegBox[i] == Color.yellow)   tYellowCount ++;
};
oRedCount = min(tRedCount, bRedCount);
oGreenCount = min(tGreenCount, bGreenCount);
oBlueCount = min(tBlueCount, bBlueCount);
oWhiteCount = min(tWhiteCount, bWhiteCount);
oBlackCount = min(tBlackCount, bBlackCount);
oYellowCount = min(tYellowCount, bYellowCount);
int totalMatch = oRedCount + oGreenCount + oBlueCount +
oWhiteCount + oBlackCount + oYellowCount;
for (int i = 0; i < 4; i++)
  if (this.pegBox[i] == b.pegBox[i]) exactMatch++;
for(int i = 0; i < 4; i++)
  pass.pegBox[i] = Color.lightGray;
for(int i = 0; i < exactMatch; i++)
  pass.pegBox[i] = Color.black;
for(int i = exactMatch; i < totalMatch; i++)
  pass.pegBox[i] = Color.white;
pass.noInBox = 4;
return pass;
}

public int min(int a, int b){
if (a > b) return b;
else return a;
}

public boolean allSameColour(Color c){
int count = 0;
for(int i = 0; i < 4; i++)
  if (this.pegBox[i] == c) count++;
```

```
return count == 4;
}
```

This rather long method counts the number of occurrences of each colour in the two boxes. For each colour it then finds the minimum value of the counts. This will be the number of guesses which are correct for each colour irrespective of whether the guesses are at the correct or incorrect positions. It then discovers which of these guesses were in the correct positions. In the end it fills the boxes with the white and black colours having first initialized the box with a light gray colour which for the Navigator browser is the background colour.

12.8 Adding HCI to the running example

Let us return to the running example. In this section we shall turn the code into an applet which includes facilities for searching for the locations where a particular word can be found. In order to do this we shall use the methods checkWordIn and getLocations which have been defined in Section 5.8. The former checks whether a word is contained in the data structure used to hold the relationship between a word and its locations; it returns true if its argument is found in the data structure. The latter returns with a vector containing all the locations associated with the word which is its argument.

The HCI for the applet will contain a text field which will contain the word to be searched for, a list which will contain its locations, a button which has to be pressed to start the search process and a label which points the user at the text field. The code for the applet is shown below:

```
public class Search extends Applet{
TextField tf;
List ls;
Vector v = new Vector(30);
Label l;
Button b;
Panel p;
LinksData ld;

public void init(){
p = new Panel();
ld = new LinksData(50);
tf = new TextField(40);
ls = new List (10,false);
b = new Button("Search");
l = new Label("Type in word to be searched for here" +
    "--------------------->");
setLayout(new GridLayout(2,2,30,30));
p.setLayout(new BorderLayout());
```

```
p.add("West",b);
add(l);
add(tf);
add(ls);
add(p);
// Code which initializes the data structure
// with word-location data.
}

public boolean action(Event evt, Object arg){
if(evt.target.equals(b)){
  String word = tf.getText();
  if(ld.checkWordIn(word)){
    v = ld.getLocations(word);
    ls.clear();
    showStatus("Word found");
    for(int i = 0; i < v.size(); i++)
    ls.addItem((String) v.elementAt(i));
  }
  else{
     showStatus("word "+ word + " not found");
     ls.clear();
     ls.addItem("");
  }
}
return true;
}

}
```

The init method sets up the HCI elements. This includes a panel which contains one button. We have used the panel to force the size of the button down so that it does not look too ugly. We have not included the code which initializes the data structure holding the word-location data. Normally this would involve the use of stream methods to copy data from a file on the applet host. The interface is shown in Figure 12.4.

The main processing that occurs in the applet is carried out in the action method. This monitors the pressing of the button and then reads the word that has been typed within the text field. A check is made that the word is contained in the data structure; if it isn't then a message is sent to the status bar of the browser and the List element cleared.

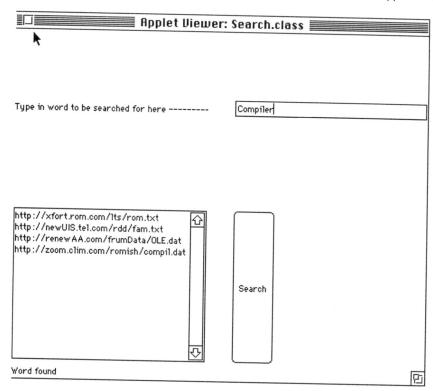

Figure 12.4 The search applet.

If the word is found then the locations associated with the word are retrieved using the method `getLocations`. Each location is then cast to a string and added to the `List` element.

12.9 SUMMARY

This chapter has described the main components of an applet and has shown how when you develop a number of serious applets within the same HTML document you will often need to make use of multi-threading. The final part of the chapter showed the development of an applet which made extensive use of drawing within a graphics context.

CHAPTER THIRTEEN

Network Programming

AIMS

- To provide an overview of the network support within Java.
- To outline the network library classes.
- To build and analyse simple network software.

13.1 Introduction

One of the key packages in the Java system is the `java.net` library. This provides support for accessing the Internet both as a client accessing remote services and as a server providing services to remote clients.

The role of the network in the life of the Java language is critical. The most popular application areas for Java code will be those supported by mixed-platform environments where the ability to access remote information and services will be of prime concern. The `java.net` package includes support for creating clients and servers, as well as classes for related requirements, such as those connected with network addresses. In this chapter we will demonstrate the power of the `java.net` package by developing a number of client–server programs.

Before looking at the facilities of the `java.net` package it is worth describing some concepts. Some of these you will have met before; however, a number will be new to you:

Internet. This is a network which itself is made up of a large number of networks. These networks will be either commercial, governmental or educational.

Host. A host is an individual computer on the Internet. Each host has a unique address known as its IP address.

Hostname. Since numeric addresses are quite difficult to remember, hosts on the Internet are usually given a symbolic name known as the Hostname.

IP address. This is a unique number given to a computer on the Internet. It is represented by a 32-bit number.

Packet. A packet is a collection of data sent over the Internet. The contents of a packet are defined by the protocol that is used.

Protocol. This is a set of rules which determine what is going to be sent in a packet. For example, a protocol will describe the format of the redundant data which is sent in a packet and used for error checking. The common protocol in the Internet is TCP/IP.

Port. This is a very much like a connection into a computer. Many operating systems allow a large number of ports, many of which are dedicated to certain tasks such as electronic mail.

Socket. A socket is an endpoint in a network. In TCP/IP it is represented by a unique number made up of the IP address and port number of the source computer and the IP address and port number of the destination computer.

13.2 A tour of the package

The `java.net` package includes all the tools you will need to implement network support. The library is small and compact but requires a basic level of understanding before it can be used effectively. We will explain as much as is required to implement simple services and Web programs; however, it is worth pointing out that this text is not the place for a detailed explanation of network issues and we will not hesitate to sacrifice accuracy for clarity when we cover the basic topics. By the end of this chapter you should have sufficient knowledge to write code that will enable you to integrate network functions seamlessly into Java applications and applets.

The classes in `java.net` fall into three classes:

Web classes. These classes allow you to access Web documents via their URLs. The classes used for this are `URL` and `URLConnection`.

Raw classes. These classes are used to provide stream-based interfaces to hosts on the Internet. They allow the programmer to build up new protocols, connect to existing files and develop client-server software. The bulk of the remainder of this chapter describes the use of these classes. The classes which fall into this category are: `Socket`, `ServerSocket`, `DatagramSocket` and `InetAddress`.

Extension classes. These classes are used to extend the Web classes described above to cater for new document and content formats. For example, if a new graphics standard was developed and you needed to access documents using this standard on the Web, then you would have to use these classes to write software to help the Web interface classes recognize and process the documents. The classes which come under this category are ContentHandler and URLStreamHandler.

These, then, are the main categories of classes. In the next section we shall examine the three most important ones and then use one of them (Socket) to develop a sophisticated piece of client-server software.

13.2.1 The URL class

This class handles connections to Web documents. It is associated with a number of constructors which set up URL objects. For example, the URL constructor which has a string parameter treats the string parameter as the URL. For example:

```
URL oldWeb = new
   URL("http://info.cern.ch/hyper/old.tex");
```

sets up the URL object which is associated with the World Wide Web protocol (http), a host info.cern.ch, a directory hyper, and a file old.tex. Remember from Section 4.3.4 that a URL is split into these constituent components. This is just one constructor for URLs; there are three others, which in common with the one described above, all throw a Malformed-URLException if the format of the URL is incorrect.

In order to process the text within a URL object the simplest strategy is to use the method openStream defined in URL. This opens an input stream connected to the URL object so that the input stream methods described in Chapter 10 can be used to read from the object. This is shown below:

```
URL queryWeb =
   new URL("http://infor.cern.ch/oldFin/lemor.txt");

try{
   InputStream is = queryWeb.openStream();
   DataInputStream ds = new DataInputStream(is);

   . . .

   // Code for processing the data input stream ds

   . . .

catch(IOException e){
   System.out.println("Problem with connection");}
```

Here an input stream is has been associated with the URL object, then a DataInputStream stream object ds has been created from is. This means that after this line of code the HTML and text contained in the URL object can be accessed using methods such as `readLine` defined in the class `DataInputStream`.

13.2.2 The `Socket` and `ServerSocket` classes

These two classes establish stream-based input and output between server and client computers. A `Socket` object represents the Java version of a TCP connection. When a socket is created, a connection is made to a specified computer; when a `ServerSocket` connection is made the server on which it is made listens for an incoming connection from a client and establishes it when it hears the connection.

There are four constructors for the Socket. The most popular takes the name of a host computer and a port number.

When a `ServerSocket` is created it listens for connection requests. When a connection request is accepted the method `accept` returns a socket for future data transfer between the client and the server. The code below illustrates this where conn is a socket object.

```
try {
      /* Try to be a server on this port */
      sock = new ServerSocket(port);
      System.out.println("Started on port " + port);
      conn = sock.accept();
   } catch(Exception e) {
      System.out.println("Err: " + e);
      System.exit(1);
   }
```

Here, a new ServerSocket object sock is created on a specified port `port` by using the constructor `ServerSocket` with the single argument which is the port number. The method `accept` is then used to create a socket when a connection has been created. This object can then be used for data transfer as shown in Section 13.4. The code is enclosed with a `try-catch` clause in case a problem occurs.

Once you have established such a stream you can then use methods defined in the `Stream` classes to send and receive data. This is shown in great detail in the example described in Section 13.4.

13.3 The common protocol

One criticism which has been made against the network support within the Java package libraries is that the only protocol available is TCP/IP, which is not always available as part of the standard operating system software in non-UNIX environments.

While it is true that some platforms have better support for other protocols, the selection of IP for the Java libraries is reasonable given that it is the de facto protocol for the Internet and has been ported to a whole range of platforms. In addition, supporting a range of protocols which are not uniformly available on all platforms which can run Java would inhibit the intrinsic cross-platform nature of the Java language and limit the cross-connectivity which makes Java such a useful language.

However, there are bound to be problems which require Java and the use of a protocol other than TCP/IP. In these cases all is not lost: it is possible, albeit challenging, to write methods which implement other protocols. By using native methods (methods written in other programming languages such as C) it is also possible to take advantage of existing system libraries to manage network connections.

13.3.1 Software and servers

Java allows the developer to create network connections in a number of ways. This makes embedded Java applets far more flexible than just vanilla HTML pages. While some applets will be self-contained and require no external support, most complex applications will rely on external servers and services to enrich the application/applet environment. The way that connections are handled is at the discretion of the developer, ranging from connections which the user fully controls and understands, through to connections that happen 'behind the scenes' without user intervention.

In addition, subject to security settings, Java code can connect to any arbitrary server available from the end-user machine. There is no requirement to limit access to a single machine or to a single network, especially from a Java application. In particular, the Java network libraries do not limit the developer to using only HTTP to access external services and handlers can be created for any service which uses IP as a transport.

13.3.2 Some simple examples

The examples in this chapter will concentrate on establishing and managing network connections. We will not focus on what to do with the data that is generated, except in an abstract manner. There are two reasons for this: first, because this chapter is about the network libraries only and, second, because there are so many uses for network connections that we could not possibly do justice to them.

The code that we will introduce to illustrate the `java.net` library will typically do simple tasks – after all, we are not concerned with what the application does aside from the network implications. The thing to remember when looking at these examples is that you can easily take the network aspects of the code and extend them yourself. For example, in order to extend a simple server which sends the time to network clients to carry out a more useful task, you should be able to replace the code which handles generating the time with code to carry out other tasks such as accessing a file with little effort. Once you have a set of classes which handles networking in a generic manner it is relatively trivial to add additional functionality which meets your project goals.

13.3.3 Possible applications

Even though we cannot realistically provide examples for every kind of server, it is worthwhile giving some sample uses for servers generally. The Java packages can be used to write a diverse range of servers limited only by resources and the imagination of the development team.

Examples include gateways to databases, proxy servers to navigate through firewalls, feedback systems for large-scale systems, mediators for network games, mail servers and so on – the list is endless.

One thing to consider when embarking on developing a Java server is avoiding writing something which already exists in another language. While there may be compelling reasons to port functionality to a Java applet or application – for example, writing a cross-platform mail reader – there is little point in writing the accompanying server if another application is already available. Not only will you incur expense by performing the development, but you will create a new program with the bugs and problems that immature software always suffers from.

If there is a mature, stable and usable server package available, then do not hesitate to use it. While applications may benefit from a Java client there is no reason why the code that they use cannot be written to work with the existing servers and, in many ways, it makes client development simpler since the server is a known quantity.

13.4 Writing a server

We will start our description of client–server functionality with the server end of things. Our goal will be to write a simple server that will accept network connections and then write back any strings that the client sends in. It is a simple goal. However, it serves as an excellent way of introducing the libraries. For the reader impatient to see big applications, we would advise you to imagine that instead of simply returning a string the server carries out some major set of functions such as accessing a huge database, making several complex and involved queries and then returning the string.

13.4.1 Introducing the first iteration of the server

This first version of the server will just wait for a connection and then write the string received from the connection to the out channel of the server process. When the string has been printed out the application will quit. As a rule, it is only possible to have servers running as part of Java applications because of the security constraints imposed on applet code by the Web browser which embeds the Java run-time system.

The code for the server is shown below; we have extensively commented the example:

```
import java.lang.*;
import java.net.*;
import java.util.*;
import java.io.*;

public class server1 {
    public static void main(String args[]) {

        /* Create a new instance of the simpleServer.  */
        /* Makes use of the class simpleServer defined */
        /* below                                        */

        simpleServer ss = new simpleServer(6001);
        }
}

class simpleServer {
  ServerSocket sock;
  Socket conn;
  BufferedInputStream instream;
  String str;

  simpleServer(int port) {
    try {

      /* Try to be a server on this port */

      sock = new ServerSocket(port);

      /* Server socket created            */

      System.out.println("Started on port " + port);
      conn = sock.accept();

      /* We now have a socket called conn */
      /* thorugh which data can flow      */

    } catch(Exception e) {
      System.out.println("Err: " + e);
      System.exit(1);
    }

    try {

      /* Create the stream to the socket            */
      /* We use a BufferedInputStream. This is      */
```

```
      /* just like an InputStream except that   */
      /* it stores data in a buffer              */

      instream = new
         BufferedInputStream(conn.getInputStream());

      /* getInputStream gets the input stream    */
      /* associated with a socket                */
   } catch(Exception e) {
      System.out.println("Err: " + e);
      System.exit(1);
   }

   /* Read line from the socket and then write */
   /* it out                                   */
   str = this.getline();
   System.out.println("Str: " + str.trim());
 }

 public String getline() {
   StringBuffer strbuf = new StringBuffer();
   int tmp;

      /* Reads character by character from stream    */
      /* If value returned is -1 then end of stream   */
      do {
      try {
         /* Try to read from the stream */
         tmp = instream.read();
      } catch(Exception e) {
      return(null);
      }
      if (tmp == -1) {
         /* There is nothing to read */
         return(null);
      }
      if (tmp != 0) {
         /* Add character to StringBuffer */
         strbuf.append((char)tmp);
      }
      } while (tmp != '\n');
         /* Return the String of the StringBuffer */
         return(strbuf.toString());
   }
}
```

If we compile this file and run the server, we can then telnet into port 6001 and type a string. The string is printed out on the server output and then the server exits. It is worth walking through the code to explain what is happening. The first class, `server1`, just contains the `main()` method that all applications have to implement. The class creates a new instance of an object known as `simpleServer` and passes the port we wish to use as an argument. All of the work happens in the `simpleServer` class. Looking at the constructor, we can see that the first line of code is:

```
sock = new ServerSocket(port);
```

This creates a new `ServerSocket` called `sock`. Remember that a socket is a combination of a host and a port. A host is a (possibly) remote computer which supports the TCP/IP protocol and a port is the part of the computer that you talk to for a given service. So certain ports are used for sending email, starting terminal sessions and even playing games. You can think of a port as a way of telling the computer which software or service you would like to use.

The `ServerSocket` creates a network connection on the machine which is prepared to accept connections from client machines in order to provide some kind of service. The number that is passed as an argument specifies which port we want to use. In order to let clients access our simple service the client software must have some prior knowledge of the port number that we are using. Well-known services have a set of ports which are universally recognized and ports that have a number less than 1024 are considered 'special' on many implementations of TCP/IP and require system privileges to be used. The danger in selecting a port at random is that if your software is later moved to another server, it is possible that another piece of network software is already expecting to use the port that you have selected and your software will die reporting that the port is in use.

The best way of dealing with this is to provide a mechanism for allowing the user to specify an alternative port on the command line which can override the default that the software uses. At the moment, we have created the socket connection for the server but nothing else will happen. We need to tell the socket that it should accept a connection when one arrives. This is done with the call:

```
conn = sock.accept();
```

This tells the `ServerSocket` that it should wait for a connection. Because it is impossible to predict when a connection request will arrive from a client, making the call blocks the thread of execution until a connection is made to the port. Until this happens no other lines of code are processed. This is fine when the server is expected to cope with only one client, but if there are multiple clients, having the entire execution halted until another client arrives is not workable – we will return to this problem later in the chapter and show you a solution.

Notice that the call to `accept()` is grouped with the `ServerSocket` call, so that if there are problems establishing the port the code doesn't send a message to an object which could not be created. If there are problems in establishing the

`ServerSocket`, then the error is printed to the `out` channel and the application exits by means of the code:

```
System.exit(1);
```

The argument 1 to the call of exit enables the system to provide an error code which gives an indication of the problem.

The next few lines of code create the required streams to let us read from the socket. When these lines of Java are executed, we already have a connection established from a client. We know this because the call to `accept()` blocks execution until this is true. In this example, we have chosen to use a `BufferedInputStream` from the `java.io` package. This stores data in an area of memory known as a **buffer**. We have to catch the exceptions because the call could generate a problem. The alternative would be to declare that our class can throw the same exception, but this approach has the cost of losing the resolution which is provided by catching exceptions at the point in the code where they are thrown.

If the application has successfully created the `ServerSocket`, accepted an incoming connection request and dealt with the I/O streams, we can then read a line of input from the socket connection. This line of input will be the line that the user has typed. We have defined a separate method called `getline()` to handle this task. In essence, `getline()` reads a byte from the stream we have associated with the socket (it is not possible to read and write directly to sockets – instead you must associate a stream using the `getInputStream()` and `getOutputStream()` methods). If the byte is equal to -1 then there is no input from the stream waiting to be read. If the byte is not equal to 0, then we make a cast from the integer value of the byte to a char and place the character into a StringBuffer. When the character matches `"\n"` (which is the code for the return key) we send back the String representation of the StringBuffer. At this point `simpleServer` prints out the line that `getline()` returned and since there are no other lines of code to execute the application exits.

13.4.2 Extending the server

The first example has illustrated the basics of writing a very simple server. The first step is to create a `ServerSocket` which will be used to accept incoming connections. The next stage is to accept a connection on the `ServerSocket` and to process the input appropriately. In our example we just used the standard telnet to test out the server and typed in strings from there. We will come to writing clients later in this chapter. So, we can now write lines to the server `out` channel, but what about the client? Also, what happens if we want to deal with more than one line of text? The next example covers both these cases. Because we are going to handle multiple lines of text, we will also add support so that the user can type 'bye-bye' to terminate the connection.

The constructor for `simpleServer` has the following lines to supervise reading the line and printing it out. The rest of the constructor remains the same with `getline()` still being used to handle reading from the connection.

```
/* Read line from the socket and then write it out */
  do {
      str = this.getline();
      this.putline("You said: " + str);
      System.out.println("Str: " + str.trim());
  } while (!str.startsWith("bye-bye"));
```

The first change is that we are now using a `do-while` loop to handle reading from the connection. As long as the string returned from `getline()` does not start with `"bye-bye"` then the loop keeps reading lines of text. When the string does start with `"bye-bye"` the loop is terminated and the application exits since there is no more code to execute. We have also added a new method to handle writing strings to the client, called `putline()`. The Java code for this is:

```
public void putline(String line) {
    byte tline[] = new byte[1024];

    line.getBytes(0,line.length(),tline,0);
    try {
    conn.getOutputStream().write(tline,0,line.length());
    }
    catch(Exception e) {
      System.out.println("Err: " + e);
    }
}
```

The purpose of this method is to take a string, convert it into bytes and then write those bytes out to the network connection. The first line of code places a byte representation of the whole string into an array of bytes. These bytes are then written out to the client.

You might like to compile and test the code at this stage. Using Telnet to connect to port 6001 you can type a series of lines each terminated with a CR and see them echoed back to the screen. If the string you type begins with `"bye-bye"`, the whole of the string is echoed back and then the connection closes as the application exits. It is worth saying that it is not good practice to allow socket connections to close when the application exits. A preferable method is to close the socket explicitly – we will do this in later examples.

13.4.3 Handling multiple clients

So far both examples in this section have handled only one client. Now we will introduce a technique for handling multiple clients. The way we will do this is to have each client connection handled by a different thread (if you are not familiar with the notion of threads and multiple lines of execution, then you should take the time to reread Chapter 9). In this way, it appears to each client that it is the only user of the system since the fact that the server is a multi-user server is hidden from it. The source code looks like this:

```java
import java.lang.*;
import java.net.*;
import java.util.*;
import java.io.*;

public class server3 {
  static int port;

  public static void main(String args[]) {
    try {
      port = Integer.parseInt(args[0]);
    } catch (Exception e) {
      port = 6001;
    }
    /* Create a new instance of the simpleServer */
    simpleServer ss = new simpleServer(port);
  }
}

class simpleServer implements Runnable {
  ServerSocket sock;
  Socket conn;
  int port;
  Thread kicker;

  simpleServer(int port) {
          this.port = port;
          this.start();
  }

  public void start() {
    if (kicker == null) {
      try {
        /* Try to be a server on this port */
        sock = new ServerSocket(port);
        System.out.println("Started server on
        port  " + port);
      } catch (Exception e) {
        System.out.println("Err: " + e);
      }
      kicker = new Thread(this);
      kicker.start();
    }
  }
```

```
   }
   public void stop() {
   }
   public void run() {
     while (kicker != null) {
       try {
           conn = sock.accept();
           new connectionHandler(conn);
       } catch(Exception e) {
           System.out.println("Err: " + e);
           System.exit(1);
       }
     }
   }
}
class connectionHandler implements Runnable {
   Socket conn;
   Thread kicker = null;
   BufferedInputStream instream;
   String str;

   connectionHandler(Socket connin) {
     conn = connin;
     this.start();
   }
   public void start() {
     if (kicker == null) {
       kicker = new Thread(this);
       kicker.start();
     }
   }
   public void stop() {
     try {
       conn.close();
     } catch (Exception e) {
       System.out.println("Err: " + e);
     }
     kicker = null;
   }
   public void run() {
     try {
       /* Create the stream to the socket */
```

```
    instream = new
    BufferedInputStream(conn.getInputStream());
  } catch(Exception e) {
    System.out.println("Err: " + e);
    System.exit(1);
  }
  /* Read line from the socket and
  then write it out */
  do {
    str = this.getline();
    this.putline("You said: " + str);
    System.out.println("Str: " + str.trim());
  } while (!str.startsWith("bye-bye") && kicker !=
  null);
    this.stop();
}
public void putline(String line) {
byte tline[] = new byte[1024];
line.getBytes(0,line.length(),tline,0);
try {
  conn.getOutputStream().write(tline,0,line.length());
} catch(Exception e) {
  System.out.println("Err: " + e);
}
}
public String getline() {
StringBuffer strbuf = new StringBuffer();
int tmp;
do {
  try {
    /* Try to read from the stream */
    tmp = instream.read();
  } catch(Exception e) {
    return(null);
  }
  if (tmp == -1) {
    /* There is nothing to read */
    return(null);
  }
  if (tmp != 0) {
    /* Add the character */
    strbuf.append((char)tmp);
  }
} while (tmp != '\n');
```

```
    /* Return the String representation */
    return(strbuf.toString());
    }
}
```

The source code is quite detailed so you should take a moment to make sure that you understand how it works. The basic principle is that each `Socket` is handled in a separate thread and new `Sockets` are created from another thread which monitors the `ServerSocket`.

In this server it appears to each client that it is the only client using the server, even though there could be several other users. You will also notice that when the user types a string starting with `"bye-bye"` the thread is stopped and the socket is closed cleanly using the `close()` method. As we said earlier in this chapter, sockets should be closed cleanly wherever possible – especially in a server which is maintaining multiple sockets.

A logical extension of this server would be to have the input of one client sent out to all of the other clients in the manner of a broadcast system. Looking at the way that the server above is written, you should be able to see that the simplest way to do this would be to create a method which keeps track of all of the open sockets and can be asked to write out strings to all but the sender socket.

13.4.4 Other tasks with sockets

So far we have shown you how to build a basic server in several iterations. When deploying the server code in your own projects, there are hooks to handle the application-specific processing as required. In this section we will look at some of the other methods which are related to sockets.

While some servers will be available to the whole of the Internet, others may contain information or services which could be restricted to clients from particular sites or from a certain list. The socket class provides a mechanism for obtaining the address of the client to which it is connected.

Here is a code fragment which illustrates how to get the IP address of a client:

```
...
ServerSocket ss = new ServerSocket(3000);
Socket sock = ss.accept();
InetAddress addr = sock.getInetAddress();
System.out.println("Address: " + addr.toString());
...
```

This code creates a `ServerSocket` which is listening to port 3000 (for brevity we have omitted the exception handling which is required) and then `accept()` is called which will block the thread of execution until a client connects to the port. When a connection is made, the socket is created and then we make a call to `getInetAddress()` which returns the address in the form of an `InetAddress`. We convert the address to a String and then print it out. Instead of just printing it we could have put some further processing in, for example to make a comparison to check the address matches a predefined set of rules.

This is the first time that we have used the `InetAddress` and it is sufficiently useful to be worthy of some coverage. The `InetAddress` is an object which is related to an IP address; it can be thought of as the call-sign that computers using TCP/IP will use to identify themselves. Like call-signs, IP addresses can be changed (within some constraints which are beyond the scope of this book) and therefore it is worth remembering that checking that the IP address of the client matches an address in the ruleset is not a guarantee that everything is fine. However, for simple security and usage logging, getting the IP address from the socket is sufficient.

So what can you do with an IP address? IP addresses are typically associated with hostnames. For example, the address 206.26.48.100 is associated with the machine called 'java.sun.com'. The network package provides support for looking up names based on numbers and numbers based on names. Here is a simple code fragment to illustrate the point:

```
. . .
ServerSocket ss = new ServerSocket(3000);
Socket sock = ss.accept();
InetAddress addr = sock.getInetAddress();
System.out.println("Address: " + addr.getHostName());
. . .
```

This is very similar to the previous fragment, with the exception that when we print out the line of information we make a call to the `getHostName()` method; this returns a String containing the name. This is more useful for screening hosts than working with 'raw' IP numbers. For example, if we only wanted to allow access from hosts that are part of the Sun network we could look for hostnames ending with 'sun.com' or 'sun.co.uk' instead of having to maintain a list of the network ranges that Sun uses.

It is worth noting that the call to `getHostName()` returns the name which was returned from the local name services implemented on your machine. For example, if the code was executed on a Sun, then the name returned to the call will vary depending on whether the information came from the local files, the NIS service or the DNS. Equally possible is the chance that the client has not been registered in the name services properly and so there is no entry available at all. When basing code decisions on something as potentially variable as hostnames it is advisable to make sure that the information that is returned from the call is the information that you are expecting, especially if granting access has some financial or security implications.

It is also possible to perform the operation in reverse, taking the name of a machine and obtaining the IP address. This is done through the `getByName()` and `getAllByName()` methods which return the addresses associated with a hostname. The `getAllByName()` method returns all of the IP addresses that a machine has registered; typically this is applicable to large server machines which require multiple network connections for increased speed or robustness or service.

One other useful method which is associated with `InetAddress` is `getLocalHost()` which returns the IP address of the local machine. This is useful for all sorts of applications, not least of which is having a network client report the IP address of the machine it is using for logging purposes.

13.4.5 Summary of server applications

This section has shown you how to build moderately complex servers using Java. The examples described have focused on the mechanism of creating the server process and managing connections, with little emphasis on the overall functionality of the server. The point of this approach is to remove the extraneous issues of additional functionality for the sake of clarity and simplicity of code. It is a small matter to take the example server and add functionality specific to your application requirements.

We have also discussed the benefits and costs associated with writing a server process in Java. The primary cost is that the interpreted nature of the language means that the overall latency of the system will be unsuitable for some requirements. The advantages of using Java can be quite compelling, especially the ability to deploy an identical server application onto a whole range of platforms with no changes to the source code.

When writing Java applications the developer has access to the Thread support as we have shown in the example above and can use a familiar language to develop both the server and the applet for a system solution. When writing a large-scale server the attractions of the language and the problems associated with using it both become more significant. Our advice in this matter is to choose the best tool for the problem and the project – this includes considering the abilities of the developers. The long-term maintenance of the server will be a time-consuming task and an inappropriate selection of programming language will only make this more so.

13.5 Writing an applet

The previous section covered the use of the network package to develop a server process for a Java application. Java also supports network access for applets. In this section we will illustrate the use of the network package within applets.

13.5.1 Applet security

As mentioned briefly at the start of this chapter, network access from applets is subject to some constraints. The most significant limitation is that applets can only make network connections to the host that they were downloaded from. This constraint is imposed by a Web browser which operates a strict security policy.

Each browser is allowed to implement a different security model or to allow the user to switch between models; at the time of writing the browser that is most likely to have the majority of users, Netscape Navigator, will implement a heavily constrained model which is not modifiable by the user.

There have been some releases of code which allows the developer to bypass the security model by taking control of network connections that were intended for other purposes and were therefore not subject to the same constraints as applet socket connections. While these approaches may work, we would advise against using them for two reasons: first, such security loopholes are likely to be addressed as Java products become more stable and may make your code break in later releases of the system and, second, subverting other connections without the express knowledge of the user violates any trust that the user has in the software. Applet developers are constrained within a tightly controlled environment, and violating the rules undermines user confidence in the applet and in Java as a whole.

13.5.2 Our first look at a client

A simple example of a client will be described in this section. This client will connect to a port and then print out whatever output the server produces. This is not very useful for interactive services such as Telnet or ftp but does work with the daytime service which simply prints out the current time and exits. Our code will make a socket connection to the server and then read back a line of output which will be printed to the standard channel out. Here is the code for it:

```
import java.lang.*;
import java.net.*;
import java.util.*;
import java.io.*;

public class simpleClient {
  static int port;
  static String host;

  public static void main(String args[]) {
    try {
      host = args[0];
      port = Integer.parseInt(args[1]);
    } catch (Exception e) {
      host = "localhost";
      port = 13;
    }

    /* Create a new instance of the simpleServer */
    simpleHandler ss = new simpleHandler(host, port);
  }
}
```

```
class simpleHandler {
  BufferedInputStream instream;
  Socket conn;

  simpleHandler(String host, int port) {
    try {
      conn = new Socket(host,port);
      instream = new
      BufferedInputStream(conn.getInputStream());
    } catch (Exception e) {
      System.out.println("Err: " + e);
      System.exit(1);
    }
    /* Read line from the socket and write it out */
    String str = this.getline();
    System.out.println("Str: " + str.trim());
  }

  public String getline() {
    StringBuffer strbuf = new StringBuffer();
    int tmp;
    do {
      try {
        /* Try to read from the stream */
        tmp = instream.read();
      } catch(Exception e) {
        return(null);
      }
      if (tmp == -1) {
        /* There is nothing to read */
        return(null);
      }
      if (tmp != 0) {
        /* Add the character */
        strbuf.append((char)tmp);
      }
    } while (tmp != '\n');
    /* Return the String */
    return(strbuf.toString());
  }
}
```

The arguments are used to supply a hostname and a port to connect to. For example, to access the day/time server on aUNIX machine, you should type:

```
java simpleClient localhost 13
```

and the output would be the date and time. Because the arguments are expected to be a String and an int representing the hostname and the port, using the names of the service will not work. For example:

```
java simpleClient localhost daytime
```

would not work because the call to `Integer.parseInt()` would generate an exception and the default settings would be used. If this were a real-world application and not an example, it would be a good idea to give the user some indication that the arguments that have been supplied have failed and the defaults are being used. If this is not done, the user could make any kind of mistake and not notice that the software has defaulted to other parameters.

Once the arguments have been processed, we create a new instance of a class called `simpleHandler` which will do all of the work. The first thing that `simpleHandler` tries to do is to open a network connection to the specified host, using the arguments passed from `main()`. The next line of code tries to establish an input stream from the socket connection in much the same manner that the server examples did in the preceding section. Since both of these calls could generate exceptions we have used a `try...catch` statement which will either succeed and the execution of the code will continue, or fail and it will exit reporting the exception to the user by using `println()`.

Once the connection has been established, a call is made to the `getline()` method which was first used in a server class and then the line that is returned is printed. In the case of the daytime service this will be the current time and date from the viewpoint of the server.

One of the things that you should note is the amount of replicated code which is shared between the server examples and the client examples. This is a deliberate ploy: we could have written the code to look completely different, but using code which is very similar has the benefit of illustrating the close ties between servers and clients. This is something that should be expected, considering that both types of application are written using the same classes from the same package. This similarity is a great strength of the `java.net` package, mainly because it uses well-understood principles developed in one area that can be effortlessly deployed in the other.

In fact, the basic principles which apply to servers are exactly the same as those which apply to clients. The essence of the network package is to create a socket (either using a ServerSocket in a server or directly in clients) and then to create the input and output streams using the `getInputStream()` method and the `getOutputStream()` method. Once these steps have been taken, it is possible to read and write to the network connections using the methods that we have already illustrated. With this in mind, it is a small matter to create a set of classes and methods which deal with the nitty-gritty of managing network connections, thereby increasing the amount of code that can be reused in a project.

We should also note that the `sun.*` package hierarchy includes a network library that replicates a good deal of the functionality of the `java.net` package and often includes classes that are more flexible and require less coding to reach the same level of support. However, since Java ports to other platforms are only required to implement the java.* packages there is no guarantee that a target system will be able to use the classes in the sun.* packages. We have deliberately chosen not to illustrate the use of these packages for that reason – after all, this book is about the generic Java language and as far as possible is not tied to any specific implementation.

13.5.3 Making constrained connections

We have already mentioned the limitations that are imposed on network connections made by applets. However, since it is possible that applet code will be available from a number of servers other than the original distribution point, how is it possible to make connections? One approach is to hard-code the network address of each server into different versions of the applet. Clearly this is a clumsy and inelegant solution. In this section we explain how to obtain the name of the machine that the applet was downloaded from. This can then be used to make a connection that will not fall foul of the security model.

The Applet class contains a number of methods which return information about the document that an applet is embedded in and we will use these to get the information. The following example is an applet which determines the host from which it was downloaded and then makes a connection to the daytime service, displaying the results using paint(). The code is shown below:

```
import java.applet.*;
import java.net.*;
import java.io.*;
import java.awt.*;

public class safeConn extends Applet {
    Socket conn;
    int port = 13;
    String host;
    BufferedInputStream instream;
    String time;

    public void init() {
      try {
        URL tt = new
        URL(this.getDocumentBase(),"somefile");
        host = tt.getHost();
      }catch(Exception e) {
        System.out.println("Err: " + e);
      }
      try {
        conn = new Socket(host,port);
```

```
      instream = new
      BufferedInputStream(conn.getInputStream());
    } catch (Exception e) {
      System.out.println("Err: " + e);
      System.exit(1);
    }
  }

  public void start() {
    /* Read a line from the socket */
    time = this.getline();
  }

  public void paint(Graphics g) {
    g.drawString("Host: "+host+" Time: "+time,10,10);
  }

  public String getline() {
    ...
    /* As before in examples */
    ...
  }
}
```

The most significant lines in the context of this chapter are:

```
URL tt = new URL(this.getDocumentBase(),"somefile");
host = tt.getHost();
```

The first line creates a new URL which comprises the document base of the applet (that is, the Web page into which the applet has been embedded) plus a spurious String which is only used to satisfy the parameter requirements of the class. The next line asks the URL for the host element; this is returned as a String. After that, the code is a simple adaptation of the simpleClient class illustrated above ported to be a simple applet.

One potential problem with using this technique to get the hostname is that when pages are loaded from disk (using the 'Load File' option or similar) the hostname will be returned as an empty String. This will generate exceptions if passed directly to Socket. Be aware that users may have local copies of your class files, and code accordingly.

13.5.4 Guidelines for applets and applications for client–server applications

The same basic guidelines apply to both servers and clients. For example, it is always preferable to close a socket explicitly using the close() method rather than let it be closed when the application dies or when the connection times out.

This is especially important with an applet which must ensure that all open sockets are handled appropriately when the applet is unloaded and reloaded.

Equally, when using network connections, it is essential to keep the user informed of what the applet is doing and why. Recently, there has been increased awareness of the potential of malicious software and it is prudent both for the prolonged life of your code and the reputation of you and your organization if the user knows what connections are being made and why. We would also advise you to avoid hijacking other connections to bypass the security model for much the same reason. There is no justification for not keeping the user informed of progress and functionality and a carefully considered approach to this will pay dividends.

13.6 General considerations

Having discussed some of the specific issues surrounding using the `java.net` package we will now move on to some of the more general issues. These are considerations that are not directly related to the coding of a project, but should be considered when the overall design of the system is being developed.

13.6.1 Network bandwidth constraints

One of the biggest problems facing Java and related technologies is the limited capacity of the Internet. Java invites users to download and manipulate a rich content set which can include images, sound clips and motion video, in addition to the requirement to download the class files associated with the execution of the code.

When designing an applet, you should consider carefully the impact of poor network quality on your application. For example, if your system consists of an applet which feeds back user response to a remote server controlling the animations that are transmitted to the applet, what impact will poor performance have? In this instance it is easy to imagine that network congestion will delay the user feedback to the server by several seconds. This will frustrate the users so they provide the same feedback again – and when the server gets the messages the action will be executed twice.

Equally, from an attention-span perspective, not many users are going to wait an hour for your meticulously crafted full-motion video to be downloaded over an already crowded network. As a developer, you have but a limited period of time from when the user clicks on the link to your applet to losing interest to show your wares – regardless of whether your content is commercial, educational or recreational. If you want your applet to be viewed, then carefully consider how you can minimize the amount of network resources you will consume.

One approach that is being considered on a project one of the authors is involved with is to have the user install the majority of bespoke classes in advance of using the applet. However, this approach is not suitable for every application;

this project is supporting many tens of thousands of users and the applet code will frequently be reused. Another approach is to optimize the structure of the code to use as many components as possible from the standard Java packages. While this may force a slightly more generic appearance on applets, it does significantly reduce the network demand.

Whatever way you decide to optimize your applet it is worth doing. The amount of time it takes for a user to become bored is very small, and to capture the imagination in spite of generally poor network access is a skill which is worth honing.

13.6.2 Good behaviour

Another aspect of using the network library is to ensure that the user has control over the network processes. For example, if you write some code which plays an audio stream over the network as it is downloaded you should also take precautions to ensure that the user can control what could be an irritating behaviour. If the audio stream accompanies a transcript of a speech, a user visiting the software in a shared office may well want to switch off the audio and concentrate on the text. In our experience, there is no other aspect of control in software which gets more overlooked or underestimated than network connections. When writing any kind of code, make sure that the user has control and not the developer. Users who get tired of software will not revisit it.

13.7 SUMMARY

One of the outstanding features of the Java language is the java.net library. This contains a large number of facilities for communicating with computers on the Internet. The means whereby this is done is very simple: it just involves treating the data emanating from one computer or being sent to another computer as a stream.

CHAPTER FOURTEEN

Applications

- To describe the differences between an application and an applet.
- To describe a simple application.
- To outline the advantages and disadvantages of using applications.

14.1 Introduction

The difference between applets and applications should be clear to you by this stage of the book. To make it even clearer, applications are standalone, requiring only the presence of the Java run-time interpreter, and are self-contained. Applets, by contrast, are dependent on a host, typically a WWW browser, to support execution and to handle the more direct interfaces with the underlying client system. Applets are normally embedded in HTML documents.

This chapter is about applications, which are the most well-known type of code, although paradoxically the first wave of Java code is likely to be almost entirely applets as developers experiment with the possibilities that the applet provides. However, applications written in Java should not be ignored and will solve problems where applets are not appropriate.

Naturally, since Java is the language used in both applets and applications, both share a common set of characteristics which embody some of the strengths of the Java system. However, there are some differences which are important and so we will take the time to tell you when you should be using an applet and when an application would be better suited.

14.1.1 Introducing an application

We will introduce applications using the minimal Hello World approach. As you will have seen before, the Hello World code simply prints the string "Hello

World" to the output. In the case of a Java application this is the standard output: the command line interface which was used to start the application off.

Here is the code for the Java version of Hello World:

```
public class HelloWorld {
      public static void main (String args[]) {
            System.out.println("Hello World");
      }
}
```

Applications are required to define a static method called main. The Java system guarantees to call this method with the arguments that were supplied as the command line passed as the sole parameter, with it being up to the application to process the arguments and act accordingly. In our simple application, there are no arguments, and the only line of code in the main method prints out a String to the output of the system.

The main method is the basic building block of a Java application, as it is with some other programming languages such as C. The main method is the core of an application, and it is from here that your code will allocate resources, load external entities and generally control the flow of the application. In Java, the main method is defined as static. This means that it is associated with the class rather than with an instance of the class.

Our first example doesn't make use of the fact that the system will pass on the command line arguments that were given to the application when it was called. The command line arguments are whatever the user has typed after the name of the application; for example, if the user types:

```
java myApplication fast yellow loud
```

at the system prompt, then the Java run-time interpreter executes the Java class called myApplication.class (which will contain the class for your application) and the words 'fast', 'yellow' and 'loud' will be passed on to the main method in the application. These arguments are typically used to specify optional behaviour within the application. For example, the argument -fast might ask the application to use a faster algorithm to process images in preference to the slower but more accurate algorithm that the application would use by default. The use of the minus sign in arguments is not a requirement, but is common on some systems, especially UNIX. It doesn't really matter how you process the arguments that the user supplies to your application as long as the arguments make sense to the user and the user is given a clear and reasonable message when incompatible or unsupported arguments are given, ideally with a list of the arguments that are supported.

Some systems, again notably UNIX, lean towards using single letters. However, the use of more friendly arguments may look more useful and will not require the user to consult the help system before use. The downside is that lengthy arguments tend to be tedious to repeat frequently, and an application which may require a large number of arguments becomes a real chore to use.

Our advice is to support a flexible combination of both one-letter and full-word arguments whenever possible. For example, the example given for `myApplication` could support both `-fast` and `-f` to indicate that the user wants to use the fast algorithm. By carefully choosing your arguments it is possible to create a usable system which is both friendly for novices and quick for experienced users.

This system fails when you have a large number of arguments; for instance, if we wanted to have arguments to specify a fast algorithm `-fast` and to make the application write out the final production file `-final`, how do we implement both arguments as single letters? Do we have `-final` implemented as the next free letter of the alphabet `-g`? The answer is an emphatic no. If your application requires more than a few arguments then you should seriously consider implementing an interface to allow the user to select options on-screen. The use of huge lists of command line arguments is an unwarranted abuse of your users' time and patience and should be avoided at all costs.

Given that you do require some arguments, how do you process them? Let's illustrate this by extending the `HelloWorld` example from earlier in the chapter. The code looks like this:

```
public class HelloWorld2 {

  public static void main (String args[]) {
    for (int i = 0; i < args.length; i++) {
      System.out.println("Arg " + i + ":" + args[i]);
    }
  }
}
```

If you run and compile this code and then execute it as:

```
java HelloWorld2 Java is cool!
```

you should get the following output:

```
  Arg 0:Java
  Arg 1:is
  Arg 2:cool!
```

You can see that the new code takes each argument that has been passed to the application and prints it out on a new line, indicating which argument it is. The number of arguments passed to the method can be obtained by using the `length` method.

What if you want to do something with the arguments? Let us take the example given above for specifying that the type of algorithm used is to be faster than the default. The code to handle this is as follows:

```
public class HelloWorld3 {

  public static void main (String args[]) {
    String algorithm = "slow";
    for (int i = 0; i < args.length; i++) {
      if (args[i].startsWith("-f")) algorithm = "fast";
    }
  System.out.println("Algorithm: " + algorithm);
  }
}
```

In this example, each argument is checked to see if it started with '-f'. Here we use the method startsWith provided as part of java.lang.String. This includes arguments such as '-fast' and '-f', but also would match the arguments '-fish' and '-friday'. Another approach would be to explicitly look for the supported arguments '-f' and '-fast'. If an argument matches, then the algorithm is changed from the default slow algorithm to our faster option.

Exercise

A Java application which generates machine code has two command line arguments. The first is either -v or -vax for generating code for a VAX computer, -s or -sun for a Sun computer or -p or -pc for a PC computer. Write down the code which handles this; don't worry about calling System.out. The default is the Sun computer.

Solution

The code is shown below:

```
public class HelloWorld3 {

  public static void main (String args[]) {
    String computer = "PC";
    for (int i = 0; i < args.length; i++) {
      if (args[i].startsWith("-s")) computer = "Sun";
      else if (args[i].startsWith("-v"))
        computer = "VAX";
    }
  }
...
```

One last thing to watch out for when handling arguments is always to specify a default behaviour. Instead of requiring the user to specify one of '-fast' or '-slow' to select an algorithm, define a default behaviour and only require the user to override this when needed. If you don't do this, you will have to cope with the possibility of the user calling both arguments, one after the other, which will require a good deal more supporting code and effort on your behalf to ensure that the behaviour that the user expects is what is really happening inside your application.

14.2 The application life cycle

You saw in Chapter 12 how the Java system creates a 'life cycle' for applets. At key points in the life of an applet, certain methods are guaranteed to be called by the system. These key points allow the developer to design an applet which will cooperate with other applets and the Java host system, as well as providing a general model for designing an applet.

Applications are not required to cooperate with other applications in the same manner. This means that if you implement a method that would be called automatically in an applet, you must arrange to have this method called manually in your application. Some of the applet methods may not be directly related to the operation of your application but others are more useful, especially the Runnable interface.

The main method has already been introduced as the core of an application, and it is from here that methods must be called (although, of course, methods can be called by other methods which were, in turn, called from main). If you wish to define a life cycle for your application, main is the method you should start from.

Why would you require this kind of execution model? After all, when your application is closed by the user the thread of execution is ended. Well, while it is true that most applications will not require the kind of rigorous model that the Java system demands of an applet, there is a need to ensure that any external resources are handled cleanly when the application exits. For example, if an application connects to a remote server to perform some kind of search, then it is far better, and preferable, to ensure that the server knows that the client has been closed by the user as soon as possible in order to avoid consuming valuable resources by performing a search for a client that is no longer able to take the results.

Equally, if an application shares information with other applications, or provides some kind of service, then the code should take precautions to ensure that when the thread of execution is terminated the dependent resources are released cleanly. The advantage of the model imposed by applets is that developers are required to implement at least the basics of the life cycle in order to have code executed. Our advice is to follow a similar model when writing applications.

14.2.1 Using threads in an application

When using threads in an applet the Java system provides a certain amount of
support for starting threads if the applet subclass implements the Runnable
interface. For example, when your applet has been sent the call to the init()
method, a call will be made to the methods that make up the Runnable
interface, which will allow you to ensure that your threads are running and
stopping when they are supposed to. The reason that a Java browser does this is
to ensure that threads are killed or suspended when a page of HTML (including
applets) is no longer on screen or is reloaded. None of this is required with an
application – after all, once the user has called the application from the user
interface or the command line interface the code will be executed until all the
intended functions have been completed or the user terminates the execution.

Therefore, applications wishing to implement threads must make sure that they
are executed from the main method. The most effective way of handling threads
in an application is to provide separate classes which extend the Thread class and
which are created and managed from the main application class. A simple
example is shown below:

```
class appThread {

public static void main (String args[]) {
    new myThread("One").start();
    new myThread("Two").start();
  }
}


class myThread extends Thread {

  public myThread(String str) {
  super(str);
  }

  public void run() {
    for (int i = 0; i < 10; i++) {
      System.out.println("Thread "
                         + getName() + " :" + i);
      try {
         sleep(100);
      } catch (InterruptedException e) {
      }
    }
  }
}
```

In this code, the top-level class `appThread` creates and starts two instances of the `myThread` class. `myThread` extends the `Thread` class and so we only have to call the `super` method to instantiate it and then implement `run` in order to provide the code to be executed in the thread. By passing a string to `myThread` (and so to `Thread`, by the use of `super`), we call a constructor which defines a name for the thread. Then, in the `run` method we determine which thread we are by calling `getName`. This is one approach; another approach would be to pass a String to `myThread`, which is then made available to other methods in the class. We prefer the method in the example because it maintains a level of consistency with the constructor for the subclass and the superclass. If you compile and execute this example, you will see each of the threads counting up from zero to nine, with the output being interleaved as the `sleep` statements free up the logical execution stream for the other thread.

This example illustrates how to start threads. As we have already mentioned, you should make some effort to ensure that when threads die or an application exits, any resources such as network connections and files are closed cleanly. You can see from the example that threads can be started in the normal manner, and equally threads can be stopped by calling the `stop` method. If this method has not been overridden, then the default behaviour is to stop the execution of the thread.

14.2.2 Dual-purpose code

One other reason for implementing methods which define a life cycle for an application is that it is possible to write code that can be executed both as an applet and as a standalone application. A good reason for this would be to extend cross-platform support to platforms which may have a browser but not a run-time system, or which have a run-time system but no browser.

However, while the idea of writing code which can be run both as an application and as an applet may be appealing, there are some important differences between applets and applications which should be seriously considered. Before discussing these issues it is worth introducing a simple example which can run both as an applet and as an application:

```
import java.applet.Applet;
import java.awt.*;

public class dualCode extends Applet {

  public static void main (String args[]) {
    Frame f = new Frame("Dual Applet/Application");
    f.setLayout(new FlowLayout());
    dualCode dc = new dualCode();
    dc.init();
    f.add("Center",dc);
    f.resize(100,100);
```

```
    f.show();
  }

  public void init() {
    setLayout(new FlowLayout());
    add(new Button("Button"));}
```

When this code is run as an applet the first method that is called is `init`. The `init` method simply defines the layout model for the applet and creates a button. However, when the code is executed as an application the first method that is called is `main`, as we have described at the start of this chapter. In this example, `main` creates a new top-level `Frame`, called `f`. The `main` method sets the layout model and creates a new instance of the example class – this is done because `main` is static. Then, the new instance of the example class, `dc`, is added to the `Frame` `f`. The `Frame` is then resized and displayed. So, once the `Frame` is displayed the code operates in the same manner regardless of whether it is being executed within the hosting environment of a browser or as a standalone application. However, while this looks like a perfect solution and makes you wonder why Java even bothers to differentiate between applets and applications, there are some severe constraints on using this approach.

The problems arise when differences in functionality between applets and applications make the use of the same Java code impossible. As an example, the security model imposed on applets by the browser means that opening network connections is very constrained, while an application can open and manage connections freely. Therefore, in order to write code which can function as both an applet and an application, it is necessary to write to the lowest common feature set. In the case of network connections this means imposing the constraints of the browser security model on applications as well as applets and in the process severely limiting the functionality of the resulting code.

The next section discusses some of the differences between applications and applets. Each can be regarded as an obstacle in writing dual-purpose code. However, if you find that the requirements of your project are served by the constrained feature set that allows the generation of dual-purpose code, then using this technique can be an elegant and simple solution to reaching a larger number of users on a wider range of platforms, as well as facilitating development of applet code in the absence of browsers.

14.3 Differences between applets and applications

Although applets and applications are both written in Java and have access to the same library packages, there are some significant differences between the functionality available in each. In this section we will discuss some of the more important differences and the impact this has in making the decision to develop either an application or an applet. It is very easy to be seduced by the charm of developing an applet which can be downloaded and executed on the fly. However, there are some limitations to applets. These are primarily imposed by security models adopted by Java-compatible browsers which make applet development unsuitable for some requirements.

14.3.1 Loading images

Loading images into applications is extremely difficult. Applets rely on the getImage method to pull in an image from a URL. Unfortunately, this method does not work with applications, even if the application class extends Applet. The reason for this is that the getImage method always makes a call to getAppletContext, and getAppletContext calls the stub of the applet, which is defined automatically when an applet is hosted by a browser, but is not set in an application. Consequently, calls to getImage within an application will generate an exception. There is a short-term solution to this problem, reported to the *comp.lang.java* group, which is to:

```
import sun.awt.image.URLImageSource;
```

at the start of the code and then use the call:

```
img = Toolkit.getDefaultToolkit().
createImage(new URLImageSource(url));
```

to load in the images. While this is a workable solution, the use of the sun.* packages is not recommended, since not all implementations of Java are guaranteed to implement the Sun libraries, and so your code could well break on some Java systems.

Java implementations are only required to supply the java.* hierarchy, which means that betting on the availability of a package that may not be included in the port that a client is using is a recipe for disaster in the long term. In general, it is very strongly recommended that developers use the java.* classes wherever possible, as adopting this approach will ensure that code makes the most of the Java cross-platform support.

14.3.2 Applet security limitations

Because the model of applet execution includes the dynamic loading and running of unknown code from anywhere on the network, there is the chance that malicious code will be written which will try to abuse the local client machine in some manner. Therefore, the designers of Java have implemented a security model for applet execution which limits what an applet can do with the local system. These limitations are important components in deciding between developing application code or applet code for a particular application. Although an applet can make calls to the libraries which have been constrained for security reasons the results from these calls will not be as expected. The following paragraphs discuss the limitations that the security model imposes on applets.

For security reasons, applets have very limited access to the local file system. In fact most of the basic file operations which are available to an application (including checking if a file exists, and seeing what type of file it is) are not available to applets. In addition, the use of the `FileInputString` and `RandomAccessFile` libraries is constrained and applets cannot create new file handlers in the I/O packages. The reasons for this are sound – after all, the thought of an unknown applet having unlimited access to the local file system would compromise system security. The Java security model defines a series of Access Control Lists. If the file that your code requires is not on the list, then you cannot:

- check for the existence of the file

- read the file

- write the file

- check the file type

- check if the file is a directory

- get the timestamp from the file

- check the file size

- create a directory

- name the file.

Since your applet code cannot define the files in the access list the access you can have within applet code is almost non-existent. Therefore, if you need access to files on the local machine, you must write an application. At the time of writing, the definitions of the control lists are vague, especially as the browser that will almost certainly have the greatest distribution (Netscape) has yet to decide on an implementation model. However, regardless of the model that Netscape adopts, it is not possible to assume a given security model on a browser without making assumptions about which browser the user is running – and making this kind of assumption eats deeply into the cross-platform nature that makes Java a flexible language.

Applets are unable to open network connections to arbitrary hosts. In fact, an applet can only make connections to the host from which it was downloaded. This does pose some problems regarding scalability for large-scale systems, since one machine must be responsible for delivering applets using HTTP as well as maintaining services for all of the other aspects of applet operation. While this model prevents connections being made to 'hidden' hosts (that is, hosts that the user has no knowledge of), it does mean that one machine has to deliver a complete range of services to all clients instead of adopting an approach of separate machines running specialized services.

In addition, applets cannot create socket factories. Socket factories are the handlers which process incoming socket connections and process the raw data from the network layer. By removing the ability to create socket handlers the designers of the Java system have removed the possibility that malicious code can use this route to subvert network streams. Again, however, there is a direct separation between the functionality of the Java libraries and the functionality of the Java applet.

Applets are not allowed to access packages in the sun.* library. These functions contain classes which could potentially be used for subverting local functionality. Additionally, applets are not allowed to create new class loaders. The class loaders that are supplied as part of the Java system run a comprehensive series of checks before allowing a class to be referenced, and therefore allowing an applet to create new loaders would defeat the notion of that aspect of the security system.

Applets are not allowed to link libraries using the System.loadlibrary() call, which is not the case with applications. Also, applets cannot modify the AppletSecurityManager which implements these rules, for much the same reason.

The creation of classes in the java.* library is also not permitted. This prevents applets from creating packages which contain subversive code to be called by other (benign) applets loaded later by the user.

Applets cannot define native methods. These are methods which are written in another language and compiled to machine code. The lack of native methods means that malicious applets cannot define methods which the Java system cannot manage or analyse. Stopping forked processes prevents applets starting processes which are outside the control of the Java system (for example, starting a process which deletes files in the user space).

In addition, applets cannot manipulate threads which are not part of the applet thread group. While this does not reflect directly on the functionality of an application (which doesn't require the same notion of thread control), it is an important limitation of the scope of thread control within the browser space.

14.3.3 Creating servers

Applications can be written to support server functionality using the network libraries. Applets, however, do not support this, and the use of the accept and listen calls is not permitted. This has been done to stop applets bypassing the constraint of only opening connections to a single remote host (where the applet was loaded from) by becoming servers and accepting connections from 'hidden' machines.

14.3.4 Summary of differences

Most of the differences between applets and applications exist because of the important requirement to provide a reasonably secure mechanism for executing unknown applet code, while minimizing risk to the local machine. Other differences, such as loading images into applications, can be regarded as design deficiencies in the Java system. These may well be addressed in later releases of the Java environment or by the availability of third-party libraries.

In essence, it is important to consider the needs of a specific project before deciding to develop either an applet or an application. The novelty value of developing applets is not sufficient motivation when the demands of the system require access to facilities that the security model denies to applets; equally, working around the limitations that an application inherits from the bias of the Java packages towards applet development may render some application initiatives useless. As has been mentioned previously, the first wave of Java development is expected to be centred on applets, although this may change with time.

14.4 Application limitations

One other topic worthy of note is the latency incurred when a Java application is started. Because the compiled Java byte codes are interpreted and then executed in the Java virtual machine there is a period of time which elapses between the start of the execution and the Java code being executed. For most applications this is not important. For example, it doesn't matter if a simple game or a spreadsheet takes an additional 10 seconds to start before being available to the user. However, there are systems which cannot tolerate the latency of the interpreter. As an example, consider a large-scale network system which has a series of synchronized servers. When a server crashes, the lag between the server being restarted and the server code rejoining the other servers in providing functionality can be very significant.

Another, smaller, issue with using applications is that if path names to external files and resources are hard-coded into the classes, then the different file structures on different platforms will cause the code to break unless it is specifically ported. For example, the file:

```
/home/adam/development/java/project/images/someimage.gif
```

on a UNIX host will not be the same as:

```
C:\users\adam\development\java\project\images\someimage.gif
```

on a Windows NT host. This also doesn't take into account the limitations that some operating systems impose on file names (for example, Windows 3.1). One approach to addressing this is to have the path to the resource files specified as an argument or contained in a separate configuration file, but neither approach is entirely without limitations. This does affect the cross-platform nature of Java in a small but significant way, since there will be few applications that will run without requiring access to some external data or resources. When developing an application, our advice is to make as few assumptions as possible about the underlying file system in order to preserve as much interoperability as possible.

14.5 Adding user interface elements to applications

It is easy to add elements from the AWT library to applets, mainly because the
`Applet` class inherits from the AWT hierarchy. Applications do not automatically
provide a mechanism for doing this, and so it is the responsibility of the developer
to create a suitable holder for the user interface elements. There are many
approaches to doing this and, in fact, there are many approaches to writing
applications in general. Our approach, which we have developed with both Java
and other languages, is to keep the amount of code in the `main` method to a
minimum and create a separate class which contains the bulk of the code for the
'body' of the application.

Our preferred approach is to keep the `main` method as simple as possible and
use it only to maintain top-level control within the application as a whole,
although often these high-level tasks which affect the whole of the application can
also be pushed down into other classes.

As an example of adding AWT elements to applications, consider the
following:

```
import java.awt.*;

public class uiApp {

    public static void main (String args[]) {
            frameClass fc = new frameClass("UI Demo");
        }
}
```

In this class, the only method is `main()`. The only line of code in the method
creates a new instance of the `frameClass` class. The class that is called looks like
this:

```
class frameClass extends Frame {

  public frameClass(String str) {
    super(str); addElems();
    resize(100,200); show();
  }

  public void addElems() {
            setLayout(new FlowLayout());
            add (new Button("Button 1"));
            add (new Button("Button 2"));
            add (new Button("Button 3"));
            add (new Button("Button 4"));
        }
}
```

The constructor which has been called from the first class calls `super` with the string as an argument. Since this class inherits from `java.awt.Frame` this has the effect of creating a top-level frame with a title set to the string passed into the method from `main` in the other class. At this point another method `addElems` is called which defines the layout model for the frame and then inserts four buttons which are named sequentially. In fact, although these buttons are created by four separate lines of code, there is no reason why a simple loop could not be used. Once the buttons have been added, the constructor resizes the main window and then maps it to the display. At this point, of course, the buttons have no actions attached to them, since we have not overridden any of the methods which handle incoming user events. Since the same AWT elements are being used for applets as well as applications, the technique remains the same for processing external input.

14.6 SUMMARY

This chapter should make clear that there are many similarities between applets and applications, and that one of the differences is the lack of external calls which are provided for applets by a browser. We have also introduced the notion of code that will execute as both an applet and an application and made clear the advantages and disadvantages that this technique involves. Finally, we described the additional information required to use AWT elements and threads in an application. Although the same libraries are used in both applets and applications, applications require some 'glue' code which compensates for the lack of external messages and inheritance which is implicit with an applet.

CHAPTER FIFTEEN

Database Access

- To introduce the main relational concepts required to understand database access in Java.
- To introduce that small subset of the SQL query language necessary to understand database access in Java.
- To describe the command interface between Java and relational database systems.
- To show some very simple examples of Java code which access relational databases.

15.1 Introduction

Most of the hype that has been generated by the Java language has centred around its use for Internet applications. While such applications represent an important area for Java, the main area where commentators feel that it will take off is that of the intranet. The term **intranet** is used to describe the use of technologies such as Java and Netscape to implement company-wide information systems. The users of such systems would not interact with company data using an operating system such as Windows 95, but would use a browser to carry out functions such as retrieving sales data, updating personnel files and calculating future market growth.

Intranet applications will usually be based on large databases that have been implemented using relational database technology and, ever since Java appeared in 1995, there has been a requirement for the language to provide interfaces to the main relational database systems such as Ingres, Oracle, Access and SQL Server. In late 1996 this need was recognized by the incorporation within version 1.1 of the Java system of database access facilities. Such facilities can be found in the `java.sql` package. In order to understand these facilities we will have to digress for a moment in order to describe the main relational concepts that you will require in order to follow the remainder of this chapter.

15.2 Relational databases

Relational databases have been in existence since the early 1970s. The concept which underlies relational database systems is the storage of data within tables. An example of such a table is shown in Figure 15.1.

This table, which might form part of a personnel system, consists of four columns or fields which contain data describing the employees of a company: the second column contains the name of the employee, the third column contains the salary and the fourth column contains the name of the department in which the employee works. The first column is a number which uniquely identifies each employee, in that no two employees will have the same number; in relational database terms this number is known as a **key**. The table is identified by a name; in Figure 15.1 this is *Personnel.*

A database, implemented using relational technology, will consist of a number of tables similar to that shown in Figure 15.1. Each will be associated with a key and will also contain information which is common to other tables. For example, the table shown in Figure 15.2 shows the data held on the departments which are referenced in the table shown in Figure 15.1. Here the table contains data which identifies a department, the city in which it is based and the number of employees who work in the department.

The table in Figure 15.2 contains a column which is identical to one in the table shown in Figure 15.1: this is the column which identifies a department. This shared data is known as a **foreign key**.

Personnel			
PersonnelId	Name	Salary	Department
3458	Lewis	23500	Sales
3345	Ince	12000	Sales
1001	Freeman	14000	Research
5589	Thomas	12800	Accounts
2999	Davis	23000	Accounts

Figure 15.1 A relational table.

Departments		
Department	Location	Size
Sales	Manchester	34
Research	London	23
Accounts	Paris	10
Marketing	Paris	50

Figure 15.2 Another relational table.

Such data allows a high degree of sophisticated processing to be carried out; for example, a program can be easily written to access the tables and list those members of staff working in Paris. Such processing is normally carried out using a programming language known as SQL (Structured Query Language).

15.3 SQL

SQL was invented by Donald Chamberlin, who worked for IBM in the 1970s. It consists of a number of statements which carry out the functions of writing data to and reading data from a database made up of tables such as the ones shown in Figures 15.1 and 15.2.

SQL is implemented either as a standalone language or as a command interface within an existing language such as C or Java. The aim of this section is to describe a small enough subset of the language necessary to understand the facilities which Java provides for accessing relational databases.

We shall concentrate on one SQL statement: the `SELECT` statement. There are many others available. However, since this is not an SQL programming text we will not describe them.

The `SELECT` statement will select a number of rows from a table according to some criterion. An example of a `SELECT` statement which accesses the table shown in Figure 15 .1 is shown below:

```
SELECT * FROM Personnel WHERE Department = 'Sales'
```

What this statement does is to select those rows of the `Personnel` table which contain the string `'Sales'` within their `Department` field. The asterisk indicates that the rows which are to be retrieved will contain all the fields of the table. Another example of the SELECT statement is shown below:

```
SELECT Name, Department FROM Personnel WHERE
   Salary > 15000
```

This selects the rows of the Personnel table associated with an employee who has a salary greater than £15 000. This example differs from the previous one in that the asterisk is replaced by the names of two fields (Name and Department). This results in a table being formed which only contains the Name and Department columns of the Personnel table which satisfies the condition Salary > 15000.

A final example of the SELECT statement is shown below:

```
SELECT Name, Salary, Department FROM Personnel WHERE
   (Salary BETWEEN 20000 AND 30000) AND
   Department IN ('Sales', 'Research')
```

This produces a three-column table which contains the name, salary and department of all those staff who have a salary between 20 000 and 30 000 pounds and who work in the Sales or Research departments.

This, then, is a brief description of SQL as exemplified by the SELECT statement. The important point to make about all these statements is that they create tables. The implication here is that any programming language into which SQL is embedded must implement some means of processing these tables. This topic will be dealt with in Section 15.5.2.

15.4 Connecting to SQL databases

The first thing you need to do when accessing a relational database within a Java program is to connect to it. Two things need to be done. First, the Java program must load a database driver. This is a piece of software which carries out the transfer of data between a stored relational database and the Java program. This loading is mainly carried out by the static method forName which is found in the class Class.

For example, the code:

```
Class.forName("Drivers.newDriver.JdbcOdbCDR");
```

loads the driver found in the file Drivers.newDriver.JdbcOdbCDR into memory so that it can oversee the transfer of file-based relational data to a Java program. There are a number of commercial drivers available.

The second task is to connect to the file containing the relational data. This is achieved by means of the method getConnection found in the class DriverManager. This method has three string arguments. The first is the URL of the database containing the tables, the second is the name of the user who is trying to access the database and the third is a password (this may be empty). An example of the use of this method is shown below:

```
Connection dbConnection =
  DriverManager.getConnection("jdbc:odbc:employee.dta",
    "D.Davis","Pli00&j0");
```

Here the name of the user is D.Davis who uses the password Pli00&j0. The URL for the database has three components. The first (jdbc) informs the Java system that the URL references a database, the second component (odbc) informs the Java system that the database is ODBC compliant. An ODBC-compliant database is one which conforms to the Microsoft ODBC standard. Current drivers for Java will only access databases that conform to this standard. The final component of the URL (employee.dta) gives the name of the file containing the relational tables. The code references an object defined by the class Connection. The object created by this statement (dbConnection) is the conduit through which access to the database occurs.

Every Java program which manipulates relational databases must contain calls to getConnection and forName in order to load a database driver and establish a connection to a database. In the programs which follow we shall usually assume that these calls have been made.

15.5 Java and SQL

15.5.1 Executing SQL statements

This section describes how a variety of statements found in SQL can be executed and how the data that is returned from such executions can be accessed.

There are two classes which are used for simple SQL processing. These are Statement and ResultSet. The former corresponds to SQL statements while the latter corresponds to the collection of data that is returned after an SQL statement is executed. In order to understand how these classes are used, consider the code below:

```
Connection dbConnection;
Statement sqlStatement;
ResultSet results;
...
// Database driver will be loaded here
...
try{
  dbConnection =
    DriverManager.getConnection("jdbc:odbc:employee.dta",
      "D.Davis","Pli00&j0");
```

```
   sqlStatement = dbConnection.createStatement();
   results = sqlStatement.executeQuery(
     "SELECT Name, Address FROM EmpTable");
   while(results.next()){
     // Some processing of the ResultSet results
 }
 catch(SQLException){
   System.out.println("SQL Error occurred);
 }
```

Here the `Connection`, `Statement` and `ResultSet` objects are declared. The first statement within the `try-catch` clause establishes the connection to the database. The next statement uses the method `createStatement` to create an SQL statement object and the third statement executes the SQL statement:

```
SELECT Name, Address FROM EmpTable
```

This uses the method `executeQuery`. This has a single argument which is a string in which the SQL statement to be executed is embedded.

A loop terminates the statements in the `try-catch` clause. This loop processes the result set which has been created by the execution of the SQL statement. In the code fragment above we do not show this processing; what we do show is how the loop is constructed. When the SQL statement is executed a `ResultSet` object is created. Each element of this set contains a row of the table that has been formed by executing the statement.

The method `next`, which forms part of the class `ResultSet`, moves to the next row to be processed and returns true while there are results to be processed. Thus, the loop above will iterate over the result set until the last row of the set has been encountered.

An important point to make is the use of the `try-catch` clause. It is quite easy to make errors when accessing a relational database, for example specifying a column which does not exist, and so it is necessary to monitor any exceptions that arise. The `java.sql` package contains the exception `SQLException` which is used for this purpose.

The example above poses the question: how do we carry out the processing in the loop? The aim of the next section is to describe this.

15.5.2 Processing ResultSet objects

Within the class `ResultSet` there are a number of methods which access the current element of a `ResultSet`. Two methods you will use frequently are `getInt` and `getString`. Each comes in two versions: one with an `int` argument and the other with a `String` argument. The method `getInt` returns an integer and the method `getString` returns a string.

The argument identifies the column number or name of the `ResultSet` element that is being processed. For example, if the SQL statement:

```
"SELECT Name, Address FROM empTable"
```

has been executed and we are in the middle of the loop processing the resultant `ResultSet` object `results` which has been created from this execution, then the statements:

```
String fName = results.getString("Name"),
fAddress = results.getString("Address");
```

will place in `fName` the string which represents the name field of the row which is being processed and place in `fAddress` the address. The example above uses string arguments to identify the fields within the row which is being processed. A more efficient alternative is to use the `int` argument versions of the methods. For example, the code:

```
String fName = results.getString(1),
fAddress = results.getString(2);
```

is equivalent to the previous fragment which uses string arguments. The `int` argument refers to the number of the field within a row with the first field starting at one. There is a problem with using `int` arguments: it produces Java programs which are difficult to read. This can be overcome by the use of `final   int` variables (constants). For example the code above can be written as:

```
String fName = results.getString(Name),
fAddress = results.getString(Address);
```

provided the declaration:

```
final int Name = 1, Address = 2;
```

precedes it somewhere. The example below illustrates the use of methods such as `getInt` and `getString`:

```
Connection dbConnection;
Statement sqlStatement;
ResultSet results;
final int Name = 1, Address = 2, Age = 3;
// Database driver will be loaded here
try{
   dbConnection =
   DriverManager.getConnection("jdbc:odbc:employee.dta",
      "D.Davis","Pli00&j0");
   sqlStatement = dbConnection.createStatement();
   results = sqlStatement.executeQuery(
      "SELECT Name, Address, Age FROM EmpTable");
   while(results.next()){
      System.out.println("Name =" + getString(Name) +
```

```
            " Address = " + getString(Address) +
                    " Age = " + getInt(Age));
   }
catch(SQLException){
   System.out.println("SQL Error occurred");
}
```

Here, the rows from the table `empTable` containing two strings and an `int` are retrieved and then processed one by one. This processing merely consists of their values being displayed on the `out` channel.

15.5.3 Prepared statements

The process of executing an SQL statement can consume a large amount of system resources. First, the statement has to be checked for its correct syntax, it then has to be compiled and then a strategy has to be developed to ensure that the access is as efficient as possible. After these three steps have been carried out the SQL statement is executed.

There will often be a requirement for an SQL statement to be repeatedly executed. When this happens there is only a need for the first three steps detailed above to be carried out once. In order to ensure this, Java provides facilities for what are known as **prepared statements**. Such statements are stored in a compiled form ready for execution. The class `PreparedStatement` fulfils this function. For example, the code:

```
Connection dbConnection;
PreparedStatement pSqlStatement;
ResultSet results;
final int    Name = 1,
             Address = 2,
             Age = 3;
// Database driver will be loaded here
   dbConnection =
   DriverManager.getConnection("jdbc:odbc:employee.dta",
      "D.Davis","Pli00&j0");
   pSqlStatement = dbConnection.createStatement(
      "SELECT Name, Address FROM Emptable WHERE Salary >
         20000");
```

creates a prepared statement which exists in a compiled form that can be used time and time again.

Prepared statements are at their most useful when they are parameterized. For example, let us assume that we need to retrieve employee data which depends on the salary of each employee: sometimes we want employee details for those employees earning more than 20000 pounds and sometimes we want employee details for those employees more than 30 000 pounds. One way to do this is to execute the statement:

```
SELECT Name, Address FROM Emptable WHERE Salary > 20000
```

and the statement:

```
SELECT Name, Address FROM Emptable WHERE Salary > 30000
```

However, this defeats the aim of prepared statements. What is required is to be able to create parameterized prepared statements. Ideally we need some way of specifying our SQL statement as

```
SELECT Name, Address FROM emptable WHERE Salary > ?
```

where the question mark indicates a value which is provided at run time. Java provides a facility whereby this can be achieved. Consider the code shown below:

```
Connection dbConnection;
PreparedStatement pSqlStatement;
ResultSet results;
final int Name = 1, Address = 2, Age = 3;
...
// Database driver will be loaded here
...
  dbConnection =
  DriverManager.getConnection("jdbc:odbc:employee.dta",
    "D.Davis","Pli00&j0");
  pSqlStatement = dbConnection.createStatement(
    "SELECT Name, Address, Age FROM empTable
        WHERE Salary > ?");
...
pSqlStatement.setInt(1,20000);
pSqlStatement.executeQuery();
...
//Processing of staff earning more than 20000
...
pSqlStatement.setInt(1,30000);
pSqlStatement.executeQuery();
...
//Processing of staff earning more than 30000
...
```

The parameterized prepared statement is first set up and then is executed twice. However, before each execution the argument of the statement is set using the method setInt. This has two arguments: the number of the argument and the value which is assigned. Arguments in a prepared statement are numbered from left to right starting at one. setInt is just one example of a whole series of methods which set arguments; for example, setString will set string value arguments.

15.5.4 Stored procedures

Stored procedures are collections of SQL code which carry out functions that have been identified as being of use to many users of a relational database application. For example, in a personnel system there may be a frequent need to retrieve the address of a member of staff, given their name. Such facilities would be implemented by means of a stored procedure. The general form of a stored procedure is:

```
result = CALL Procedure Name(Arg1, Arg2,..., Argn)
```

where the result of a call is given by result and the arguments to the call are written within round brackets and separated by commas. The class CallableStatement describes such statements and arguments are specified using question marks in a similar way to their use in prepared statements. In order to read data from a result argument there is a need to register the result as being of a Java type and also to access that value. The code below shows this in action:

```
Connection dbConnection;
CallableStatement cs;
...
cs = dbConnection.prepareCall("? = Call getEmpls(?)");
cs.registerOutParameter(1,java.sql.Types.INTEGER);
cs.setString(2,"Sales");
cs.executeUpdate();
int val = cs.getInt(1);
...
```

First, a callable statement object is created. This statement has the name getEmpls and has an output argument which is an integer and one input argument which is a string. The output argument is then registered with the Java program as being of SQL type INTEGER; this corresponds to int in Java. Next, the second parameter, a string, is set to the value "Sales"; the callable statement is then executed and the value returned accessed using the method getInt.

15.5.5 Portability concerns

Java programs which incorporate SQL statements are portable across a wide range of relational database systems. Provided the systems are ODBC compliant then there should be few problems involved in, say, transferring from an Ingres database to an Oracle database. One of the problems that does occur is the different ways that relational database manufacturers have dealt with entities such as dates and time of day, where the format may differ from implementation to implementation. The way that the Java relational database interface gets over this problem is via escape characters. An example of the use of these characters is shown below:

```
PSqlStatement = dbConnection.createStatement(
    "SELECT Name, Address, Age FROM EmpTable
        WHERE BirthDate > {d'1966-03-11'}");
```

Here the escape character d specifies that the characters enclosed by the escape ' characters are meant to be a date. The escape characters are intercepted by the database driver which translates to the format required by the database management system being used.

15.6 SUMMARY

Database access is an important facility in intranet applications. Java has a command-based interface which requires programmers to insert SQL statements as strings within methods which access relational databases. Java contains facilities for virtually all types of SQL statements including prepared statements and callable statements. It also contains facilities for communicating SQL arguments and processing sets of data that result from SQL statement execution.

The Java Development Kit

A.1 Introduction

This appendix does not cover the Java language directly but, instead, focuses on the background information that a developer needs to know in order to develop Java applications and applets. We will outline the essential information required to make the most of the tools which are supplied as part of the Sun Java Development Kit (JDK). The examples given in this chapter are based on the Sun JDK distribution for the Sun Solaris operating system – although most other platforms will operate in a similar manner. We have not chosen to give specific examples for other operating systems simply because we would not be able to create a complete list.

A.2 First steps

This section will show you how to take a Java file and compile it. This will allow you to work through any of the examples shown in this group as well as allowing you to access and work through any code fragments that are available for downloading on the Internet or any of the commercial networks.

A.2.1 Compiling a Java source file

The basic sequence for compiling a Java code file is to create the file, either by typing in the code or by downloading the code from another site, and then instruct the compiler to process the file. The compiler will take the source file and produce a file which either can be used by a browser or the appletviewer or is a standalone application.

Let us take the standard HelloWorld Java application and step through the compilation process. In this example we will describe an application rather than an applet; however, the process for compilation is the same. The code is:

```
public class HelloWorld {

  public static void main (String args[]) {
```

```
            System.out.println("Hello World");
    }
}
```

A.2.2 Creating the source file

As a developer you can use a text-editor or word processor to create your source code files as long as the saved files are in ASCII format. Source files must end with the .java extension and, by convention, the name of the file is the same as the name of the class which is defined within the file, so we would create a file called 'HelloWorld.java' to contain the source in the example above.

It is important to point out that you can only have one public class per Java source file – although it is quite acceptable to include as many non-public classes as you like.

The convention of naming files after classes is an important one. As the amount of code required for a project increases, the importance of a consistent naming system to handle a large number of files becomes increasingly vital for keeping track of classes.

So, for this example, we create a text file called HelloWorld.java and type in the simple example as above. Note that the name of the file is case-sensitive to match the class name.

A.2.3 Compiling the source file

Once you have constructed a source file you can use the compiler to translate the Java instructions into byte codes. These will later be used by the Java interpreter. When the compiler compiles a Java source file it writes out a file named after the class that has been processed with .class appended. This is another reason for naming the source files after the class names, since the compiler will create files named after classes regardless of the naming strategy you have adopted. The one-to-one mapping of classes to sources and classes to compiled class files is useful for keeping track of large amounts of code.

The Java compiler is called javac. It is invoked simply by typing:

```
javac <filename>.Java
```

If the JDK has been installed correctly, the compiler will be in your search path and will not have to be specified explicitly. If your shell returns an error reporting that the javac binary cannot be located, you should return to the installation instructions and ensure that you have followed all of the steps laid out. Some readers will look to this book to help diagnose installation and configuration problems, but even with the best will in the world we cannot cover the range of platforms that Java will support. The best place to look for guidance in this area is the documentation which is supplied with the JDK and the Sun Java Web servers.

So, for our example, we just type:

```
javac HelloWorld.java
```

The compiler will take the source file and generate a byte-code file called `HelloWorld.class`.

A.2.4 Dealing with syntax errors

The Java compiler, as with most compilers, will perform syntax checks on the source code as part of the compilation process. These check for syntax errors and ensure that you have created source code which conforms to the definition of the Java language. So, for example, if instead of typing this line in our example:

```
public static void main (String args[]) {
```

we typed:

```
main (String args[]) {
```

and recompiled it, the `javac` compiler would report the following error:

```
HelloWorld.java:4:  Invalid  method  declaration;  return
type required.
  main (String args[]) {
  ^
  1 error
```

This error indicates that a method in Java must declare what will be returned to the calling method. Even methods that do not return anything must explicitly say so by using the `void` keyword. You can see that the compiler has also stated that the error has been encountered in line four of the source file. Since blank lines are taken into account this may not be the fourth line of code. The Java compiler tries to continue compiling after encountering an error, so that as many problems can be identified in one pass as possible. However, this may mean that the same error can generate a whole raft of errors as the compiler finds related problems further into the source file. For example, instead of declaring a String correctly we could have typed:

```
sTring someString;
```

and then compiled the source file. Not only would the compiler complain about the real error but it would also generate an error each time that the String was referenced. For example, if `someString` was assigned a value from calling a method which returned a String, the compiler would complain about an invalid cast between `String` and `sTring`. Most compilers do this and it is not something specific to the Java system, but it is worth looking at the errors that are generated from a source file and seeing how many of them are caused by one problem being encountered over and over again.

In addition to errors, the Java compiler can also issue warnings. A common warning is creating a file which contains a public class that is not named after the file. The compiler will continue to compile after a warning, but it is an indication that the developer is not following the guidelines that the compiler expects to work with. In our experience it is worth fixing the problems that the warnings disclose, if only to prevent you becoming desensitized to real errors when they are reported.

Syntax errors are, of course, the simplest to handle and report. After all, the design of the Java language is well defined and the compiler knows what the rules are. When source code does not conform to these rules there is a clear case of an error and the compiler can make a clean-cut decision about syntax based on the relatively simple model of the language definition.

There is another kind of error which a compiler rarely detects and that is a conceptual flaw in the design of the program. This can be thought of as the developer writing code which is *syntactically* correct but which is flawed in the logic of the design. You will encounter these errors more frequently than you would like and you will often have to trace the progression of your code through execution to determine what is happening.

There are two main approaches to debugging code in this manner. The first, and most basic, is to insert lines of code at key points in the source code which print out a line of information regarding the progress of the execution or possibly the value of a variable. These lines would typically be moved by the developer as the problems are narrowed down to a specific area of the code. This approach is effective for simple problems in small amounts of code, but does not scale up to handling complex problems in large code bases. The other approach is to use a debugger. This allows the developer to control the execution of the program manually on a step-by-step basis and check the way that methods are called and the value of variables at each step of progression.

A.2.5 Dealing with run-time errors

In order to make use of the Java debugger jdb, you must compile your source code using the -g flag for the javac compiler. This flag allows the compiler to build into the final class file the required information that jdb will use to debug the file. To use the debugger, you simply call the binary and specify the Java target. So, for example, if we wanted to debug our simple example, we would first compile the .java file using the debug flag for the compiler:

```
javac -g HelloWorld.java
```

and then call the debugger with:

```
jdb HelloWorld
```

The model of operation for this type of debugger is to specify a break-point somewhere in the code. A break-point is a point in the source code which will cause the debugger to stop execution and hand over control to the developer. Exceptions that are not caught by methods, or are unexpected, are also considered as break-points so the debugger will stop there as well. The use of break-points lets the debugger run the program automatically until the execution reaches the area which interests the developer. At that point, it is possible to step through the execution of the code, one line at a time, to see in greater detail what is happening. Because, after each line is executed, the debugger can read the value of any variable it is a useful way of seeing where design problems manifest themselves.

A.3 Running Java code

Once you have created a Java file and compiled it so that there are no syntax errors you will want to run the code. We have covered the general debugging concepts before this section because they fit more comfortably with the compilation process. However, only the syntax errors will have been detected and fixed by the time that the compiler generates a usable class file, so any conceptual errors which you have made will not show up until you try to run the software. Some errors may take hours or weeks of use to show up, because the problems increment slowly and the effect takes some time to become noticeable, or because the code which generates the problems is so deeply tucked away into the program structure that it is not often called during normal use. Regardless of this, you will still need to run the code.

A.3.1 Running an application

To run an application you will need to call the Java run-time interpreter and ask it to process the class file that you have compiled. If your application consists of multiple classes, and hence has multiple class files, you need only enter the name of the class which contains the `main()` method.

Continuing with our example, to run the HelloWorld application we would type:

```
java HelloWorld
```

Notice that we did not need to tell the Java interpreter that this is a class file. The `java` binary knows that this is the case and, in fact, will not run if you specify the `.class` part of the file name. When your application requires access to additional classes the Java interpreter will take care of loading them. The class files in the same directory as the class which has been passed to `java` and the default Java packages will be available to the interpreter automatically. However, if you have a development structure which spans multiple directories and includes packages which you have written yourself, then you need to set the CLASSPATH environment variable to include all of the places that you want the run-time system to look for additional classes. There are some interesting arguments that can be supplied to the Java interpreter. We shall describe them here:

`-debug`

This allows the Java debugger to attach itself to the Java session. When you start a session with the `-debug` flag a password is displayed which must also be used by the remote debugger.

`-cs`

When this flag is used, the Java interpreter checks the class files against the source files and recompiles any classes which have been modified. The recompiled classes are then loaded. While useful, this can take some time to happen especially in projects with large amounts of source code.

`-noasyncgc`

This flag disables the automatic garbage collection to free up resources occupied by objects which are no longer in scope. Under other circumstances, the garbage collector runs as a background thread which is executed in parallel with the main system and program threads.

`-verbosegc`

Causes the garbage collector to print out a message to the standard channel out every time memory is freed from objects which are no longer in scope.

`-verify, -noverify`

Controls the operation of the code verifier.

`-verbose`

Asks the interpreter to print out a line to the standard output for each class that is loaded. In addition to the `javac` interpreter, there is also a non-optimized version which is invoked by calling '`java_g`'. An additional flag which applies to this is '`-t`' which prints out a trace of the instructions as they are executed.

A.3.2 Running an applet

There are two ways of viewing applets. The first is to use a Java-compatible browser such as Netscape Navigator 2.0. The second is by using the Appletviewer which is shipped as part of the Sun JDK.

Both the browser and the Appletviewer work in much the same way. A page of HTML containing references to applets (we will discuss these references in detail in Section A.6) is loaded and then the class files and associated resources (images, sound, and so on) are located and loaded, as the applet code is executed. The fundamental difference between a browser and the Appletviewer is that the browser will display all of the HTML that it understands – this includes text, Java code and images – whereas the Appletviewer ignores all of the HTML tags except for those which are Java applets. The Appletviewer then loads each of the applets and associated resources and displays each of the applets in a separate top-level window.

To use the Appletviewer you must create an HTML file which references your applet. You can place other entities into the HTML file but the Appletviewer will ignore them. A simple file to view our HelloWorld applet would look like this:

```
<HTML>
<HEAD>
<TITLE> Appletviewer Test </TITLE>
</HEAD>
<BODY>
<APPLET CODE="HelloWorld.class" WIDTH=150 HEIGHT=25>
</APPLET>
</BODY>
</HTML>
```

We will not discuss the basics of HTML at any length, except to cover the extension of HTML which allows applets to be embedded into Web pages. The example above simply defines an HTML document which has a title of 'Appletviewer Test'. In the body of the Web page the tag that interests us is <APPLET>. This is the agreed extension to HTML which allows Web page writers to include references to applets in pages. We have used the most basic form of the tag:

```
<APPLET CODE="HelloWorld.class" WIDTH=150 HEIGHT=25>
</APPLET>
```

The first word in the line, 'APPLET', is self-explanatory. In developmental alpha versions of the Java system the tag used to declare Java applets was APP. You may still see some references to this as the alpha release of the software will take some months to disappear completely. The next word is CODE. This flag tells the browser which class file to load. In this case we have chosen to use the HelloWorld.class file that we compiled earlier. It is important to remember to put the .class suffix after the name of the class you wish to load. The name of the class is the top-level class in your applet. Other classes which are called or defined by your top-level class will be loaded automatically. The next two arguments are used to define the amount of browser window space that the applet will occupy. These tags have been made compulsory in the beta release and are included so that browsers such as Netscape can determine the layout of a Web page before waiting for all of the classes and resources to load and the applet to initialize. The cost of this is that you may find that some of the methods in the `Applet` class relating to size are not implemented correctly in all the browsers supporting Java. The final tag `</APPLET>` defines the end of the tag for this applet.

These five small elements define the minimum amount of HTML that is required to include an applet into a Web page. There are some other tags which can be used, as well as a mechanism for passing arguments into applets using HTML, but we will return to this topic later for a more in-depth coverage. For the moment, it is sufficient to understand that this small amount of HTML will specify to the Appletviewer (or a browser) that a Java applet is embedded into the page.

Having created the HTML file, we now need to have the AppletViewer load the applet and execute it. It is not possible to load an applet directly into the AppletViewer without creating and loading an HTML page. Having created a file such as the one above, it is possible to load the file by calling the viewer with the name of the file as the argument:

```
appletviewer myfile.html
```

This approach assumes that the file is located in the current working directory. It is also possible to have the viewer load and process a page of HTML containing applet references from a remote machine by specifying a URL as the argument in the place of the local file name, for example:

```
appletviewer http://host.domain.com//some/path/myfile.html
```

Naturally, this assumes that the remote machine is running as a server for HTML pages and that your machine is allowed access to the page that you specify. If both of these are true, then the Appletviewer will load the HTML page, looking for `APPLET` tags. For each tag that is found the viewer will try to download and execute the applet - each in a separate top-level window.

There is only one command line option which can be specified to the Appletviewer, and that is '-debug' which allows the `jdb` debugger to connect to the process and perform debugging remotely.

A.4 Other JDK tools

So far we have discussed the Java compiler (`javac`) which takes source code and generates byte-code class files. We have also touched on the debugger (`jdb`) which allows the developer to trace the execution of Java code to track down programming problems. In the last section we described the basics of the Appletviewer, which allows the developer to test out an applet without needing to use a browser. There are other tools in the JDK, but in our experience the ones that we have already described are those that are most commonly used. The remaining tools are included in this section.

A.4.1 Native method support – Java

This tool generates the header files for use in native methods that are written in C. Native methods are methods which are written in another language (for example, C), but called within Java applications.

A.4.2 The Java disassembler

The JDK also includes a Java disassembler which can be used to obtain information from compiled class files. The first thing to note about the disassembler is what it cannot do, namely take a piece of compiled Java and generate the source code for the classes. In theory it would be possible to analyse the byte codes which are generated by the compiler and then reverse-engineer the results to create a form of the sources, but it is our opinion that the amount of effort this would require to render a mildly useful form of the source code will ensure that this is very rarely done.

The disassembler is called `javap` and we will illustrate its use in this section. For this we will need a sample class to work with. The class we have created is as follows:

```
class myClass {
   static int a = 1;

        public static void main(String args[]) {
             myClass mc = new myClass();
   }

        public void methodA() {
             int b = 2;
             System.out.println("b: " + b);
             this.methodB(b+1);
   }

        private void methodB(int i) {
             System.out.println("i: " + i);
        }
}
```

This is a very simple Java application which prints out two lines of output and then exits. The static `int` a is used for illustration only and is not used in the code. The first step is to put this class into a file and then compile it. We will call the file `myClass.java` following the naming scheme which we described at the start of this chapter.

The file must first be compiled:

```
javac myClass.java
```

The `javac` command takes the Java source code and produces the byte codes which are used by the Java run-time system, either as a standalone interpreter or as a part of a Web browser. Once the code has been successfully compiled, you may want to execute the code to make sure that it behaves as expected. To run the program all you need to do is type:

```
java myClass
```

This piece of sample code is an application and will not run in a browser or with the Appletviewer. When running the compiled code, you should see the following:

```
b:  2
i:  3
```

The next stage is to use the disassembler to look at the compiled code in more detail. If used without any arguments `javap` takes the compiled code and prints out a list of the public files and methods which are in the class. So if we pass the disassembler over our example class with no arguments:

```
javap myClass
```

you will see the following output:

```
Compiled from myClass.java
class myClass extends java.lang.Object {
    static int a;
    public static void main(java.lang.String []);
    public void methodA();
    public myClass();
    static void <clinit>();
}
```

The first line of the output shows what file contained the source code that generated the class. In our case we used the filename `myClass.java`, and so this is reflected in the output.

The next line shows the class definition. In our example, the class `myClass` did not extend anything, but if you look back in this book you will see that all classes either extend another class or extend `java.lang.Object` which is the basic building block for the whole of the Java language. In our example, because we have not explicitly extended from another class, we inherit automatically from `Object`.

The next line shows the presence of the (unused) static integer, and the next four lines show the methods that exist in the class. There are two things to notice: the first is that the disassembler has listed a class, `clinit`, which is not in the source code above; the second is that `methodB` is not listed at all in the output.

Why is this? Well, the additional class `clinit` is added by the system for internal use and the private `methodB` is not displayed because the default set up with `javap` is to list only the public methods. There is a command line argument that can be supplied to `javap` to list both the private and protected methods in a class in addition to the public ones. The flag is –p and if we call `javap` again using the flag:

```
javap -p myClass
```

we see the following:

```
Compiled from myClass.java
class myClass extends java.lang.Object {
    static int a;
    public static void main(java.lang.String []);
    public void methodA();
    private void methodB(int);
    public myClass();
    static void <clinit>();
}
```

As you would expect, much of the output is the same, with the addition of the extra line which lists the private `methodB`.

Javap is also capable of listing the instructions which comprise the Java byte codes, using the –c flag on the command line. So if we call `javap` as:

```
javap -c myClass
```

we see the following result:

```
Compiled from myClass.java
class myClass extends java.lang.Object {
static int a;
public static void main(java.lang.String []);
public void methodA();
public myClass();
static void <clinit>();

Method void main(java.lang.String [])
0 new #5 <Class myClass>
3 dup
4 invokenonvirtual #11 <Method myClass.<init>()V>
7 astore_1
8 aload_1
9 invokevirtual #10 <Method myClass.methodA()V>
12 return

Method void methodA()
0 iconst_2
```

```
1 istore_1
2 getstatic #16 <Field java.lang.System.out
  Ljava/io/PrintStream;>
5 new #3 <Class java.lang.StringBuffer>
8 dup
9 invokenonvirtual #18 <Method
java.lang.StringBuffer.<init>()V>
12 ldc #1 <String "b: ">
14 invokevirtual #15 <Method
java.lang.StringBuffer.append(Ljava/lang/String;)Ljava/lang/
StringBuffer;>
17 iload_1
8 invokevirtual #9 <Method
java.lang.StringBuffer.append(I)Ljava/lang/StringBuffer;>
21 invokevirtual #13 <Method
java.lang.StringBuffer.toString()Ljava/lang/String;>
24 invokevirtual #17 <Method
java.io.PrintStream.println(Ljava/lang/String;)V>
27 aload_0
28 iload_1
29 iconst_1
30 iadd
31 invokenonvirtual #8 <Method myClass.methodB(I)V>
34 return

Method void methodB(int)
0 getstatic #16 <Field java.lang.System.out
Ljava/io/PrintStream;>
3 new #3 <Class java.lang.StringBuffer>
6 dup
7 invokenonvirtual #18 <Method
java.lang.StringBuffer.<init>()V>
10 ldc #2 <String "i: ">
12 invokevirtual #15 <Method
java.lang.StringBuffer.append(Ljava/lang/String;)Ljava/lang/
StringBuffer;>
15 iload_1
16 invokevirtual #9 <Method
java.lang.StringBuffer.append(I)Ljava/lang/StringBuffer;>
19 invokevirtual #13 <Method
java.lang.StringBuffer.toString()Ljava/lang/String;>
22 invokevirtual #17 <Method
java.io.PrintStream.println(Ljava/lang/String;)V>
25 return
```

```
Method myClass()
0 aload_0
1 invokenonvirtual #14 <Method java.lang.Object.<init>()V>
4 return

Method void <clinit>()
0 iconst_1
1 putstatic #12 <Field myClass.a I>
4 return

}
```

This lists the byte-code instructions for all of the methods. A discussion of what the byte-code instructions represent is beyond the scope of this book, but an idle glance over the output from javap reveals a surprising amount of information to the casual user. We do not recommend that developers spend time understanding the byte-code system unless there are very good reasons, such as implementing a Java system on a new platform, but javap does provide a useful tool for working at that level. One of the benefits of the Java system is that there is no need for most developers to understand the intricacies of the underlying system: if you are working at that level then you are probably doing something wrong or have selected the wrong programming language.

A.5 API documentation

If you have downloaded a copy of the JDK, you will be familiar with the style of the API documentation in HTML. All of the API pages follow a similar and clear format which summarizes information at the top of the page and then provides more detail further down the page. The JDK provides a tool to assist in the production of documentation for classes in a format which matches the Sun API HTML pages. Unlike the previous tools, the documentation generator (javadoc) works with source files and not with compiled class files.

The basic method for generating the documentation is to call javadoc with the name of the source file:

```
javadoc myClass.java
```

Javadoc will load and process the file and then write out an HTML file to the local directory called <classname>.html. The output from this process is pretty basic. A better solution is to include comments in the source file that javadoc can understand and therefore add to the HTML output. The comments which javadoc can work with start with @. Extending our example, if we added the following lines to the Java source code file before the class definition:

```
/**
 * A class used for illustrating javadoc
```

```
 * For example:
 * <pre>
 *     javadoc myClass.java
 * </pre>
 *
 * @version 1.2 21st November 1995
 * @author  Adam Freeman
 */
class myClass {
    ...
```

then the documentation produced would look like that found in the Java API documentation. The forward slash and double star identifies comments that can be used in automatic documentation generation tools.

The codes have been interpreted and formatted in the output file. It is important to provide all of the information that someone using the class might need to know, without providing extraneous information. javadoc will only document methods in the class that are available for external use, and it is possible and desirable to document the methods as well as the class as a whole. The following is an example:

```
/**
 * Prints the value of the int to the standard out
 *
 * @param someint The integer to print out
 *
 */
public void someMethod(int someint) {
    ...}
```

This comment, immediately before the method, allows javadoc to provide information about how the method should be used and what it does. The '@param' tag is one of three such tags which can be used in method comments:

```
@param parameter-name description
```

This adds a reference for a parameter to the method comment. The name of the parameter should be the descriptor and not the type.

```
@return description
```

This adds a return section, which describes the value that the method will return.

```
@exception class-name description
```

This adds a 'Throws' entry which lists the exceptions that the method may throw. It is important to specify the fully qualified exception name since javadoc will automatically create a hot-link to the documentation for the exception that the method could throw.

The value of using `javadoc` to automatically document usage details for your developed classes cannot be underestimated. Not only will `javadoc` provide a documentation format which is consistent with other classes that you write but also with the Sun API specs. In addition, using the tags within the source file imposes a level of comments which is both plentiful and consistent across multiple source files. If you are considering permitting other developers to access your package library, then it is our advice that you consider the use of `javadoc` to be essential before shipping the code to other sites.

A.6 HTML tags

This section will cover the essentials of using HTML to embed applets into Web pages. You have already seen the basic building blocks which are used to tag Java code, namely:

`<APPLET>, CODE, WIDTH, HEIGHT` and `</APPLET>`

Using these tags it is possible to include applets into Web pages. The example we gave above was for the HelloWorld applet which is discussed at length in Chapter 12. The HTML tags to embed this into a Web page were:

```
<APPLET CODE="HelloWorld.class" WIDTH=150 HEIGHT=25>
</APPLET>
```

To recap, the first `APPLET` tag states to the browser (or the Appletviewer) that this is a Java applet. The next tag, `CODE`, tells the browser that the code for the applet can be found in the `HelloWorld.class` file.

There are other tags that can be used when embedding an applet. The `CODEBASE` tag specifies where the browser should locate the class file which is specified with the `CODE` tag. It is also possible to pass arguments to applets through HTML. This is of most use when the Web pages are being generated dynamically through CGI (Common Gateway Interface) or when one applet is likely to be widely used and is therefore capable of supporting a range of operation modes. The way of doing this is to include `PARAM` tags between the `<APPLET>` and `</APPLET>` tags, like this:

```
<APPLET CODE="HelloWorld.class" WIDTH=150 HEIGHT=25>
  <PARAM NAME=param1 VALUE=value1>
  <PARAM NAME=param2 VALUE=value2>
</APPLET>
```

Within the applet code that is invoked by this HTML it is possible to read these values. For example, in the `init()` method of the example class we could have changed the line which prints out 'Hello World' to read the value of `param1` and print that out instead. The code to do this is shown below:

```
String str = getParameter("param1");
System.out.println(str);
```

This line of code gets the value of the parameter called `param1` (listed in the example above) and then prints out the value of the string holding the parameter. One thing to be careful of is cases where your code expects to receive a parameter through HTML and it has not been added. This is most likely to happen if others use your code. One simple way of handling this is to check the value that has been returned from the call to `getParameter()` and supply a default value if there is nothing available from the Web page. For example:

```
String str = getParameter("param1");
if (str == null) {
  str = "HelloWorld!";
}
System.out.println(str);
```

This small change ensures that the value has been initialized with something – even if the Web page that called the applet failed to specify a value. Supplying a default value is a very useful strategy, especially when not initializing a variable correctly could cause exceptions later in the execution of the applet code.

A.6.1 Non-Java browsers

It is possible to include tags between the `<APPLET>` and `</APPLET>` tags in the HTML page. HTML that is included here will be displayed by browsers which do not recognize the `<APPLET>` tag and therefore do not support Java applets. This facility can be used to include explanatory messages or even screen-shots of Java applets to non-Java browsers; this is an important feature since a large number of browsers will not support Java for some time to come. As an example of this feature, consider the following HTML code:

```
<APPLET.....>
<blockquote>
<hr>
<em>
You are using a browser which does not support Java.
If you had a Java-aware browser, then you would
currently see the HelloWorld applet at work...
</em>
<hr>
</blockquote>
</APPLET>
```

Java-compatible browsers will recognize the APPLET tags and load the applet, but other browsers will skip the APPLET tags and display the text instead. We strongly recommend taking advantage of this facility when writing Web pages that will embed Java applets, not least because seeing a nearly-empty screen because an applet should be there is disconcerting to the user unless there is an explanatory message.

A.7 SUMMARY

We have described the system facilities for carrying out common tasks such as compiling Java code and including Java code within HTML documents. Many of these facilities look like those available in a UNIX-based system. However, as more and more implementations of Java are made we expect different instantiations of these facilities together with extra facilities which may be specific to the host system.

Index